REVISED EDITION

Month-By-Month™

WHAT TO DO EACH MONTH TO HAVE A BEAUTIFUL GARDEN ALL YEAR

GARDENING
MICHIGAN
IN

Published by Cool Springs Press, a Division of Thomas Nelson, Inc., P. O. Box 141000, Nashville, Tennessee, 37214.

Fizzell, James A. (James Alfred), 1935-
     Month-by-month gardening in Michigan : what to do each month to have a beautiful garden all year / James A. Fizzell.– Rev. ed.
               p. cm.
     Includes bibliographical references and index.
     ISBN 1-59186-226-4 (pbk.)
     1. Gardening–Michigan. I. Title.
SB453.2.IM525F59 2006
635'.09774–dc22

                              2005008037

Revised Printing 2006

Printed in Singapore
10 9 8 7 6 5 4 3 2 1

Managing Editor: Billie Brownell
Horticultural Editor: Robert F. Polomski, Extension Consumer Horticulturist,
               Clemson University
Designer: James Duncan, James Duncan Creative
Production Artist: S.E. Anderson

On the cover: Calendula, photographed by Thomas Eltzroth; page 7: Dency Kane (aster, middle of page)

Visit the Cool Springs Press website at www.coolspringspress.net

REVISED EDITION

Month-By-Month™

WHAT TO DO EACH MONTH TO HAVE A BEAUTIFUL GARDEN ALL YEAR

GARDENING in MICHIGAN

JAMES A. FIZZELL

COOL SPRINGS PRESS

Nashville, Tennessee
A Division of Thomas Nelson, Inc.
www.ThomasNelson.com

DEDICATION

To Janie—wife, business partner, best friend—for her loving assistance and support for these many years. And to our great-grandchildren Emma, Mikaela, and Brooklyn Grace, another generation being brought up in the gardening tradition.

ACKNOWLEDGEMENTS

Some very special people have lent their expertise in preparation of the *Month-by-Month Gardening in Michigan: Revised Edition* manuscript:

Most important is my wife, Jane. The hours I spent writing this book are hours we could have spent together. Without thought for her own time, Jane read copy, edited, researched, fended off impatient clients, and offered help any way she could to make this and all of our books possible.

Julie Morell-Greve, Naturalist, supervises maintenance of natural plantings and ponds for the Park Ridge Park District; she is a knowledgeable resource and friend. Jerry Hohla, Soil Scientist, has provided much of the information on the history of Midwest soils. Greg Soulje, Meteorologist, known for his expertise in providing long-range prognostications, was a ready resource for most of the weather statistics. Gregory R. Stack, University of Illinois, Matteson, friend and fellow horticulturist, shared an office with me for years at the University. Greg is an outstanding horticulturist and offered resources and moral support. Providing additional assistance for this addition are Dr. Phil Nixon and Dr. Raymond Cloyd, Entomologists, University of Illinois, who developed the revised list of pest control materials and recommendations for controlling the troublesome creatures in the garden.

Also, sincere thanks is due to the good people at Cool Springs Press . . . to Roger Waynick for making our books possible, to Hank McBride who is responsible for scheduling Cool Springs production schedules and seeing that books are published on time, and a real debt of gratitude is due to my editor, Billie Brownell. Billie edited this edition of *Month-by-Month Gardening in Illinois*, and is responsible for several others of our books published by Cool Springs Press. Billie is a tireless and skillful editor who makes sure everything is absolutely correct.

Thanks to all of you for the many hours you have spent on the editing, layout, and production. Finally, thanks to Cindy Games for her tireless efforts working on the distribution of all our books.

God Bless You All!

CONTENTS

INTRODUCTION

Why *Month-by-Month Gardening*? Because gardening is
a journey, not a destination.

THE BENEFITS OF A MONTH-BY-MONTH GARDENING SCHEDULE

The enjoyment in gardening comes not so much from completing a garden, but in doing it: the daily experiences, such as planting a few onion sets in the first warm afternoon of spring, the surprises, such as seeing a purple crocus before the snow has even gone, and the satisfaction, such as having fresh green beans on the dinner table or tomatoes, bright and red, safely canned in quart jars, keep us gardeners coming back year after year.

Month-by-Month Gardening in Michigan is designed to help you get as much out of this wonderful experience as possible. It answers questions like these:

• When is it safe to put out tomatoes?

• When should I plant my oak tree?

• Can I divide iris now?

You may become so involved in other activities that you miss important gardening chores or start them too late to do them right. If you have ever been in this situation, you can understand the importance of reminders. Maybe you have wished, when the perfect spring day arrived to set out transplants, that you had sown seeds earlier. How about that cold frame you

wish you had put together last winter? Most of us can benefit from prompting.

Ten categories of plants are described in the book. Each is followed through the year to alert you to things that need to be done. If you are concerned about what to do in the annual garden in March, for instance, turn to that chapter for specific tasks that will make your annuals even more enjoyable.

As you garden, you will certainly discover many other ways to increase your pleasure and to make you a better gardener. Keep a journal as you work through the gardening season. Record planting dates, sources of plants or seeds, flowering dates, successes, and failures. We all have gardening disappointments. If you do not document them, you risk repeat-ing them.

Seasons vary considerably. Some arrive very early, and some are cold and disappointingly late. Timing from one end of this state to the other can vary more than three weeks. I have tried to provide the best guess for the proper times for gardening activities.

In some cases I have coordinated them with other events such as the blooming of certain

THE BENEFITS OF A MONTH-BY-MONTH GARDENING SCHEDULE

plants, a system known as phenology. By watching how the plants are developing outdoors, you can know whether the season is early or late. Dates in this book are averages. Adjust them once you decide how the season is turning out.

GARDENING IN MICHIGAN

Gardening has been important in Michigan since the first settlers arrived. They found much of the land to be flat-to-rolling grassland suitable for farming, with plenty of hardwood forest along rivers and streams to provide timber for homes and buildings. The northern part of the state was much more rugged, wooded and hilly. Soon after their arrival, settlers began to plant gardens.

Gardening was considered women's work, and the garden was next to the house where the women could watch over it. It was fenced to keep out wandering livestock and to be easily accessible to the kitchen. In the garden grew all the vegetables, greens, and herbs needed for meals, as well as herbs used for making medicine, flavoring foods, freshening the air, dyeing cloth, and repelling bugs and vermin.

Hollyhocks and sunflowers, cosmos and wild roses often shared space with cabbages and beans in the vegetable patch. Life was hard, and flowers provided beauty and fragrance. A few on the dinner table brought a little joy to an otherwise dreary existence.

As settlements appeared and more folks moved from the farm to town, gardens went with them. Town gardens combined herbs and vegetables, but the flowers moved from the garden to the front yard.

Gardening, no longer necessary just for existence, became a hobby. Even the well-to-do were participants. Flowers soon became a necessity in the genteel homes of the Victorian age. Victorian gardens were elaborate with masses of color, trees, evergreens, and fixtures such as cast iron benches, gazebos, arbors, fountains, and glass-gazing balls.

Lawns became possible with the invention of the lawn mower. And with the appearance of fine lawns arrived lawn games such as croquet and badminton.

To satisfy the demand for more and unusual plants, explorers were bringing all kinds of new plants from all over the temperate world. Asia was a particularly fruitful source, and many of the plants we grow today were introduced during those years. Seed companies got their start about that time as well, and landscape architecture became a recognized profession in this country.

In the mid-1800s, horticulture societies were beginning, and in 1855 the Michigan A and E College was established at East Lansing. One of the pioneering horticulture research projects was started there by Professor William J. Beale. He planted weed seeds in bottles for digging up every few years to see if the seeds would germinate. The year was 1888, and the project is still operating and some seeds still germinate—after more than 100 years.

Michigan State University, as it is known today, provides teaching, research, and Extension services to the garden hobbyists and commercial horticulturists throughout the Midwest.

By the turn of the century, massive gardens appeared in parks and public places. Several are still prominent in the Detroit area and on the grounds of the state capital at Lansing. Garden clubs were springing up in nearly every community. The Garden Club of Michigan was organized in 1912.

In the 1920s, wealthy industrialists including

THE BENEFITS OF A MONTH-BY-MONTH GARDENING SCHEDULE

Henry Ford enticed landscape architects to design magnificent estate gardens, most of which did not outlast the Depression.

World War I and World War II added incentives to garden. Rationing and food shortages were common, and home Liberty Gardens or Victory Gardens provided many city dwellers with produce. Many of us got our start in gardening by tending Victory Gardens.

A tremendous boom in home building followed World War II as returning veterans and crowded city dwellers made a dash to suburbia. Large lots and the absence of landscaping stimulated an interest in gardening that has not stopped.

Nearly everyone does some kind of gardening, even if it is limited to mowing the grass on Saturday morning. Most homes have landscaping of some sort and flowers. Spring and fall are planting seasons. Garden centers are forced to hire security firms to direct traffic on busy spring weekends.

Michigan State University provides support for an extensive Master Gardener program in which gardeners receive several weeks of intensive training in return for volunteer time serving the public. Many of these volunteers serve at the botanic gardens and arboreta of the state.

Gardening is a very popular hobby. Garden centers provide the latest improved plant materials and anything a gardener could want to make the hobby more fun and more successful. Expenditures for plants, fertilizers, seeds, landscape care, and other garden items or services are in the hundreds of millions of dollars each year. Gardening is like no other hobby. Gardeners share their knowledge with anyone who asks, and it is a camaraderie that includes all segments of society.

Even the municipalities have gotten into the act. No more plastic flowers. Flower gardens, planters, intimate parks in the business districts, and tree pits in the sidewalks all bring the joy of plants to soften the harshness of the concrete jungles. Municipal foresters and horticulturists are employed to keep the plantings attractive and healthy. City budgets provide for the flower beds, flower boxes, planters, and various other appropriate plantings.

Botanic gardens and arboreta have been developed in all parts of the state. Flower or garden shows are held throughout the year. Community colleges and universities teach all kinds of gardening courses for hobbyists and professionals.

The Beal Botanical Garden, established in 1873, is one of the oldest continuously operating gardens in the country. Fantastic floral displays are planted to beautify other parts of the city throughout every summer. Other metropolitan areas— Detroit, Grand Rapids, Midland, Ann Arbor, Battle Creek—do the same. Even smaller rural communities often line their Main Streets with flowers.

Gardening in Michigan is a challenge. The soils are quite fertile, but some can be difficult to handle. The weather can be extreme and changeable. Residents commonly agree that if you do not like Michigan weather, wait a few minutes. It will change. This makes gardening all the more interesting. You never know what to expect.

In this book, I attempt to reduce the number of unknowns that can adversely affect your gardening pleasure and success. Some of the secrets of handling the soil are revealed as well as contending with the vagaries of the weather.

I hope this book adds to your gardening pleasure. Gardening, horticulture, is an art. We learn it by doing, making mistakes, correcting them, and going on. Every season is different. I always look forward to each season, and during the season to

USDA COLD HARDINESS ZONES

ZONE	Average Minimum Temperature
3A	-35 to -40
3B	-30 to -35
4A	-25 to -30
4B	-20 to -25
5A	-15 to -20
5B	-10 to -15
6A	-5 to -10
6B	0 to -5

THE BENEFITS OF A MONTH-BY-MONTH GARDENING SCHEDULE

each new day. What a joy it is to get out bright and early in the morning to see what is new.

CLIMATIC CONDITIONS

The climate of Michigan is described as moist, temperate, and continental. Spring can be cool and wet. It can snow until mid-April, and flurries will occur well into May or later in the northern part of the state. Spring weather can be quite changeable with temperatures in the range of 70 degrees Fahrenheit in March followed by lows in the teens in April. It is often so wet that planting must be delayed, and it can be so cool that trees do not leaf out until the end of April. Spring can have a hard time arriving, especially in the northern part of the state.

The four Great Lakes surrounding the state have a big effect on the weather. As the air over the land warms and rises in spring, cool air off the lakes flows inland. Water temperatures at that time of the season are generally in the low 30s and the air is cold. Along the Lake Michigan shore because of the prevailing west winds, this effect can be felt as far as 20 miles inland, sometimes even more. Often lakeside communities are shivering in cold, foggy weather while inland it is warm and sunny.

This lake effect can delay the growing season as much as 1 or 2 weeks. Often development of spring-flowering shrubs in Kalamazoo can be 2 weeks ahead of the same plants in South Haven on the lake shore.

Summers throughout Lower Michigan are warm with temperatures in the 80s and 90s in the southern two-thirds of the state, and reaching 100 or more on occasion.

Southern Michigan is in USDA Heat Zone 5 with 30 to 40 heat days in which temperatures may reach 86 degrees or higher. When daytime temperatures exceed 30 degrees centigrade, about 86 degrees Fahrenheit, plant tissues begin to be injured. Central Michigan is in Heat Zone 4 with 14 to 30 heat days. The Northern part of the state is in Heat Zone 3 expecting only 7 to 14 heat days every summer.

Summer heat waves are interrupted by weather fronts bringing rain in the form of thunderstorms as humid air is pulled north by passing low-pressure areas. Behind the fronts, high pressure and cooler Canadian air provide relief from the heat for a few days.

Rainfall in the summer averages about 3 inches per month. When the normal movement of weather fronts is interrupted, droughts can develop, lasting two or three weeks. In some years fronts can stall, resulting in excessive rainfall, and heavy thunderstorms can cause localized flooding.

Fall is often the nicest season of the year. Average high temperatures in early fall throughout most of the Lower Peninsula are in the 70's falling to the 30's by late November. Days are generally clear and warm, nights cool with heavy dew. Rainfall generally becomes more frequent as fall progresses although some autumns are dry.

The first snow can be expected about the middle of October, and a 3-inch snowfall often occurs by Thanksgiving.

Winters can be quite variable. The climatic zones range from 5a in the center of the state with anticipated lows of -15 degrees, to 6b in the far southwestern part of the state where temperatures rarely get much below zero, and to an extreme of zone 3b (-30 to -35) in the Houghton Lake area and some of the Upper Peninsula. Two winter hardiness rating systems in general use are the U. S. Department of Agriculture (USDA) which is used in this book, and the Arnold Arboretum which indicates Michigan is in Zones 3 and 4. Be sure to

notice which rating system is being used for the plants you buy.

The progressions of high- and low-pressure weather systems that affect the weather the rest of the year also affect the winter weather. The lows bring warmer weather and snow. The highs that follow the lows usher in clear, crisp, Arctic cold.

Some years there is snow though there may be little cold weather. Some years it is cold with not much snow. Once in a while, we get lots of snow and Arctic cold. Temperatures can usually be expected to fall below zero degrees Fahrenheit several times throughout most of the state, and we can expect about 3 feet of snow. In the Upper Peninsula, intense cold and heavy snow are common.

As in the summer, Lake Michigan moderates the winter weather, keeping shoreline communities warmer but increasing the snowfall. Lake effect snows can be substantial as far from the lake as Dowiagiac or even Kalamazoo.

The growing season is about 170 days along Lake Michigan, and about 70 days in the coldest areas of the Lower and Upper Peninsulas. The average date of last frost is about April 25 in the southwest corner of the state, and May 25 in the far northern part. The first frost in fall can be expected anytime after Labor Day but usually occurs in October.

SOIL CONDITIONS

Glaciers were responsible for most of the soils in Michigan. As they retreated, they deposited the ground-up rock they were carrying. Glacial outwash soils are common in the southern part of the state. Outwash soils contain rocks, sand, and finer silts and clays. Sandy soils occur along Lake Michigan and throughout much of southwestern lower Michigan. An area of highly organic muck soils in the west central part of the state is the loca-

tion of some of the best vegetable-growing farms in the country.

Throughout much of the rest of the state, glacial till soils predominate. The many lakes are the result of scouring out by the glaciers, or they are from huge ice chunks that were left mixed with the other debris when the glaciers melted. As the ice melted, the land sank, leaving these delightful water features.

Soils are classified according to the size of the soil particles as sands, silts, or clays.

These are characteristics of sands:

• Sands consist of larger-sized particles.

• The grains are visible to the naked eye.

• Spaces between the grains are large, too, so that water drains away easily.

• Sands are described as light soils.

They tend to be infertile because the nutrients are easily washed away.

• If provided with sufficient water and fertilizer, sands are easy to handle, never becoming sticky or compacted.

These are characteristics of silts:

• Silts are medium-sized particles.

• They are too small to be seen individually without a hand lens.

• Silt soils are usually difficult to handle.

• They do not drain well and are easily compacted.

• Silts retain nutrients and, if handled correctly, can be productive.

These are characteristics of clays:

• Clays are made up of tiny particles, molecular in size.

THE BENEFITS OF A MONTH-BY-MONTH GARDENING SCHEDULE

They hold large amounts of water and fertilizer elements.

• Clays can develop a granular structure that allows good aeration.

• Without structure, clays are waterlogged and very hard.

• With good structure, clay particles stick together into tiny lumps called aggregates.

The aggregates hold lots of water and nutrients, but the spaces between them allow air to enter the soil.

Aggregates form naturally in clay soils. Wetting, drying, freezing, and thawing cause aggregation. That is why garden soils are in such good condition after a hard winter. Adding organic matter and working in the soil only when it is dry enough will aid aggregation.

Loams consist of soils with the right amounts of sand, silt, and clay so that none of the characteristics of any predominates. Loams are the most productive soils and are found in the major food-producing parts of the world. In Michigan, most of our soils are loams.

Organic matter is a vital part of good soils. It enhances aggregation of heavy soils and improves the water-holding capacity of light soils.

Organic soils (peats and mucks) form where water stood and the plants that grew there did not completely decompose. Peat and muck soils are used for production of vegetables and for sod production. They can be quite productive, but if allowed to dry out, they are hard to rewet.

Good gardeners continually add organic matter to their soils—old plants, grass clippings, leaves, compost, manures, anything that they can acquire free or at minimal cost.

PLANNING THE GARDEN

Drive down any residential street and look at the plantings around the homes. Some are attractively planted. Others are without plants. Some cannot be seen because of the overgrown plants. Others consist of a hodgepodge of plants set wherever there was room.

Attractive gardens require planning. Your home deserves the most attractive setting you can provide. Most gardens consist of trees, shrubs, turfgrass, flowers, possibly a vegetable garden, and maybe a water feature, hardscape, or sculpture. Collectively, this is called landscaping.

Obviously, certain areas of your grounds are better suited for the various kinds of plants. Vegetable gardens generally are not to be situated in the front yard, for instance. There is a place for everything.

Planning starts with a scale drawing of your property:

• Include all structures and adjacent features that will affect your enjoyment in your yard.

• Indicate attractive features, such as natural areas, streams, and rivers, to be enhanced, and unattractive features to be screened out.

• Identify North on the plan.

• Indicate windows from which you want to provide an attractive view.

• Locate on the plan the various uses expected from the various areas of your property.

The front is usually for public view. Determine areas for privacy, for utilities, and for attractive features.

Once the general layout has been determined, decide on the kinds of plants that will provide the pictures you want.

THE BENEFITS OF A MONTH-BY-MONTH GARDENING SCHEDULE

Trees frame the picture. Place them so that they do not hide the house—on either side or to the back. Summer shade on the south and west sides of the house can reduce the heat load. Evergreen trees that break the winter wind can be helpful.

Shrubs accent the home and provide screening and often flowers. Select plants that will not outgrow their situation and require extensive pruning. Locate the shortest shrubs at the entrance of the house, the tallest farthest from the door.

The vegetable garden should not be seen from the house or interfere with the use of the yard. It should be in full sun and near a water supply. Include space for a cutting garden for fresh flowers.

Flower gardens are attention getters. In the front of the house, they should be subtle and not detract from the overall picture—the emphasis is on the home. Elsewhere in the garden, flowers can be used as accents, borders, or features.

• Plant taller varieties at the back or ends of the beds so that they do not hide smaller ones.

• Try to coordinate colors.

If flowers are in the vicinity of flowering shrubs, make sure they do not clash. In years past, this was much more important that it is today when "almost anything goes." Try to have flowers that complement instead of compete with other blooming plants.

• Consider the color of the buildings behind the flowers.

A pink-flowering crabapple in front of a pink house will never produce the spectacular display that a deep red- or a white-flowered tree would. The pink flowers will get lost.

• Plan so that something is in bloom throughout the summer.

Some flowers and shrubs do not bloom all season. Annuals flower all summer and can be used to fill in.

Features such as a water garden and statuary generally belong in the private areas of the yard, not in the front. Unless your house is not the most attractive thing on your property, why would you want to detract from it? Situate the features where you and your guests can appreciate them. If you can arrange for the pond to be seen from the picture window in the family room, or the fountain to be watched through the sliding doors off your bedroom, it will add to your enjoyment.

Plan carefully. A pond or a tree is tough to move once it is in place. Shrubs or flower gardens may be a bit easier to move, but once you have anything in place, you will find it much more difficult to move than it would have been to change it on paper.

MAKING USE OF REFERENCE BOOKS

Gardening books are fun to read, and they all have helpful ideas. Even books written for other parts of the country may have information that you can adapt for our area. Steve Still's *Manual of Herbaceous Plants* (Stipes, 1993) is filled with good information. Boland, Coit, and Hair's *Michigan Gardener's Guide* (Cool Springs Press, 1997, and revised 2002) is written specifically for this state, and it is especially good for new gardeners or those moving here from other climates.

GENERAL HORTICULTURE PRACTICES

PLANTING

Getting plants off to a good start will eliminate numerous problems.

Many of the problems I see are the result of careless planting. With annuals, the consequences of poor planting last only that season. Trees, shrubs, and perennials last for years, so care in planting them has a lasting effect.

Annuals can be started from seeds sown in the garden. More often, they are started from plants bought from garden centers or started indoors. To plant annuals, follow these steps:

1. Prepare the soil by spading or tilling to a depth of at least 6 inches.

2. Remove the plants from the containers or pots by squeezing the sides to force the plants out. Do not pull them by the stems.

3. Butterfly the little masses of roots by slicing them partially in half from the bottom.

4. Set the plants in the prepared soil at the same depth they grew in the containers.

Perennials, grasses, and bog plants are usually sold in pots or cans. Smaller trees and shrubs are also available in containers.

To plant container-grown plants, follow these steps:

1. Prepare the soil deeply, at least as deep as the container. For some perennials, preparation of 1 1/2 to 2 feet is preferred.

2. Remove the plants from the containers.

3. Make four vertical slices to cut circling roots. This will hasten root development and prevent girdling roots later on.

4. Dig the planting holes as deep and twice as wide as the balls of soil on the plants.

5. If the plants were growing in an artificial soil mix, shake off as much of it as possible, and mix the artificial soil with the soil from the planting holes. Use care to minimize root damage.

6. Refill the holes halfway with soil, water until the hole begins to fill, and replace the remainder of the soil.

7. Thoroughly soak the area to settle the soil.

Trees and shrubs can be container-grown, bare root, or balled and burlapped.

Bare-root plants are usually small. They are dug with no soil around the root systems. Bare-root plants need to be protected from drying until they are planted. Either heal-in bare-root plants in a pit, or set them in a bucket of water.

To plant bare-root plants, follow these steps:

1. Dig the planting holes large enough so that the roots can be fully spread out in their natural positions and deep enough so that the plants can be set at about the same depth they were grown in the nursery. If the soil is poorly drained, the plants may be set higher.

2. Prune out broken or diseased roots and broken or poorly shaped branches from the tops.

3. Set the bare-root trees or shrubs in the planting holes, and spread out the roots. It might be necessary to make cones of soil beneath the plants to get the roots to lie correctly.

4. Support the plants as soil is shoveled over the roots.

5. Fill the holes halfway with soil, firm the soil, and fill the holes with water.

6. When the water has drained, fill the holes the rest of the way with the remaining soil, firm the soil, and soak with water again.

Bare-root trees may need support to keep them from being blown over until roots develop.

Balled-and-burlapped plants are large and heavy. They are dug with large balls of soil around the roots. The soil is wrapped with burlap and tied with twine.

To plant balled-and-burlapped plants, follow these steps:

1. Before starting to dig the planting holes, measure the diameter of the balls and the depth from the bottom to the top of the balls.

2. Dig the planting holes one and one-half times the diameter of the balls and slightly less deep than the plants grew in the nursery. If the soil is poor, dig saucer-shaped holes several times wider than the diameter of the balls. The balls may be set as much as one-third out of the ground and soil hilled up to them to prevent drowning the roots.

3. While the plants can be laid on their sides, prune out broken or poorly shaped branches.

4. Set plants in the holes carefully to avoid breaking the balls.

5. To minimize chances of sunburning the bark, orient the plants the same way they were growing in the nursery. Be sure the plants are straight. If necessary, use clods of soil to prop up the plants so that they stay straight.

6. Cut and remove the twine around the balls. Either remove as much of the burlap as you can, or stuff it down in the holes.

7. Fill the holes halfway with the soil that was removed from the holes. Break up any clumps but do not stomp the soil down. This will compact the soil, making it difficult for roots to grow into it.

8. Fill the holes with water.

9. Backfill the remaining soil. Leave a curb of soil around the perimeter of the holes to hold water.

10. Soak the area with water to settle the soil and force out air pockets.

SOIL AMENDMENTS

Difficult soils can be improved with amendments. Amendments include the following:

• Organic matter

This is the best soil amendment material. For example, sandy soils dry out too quickly and hold little fertilizer. Organic matter improves both the water-holding capacity and the fertility of sandy soils.

• Sand

When used in sufficient amounts, two-thirds by volume, it can improve heavy soils.

• Calcined clay

• Wetting agents

Not actually amendments, but can enhance wetting of hydrophobic soils.

• Gels

When added to light soils, may increase water-holding capacity.

Whatever material is used to amend your soil, make every effort to mix it in as large an area as possible and to avoid developing layers. Mixing peat moss with the soil in a garden and digging it in 6 inches may create an excellent surface soil above a tough clay. Where the layers meet, an interface will be created that will prevent the movement of water, air, or roots.

Any situation that results in an interface will confine the root systems and prevent proper development of the plants. Changes from modi-

fied soil to the existing soil should be gradual so that roots can grow from one to the other.

WATERING

Watering is an option for gardeners in Michigan unless the soil is quite sandy. Most years there is sufficient rainfall to produce crops, to grow flowers and vegetables, and to have a lawn. Unfortunately, there are seasons when the rainfall is not evenly distributed, and watering is helpful, or even essential, for healthy plants.

Proper watering means thoroughly soaking the soil and allowing it to dry almost to the point of wilt before watering again. If the soil is kept constantly wet, roots will receive insufficient air. Either they will die, or they will develop at the surface where they are susceptible to other problems.

Soak container plants—pots, planters, or benches— until water runs out the drain holes. Do not let plants reabsorb the drainage water.

Apply a measured 1 inch of water to lawns and gardens. This amount will moisten the soil to a depth of 6 inches or more. Do not apply water again until plants show signs of wilting.

Water newly planted trees and shrub borders by setting a slowly running hose at the bases of the plants and allowing it to run until water runs off.

Thoroughly soak established trees every fifteen to twenty days in dry weather. Using a sprinkler, apply $1^1/2$ to 2 inches of water to the entire area beneath the branches of the trees.

Stage-water hydrophobic soils (those not easy to wet), powder-dry soils, and soils on slopes.

• Apply water until it begins to run off.

• Then stop and allow the soil to absorb the water.

• Continue watering again, repeating the process until the required amount of water has been applied.

• Measure the water by placing straight-sided cans in the area being sprinkled.

• Turn off the water when the desired depth of water has accumulated in the cans.

FERTILIZING

Most soils in Michigan are fertile. But for optimum growth, fertilizer is usually necessary to provide sufficiently balanced soil nutrients.

Organic matter provides some nutrients, especially nitrogen. Most organic materials such as manures are low-yield fertilizers. Sewage sludge types are higher, and some are modified with the addition of supplemental materials to a standard analysis.

The fertilizer analysis is stated on the package and is expressed as a percentage of nitrogen, phosphate, and potash. For example, the analysis of a common commercial organic fertilizer is 6-2-0.

Commercial fertilizers may have much higher analyses—10-10-10, 20-20-20, or even 45-0-0. The first two are balanced, complete fertilizers. The last one provides only nitrogen.

Soil tests determine the amount of additional fertilizer needed by your soils. Without a soil test, fertilizer is usually applied to provide 1 pound of nitrogen per 1000 square feet of garden or lawn. The other two nutrients just go along for the ride in case they are needed. One pound of nitrogen takes 10 pounds of 10-10-10, 5 pounds of 20-20-20, or 2.2 pounds of 45-0-0.

GENERAL HORTICULTURE PRACTICES

Apply fertilizers carefully:

• Use a spreader to fertilize lawns.

• Spread fertilizers on gardens by hand.

• Measure the area, and weigh out the appropriate amount of fertilizer.

Fertilize trees by broadcasting the correct amount beneath the trees with a spreader, by boring holes in the ground and filling them with the fertilizer, or by hiring an arborist to inject the material into the soil. Apply 2 pounds of fertilizer per 1,000 square feet of area beneath the tree, or sufficient fertilizer to provide $1/2$ pound of nitrogen per inch of trunk diameter at breast height.

PRUNING

Most plants benefit from periodic pruning. Some gardeners fear getting out the clippers and trimming their plants. They are reluctant to take off anything for fear they will not prune it correctly. Others go overboard, clipping merrily away without regard for what they are doing or where they are going.

Proper pruning invigorates a plant. It causes the plant to grow new shoots where the gardener wants them. Technically, pruning can be as simple as removing spent blooms from annuals or dry tops from perennials. This deadheading process stimulates renewed flowering.

Shrubs need pruning to develop new stems that flower better. Removing one-fourth of the oldest stems to the ground every year will keep the plants young and vigorous. Cutback overly long stems to keep plants in bounds. Some shrubs can be cut back to the ground every few years to renew them. Pruning eliminates scale insects and canker diseases.

Small flowering trees and fruit trees must be pruned to keep them flowering and producing. Timing and skill are important, and skill is developed by actually pruning the trees. Remove suckers and crossing branches. Strongly vertical shoots do not flower well and do not produce fruit. Remove them before they take over and destroy the shape of the trees.

Juvenile shade trees need pruning to shape them as they grow. Maintain a single leader. Remove lower branches for clearance. Try to achieve a balance of 60 to 70 percent crown to 30 to 40 percent bare trunk.

Mature trees require the services of a professional arborist with the equipment and expertise to do the job safely and correctly.

WINTER CARE

Winter hardiness is the ability of a plant to survive cold temperatures in a particular geographic location. Plants use different strategies to survive extreme temperatures:

• Some die back to the ground and rely on protected underground parts—roots, rhizomes, tubers, or bulbs.

• Other plants lose their leaves, and the sap drains down into the roots for the winter.

• Evergreen plants use other means such as moving water into the intercellular spaces to avoid rupturing cells.

Whatever the means, plants that are hardy here can survive the winter. If you plant a semihardy cultivar, it is your responsibility to assist it in surviving, or it will not.

GENERAL HORTICULTURE PRACTICES

Even hardy plants need care to get through the winter in the best shape:

• Water them.

Plants should be thoroughly watered before the ground freezes.

• Mulch them.

Evergreen ground covers will winter-burn and become unattractive if exposed to winter sun and winds. A light straw mulch can protect them. Shallowly rooted perennials can be heaved out of the ground by freezing and thawing of the soil. Mulches will keep them frozen and securely rooted in the soil.

• Protect them.

Exposed evergreens can be protected from sunburn and windburn with burlap screens attached to wooden stakes driven into the ground.

Hybrid tea roses and their relatives are not completely hardy. They will need winter protection in most years. Rose cones or hills of garden soil over the plants are usually sufficient protection.

Native plants need no protection from the elements. They and some of the introduced kinds will need protection from animals, however. Rabbits, mice, and deer can decimate a planting over a winter. To protect the plants, try the following:

• Install rabbit guards.

• Clear the ground beneath trees or shrubs to keep mice from establishing homes there.

• Spray valuable plants with deer-proofing materials or set soap bars out in strategic places.

If the deer are particularly hungry, only wire cages can be relied upon to protect plants.

In areas where snows are heavy, construct snow sheds to protect foundation plantings from the snow sliding off the roof. Plywood supported by 2-by-4 frames and sloping away from the house will work. Make them strong because snow weighs a lot.

OVERWINTERING TENDER PLANTS

Many tender plants are grown in the garden. Common tender plants include summer bulbs such as gladiolus, tuberous begonias, dahlias, and cannas. To overwinter them indoors, follow these steps:

1. Lift these plants (dig them up) after the first frost.

2. Shake off as much soil from the roots as you can.

3. Allow the clumps to dry, then separate and clean the bulbs.

4. Store them in a cool, dry place, but check that they are not shriveling during the winter.

Houseplants vacation outdoors and must be moved indoors before they freeze. Clean the pots, and treat the plants for uninvited guests such as bugs, slugs, and weeds. Keep the plants in a cool place for a while before bringing them into a heated house. The low humidity and low light intensity will cause them to drop older leaves. Do not be upset. It is the plants' way of adjusting to the change.

GENERAL OVERVIEW

For the purposes of this book, the garden plants are divided into 10 groups. Although this division may seem arbitrary, the chapters are arranged to make it easy for you to find the information you need.

The chapter on annuals describes these interesting plants and discusses how they can be used in the garden. Planning is important. To make the best use of annuals, some thought should be given to their location, their colors, and their size as they develop. In this chapter you'll find suggestions on how to grow them and how to care for them. The monthly calendar tells just what you should be doing each month to get the most enjoyment from annuals.

Bulbs, corms, rhizomes, and tubers are underground structures that allow these plants to survive unfavorable weather. Some of our most familiar and easily grown plants fall into this category. Spring-flowering bulbs are the most common plants in this group, but it includes summer-flowering plants and cut flowers as well.

Some of these plants are completely hardy. Others are not hardy and require special care. These are worth the extra effort they require because they are some of the more spectacular flowers in the garden. Unless their peculiarities are understood, however, growing them can be a hazardous undertaking.

Herbs and vegetables are usually thought of as summertime plants. But some can be grown all year indoors, and some are perennials that survive the winter. Some are cold tolerant and can be grown early in the season or late, even surviving freezing weather to provide fresh produce as late as Christmas.

Seeding and growing transplants indoors and using a cold frame or portable greenhouse can lengthen the season, adding to the pleasure of your garden. Timing is important to have plants of the proper size at the right time. Too early, and the plants become overgrown and leggy. Too late, and the advantage of an early start is lost.

Nearly every home has a lawn. In Michigan, lawn care is a major agricultural pursuit. The annual outlay for lawn-care products and services is in the multimillions of dollars, and the value of lawns is calculated in the billions.

Many of the calls we receive on our radio programs and much of the time we spend looking at turfgrass problems are the result of not doing the right thing at the right time. Most of the turfgrasses grown in the state are cool-season species. Starting a lawn, making repairs, fertilizing, and preventing pest problems need to be done when the problems can be prevented. It is much easier to prevent them than to try to cure them once they have begun.

Perennial flowers offer real challenges to gardeners. Most of us start with annuals and graduate to perennials because of the opportunities they offer. No two perennials are alike. The sizes, forms, flowering times, care, and specific requirements are unique to each. Once you learn one of them, there are always more kinds to grow and understand. Some of these plants flower at one time of the year, others at different times. Only a few of them bloom throughout the season. Their planning and care are time sensitive.

Interest in native perennial plants has never been greater. Most gardeners are just beginning to grow these splendid plants. Although they do not require a tremendous amount of care, gardeners may take steps to increase chances of success. They have certain needs that determine how and where they will grow best. Once those needs are met, wildflowers do just what they are intended to do—grow.

GENERAL OVERVIEW

Rose care is becoming less demanding with the increasing popularity of old-fashioned shrub roses and the newer landscape varieties. Many gardeners still prefer the hybrid tea types because of their superior blooms. Whether growing the hybrid teas or the less-demanding types, there are still things that need to be done in a timely manner: controlling diseases and insects, pruning, planting, dividing, and providing winter care.

Shrub plantings need regular care to keep them flowering, attractive, and within bounds. Pruning must be done at the proper time of the season so that the plants will bloom the next year. I receive many calls from gardeners who cannot explain why their favorite lilac never blooms. They have regularly removed the flower buds after they formed by pruning. Certain times of the year are best for renewing shrubs so they grow back vigorously. Diseases that affect some shrubs must be prevented long before any indication of the trouble appears. Certain insect pests are susceptible to insecticide applications for only a few days a year. Miss that window, and the plants will be forced to endure the damage for another year. Start a shrub planting when the plants have the best chance of surviving.

Whether the trees you grow are fruit trees or ornamental flowering plants, pruning can remove the flower buds and stimulate wild growth. Or it can control the growth, allowing the plant to develop productive branches that will flower and fruit in abundance. Shade trees need to be guided by judicious pruning as they develop. Protecting trees from insects and diseases must be done in a timely manner. Some pest problems require treatment throughout the season. Others are very specific and must be confronted when the pest is susceptible to treatment.

Vines and ground covers are utilitarian plants. They often serve as backgrounds for other, more conspicuous plants. Often they are neglected until something happens to them. At Wrigley Field in Chicago, for instance, the Boston ivy vines on the outfield walls were taken for granted. They seemed to grow without difficulty even though they had become part of the charm of the "Friendly Confines." Even the Chicago Cubs newsletter is named *Vineline*. When the Japanese beetles and the leaf spot appeared late one season, the importance of these plants was immediately evident.

Once the damage was done, it was too late to do anything that year. Nevertheless, these troubles are now anticipated and treatments applied before the troubles arise. Some vines are so essential to the landscape that their loss changes the entire effect of the site. Not just the vines at Wrigley Field, but the ivy-covered walls of many institutions of higher learning create their personality. Weed control in some ground covers must be done when the weeds are susceptible but the damage to the ground cover is minimal.

Some ornamental grasses are exotics; others, are native plants. Care can be simple or complex. Annual and perennial ornamental grasses have places in the landscape. They can be spectacular.

Finally, the bogs that were once considered trouble spots in the landscape are now the water gardens that have become the newest fascination in the gardening world. Whether it is just a small fountain or a pond with waterfall and koi, the water garden will make use of plants that are unique to this kind of setting.

Now, let's look at these plants in more detail.

ANNUALS

Annuals are plants that germinate from seeds, grow, flower, produce seeds, and die in one season. In the flower garden, annuals begin to flower in early summer and continue to bloom until killed by freezing weather. This long season of floral display makes them popular. When we plant flowers, we want to see them blooming!

Plant hybridizers have developed vastly improved varieties of annuals that are more prolific and more disease resistant and have better form than plants of the past. They will fit almost any situation in your garden, including shade, if you select them carefully. You can use them in the following ways:

- Edging
- Accents
- Background
- A cutting garden
- A temporary landscape until new plantings are put in place
- Fillers in the perennial garden
- Container plants in flower boxes, urns, or planters

Since annuals are removed from the garden every fall, the soil can be improved and weeds controlled before planting in spring. This is a big advantage over trying to eliminate a weed problem without damaging plants already in place.

PLANNING THE ANNUAL FLOWER GARDEN

In planning your garden, use large splashes of color. Selections of mixed colors make a better impact if there are many plants. Try to avoid planting annuals in rows along the sidewalk or driveway where they will look like toy soldiers, detracting from the looks rather than adding to the interest of the landscape.

Before buying plants or seeds, draw your garden plan to scale on a piece of graph paper. Check the seed packets or your *Gardener's Guide* for the proper spacing so that you will know how many plants of various kinds are required. In shady areas where little else will grow, plant begonias, coleus, or impatiens. These adaptable plants will tolerate the shade and provide interest, too.

STARTING ANNUALS FROM SEEDS

Annuals are available at garden centers, supermarkets, and hardware stores—any place plants are sold—sometimes your choices are limited. For a challenge and more flower options, start your own seeds indoors under lights. By starting the plants indoors, you can have flowers earlier and feel the pride of doing it yourself, too. (See page 24 for instructions on how to build a light stand.)

TRANSPLANTING ANNUALS

When the seedlings are big enough to handle, transplant them into plastic cell-packs, the kind commercial growers use (they fit into flats, too), or into other convenient containers. Keep the lights just above the plant tops. Apply a liquid fertilizer after the plants start to grow. Set plants in the garden when frost is no longer a threat.

PREPARING THE SOIL

Kill all weeds in the annual garden or flower bed by applying herbicide or by hoeing them out. Use glyphosate or a similar herbicide that eliminates vigorous underground roots and rhizomes on perennial grasses such as quackgrass. Add compost or other organic matter and fertilizer to supply about $1\frac{1}{2}$ ounces of nitrogen (1 pound of 10-10-10 or the equivalent) per 100 square feet of flower bed. Spade or till the soil to a depth of at least 6 inches. Break up any lumps and clods to make a uniform, fine soil.

Set the plants at the proper spacing and at the same depth they grew in the transplant containers. If the roots are dense, butterfly the tiny ball from the bottom to force new roots.

CONTROLLING WEEDS

Weeds are easily controlled when they are small.

Hoe them out as soon as you see them. Use herbicides to prevent germination of new weed seeds. Apply them according to the directions on the label to weed-free soil.

CONTROLLING PESTS

Insects can attack your plants.

If you notice just a few insects, pick them off. If the whole garden is infested, spray or dust as needed according to instructions of pest-control products.

Control foliar diseases by keeping the leaves dry and spraying or dusting with an all-purpose garden fungicide.

Control root rot and collar rot diseases with proper watering practices or with soil fungicide drenches.

JANUARY
ANNUALS

PLANNING

Begin planning your flower garden for this summer. Start by drawing a plan on graph paper. Draw it to scale to be able to estimate the number of each kind of plant you will need.

Check your gardening journal. Which plants were especially nice in previous seasons? Which ones were failures? Do not be tempted to try them again—no matter how good they look in the catalogs.

Use the garden catalogs to advantage:

• Note the new varieties of old, familiar plants.

• Begin a list of annuals to try this year.

The All-America Selections are highlighted by the companies that offer them. They are always good plants to try, but their success depends on your particular garden. Most of these varieties do fairly well everywhere.

• Review your choices, and complete your list of old and new plants.

• Order your seeds.

Spring is just around the corner. Start some seeds this month to have transplants by the frost-free date.

PLANTING

If you have tried starting seeds indoors and have been disappointed because the plants were too tall and spindly, now is the time to do something about it. Lack of light causes most of the difficulties with growing garden plants indoors. Solve that problem by buying or building an artificial light stand and growing your plants under lights.

Follow these steps to build your own stand:

1. Make a lighting fixture with two, 2-tube, 40-watt shop lights. (You do not need plant lights; cool-white fluorescent bulbs work well.) Fasten them side by side to a piece of $3/4$-inch plywood or to two lengths of 1-by-4s. This unit will accommodate four 10-inch-by-20-inch standard flats.

2. Use a work bench or place boards over saw horses to make a stand 4 feet long and 20 inches wide to support the flats.

3. Hang the lights so that you can raise and lower them over the plants. Attach the lights to hooks from the ceiling, or build a rack with pulleys and ropes

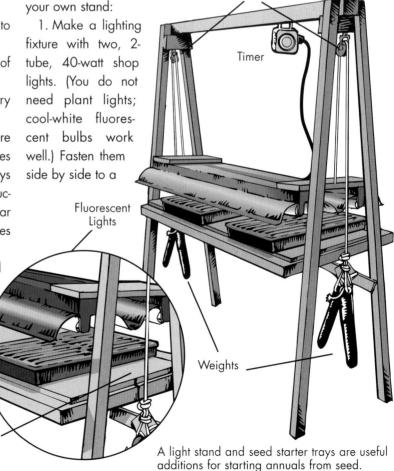

Pulleys

Timer

Fluorescent Lights

Weights

Seed-Starter Tray in 10x20" Flat Tray

A light stand and seed starter trays are useful additions for starting annuals from seed.

using bricks or old sash weights for counterbalances.

Visit your local garden center, and stock up on plastic flats, cell-packs, and miscellaneous containers for transplanting. Invest in at least one seed-starter tray. A tray has 20 rows of grooves to fill with artificial planting soil, such as Jiffy Mix, Pro Mix, Fafard, or any other brand, into which you will sow seeds.

Now you are ready to sow tiny-seeded **begonias**, **geraniums**, and **pansies** under lights:

1. Carefully sow seeds in the rows of starter trays.

2. Label each row so that you will know what is coming up. and include the variety if growing more than one kind.

3. Moisten the soil gently.

4. Cover trays with plastic wrap to prevent them from drying out.

5. Set the trays under the lights, and lower the lights to 2 inches above the trays.

If the stand is in a cold or drafty place, cover the whole setup to keep the heat from the lights in. Do not put the cover directly on the light fixture or it may burn.

CARE

As soon as the seeds have germinated, remove the cover over the light stand and the plastic cover from the trays. The seedlings will need to be hardened off so that they do not damp off in the trays. Because the lights need to be on for 18 hours out of every 24, you may want to use a timer.

WATERING

The seedlings will need water. Do not drown them, but keep them from wilting severely. When they start to look droopy, moisten them.

FERTILIZING

Seedlings will not be in the seed trays long enough to need fertilizer. If they begin to turn yellow, add a small amount of complete soluble fertilizer to the water. Use caution! These seedlings are very tender and easily injured.

PESTS

Keep alert for fungus gnats.

The larvae live in the potting soil. Drench with insecticidal soap or *Bacillus thuringiensis israelensis* to eliminate them.

Damping off is the most serious disease in the seed trays.

Having the seedlings in rows limits the spread of the disease. Drenching with a thiophanate-type fungicide may be helpful. Follow label directions carefully. Sanitation is the best defense against diseases.

HELPFUL HINTS

Inventory your garden tools. Sharpen the hoes and shovels so that they will be easier to use. Wash off all the tools, and wipe them with an oily rag to protect them.

Check the condition of the **geraniums** overwintering indoors. Leaves on plants stored in brown paper bags should be dry, but the stems should still be green. If the plants are shriveling, mist them. If they are moldy, open the bags and dry them out.

Record the source of the seeds, the varieties, the planting date, and when the first seedlings appear in your journal. Indicate difficulties, diseases, bugs, poor germination, and any other information that may be helpful in the future.

FEBRUARY

ANNUALS

 PLANNING

February is a busy month for gardeners. The days are longer, and growing-things begin to perk up.

This month your first task is to buy or make transplanting soil. The artificial mixes with brown peat moss and perlite are excellent. (Do not buy the moist, black potting soil for this use.) You may prefer to make your own soil mix; use 1/3 each loamy garden soil, #2 torpedo sand, and brown peat moss.

Moisten the potting mix. Artificial mixes are slow to wet. Unless they are wetted before they are used, they may not wet at all. Pour some in a bucket, and add water. Stir the mix once in a while to moisten all of it.

Your next task is to obtain containers for transplanting seedlings. They need drainage holes in the bottoms and should be small enough not to take up all the room under your lights. You have two choices:

1. Commercial cell-packs are available from garden centers or hardware stores. They fit perfectly into the 10-inch-by-20-inch plastic flats. Each will hold 6 or 8 seedlings.

2. Containers that you have around the house—cottage cheese cartons, bottoms of milk cartons, small pots, or peat pots—are acceptable. The containers do not have to be fancy, but they should be the same height. If the containers are different heights, getting the lights adjusted to the right distance from the plants will be difficult. Punch some drainage holes in the bottoms.

 PLANTING

Several important annuals must be sown in February, and you will need room under the lights for them.

Gerbera daisy

• Sow **gerberas**, **petunias**, **impatiens**, and **wax begonias** on February 1.

Some of these seeds are amazingly tiny, like dust. Sow them on top of artificial mix, and do not cover them—they need light to germinate. Label them carefully.

• Sow **ageratum**, **lobelia**, and **love-in-a-mist** on February 15.

Transplant seedlings started in December and January as soon as they are large enough to handle.

1. Lift them out of the seedling tray with the end of a small wooden label. Be careful not to

squeeze the stems or to break off the roots.

2. Separate them by gently pulling them apart. If the seedlings are left in the starter tray too long, they will become a jumbled mess and be difficult to separate.

3. Fill the containers with artificial mix, and firm it so that it does not settle.

4. Use the point of a pencil or a small label as a dibble to make holes in the mix.

5. Set a seedling in each hole using the dibble to push all the roots into the hole.

6. Firm the seedling down with your finger and thumb on each side.

CARE

Water the cell-packs after planting them, and set them under the lights. Lower the lights to 1 inch above the seedling tops. Did you label the packs? Include the kind of plants and the variety if you are growing more than one.

WATERING

Do not overwater the seedlings or the transplants. The first watering after transplanting settles the soil around roots and should be sufficient to keep the plants from wilting for a week or so. The plants may stay wilted from transplanting for 1 or 2 days. When the soil dries to the touch, water again. These plants can tolerate a little wilting to harden them off.

FERTILIZING

The artificial potting soils do not have any fertilizer in them, so you will need to add some. Use a soluble 20-20-20 fertilizer at $1/2$ the recommended strength. Apply the fertilizer to wet soil after the second watering. Once the plants are growing vigorously, fertilize them monthly at the normal rate.

HELPFUL HINTS

Have you run out of room yet? You may need additional room once you are in full production. Do not grow any more plants than you really need unless you are willing to develop more growing space. Another plant stand may be necessary.

If you do have a little room, take cuttings from **geraniums**, **begonias**, and **coleus** overwintering in pots. Root them in sand under the lights. They will become sizable plants by Mother's Day. Put them in an attractive pot with a cheery bow as a nice little gift for someone special.

Begonia

MARCH

ANNUALS

PLANNING

Signs of spring are all around. The plant stand is full. There is no more room for transplanting, but the seedling tray is getting overgrown. What can you do?

Consider a cold frame. Garden catalogs offer all kinds, but it does not need to be fancy. You can make your own. I use a portable one that I can set up in the part of the garden that will be planted last. Here are its ideal specifications:

• It is made of plywood, the size of an old storm window.

It is 30-by-60 inches inside and holds nine 10-by-20-inch flats.

• Its corners are made from 4 pieces of 2-by-4s.

• The back is 15 inches high, the front 10 inches.

• The sash can be slid back to permit me to work on the plants or to let in air. (I may put hinges on it this year.)

PLANTING

As soon as you can, transplant the seedlings you sowed in February. Move the biggest of them to the cold frame. If severe weather threatens, move them indoors for a night or so. Move them back out when the temperatures are moderate. Eventually, they will harden off

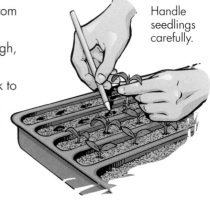

Handle seedlings carefully.

and will take the low temperatures as long as it does not actually freeze in the cold frame.

A frame will warm up on sunny days and will stay quite warm all night. Cover the frame with old blankets on a frosty night. Remove the cover when the sun comes up the next day.

In March, most of the snow is gone, and the ground is beginning to dry out. The itch to garden is probably overtaking you by now. There is something you can do.

The **pansies** you seeded last December are ready to be planted. Set them outside in the flat for a few days to harden off. If the weather is supposed to stay mild for a few days, go ahead and plant them. We like to look out the picture window in our kitchen to watch the birds at the feeder. The flower bed

A cold frame can be made from a few materials.

around the feeder is the perfect place for **pansies** with their bright, cheery faces.

On March 1, sow these seeds:
- **Coleus**
- **Dusty miller**
- **Nicotiana**
- **Pinks**
- **Melampodium**
- **Snaps**
- **Verbena**

You should be getting good at this by now. Which ones need light? Check your planting chart.

On March 15, make room to sow these seeds:
- **Alyssum**
- **Portulaca**
- **Salvia**

If the ground has dried out, you can try to spade over a spot in the flower garden where the direct-seeded annuals will go. You can sow some seeds there in a couple of weeks.

CARE

By the end of this month, the worst of the weather should be over. Spring is officially here!

Is the cold frame full, too? As long as the temperatures stay above freezing, most of the transplants can spend the time outside. If frost or a freeze is predicted, move plants indoors overnight.

WATERING

Be cautious about watering. As long as it is cool, plants do not need much water. Keep them on the drier side rather than on the wetter side. If the sun suddenly comes out after days of cloudy weather, be sure they have enough water, and then let them wilt. (They will wilt whether you let them or not.)

FERTILIZING

If the plants are growing and have normal color, they do not need fertilizer. If they are hardened off and lower leaves are turning yellow, fertilize with soluble 20-20-20 mixed according to directions.

PESTS

Mites can become a problem under lights.

If the plants are getting yellow dots in the leaves, shake a plant over a piece of white paper. Mites that fall off will look like tiny moving specks. Insecticidal soap will control them.

Damping off can be troublesome if plants are kept too wet.

Be careful with the water!

GROOMING

Pinch plants that are overly long to remove the growing tips. They will branch out, making bushier plants. Do not pinch tall **snapdragons** or **marigolds**.

HELPFUL HINTS

In addition to cold frames, a small portable greenhouse can be set up now to handle the overflow from the light stand. I have a plastic-covered, portable greenhouse that is 6 feet square and has enough head room to allow me to stand up. It has 2 shelves and can hold 25 to 30 flats. Because of its height, it holds enough heat to keep it from freezing until temperatures fall below about 25 degrees Fahrenheit.

Pick a few **pansies**. Put them in a glass on the kitchen table.

APRIL
ANNUALS

PLANNING

Daylight saving time! Isn't it amazing how the change of time makes you want to get into the garden?

April showers are different, too. They may bring May flowers, but they also make for wet gardens. Do not be in too much of a rush to work wet soils.

PLANTING

As soon as seedlings in the starter trays are large enough to handle, transplant them into cell-packs. Left too long in the seed flat, they will become overly long, and roots will be difficult to get out.

Even though there is not enough room for all the things in the cold frame or under the lights, it is still too early to plant most annuals in the garden. But some annuals can be seeded directly into the garden.

Sow the following where they will be growing:

- **Spider flowers (cleomes)**
- **Cosmos**
- **Four-o'clocks**
- **Globe amaranths**
- **Gloriosa daisies**
- **Morning glories**
- **Moss roses**
- **Snapdragons**

Or seed them a little heavily, and plan to transplant the extra seedlings to other places in the garden.

The average date of last frost is only 1 month away. The latest date of last frost is about May 5 in the southern part of the state, May 30 farther north. It is none too soon to seed the last plants under lights. Do not delay sowing **calendulas**, **celosias**, **gail-** **lardias**, **marigolds**, and **zinnias**. In only 4 to 6 weeks they will be big enough to plant outside.

CARE

Lift the sash on the cold frame on sunny days. Lower it if the sun goes behind a cloud or the North wind begins to howl. It can still be winter this time of year, especially in the north. Snow happens. Wasn't there a song about a "love that's swift and light as an April snow?" By this time of the year, snow does not stay around too long, but it does not take much of it to wreak havoc on your plants!

WATERING

Watering the flats and packs takes a lot of time now. Do not let the plants dry out. Use a water-

Squeeze a handful of soil into a clump. If you can't crumble it (and it remains in a clump), it's too wet to work.

Four-o'clocks

Use insecticidal soap to dry up the aphids and whiteflies. Drench the soil with insecticidal soap *Bacillus thuringiensis israelensis* to eliminate fungus gnats.

Damping off is the most serious disease of plants in the cold frame or under lights.

Avoid overwatering the plants.

Weedy grasses or chickweed may invade the garden. Kill them with glyphosate before turning the garden. Keep the glyphosate off anything of value. Once glyphosate hits a green weed or runs off into the soil, it is deactivated. You do not have to worry about it affecting things planted later.

GROOMING

As the plants begin to stretch, pinch the tips out to stimulate branching. Do not pinch tall **marigolds** or **snapdragons**.

When the soil dries so that a handful can be squeezed into a ball and then broken, begin to turn over the flower beds. Refer to the design of your garden to refresh your memory about which plants go where. Leave enough space for things that will be planted later.

ing rose on a long handle to gently flood the plants without knocking them over and without breaking your back.

FERTILIZING

Annuals that have been transplanted for a couple of weeks will need fertilizer. Use a complete, soluble kind that can be mixed in a watering can. Miracle-Gro™ or Peters™ 20-20-20 works. Or use whatever brand your neighborhood nursery has available. Because plants such as **ageratum** are touchy, do not overdo the fertilizing.

PESTS

Fungus gnats, aphids, and whiteflies can be problems.

MAY

ANNUALS

PLANNING

Think ahead. Where will you put all the plants you have been growing? Did you make your garden plan?

You may become so involved in growing things that you forget to do the planning. You see something pretty in the catalogs, or you cannot resist the beautiful pictures on the seed packs. When you transplant the seedlings, you cannot bear to throw out the extra plants, so you plant them, too. And suddenly the basement, the cold frames, and the garage are overflowing with plants.

It is not too late to make some sense out of the mess. Draw a garden plan. Identify the plants you will need, and give the rest away. I have neighbors who know me well enough to expect that there will be plants available. They are seldom disappointed.

PLANTING

All annuals can be set out in the garden this month. By the end of May, even the northern part of the state is frost free. Space your plants appropriately. Plant them too close together, and they will be overcrowded with poor blooming. Plant them too far apart, and they will not fill in. Check your catalogs or your *Gardener's Guide* for the correct spacing.

Set the plants at the proper depth, too. Too deep, and they will rot. Too shallow and they can fall over the first time you water them and they will dry out.

Thin out direct-seeded annuals to the correct spacing.

If you have leftover plants, pot them in planters, strawberry jugs, or whatever you have. Set the containers around the patio, on the front steps, or wherever an accent is appropriate. Mix tall, short, and creeping plants to create imaginative arrangements.

WATERING

Watering small plants is critical. Do not let them dry out, but do not keep them soaked or they will rot off. Water to soak the soil, and allow the plants to wilt before watering again. It is best to water in the morning so that the plants have plenty of time to dry before nightfall.

FERTILIZING

Mix liquid 20-20-20 fertilizer in a bucket. Apply 1 cupful to newly transplanted annuals to get them off to a good start.

Marigold 'First Lady'

PESTS

Did you plant **marigolds**? Have they turned to lace overnight?

If they have, go on a midnight safari. About an hour after dark, the nighttime pests begin their evening's activities. Take a flashlight with you, and see what is eating your plants.

Earwigs and slugs will eat **marigolds** and other pungent plants. To combat earwigs, dust or spray carbaryl on the plants. Control slugs with either metaldehyde baits. Spread them outside the flower bed to attract the pests. Or try the beer trick. A pan of stale beer will attract slugs because they like the strong smell of aldehydes. Get out early the next morning and collect them before they sober up and go home.

Other bugs make their first appearances this month. Cutworms eat off the new plants at the soil line. You are left with dead tops lying there the next morning.

Add aluminum foil collars to the stems to hide the plants from the marauding worms.

Aphids and spider mites can be problems.

Combat them with insecticidal soap. Spray the undersides of the leaves and the growing tips of the plants.

If the weather stays cool and wet, leaf spot diseases can show up.

Be alert. At the first sign of trouble, spray or dust the plants with a fungicide. Maneb or thiophanate-methyl fungicides will work.

If weeds have shown up where the flowers are to be planted, get rid of them first.

Apply glyphosate to any large weeds or grasses. It will be deactivated as soon as it dries, so there is no danger to your new plants.

Other weeds may show up in your planting later. Hoe them out.

After your plants have recovered from having been transplanted, apply a pre-emergent herbicide to prevent weed seeds from germinating.

Apply dacthal or trifluralin to weed-free soil. Read the label to be sure the material will not harm the flowers in your garden.

GROOMING

Did some of your seedlings get overly long? Pinch them down right away to stimulate side shoots and more blooms. Do not pinch tall **snapdragons**. You want long stems on them.

HELPFUL HINTS

Annuals grow very quickly as soon as the weather turns warm. But while it is still cool, they will just sit there. Do not be alarmed. Covering your plants with clear plastic on cool, dark days will keep the heat in and speed them up. Do not cover them, however, if there is a likelihood that the sun will appear. It will cook the plants.

There is always a chance that a once-in-a-lifetime late frost will happen. I remember one in late June of 1963. It froze corn as far as Kankakee, Illinois, and Lafayette, Indiana. Keep a blanket or a couple of old bed sheets handy to cover your plants if frost is predicted.

Make your journal entries. Record the dates you planted the various annuals, how they were spaced, and how well they developed from the date you sowed the seed. It is important to note how the things you try actually work out. If the plants were too small from the seeding date, for instance, plan to sow a week earlier next year.

Draw a plan of where you actually planted the annuals. You may not always follow your original garden plan.

JUNE
ANNUALS

PLANNING

Start thinking about how you will take care of your flowers when you are on vacation.

You may have a neighbor who is willing to help. Or you may need to contact plant care people who will stop by every day to see that everything is okay.

If you will be gone only a week, plan to water thoroughly, weed, and deadhead before you leave. Big gardens are like pets. They can make it difficult to get away. Usually, even after a couple of weeks, the garden will need only a little cleaning up to be as good as new.

PLANTING

It is still not too late to plant annuals. If the spring bulbs were late and you just cut back the leaves, plant the space with annuals now. If the plants are a little leggy, cut them back to make bushier plants and more blooms.

Here are some ways to use extra annuals:

• Plant them in pots, cans, or planters.

• Give them as gifts for apartment or condo dwellers who do not have room to grow their own plants.

• Let your imagination run free. A pot of red **geraniums**, purple **petunias**, and white **alyssum** makes a great display in the corner of the deck. Many combinations look good.

• Change the plants as the season progresses and things wear out.

WATERING

Watering can be quite a chore if you have lots of flowers. Watering over the top creates perfect conditions for diseases. Hand watering is still the best way to make sure all the plants get the water they need while keeping the leaves dry. But you may not have time to water during a busy day, and after work there is the chance that the plants will stay too wet overnight.

Leaky pipe or drip watering systems are the next best things. They apply the water to the soil, not to the tops of the plants. Of the various kinds of leaky pipe systems, some squirt water all over the plants. The better ones sweat the water out.

Drip systems have individual emitters spaced out so that water is applied to each plant. Some systems have spaghetti tubing that goes to each plant.

Check an automatic watering system regularly. If it is not working correctly, things may get plugged up, and plants will not be watered.

June brings the first of the really hot weather. If your plants have gone through a spell of cool, dark weather, the sun will wilt them. Wilting does not mean the plants lack water; it means that the water is leaving the plants faster than it can be replaced. The soft leaves lose water too fast. They will harden up in a couple of days. Before watering, check the soil. If it is moist, there is no need for more water.

Annuals such as some **impatiens** varieties will wilt every time they are in full sun. If wilted plants recover overnight and look fine the next morning, do not water them. If they do not recover overnight, water them in the morning.

FERTILIZING

Every month apply a complete, dry fertilizer such as 10-10-10 to keep plants vigorous and healthy. Use 1 pound per 100 square feet. Keep it off the leaves, and water it in immediately.

PESTS

If your leaves turn to lace overnight, take a midnight safari with a flashlight to see what is eating them.

Carbaryl controls earwigs. Stale beer attract slugs. Set out a pan of beer, and dispose of slugs the next morning. Insecticidal soap combats aphids and mites.

Old blooms attract botrytis, the gray fuzz that grows on old dead stuff. If you give it a chance, botrytis can attack plants such as **geraniums**, which are very susceptible to it. Botrytis causes brown edges on the leaves.

Most annual flowers have completed the first flush of bloom by now. Deadhead the plants to clean them up so that they look nicer. Deadheading also relieves them of the seed load and hastens reblooming.

In wet weather, weeds will sprout as if by magic.

Hoe weeds out as soon as you see them.

Rabbits can be a problem in your garden.

Try anything you want, but only vicious dogs and/or a sturdy fence keep rabbits out!

GROOMING

Plants fill in faster and make more blooms if they are pinched early. Just nip out the growing tip. Side shoots will show up in a few days.

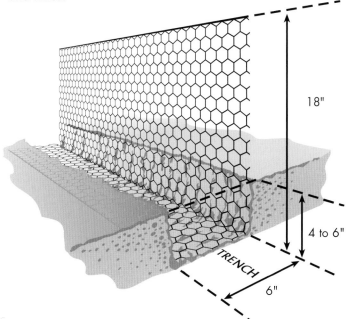

18"

4 to 6"

TRENCH

6"

Use this illustration to guide you if you construct a rabbit fence.

HELPFUL HINTS

Stake tall-growing plants so that they will remain upright. Use tomato cages for plants in the back of the garden where the cages will not be so noticeable. With plant ties or green twine, fasten plants to wooden or iron plant stakes driven behind the plants.

Mulches keep the soil moist, but they attract slugs, millipedes, and earwigs. If you are having trouble with these pests, resist the temptation to mulch the flowers. If you are not having trouble with them, apply 1 or 2 inches of shredded bark mulch. It is attractive, and it does not wash away. Or you may try compost, shredded corncobs, or pecan shells. Be aware that the shells may attract mice and squirrels looking for the remaining bits of nuts.

JULY
ANNUALS

 PLANNING

Visit the public gardens in your area. Most of them try new plants every year.

Take your notebook and camera so that you can make notes and get a picture when you see something interesting. Attend the summer field days at one or more of the following:

- Botanic gardens
- University trial gardens
- Demonstration gardens at your local community college
- Various seed companies throughout the state

These are good places to meet other gardeners and exchange ideas.

 PLANTING

If you have not planted annuals yet, your neighborhood garden center will still have plenty to choose from. Where perennials such as **poppies** or **bleeding hearts** were so beautiful a month ago, only a hole remains. Plant annuals to fill the void. Be careful not to damage the crowns of the perennials.

 CARE

Tall-growing flowers may need support with tomato cages or stakes. Do not tie the stems too tightly. The sooner you provide supports, the less obvious they will be. The plants will grow into them instead of being bundled up.

 WATERING

Unless you have an automatic sprinkler system, plan to have a neighbor water your flowers when you are gone. It is an unwritten rule: it always rains when you are on vacation, but never at home where the garden needs it. Provide clear watering instructions to the neighbor. Do not expect perfection, though.

 FERTILIZING

If the season has been wet, larger plants can profit from side dressing with a complete fertilizer now. Use a 10-10-10 fertilizer, and apply 1 pound on 100 square feet of garden. (A 1-pound coffee can holds about 2 pounds of fertilizer.) Keep it off the foliage. Water to wash any fertilizer off the plants and to get it into the soil where it will work.

 PESTS

Japanese beetles appear this month.

The big, slow-moving metallic bronze-and-green beetles eat leaves into lace. Spraying works, but picking them off your plants is easier.

Infestations of aphids and mites can seriously damage plants in a few days.

When the infestation is light, insecticidal soap works well. The soap also controls thrips (which can carry damaging diseases), whiteflies, plant bugs, and lacebugs.

Plant bugs make brown spots in the leaves.

Sometimes the damage looks like a disease, but it is not. Look for quick-moving green insects that run away. Adults can fly away.

If just one shoot of a plant is infested, clip it off instead of spraying.

Weeds can break through the herbicides and mulch after a couple of months.

If they get a good start, weeds will be tough to control. As soon as you see weeds, hoe or pull them out. Then reapply the herbicide and mulch.

Although a composting drum is ideal, there are many ways to compost.

 GROOMING

The more vigorous annuals, such as **petunias**, **impatiens**, **marigolds**, and **zinnias**, can be pretty shaggy by now. Give them a haircut before you leave on your vacation. Cut them back about halfway or even more to remove any overly long stems and stems that have fallen over. It will take about 2 weeks for them to regain their flowers. By the time you get back, they will look fine. Remove faded flowers to stimulate new blooms. Compost clippings so that they do not go to waste.

You may choose from the following methods:

• Start a compost pile.

Check with local ordinances; open composting is not permitted in all areas. Chop up the clippings and dig them into empty parts of the vegetable garden, behind the shrub border, or any place where the ground is available.

• Using a composting drum is an easier and cleaner choice than a compost pile.

• Compost small amounts in a black plastic bag.

Fill the bag with chopped clippings, a shovelful of soil, and some moisture. Turn it over whenever you think of it, and it will compost in a few weeks.

HELPFUL HINTS

Cut a bouquet for a neighbor or someone who has been ill. We gardeners take the flowers for granted because we see them all the time. Many people are not so fortunate and really appreciate a few for the kitchen table.

In Europe, no one goes visiting without a few flowers. That would be a nice tradition to start in our country.

AUGUST
ANNUALS

PLANNING

Even the best-laid plans do not always work out.

Note in your journal the annuals that have been disappointing, and plan to make changes next year.

PLANTING

Container plants need extra care. A little plant tending is in order by now. Cut back overgrown plants, and replace the ones that have seen better times. Check with your local garden center to see what is available to make a refreshing addition. Container plantings can benefit from refurbishing every month or so.

CARE

The weather can be hot and dry this month. You may be tempted to let things go because you tire of taking care of them. But do not give up.

WATERING

Maintain a regular watering routine. When the plants wilt, apply a measured inch of water. This amount will moisten the soil about 6 inches deep, plenty of water for annuals for about a week on heavy soils, about half that long on sand. Do not water again until the soil dries out.

FERTILIZING

Fertilize annuals with 20-20-20 liquid according to the directions on the package, or apply 10-10-10 again, using about 1 pound per 100 square feet of flower bed.

Container plants need regular fertilizing. Most will need fertilizer by now. Apply liquid 20-20-20, 1 ounce in 2½ gallons of water.

Spraying with a flower and garden fungicide will protect your flowers from mildew.

PESTS

Little holes in leaves are nothing to worry about. Disappearing leaves or flowers are worrisome.

Control chewing bugs with one of the *Bacillus thuringiensis* sprays. Use *Bacillus thuringiensis kurstaki* for caterpillars and use *Bacillus thuringiensis san diego* for beetles. Carbaryl or cyfluthrin will work, too.

Cool evenings with heavy dew bring on mildew and other diseases.

Protect the flowers in the cutting garden from mildew. Use a flower and garden fungicide such as triforine, or use dusting sulfur.

Even little weeds can make seeds, which means trouble for seasons to come.

Keep hoeing weeds. If you can keep the garden weed free for a year, it will be easier the next season. Fewer seeds mean fewer weeds.

Rabbits have changeable appetites. The little ones are big enough by now to be on their own. They will pick unusual things to eat. One is eating the marigold flowers in my garden right now, brazen as can be.

Pepper-garlic spray usually works. But a rabbit that eats marigolds may not mind the pepper, either.

GROOMING

Deadheading is a continuous, but necessary, job. Flowers left to go to seed will take energy needed to produce more blooms. Do a little every evening, and it will never get ahead of you. I cover my thumb with a piece of old rubber hose slit down one side, then I use a pocketknife to cut the old blooms. Eventually, you will learn to hold onto the old flower as you cut it. If you wear a gardening apron, you can deposit the clippings in it and then not have to pick up after yourself.

If the plants are getting leggy again, cut them back. If you can keep your flowers in shape through the heat and drought of August, they will reward you when cooler weather returns in fall.

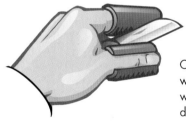

Covering your thumb and forefinger with an old piece of rubber hose will protect it from cuts when you deadhead your plants.

HELPFUL HINTS

• By now, the best and the worst of the garden should be apparent. It is time to make evaluations and record them in your journal. Indicate the names of the varieties, the places where they are growing, the conditions—wet, dry, sun, shade—so that you will know where they did the best (or worst). Sometimes the season has an effect on how well a variety performs.

• Has it been hot and dry, or cool? Has there been extended wet weather with clouds? All of these conditions can affect how well plants do. If everything did poorly or did well, record that, too.

• Make a bouquet from the cutting garden for a neighbor and one for your coffee table. The season is getting short. Enjoy the flowers as long as you can.

SEPTEMBER

ANNUALS

PLANNING

Although the annuals are almost finished by September, some look their best in the cool fall weather.

Visit some public gardens, and find out how they keep their displays looking so good even late in the season.

PLANTING

Where the plants have outlived their usefulness, pull them out.

A vacant spot in the yard now is better than an eyesore. Did you start composting in July? The old plants can go into the compost pile.

Fill in the vacated spots in the annual border with potted **hardy mums**, **asters**, **ornamental kale** and **cabbage**, or **pansies**.

You may choose to leave the spots vacant. If the soil has been difficult to work, this is the time to improve it:

1. Chop up the old, disease-free plants, and dig them into the flower beds.

2. Add any other organic matter you can find.

3. Turn the soil to at least one good spade depth, about 12 inches.

4. Leave the soil rough. It will catch water during the winter and will freeze and thaw, mellowing it. Most of the organic matter will be decomposed by planting time next spring.

CARE

Frost is not far off! Be ready. Putting a few old bed sheets or blankets over the plants for 1 or 2 nights can save them for another few weeks of enjoyment. Remove the covers the next day so that the plants do not cook.

Before they are frozen, some annuals can be brought indoors for the winter. **Begonias**, **geraniums**, **browalias**, **coleus**, and **gerberas** may be worth keeping over. If you have a place indoors with enough light, they can flower all winter, and you can set them back in the garden in spring. Lift whole plants, knock

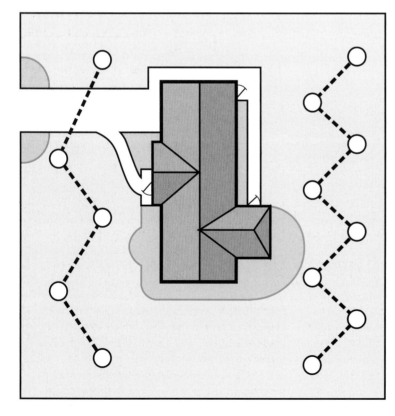

Collect soil for testing from several spots in your landscape.

the soil from the roots, and pot them in artificial mix, or take cuttings. **Geraniums** can be lifted and stored upside down in brown paper bags until spring.

WATERING

Rainfall is usually adequate in autumn. If it is not, apply 1 inch of water after the plants begin to wilt. If they do not wilt, they do not need water.

FERTILIZING

Collect soil for testing now. The results will be back in time to apply remedial fertilizers this fall or early next spring.

PESTS

As weather becomes cool and moist, slugs become active again.

Control them with slug bait or with pans of stale beer. Get out early in the morning to collect them before the slugs sober up and head home.

Mildew develops on susceptible plants when nights are cool and damp.

Fungicide treatments are probably not necessary at this late date. Plan to select mildew-resistant varieties next year.

Do not give up on weed control even where the garden is empty.

Many of the garden weeds make seeds in the fall. If they get a chance, they will drop seeds, providing plenty of weeds next year. Winter annual weeds such as chickweed and annual bluegrass get their start now. These plants will live over winter, sometimes even making flowers under the snow. Hoe them out as soon as you see them.

Perennial grasses can invade the garden.

Spray them with glyphosate while they are still growing. Glyphosate will kill broadleaf weeds, too, even **elm** and **maple** seedlings. It is much easier to get rid of weeds when the garden is empty and there are no flowers to worry about damaging.

The holes in the flower beds could be caused by squirrels burying **walnuts**, **peanuts**, or for even **crabapples**.

Squirrels are . . . squirrely.

HELPFUL HINTS

Cooler weather and some moisture should have annuals looking their best now. If you have kept the plants cut back when they were leggy, and if you have protected them from bugs and diseases, they should reward you with another month of beautiful blooms.

If annuals are not at their peak now, try to figure out why. Should you have trimmed them back one more time? Did you neglect to spray for earwigs? Were they planted too far apart? Make notes in your journal.

Look at the entries made during the season, and list some ways you might avoid the same difficulties next year.

Varieties have a lot to do with the behavior of plants in your garden. The descriptions in the catalogs and my success with the varieties in my garden have no bearing on what you can expect in your garden. Note the varieties you are growing. If your 'Super Elfins' **impatiens** are just the right size this year, buy them next year, too.

OCTOBER

ANNUALS

 PLANNING

By the end of the month, a few stragglers will be the only remaining plants in your annual garden.

Notice how some plants survive the frost. Remember the plants with frost tolerance when you decide to set out plants in the spring. **Petunias, snapdragons, moss roses,** and **verbenas,** for example, can stand a little cold and can be set out earlier.

Other plants survive because they are protected. Overhanging trees, the warm, south side of the house, taller garden plants—all create microclimates that ward off the cold. You can plant these areas earlier in the spring, too.

Good records make planning easier. If you have resisted starting a journal (maybe the name discourages you), make a few notes now. Call it a gardening notebook if you want, but record the successes and disappointments of the season. Next year, you can avoid the problems and concentrate on the good things that happened.

 PLANTING

It is not too late to move **geraniums** indoors for the winter. Save only the best, cleanest plants. Unless you have a bright, cool place to grow them indoors, simply knock the soil off the roots and cut the tops back so that they fit in a brown paper grocery bag. Hang them in a cool place in the basement until spring.

 CARE

Finish cleaning up the garden. Chop up the old plants and spread them over the garden. Make good use of fallen tree leaves to improve the soil in your garden. Any kind of organic matter will improve the soil, whether it is heavy clay or sand. Spade the organic matter into the garden. Leave the soil rough so that winter rains and frost will mellow it. The freezing and thawing make the soil friable in spring.

 PESTS

Weeds will go to seed now. Hoe out any remaining weeds.

November

ANNUALS

 PLANNING

November is a time for finishing up. You may not be not concerned with planning, but you need to do some things during the winter to be ready for spring.

Make a list of things such as broken or missing tools, materials that you ran out of, a tool you always wished you had, or something frivolous that someone might get you as a gift. You might leave a note where someone making a Christmas list could "accidentally" find it.

On another list, write down the chores (such as building the plant stand or cold frame) that can be done this winter.

 PLANTING

If you plan to grow **pansies** for next spring, it is time to get the supplies and the seeds. If the new catalogs have not yet arrived, order from this year's spring edition. It will still work.

 CARE

Annuals moved indoors for the winter will need a cool, bright place. Do not try to force them to grow. Let them find their own way. Once they have adjusted, they may bloom.

 WATERING

Be stingy with water on annuals kept indoors for the winter, unless the soil actually dries out. Plants kept too wet will rot.

 FERTILIZING

Since you are maintaining rather than growing the plants, you probably do not need to fertilize them.

 PESTS

Whiteflies and spider mites often infest plants moved in for the winter.

Insecticidal soap will control these pests. Spray the undersides of the leaves thoroughly.

Indoors, overly wet plants will damp off.

Use care in watering plants.

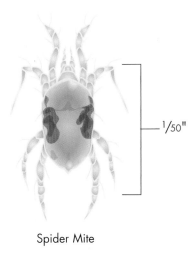

Spider Mite

1/50"

 GROOMING

Plants may become spindly indoors. Pinch back overly long shoots to force branching.

HELPFUL HINTS

- The annual flower garden is just a memory except for the **flowering cabbage**, **kale**, or **pansies**. But while the memory is still good, finalize the notes in your journal. Be critical of the season. Record your impressions, and make particular note of things you need to do differently next year. Read comments from past years, too. Make preliminary notes of things to do during the winter.

- Before the ground freezes, collect soil for testing. Your local Extension Service office and many garden centers can send soils to testing labs. The report will be back in time for ordering and applying the fertilizer next spring.

December

ANNUALS

PLANNING

Cold and snow will soon put the garden to sleep for the winter.

If you have ever lived in a part of the country where there is no winter, you know what that means. There is no end to the bugs or the weeds, and the diseases worsen at this time of year. So we can count our blessings. Each season starts anew. Finish up the year by taking stock of the joys your garden has provided during the year. Garden catalogs arrive this month, and it is time to begin planning the garden. But for now, it is enough to just relax and look at the pictures.

For us avid gardeners, though, the season never ends. We are always looking forward to the next year. There are some things that need doing this month.

PLANTING

Seed **pansies** this month so you will have sizable transplants to go out in March. You will need a bright, cool place to grow the plants all winter. A plant stand with artificial lights is the next best thing to a greenhouse. (Look on page 24 to learn how to construct one.)

To seed the plants, you need transplanting soil and a seed-starter tray. The artificial mixes with brown peat moss and perlite are excellent. (Do not buy the moist, black potting soil for this use.) You can make your own soil mix with 1/3 each loamy garden soil, #2 torpedo sand, and brown peat moss.

Moisten the potting mix. Pour some in a bucket, and add water. Stir the mix once in a while to moisten all of it. Fill the grooves in the seed-starter tray with the soil. Now you are ready to sow the seeds:

• Sow the seeds in the rows of the seed-starter tray. You will not need all 20 of the grooves now.

• Moisten the tray. Cover it with plastic wrap to keep it moist.

• Set the tray under the lights or in a bright place. The temperature should be kept at 70 degrees Fahrenheit.

• Lower the lights to 2 inches above the tray. Seeds will be up in a week or so.

• Remove the plastic.

Seedlings will stay in the tray until they are large enough to handle, within 2 or 3 weeks. Lift them out of the seedling tray with the end of a small wooden label. Be careful not to squeeze the stems or to break off the roots. Separate them by gently pulling them apart.

Fill the containers (cell-packs or something similar) with artificial mix, and firm it so that it does not settle. Use the point of a pencil or a small label as a dibble to make holes in the mix. Set a seedling in each hole using the dibble to push all the roots into the hole. Firm the seedling down with your finger and thumb on each side.

Did you label the packs? Be sure to do so. Include the kind of plants and the variety if you are growing more than one.

WATERING

Once the seeds have germinated, water to keep the seedlings from wilting.

Water the cell-packs after planting them, and set them under the lights. Lower the lights to 1 inch above the seedling tops.

FERTILIZING

Seedlings will not be in the seeding tray long enough to need fertilizer. As soon as they are transplanted, fertilize them with liquid 20-20-20 at half the recommended rate on the package.

BULBS, CORMS, RHIZOMES, & TUBERS

Plants with several kinds of underground structures are included in this chapter: bulbs, corms, rhizomes, and tubers, all structures that allow the plants to survive unfavorable weather.

Bulbs are important throughout the yearly flower garden pageant: in spring and summer and even moving indoors for winter. Crocuses burst forth before the snow is gone, followed by daffodils and majestic tulips. Then summer bulbs take over with cannas, tuberous begonias, gladiolus, and the stately lilies.

Plants that arise from bulbs are some of the easiest plants to grow. Bulbs are compressed, underground buds. Within a bulb is a tiny plant, complete with roots, stem, leaves, and flowers.

A true bulb consists of concentric layers that are bases of modified leaves. (These are called turnicated bulbs.) Daffodil or tulip bulbs are typical. Lily bulbs have individual overlapping scales.

Bulbs may be hardy or tender. Hardy bulbs stay in the ground, perfectly able to stand the winter cold. Since they stay in place for years, take some time when planning where they will be planted and when preparing the soil.

The most widely recognized bulbs are the spring- flowering types. In addition to tulips and

daffodils, crocuses, trout lilies, grape hyacinths, and many other kinds fit within this grouping. These bulbs are completely hardy and will flower year after year with little care.

Other hardy bulbs flower in summer or fall. Lilies and flowering onions (*Allium*) bloom in summer. Resurrection lily, montbretia, and autumn crocus bloom in late summer or fall.

Tender bulbs flower in the summer. Some of the most outstanding garden flowers— dahlias, gladiolus, cannas, tuberous begonias, and caladiums—are in this group.

Tubers and corms are really stems. Tubers are swollen underground stems that store starch. The new plant grows from a single bud. Potatoes, dahlias, and tuberous begonias grow from tubers. The eyes are the buds. Corms are short stems. Leaves grow from the pointed end and roots from the bottom.

PLANNING THE BULB GARDEN

Since hardy bulbs will stay in the same place for several years, plan their location before buying bulbs:

• In the flower bed

Spring-flowering bulbs produce flowers early, and the foliage must be left on until it ripens. If leaves are cut back too soon, the bulbs will deterio-

rate, and flowering will cease. When the leaves die down in early summer, a void will be left in the flower garden unless there is something to replace them. Some gardeners plant bulbs deeply and interplant them with annuals.

• In the lawn

Sometimes smaller bulbs such as squills or crocuses are planted in the lawn. A lawn covered with blue in spring is a beautiful sight, but the grass will get quite long before the leaves of the bulbs die down and it can be mowed.

• In a natural area

• In a display garden

In many display gardens, bulbs are discarded after blooming and are replaced with annuals.

Generally, spring- and summer-flowering bulbs should be planted in groupings. But do not plant either spring or summer bulbs like rows of wooden soldiers, especially along the front walkway.

SOIL PREPARATION

Well-prepared soil is important for success with bulbs.

1. Once you have decided where to plant them, spade over or till the soil 6 to 8 inches deep. In naturalized areas or in the lawn, this is not necessary.

2. If the soil is heavy and tends to get hard and crack, add organic matter.

3. At the same time, work in a complete fertilizer with a high percentage of phosphorus, or use bone meal.

Bulbs need good drainage or they will rot. If the soil is poorly drained, consider constructing raised beds or installing a means of drainage.

PLANTING

If the soil is well prepared, plant the bulbs by hand, or use a trowel or bulb planter.

1. Plant bulbs and corms with the pointed end up. Plant tubers on their sides with the bud toward the surface. If you make a mistake, the plant is perfectly capable of finding its way to daylight. In fact, planting some bulbs upside down, some on their sides, and some upright will extend the blooming time because the first two will take longer to reach the surface.

2. Plant bulbs deep enough so that the top is about 3 times the height of the bulb below the surface. This is not a hard-and-fast rule, but after a few years when you dig up bulbs to divide them, note the depth at which they have been growing. That is their preferred depth in your soil.

3. Cover the bulbs with soil, firm it, and water it thor-

CHAPTER TWO

oughly. If the weather is dry, more water may be needed.

Spring bulbs make the most impact when planted in masses. In natural areas, scatter the bulbs, and plant them where they fall. In the flower garden, plant groups of bulbs, 8 or 10 of one kind together. Plant the earlier, lower-growing kinds to the front and later, taller ones to the rear of the flower bed.

If room is at a premium, plant several kinds of bulbs in the same place:

1. Dig the area to be planted at least 8 to 10 inches deep and as big around as you want.

2. Remove the soil to the side and plant large bulbs—tulips or daffodils—in the bottom.

4. Space the bulbs appropriately and cover with 1 inch of soil.

5. Plant another layer of smaller bulbs such as crocuses or small-flowered narcissus.

6. Cover with another inch of soil.

7. Plant the smallest bulbs—squills, snowdrops, windflower, or muscari. The smaller bulbs will be up and finished flowering by the time the next level flowers.

Tender bulbs are unable to survive the freezing temperatures of winter. A few kinds are semihardy and may be killed if the winter is unusually cold with no snow cover.

Most tender bulbs are set out in spring after the frost-free date. Gladiolus corms can be set out starting about the time daffodils bloom. They will not be up until the danger of frost is over.

Do not be too hasty planting tuberous begonias, dahlias, or cannas in spring.

1. Get a head start on the season by starting them indoors in pots.

2. Use a commercial artificial potting mix of brown peat moss. Some can be grown in the pots all season. Others do best if removed from the pots and planted in well-prepared soil.

3. When danger of frost has passed, set the plants in the garden.

4. Plant the bulbs, tubers, or corms at the depth indicated in the planting chart.

CARING FOR YOUR BULBS

Hardy bulbs need little care. Divide clumps that become overgrown. Remove faded flowers, but protect the leaves until they wither.

Tender bulbs must be removed from the garden before they freeze.

1. Carefully lift the plants.

2. Cut back the tops.

3. Shake off as much soil as possible, and bring the clumps indoors to dry.

4. After they have dried, separate the bulbs, and store them in a cool, dry place for the winter.

5. Check periodically to make sure they are not shriveling. If they are shriveling, moisten them.

PEST CONTROL

Few diseases affect bulbs. Botrytis may attack ripening blooms or old foliage. Mildew will affect begonias. The most common disease problem is bulb rot due to excessively wet soil. Be sure soil is well drained and do not overwater.

Japanese beetles and earwigs may eat flower petals. Thrips discolor flowers. Control them by applying carbaryl insecticide.

Stalk borers will affect lilies and other tall-growing plants. Use carbaryl or acephate.

Mites will damage summer bulbs. Treat them with insecticidal soap.

Rabbits like to eat the blooms, and squirrels dig up the bulbs. Use garlic-hot pepper spray, which may discourage rabbits. Cover newly planted bulbs with chicken wire. Remember to remove it before the leaves grow through it.

JANUARY
BULBS, CORMS, RHIZOMES, & TUBERS

PLANNING

Garden catalogs are arriving, each with fantastic pictures and glowing descriptions. Whether or not you plan to grow any of the plants being offered, it is great to sit in front of the fireplace on a cold winter evening and dream about next summer.

Among all the hyperboles in the catalogs, you can find summer bulbs that will grow very nicely here, providing something different in your garden.

• List the plants that look interesting to you.

• Select a spot in your garden where you can do trials.

Plant 1 or 2 of various plants in rows, just to see how they grow under those conditions.

• Space the plants out so they will have sufficient room to grow.

Every garden needs an area for experimenting. As it turns out, most of my garden is experimental. One day I will put all of my experiences together and have a garden to enjoy. Not that my wife, Jane, and I do not enjoy it now, but there is always something new to try, which I will put wherever there is room. And many experiments do not go well. That is why I try them. So, there are disasters in the garden, sometimes where I wish something really nice was growing.

These experiences provide good information and help when writing books. Do the cobbler's kids have shoes?

CARE

With the January thaw, customary in the Midwest, we get a glimpse of the ground after weeks of snow cover.

To the surprise of many gardeners, the spring-flowering bulbs have been doing their thing under the snow, and nice green leaves are poking out of the ground. In the southern part of the state, **crocuses** and **snow drops** will be blooming, but in the north, winter will soon make an encore appearance.

But what about those poor little leaves? Not to worry. They are perfectly able to stand the winter weather, and the flower bud is still safely below ground. Even if severe weather damages the few

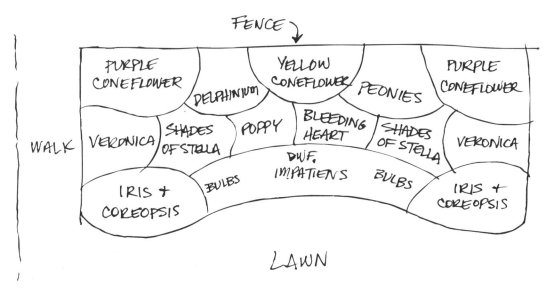

Sketch a garden plan that includes bulbs and perennials for season-long color.

leaves that are exposed, there will be more to come. It is not necessary to help these plants along. They will be fine.

The first bulbs potted for forcing can be removed this month.

1. Remember to count the weeks. Plants ready for forcing will have roots growing out of the bottoms of the pots, and shoots about 2 inches out of the bulbs.

2. If the plants being forced in outdoor beds are frozen, be very careful not to break them.

3. Move the pots into an area where the temperature is about 45 degrees Fahrenheit for a few days, and then to a warmer place (55 to 60 degrees Fahrenheit) to force them.

4. If you have room, force the plants under your lights on your plant stand.

5. Check the temperatures. If it is too warm, the flower buds may blast. If it is too cool, blooming will take forever.

WATERING

Plants being forced will need to be watched. Do not let them dry out, but do not keep them soaked, either. Test the pots by lifting them. A dry pot will be much lighter in weight.

FERTILIZING

As the plants begin to develop, fertilize with soluble fertilizer at $1/2$ the recommended rate. Fertilizing once should be enough.

PESTS

Aphids and fungus gnats will sometimes attack potted bulbs.

Drench the soil with *Bacillus thuringiensis israelensis* or insecticidal soap for the fungus gnats. Use insecticidal soap on the aphids, also.

Little can be done about diseases affecting the potted bulbs now. Bulb rots are the result of excess moisture as the plants were being cooled.

HELPFUL HINTS

• Continue to check the tender bulbs being stored indoors. If any seem to be sprouting, move them to a cooler place, and reduce the moisture. Is the peat moss wet? If it is, remove the bulbs, and replace it with dry peat.

• For success in forcing bulbs or storing summer bulbs, document what you are doing. This means keeping records. Because these activities are arts, they require learned skills. You should keep track of what you have done each year, and a journal is the easiest way to do so.

A journal does not have to be fancy; mine is a spiral notebook. At the top of a page,

I note the year. Then every time something important comes to mind (that is when something worth remembering happens), I write it down with the date.

• Where did you buy the bulbs?
• What are the varieties?
• When did you plant them?
• What was the weather like while they were rooting?
• Which ones did okay, and which ones were disasters?

Record the failures as well as the successes. Memory is short, and it is too easy to repeat the same mistake.

FEBRUARY
BULBS, CORMS, RHIZOMES, & TUBERS

 PLANNING

One of these days, the sun will be out brightly, and suddenly, the snow will be melting with streams of water running down the driveway or along the curb. I remember Februarys when I was small. We floated little stick boats down the stream in the street. We noticed the different feel to the air. Spring was just around the corner.

The first **crocus** would bloom on the south side of the house. It was always a purple one, Grandma's favorite color.

Have you noticed how much longer the days are?

Plants notice it, too. Where the snow has melted, **crocuses** and other small bulbs may bloom by the end of the month.

Make plans now for the summer bulbs snoozing in the basement. As usual there are more this year than there were last season. That means you will need more room, too.

Make a drawing of the garden, and locate spots where these lovely plants will go. The **begonias** are especially good in the shade—nothing gives more color in the shade with so little work.

Schedule plantings of **gladiolus** every week in the cutting garden. Then you will have a continuous supply all summer.

Plan to try a new kind of summer-flowering bulb. There are many to choose from. Have you noticed the newer varieties of **lilies**? They come in fantastic colors that flower for many weeks in midsummer.

PLANTING

Paperwhite narcissus can still be grown now. The bulbs are in the stores all winter. Follow these steps to grow them:

1. Set them on a bed of pea gravel in a shallow dish.

2. Add water up to the bottoms of the bulbs.

3. Set them in a cool place to make roots.

4. Once the tops start to sprout, move them to a bright, cool place until they flower. It takes only a few weeks. This is a good project for stay-at-home kids or those home for semester break.

Narcissus 'Soleil d'Or'

Amaryllis bulbs are available in hardware, discount, garden, specialty, and even grocery stores. Sometimes they are potted and ready to grow. These easily grown bulbs provide spectacular blooms without any effort on your part. They will cure you of the winter blues.

Follow these steps to grow an **amaryllis** bulb:

1. If the bulb is not already potted, plant it in a pot slightly larger than the bulb.

2. Set the bulb so that it is halfway above the pot rim.

3. Use any commercial potting soil.

4. Moisten the soil in the pot, and put the plant in a cool, bright place. In a few days, 1 or 2 shoots will begin to grow from the tip of the bulb. Eventually, it will grow 1 or 2 feet and separate into buds. The flowers will soon open, 6 to 8 inches in diameter in pastel or bright colors. Later the leaves will begin to grow.

5. Set the plant out after danger of frost has passed.

6. Bring it back in so that it can rebloom year after year.

 CARE

The bulbs are snoozing in the cellar. Potted ones for forcing are stretching their necks, ready to burst forth as they are released from their chilly prisons.

Check the condition of the stored bulbs. They may sense the increasing day length and be starting to develop. Do not rush them. There are still months of cold weather before they can be put outside. They could be potted now, but they will be quite large and will take a lot of room before they can be moved out.

Moisten shriveled bulbs. Dust with captan any that have begun to mold.

Bulbs being forced now should be showing buds. Do not push them. If it is too hot, the buds may blast. Keep the temperatures in the range of 50 to 60 degrees Fahrenheit. Some of these flowers should be in bloom for Valentine's Day. What a nice bright accent for the coffee table. What a nice gift.

Bring more bulbs out of the cold storage now. Those potted in late September will be ready for the first day of spring or maybe early Easter or Passover.

 WATERING

While the bulbs are being forced, be careful in watering them. If they are too dry, they will not develop all the way. If they are too wet, the roots may drown, and the buds will blast.

 PESTS

Watch for insects on the bulbs being forced.

Control aphids with insecticidal soap.

The cat may take a fancy to your potted bulbs or **amaryllis**. Other than that, there are no animals that will affect your plants.

Did I hear a mouse? Oh, yes, the bulbs stored in the garage might attract mice. They sometimes appreciate the warmth provided by the peat in which the bulbs are stored.

HELPFUL HINTS

Keep a record as you remove bulbs from cold storage for forcing. Include the date, the temperatures where they will be forced, how well the roots and tops have developed, and varieties that have done well or not so well. Since forcing is an art, the better records you keep, the better you will become at it.

If you have not started a gardening journal, begin it now. Do not make it a chore.

MARCH

BULBS, CORMS, RHIZOMES, & TUBERS

PLANNING

A little planning now will be helpful when the summer bulbs are ready to go outside. Without thought beforehand, you may plant things wherever you see room instead of where they will be at their best.

Unpack dahlia tubers, clean, and divide them to prepare for planting.

The tender summer bulbs are dug up and stored each winter. That means you can plant them in a different place every summer. Try to remember where you needed color last summer. Look in your journal. If you kept good notes, you should have recorded what did and did not do well. Other notes should have suggested changes for the future.

Use summer bulbs to advantage to fill in where something else has faded. Many of the perennials disappear after blooming, and so do spring bulbs. Put summer bulbs in those places to provide interest and color where there would otherwise be a void.

Move potted summer bulbs, particularly **tuberous begonias** and **dwarf dahlias**, from place to place as the situation dictates. If you run out of plants in pots, good garden centers carry them all summer. Pick up whatever you need. Then you can keep them over for use in seasons to come.

All the bulbs cooled for forcing should be out now and in full bloom. How did you do? Make notes and preliminary plans for next year. During the summer you may want to build a better place to cool the bulbs. Read up on forcing. The libraries at the botanic gardens and arboreta have excellent references. The *Holland Bulb Forcer's Guide* is one of the best.

PLANTING

If you did not clean and divide the tender bulbs, corms, rhizomes, and tubers before you stored them for the winter, it is time to do so:

• Clean the old mummy corms from the bottoms of the new corms.

• Separate the sizes.

Large corms will flower this year. The smaller cormels will need 1 or 2 seasons to reach blooming size.

• Divide clumps of **dahlias**, leaving a piece of stem and the little eye on each tuber.

Without an eye, that tuber will not grow.

• Clean the old stems from **begonia** tubers.

• Dust the bulbs and tubers with fungicide, and put them back in storage for a couple of weeks.

CARE

If you mulched the bulbs, remove the mulch as soon as you see shoots developing.

If you covered them with chicken wire, pull it up so that the shoots do not grow through it or you will not be able to get it off without damaging the new leaves. Support the wire above the shoots with sticks or coat hangers. It will keep the rabbits away until the plants are so big that the chicken wire must be removed.

WATERING

Bulbs growing outdoors seldom need watering at this time of the year.

Check the stored tender bulbs to be sure they are not shriveling, or wet and molding.

PESTS

Rabbits, squirrels, and mice are the biggest problems in getting bulbs safely into bloom. Lately, deer have moved into more urban areas and will efficiently eat off **tulips** as they flower. Most of these animals will leave **daffodils** alone. **Daffodils** contain compounds that irritate the animals' mouths.

If you find it impossible to grow other bulbs, plant various kinds of **daffodils** and forget the more troublesome kinds.

GROOMING

As the earliest bulbs finish flowering, pick off the dead blooms. Protect the leaves so that they can replenish the bulbs.

HELPFUL HINTS

Easter means **Easter lilies**.
- Incorporate these potted plants into the garden after they have served their purpose for the holiday.
- Keep them growing in the pot after the flowers fade.
- Set them in the garden when danger of freezing is over.

Set other potted bulbs, forced for Easter or received as gifts, in the garden, too.
- Remove the spent blooms but do not damage the leaves.
- When the ground is dry enough to work, knock the plants out of the pots.
- Set them in the garden where they can be left alone for a couple of seasons.

They may not bloom the next year, but after that, they should flower normally.

Easter **amaryllis** plants usually have white or pastel-colored flowers.
- When the blooms fade, remove them.

The plants will soon shoot up leaves from the bulbs.
- Keep the plants in a cool, bright place indoors until danger of frost has passed.
- Then set them, pot and all, in the garden for the summer.

Lady tulip

APRIL
BULBS, CORMS, RHIZOMES, & TUBERS

 PLANNING

Spring is here! What a joyous time for gardeners. The air has a distinct feel to it. The earliest bulbs are in bloom. There is much for you to do in the garden.

Before things get too hectic, begin to record the events of spring:

• When did the first **crocus** bloom?

• When were the **daffodils** at their peak?

• Which plants looked particularly good, and what was disappointing?

• Has the weather been colder or warmer than normal?

• What about moisture?

This information has a bearing on your plans for next season. By the time fall arrives and you are trying to decide how to proceed, your memory may not be too accurate. (It gets worse each year!)

 PLANTING

Awaken **tuberous begonias** from their winter slumber. If they were stored in pots, start watering them, and set them in a warm place. They will soon show new growth and will be well on their

Tulips and grape hyacinths make a beautiful spring show.

way by the time you set them out in late May.

Pot **tuberous begonias** that were stored in peat moss for planting out later.

1. Use commercial potting mix and preferably clay pots. They stand up better, dry out more evenly, and last longer than other pots.

2. Set tubers hollow sides up with the tips 1 inch below the soil surface.

3. Water them to settle the soil.

4. Put them in a warm place.

Start potted **dwarf dahlias** at the same time.

If you do not have room for all the pots, keep the tubers stored for a few more weeks. It is too early to put tender plants outside.

As soon as bulbs forced indoors finish flowering, cut off the faded blooms, and transplant the clump into the garden. You may want to put the plants in the cutting garden where they can be grown for 1 or 2 seasons to replenish the bulbs. Forced bulbs usually do not bloom the following year. Often it is just as well to discard the old bulbs.

CARE

Deadhead **tulips**, **daffodils**, and other larger-flowered bulbs as soon as the flowers fade. This will direct the energy that would have been expended making seeds into rebuilding the bulbs.

Protect the foliage. It is the factory that produces carbohydrates for the bulbs.

WATERING

Spring is usually a wet time of year. To reduce the chance of diseases, try to keep the foliage and flowers dry if you water.

FERTILIZING

Fertilize bulbs as they finish blooming to help them grow. Flowering next year is determined now, when the bulbs are storing up energy. If they do not do it now, it will be too late.

PESTS

It is too early for most insects. The ones you see outdoors now usually pose no danger to your bulbs. Swarms of gnats are common at this time of year.

When spring is wet and mild, bulbs can be infected by diseases that damage or kill leaves and flowers.

To control botrytis blight, leaf spots, and tulip fire, keep the foliage dry if possible, and spray or dust with a fungicide which contains thiophanate-methyl. You find this material under several brand names. See the list of suggested Pest Control Materials beginning on page 281. Treat the plants as soon as the disease is noticed.

Perennial weeds and winter annuals are active now. Chickweed, mouse-ear chickweed, annual bluegrass, and oxalis must be controlled now to prevent reseeding.

Hoe or pull the weeds as soon as you see them.

The rabbit thinks I plant the red **tulips** just for him. He munches the flowers off every spring, ignoring any threats.

Pepper spray works on the flowers that are just opening, but if I miss a day, the ones that open overnight are gone. A fence seems to be the only reliable prevention. Sometimes planting more bulbs provides for rabbit and leaves some for us to enjoy. He will not eat **daffodils**. Fortunately, rabbit tastes change every few years. Maybe next year he will not like red **tulips**.

HELPFUL HINTS

If foliage of **tulips** and **daffodils** looks too messy, tie it up. Lift all the leaves on each plant up into a loose bundle, and slip a rubber band or twist tie around it. It may not be beautiful, but at least it is neater than having them sprawled all over the garden. Some gardeners discourage this practice, saying it reduces the size of the bulbs. That has not been my experience and it's better than cutting off the foliage.

MAY

BULBS, CORMS, RHIZOMES, & TUBERS

 PLANNING

The average date of last frost, also called the frost-free date by some gardeners, occurs this month.

Finalize plans for the summer bulb garden. Check the locations where you expect to plant your bulbs. Make sure the other plants in the area have not grown so large that there is no longer room. Is there a place where something did not survive the winter? That could be a perfect spot for bulbs.

 PLANTING

After the frost-free date, it is safe to set out the first of the tender bulbs you have been storing over winter. Follow these steps:

1. If you have selected the spots for the bulbs, prepare the soil by tilling or spading.

2. Be sure the soil is not too wet or it may end up like modeling clay. Wait until a handful can be squeezed into a ball and then crumbled. If you are fortunate enough to have a sandy soil, it can be worked when quite wet.

3. Plant the tubers of **montbretias**, **caladiums**, **cannas**, **dahlias**, and **tuberoses**. They will not be up for 1 or 2 weeks, plenty of time to be sure there will be no frost after they emerge.

4. Set stakes for tall **dahlias** before backfilling the planting holes so that you do not skewer the tubers. Once they are covered up, you will not be able to find them.

Plant dormant **tuberous begonias**, but do not set out pots until you are sure there is no danger of frost (about 2 weeks after the frost-free date in your area).

Make the first planting of **gladiolus** corms early this month. Plant more corms every 7 to 10 days to have a continuous supply of blooms all summer.

If you saved the **Easter lily**, plant it in a spot in the garden. Keep the leaves growing as long

Staking provides support for tall bulbs.

as possible. The plant will grow next year and bloom in June.

 CARE

As soon as the first tall **glads** emerge, set stakes to support them. Staking is necessary to develop straight stems for cutting.

Soil that is not too wet for planting will crumble after you squeeze a handful.

 ## WATERING

Soak the newly planted bulbs as soon as they have been covered. This will settle the soil around them. Water if there is no rain for about 10 days.

 ## FERTILIZING

Once the summer bulbs begin growth, use a balanced fertilizer such as 10-10-10 at the rate of 1 pound per 100 square feet of bed. Water in the fertilizer thoroughly to keep it from burning the plants.

 ## PESTS

Aphids are commonly the first insects to attack garden flowers in the spring. Mites attack **dahlias** and other plants.

Use insecticidal soap to control them.

HELPFUL HINTS

• Tying up the foliage of spring-flowering bulbs will keep it out of the way and will be neater than letting the plants fall wherever they will. It also keeps them from getting mowed off. Interplant spring bulbs with annuals or with summer bulbs. Or you may follow the lead of some gardeners who dispense with all this work and pitch out the spent bulbs, replacing them with annuals.

• Summer bulbs are available in garden centers now. Some are already potted and have started to grow. Some have been forced into a flower. If you have not grown tender summer bulbs, this is a great way to get a start. If you are growing them, this gives you a chance to expand your planting or fill in where something is missing.

Stalk borers enter the stems of tall-growing plants, causing them to fall over.

Use acephate from a hose-end sprayer or carbaryl to protect susceptible plants.

Do not spray unless you see the kind of insect that is attacking your plants. If you can identify it, you can initiate the proper control.

Several leaf spots will infect summer bulb plants.

Use one of the thiophanate-methyl type fungicides to control most of them. These fungicides are listed in the Suggested Pest Control Materials beginning on page 281.

Weeds may pose a problem.

Keep hoeing to eliminate weeds. Preemergent herbicide such as dacthal will prevent weed seeds from germinating. Be sure the beds are perfectly clean before applying the material, however. It will not affect plants that are up and growing.

Squirrels may try to dig in the beds.

Place chicken wire over beds. The chicken wire will also keep cats from using your garden as a litter box, and chicken wire fences will discourage rabbits.

JUNE
BULBS, CORMS, RHIZOMES, & TUBERS

PLANNING

Now that the spring bulb season is over, make notes in your journal.

Before you cut off the ripening tops, make a drawing of the garden, showing where the bulbs are planted. You might need this later if you forget what is planted where.

PLANTING

It is safe to set out the **tuberous begonias** started in pots last April. These plants do best in shade. They are more colorful and flower better in the shade. Other plants do well in sun. Prepare the soil deeply where the **begonias** will be planted. They need well-prepared soil and good drainage.

Keep planting **gladiolus** corms every week until the end of the month. These will bloom late, so keep in mind colors that will be appropriate then—fall colors such as oranges, reds, yellows, and bronzes.

Plant **autumn crocuses** (*Colchicum*) now, too. Plant the corms as soon as you get them. They are available from June to September in garden stores, but the earlier you get them in the ground, the better the flowers will be. These strange plants make flowers on bare stems in fall and leaves the next spring. Remember where they are so that you can plant something else to cover the void when the leaves die down next summer.

As soon as the leaves die down on spring bulbs, lift and divide them. Plant the bulbs immediately or store them in a cool, dry place until fall. The largest bulbs will flower next year. The smaller ones can be grown in a nursery bed until they are large enough to flower, or they can be discarded. (I usually throw them away. I collect too much stuff!)

CARE

Drive stakes next to the tall plants such as **dahlias** and **cannas** to keep them from falling over. Avoid staking the tubers under the plants in the ground. Did you remember where the tubers were planted?

Loosely tie **glads** for cutting to stakes in order to keep them straight.

It's time to plant dahlias.

Autumn crocus

wigs, caterpillars, and beetles—with carbaryl.

If the season is wet, foliar diseases can be severe.

Protect the leaves with a fungicide containing thiophanate -methyl. See the table on page 277 for suggested trade names.

Hoe out weed seedlings as they appear. Once the garden is free of weeds, apply pre-emergent herbicide such as dacthal to the soil. Check the label to be sure it is safe for your plants.

 ## WATERING

June can be dry. Be prepared to water if the rains do not cooperate. Keep the water off the foliage, especially on plants in the shade. Water early in the day so that the plants have a chance to dry before evening.

Plants in the shade are at risk for foliar diseases, so try to keep the leaves dry. The plants need decent air movement, too, or they will mildew.

 ## FERTILIZING

Apply a complete fertilizer such as 10-10-10, 1 pound per 100 square feet, alongside the **glads** or **dahlias**. Feed **begonias** with liquid fertilizer according to directions on the label.

 ## PESTS

Numerous kinds of insects may adversely affect the plants.

Use insecticidal soap to eliminate aphids and mites. Control chewing insects—ear-

 ## GROOMING

Bedding-type **dahlias** and **begonias** may need pinching to force branching. Usually, this is not necessary unless the stems become overly long.

Remove spent **tuberous begonia** blooms. They will attract botrytis that may then infect the leaves of your plants. **Begonias** are susceptible to bacterial leaf spot if the foliage stays wet. Protect them with copper fungicide. See the recommendations beginning on page 281.

HELPFUL HINTS

Flowers of **lilies** and some of the other bulbs are excellent for cutting. Take in some of these blooms to be enjoyed. Too often we appreciate the flowers from afar, but hesitate to bring them indoors where we can really see them all day long. Some have wonderful fragrance that is all but missed outdoors. Indoors, it can be enjoyed to the fullest.

If there are not enough in the border garden to cut, plan to plant some in the cutting garden.

JULY
BULBS, CORMS, RHIZOMES, & TUBERS

PLANNING

Now that the spring bulbs have finished flowering and the first of the summer bulbs are beginning to bloom, evaluate your garden.

So often, we begin journaling with good intentions, recording everything faithfully. As the season progresses, however, we become busy or just forget—when the most important part to record is results. That includes both successes and failures. In fact, it is probably more important to document failures so that they are not repeated.

Take a trip around the garden:

• Did the color combinations work out as expected?

• Did the varieties flower at the right times so that the colors blended?

• Did the tall **tulips** turn out shorter than the middle-sized ones, or were they just about the right height?

Record the blooming sequence and approximate blooming dates. The dates will change every year, but the sequence should be the same.

In bloom now are the **tuberous begonias**, **alliums**, and the first **lilies** and **glads**. Make note of their performance, too.

These records will be very helpful next fall as you plan for the following spring and summer.

PLANTING

Plant **resurrection lilies**, sometimes called **summer amaryllis** or **lycoris**, this month. Keep these points in mind about them:

• These interesting plants make leaves in the spring.

• As soon as the leaves die down, the bulbs can be lifted, divided, and replanted.

• In late summer, solitary stalks emerge, bearing clusters of flowers. They can be planted in early spring before leaves start to emerge, or late fall after the blooms fade as well.

• Since you know there will be times when these flowers leave a void in the garden, plant them behind lower-growing perennials so that they will just show up when the blooms appear.

As spring-flowering bulbs die down, lift and divide them. Replant them immediately if you know where they will go, or wait until fall.

CARE

Tall-growing **lilies**, **dahlias**, and **glads** need to be supported:

1. If you did not set up stakes as the tubers or corms were planted, set up stakes now.

2. Be careful not to drive a stake into the tubers or they will be subject to rotting. Corms are so small that there is little danger of hitting them.

3. If you are growing flowers for show, guide their growth by carefully tying the stems to keep them straight as they grow. It is too late to straighten them after they are fully developed. Use strips of cloth to guide the stems up the stakes.

For general use, the supports are necessary just to keep the plants from falling over and not for producing perfect stems every time.

Hoop stakes support tall flowers very well.

WATERING

Bulbs demand careful watering. They need water, but they need excellent drainage, too. Do not keep them continuously wet. Keep the water off the leaves to reduce the chances of disease problems.

Potted **tuberous begonias** and **caladiums** in the shade need careful attention. Water them almost every day in hot, dry weather. The water that drains from the pots must be allowed to empty out; drainage water must not be reabsorbed into the pots. Keep the leaves dry, or water early enough in the day so that the foliage dries before dark.

FERTILIZING

Side-dress bulbs with a complete fertilizer monthly while they are vigorously growing. Use dilute liquid fertilizer for potted plants. Be sure soil is moist before applying fertilizer to potted plants.

PESTS

Earwigs will eat holes in the leaves and edges from flower petals at night.

Use carbaryl to control them.

Aphids may appear on the leaves or shoot tips, and mites on the foliage.

Eliminate them with insecticidal soap.

Stalk borers can severely damage tall-growing plants. The borers enter the stems and hollow them out. The plants collapse at that point.

Spray the plants every week or so with carbaryl or acephate to protect them. Once the insect is in the stem, it is impossible to kill, and the damage is done.

Thrips are tiny, fast-moving insects that mark up the flower petals. They are especially damaging to **dahlias** and **glads**.

Spray with insecticidal soap while they are small. When the flowers open, use acephate. These insects hide well down in the shoot tip or in the flowers.

Foliar diseases, leaf spots, anthracnose, and mildew may occur.

Keep leaves dry. If the weather is wet, apply one of the thiophanate-methyl fungicides listed beginning on page 281.

After a rainy spell, weeds are to be expected.

Hoe out weeds as soon as they appear. Spending a few minutes every evening with hoe in hand will accomplish more than going out once a week and making a chore of weeding.

Potted plants will attract squirrels that dig in them and throw the plants out, or knock the pots off the bench. Maybe they are looking for a place to bury something; maybe they are just squirrelly.

GROOMING

As flowers finish, remove the faded blooms. Some of these plants will try to make seeds. It is more important for them to replenish the bulbs for next year. Old flowers on **begonias** will attract botrytis, which also can move to the leaves.

HELPFUL HINTS

Pick **glads** just as the bottom buds begin to open. Stand them straight up in a bucket of warm water, and hold them in a cool place to harden them. This may keep the tips from turning up when they are used in arrangements.

AUGUST
BULBS, CORMS, RHIZOMES, & TUBERS

PLANNING

August is a lazy month. The weather is warm, we have spent several months getting the garden into shape, and now it is time to stop and enjoy it.

While you are dozing in your hammock, notice the plants that are especially pleasing this year. If you can roust yourself into a vertical position, record them in your journal. Since gardening is a process, not a destination, there will be times when you will think, I wish I hadn't done that.

Make sure that it does not happen again. How often we brag about the successes, but forget the other things. Eventually, we smarten up. Writing down the mistakes is as important as recording the successes.

PLANTING

Although it is early to find bulbs in garden centers, plant bulbs you divided and have stored for the summer. **Crocuses** or **squills** to be planted in the lawn do not need soil preparation and can be plugged in without disturbing the grass.

1. Use a bulb planter that pulls a plug of soil.
2. Set the bulb.
3. Replace the soil.
4. Step on the plug to firm it down.

Remember not to mow the grass in spring until the leaves of the bulbs ripen.

CARE

Protect foliage of summer bulbs so that it lasts as long as possible. Foliage replenishes the bulbs. Even though the leaves become shaggy and may be unattractive, do not cut them off until they turn yellow. If they are too obvious in the garden, make plans to locate them in a different place, or plant something else that will hide them.

Allow **lily** stems to die down naturally. Then cut them off a few inches above the ground. Do not pull them out or water may accumulate in the tops of the bulbs, rotting them.

WATERING

The garden needs about 1 inch of water per week. If nature does not provide it, you will need to do so. Try to avoid watering over the tops of plants. To lessen disease problems, water early in the day so that leaves dry before dark.

Do not water potted **begonias** over the top. They are very susceptible to foliar diseases.

PESTS

The foliage and stems continue to need protection from insect damage. Mites are especially troublesome in the often hot, dry weather of August.

Apply insecticidal soap to the bottoms of the leaves. Since it does not kill the eggs, repeat the treatment every 1 or 2 weeks. Mite damage shows up as stippling of the leaves. Examine the undersides of the leaves where the mites can be seen with a hand lens.

Thrips and aphids carry virus diseases that may infect and destroy your plants.

Control thrips and aphids with acephate or insecticidal soap.

When days are hot and evenings clear and cool with heavy dew, mildew begins to appear. It reduces the efficiency of the leaves and can be unsightly.

Dust the foliage with sulfur, or spray with a fungicide that contains thiophanate-methyl.

Dahlias are susceptible to several virus diseases that show up as yellow rings or spots in the leaves. They may cause malformed blooms. "Yellows" can cause flowers to turn green and not open.

Remove and destroy affected plants. These diseases are carried to the plants by insects. (See insect control suggestions.)

Weeds are not as much trouble at this time of the year, most of them having succumbed to the hoe, but they will pop up after a good rain.

Do not ignore these few now because this is the time of year when they make seeds—and they will make enough seeds to give you problems all next year. Hoe them out as you see them.

HELPFUL HINTS

It will soon be time to plant spring-flowering bulbs.

• Since the ones that have summered in the garden are well hidden below ground, try to locate them so that you do not plant on top of them.

If you drew a garden plan last spring, you should be able to find them without difficulty.

If not, try to reconstruct one now. Next year, set labels in the clumps so that they are easily identified.

• Where places in the garden have been vacated, begin to work up the soil for planting.

• Add organic matter, and turn it in at least one spade deep.

• If you have not ordered your bulbs, order them now.

The bulb catalogs have been out for weeks. If you cannot find yours, check with your local library or with your garden club members. Orders placed now will arrive soon enough for planting this fall. By waiting to order later, you may find that supplies of popular kinds are gone.

• Attend a local garden show.

Flowers are at their best now. Plant societies such as the Dahlia Society and Lily Society hold single plant shows where the competition is fierce. These are good places to learn what constitutes a top-quality flower.

 GROOMING

Remove spent flowers as they fade. If the weather is very hot, blooms may not last very long outside. Cut them for use in arrangements or in a vase to put on the kitchen table. **Lilies** and **tuberoses** are delightfully fragrant.

Tuberose

SEPTEMBER
BULBS, CORMS, RHIZOMES, & TUBERS

PLANNING

Spring-flowering bulbs must be planted in the next couple of months.

Decide where plants will go. Take a tour around the yard, and imagine what various areas will look like in spring. Where will the annual flower garden be? The ground will be barren until May. Is there room in front of the shrub border for some splashes of color? In the perennial border, there may be places where nothing will have started by then and there is room to plug in bulbs.

Decide what to plant. Keep these points in mind:

• Small bulbs are unobtrusive and will be out of the way early.

• Smaller things should be placed at the front so that they will not be hidden.

• Larger, taller kinds will last longer, and the leaves will need to be tolerated until as late as June.

• Taller **tulips** or **daffodils** can go to the back where their leaves will be hidden by other developing foliage.

Where will you store the tender bulbs for the winter? Bulbs will need a moderately cool, dry place. The bulbs are fragile, too. Bins in which to sort them and to protect them are helpful. Arrange a place in the basement or a heated garage where the temperatures and humidity can be controlled, and where the bulbs will not be disturbed. Be sure mice cannot get into the garage because they will feast on bulbs.

PLANTING

As soon as the bulbs appear in the garden displays, they can be planted in the garden. Remove shabby annuals and plant bulbs. Leave the area bare, or set hardy **mums**, **asters**, or **kale** over the bulbs for a spot of fall color.

Pot bulbs for forcing. Those started now will be ready to force in January. They can stay outside in a cold frame or be buried in a sand pit until there is danger of their being frozen in. Or an unused refrigerator will suffice if you can adjust the temperatures. The bulbs need time to make roots before the cold treatment begins.

Fall is an excellent time to divide spring bulb plantings if you can remember where they are.

1. Dig up clumps with a fork or spade, being careful not to skewer or guillotine the bulbs.

Caladium 'Candidum'

2. Separate the largest bulbs from the clump.

3. Replant them.

4. Line out smaller ones in a nurse bed for growing to flowering size, or discard them. Maybe a neighbor can use them. Small bulbs usually will not flower the first year or so.

CARE

Frost can occur at anytime. Be prepared to protect exposed **tuberous begonias** and **caladiums** so they can provide another few weeks of color. Old blankets or bed sheets are good enough.

Move the potted **amaryllis** indoors.

1. Start by withholding water to dry them.

2. Remove the foliage as it turns yellow.

3. Indoors, place the pots on their sides and leave them that way for 6 weeks to 3 months.

4. Then stand them up and water them. In a few weeks they will be blooming.

WATERING

Fall can be dry. Give newly planted bulbs sufficient water, but do not drown them. Start drying down the **dahlias**, **glads**, or **cannas** that have finished blooming for the season.

FERTILIZING

Did you fertilize the bulbs you just planted? If not, apply a complete fertilizer such as 10-10-10 or the equivalent at the rate of 1 pound per 100 square feet of bed. Water it in well.

PESTS

The tender bulbs you will bring indoors in the next few weeks must be free of bugs.

Control mites, whiteflies, thrips, and aphids with insecticidal soap. Use baits or stale beer in pans to trap slugs.

Mildew appears on summer-flowering bulb plants as the days are bright and evenings are cool and damp. Usually, it causes no damage to the plants this late in the season.

Use copper spray on **tuberous begonias** for bacterial leaf spot.

Weeds may get ahead of you in the fall.

Hoe them out as you see them. Grasses in bulb plantings are especially hard to eliminate. While the bulbs are safely belowground and the garden is empty, kill grassy weeds with glyphosate.

Squirrels think you plant bulbs just for them.

If they have found the bulb garden and are excavating it for you, cover it with a piece of chicken wire. Stake it at the edges or the squirrels will get under it or pull it away.

HELPFUL HINTS

Make a drawing of the bulb plantings as you are planting them. Indicate the kinds, colors, sizes, and other interesting facts. Maybe the year you planted them is important. Note the place you got them. If they were a gift, make note of that, too. Sometime after they have died down for the summer, you will want to know exactly where they are. Keep the drawing in your journal.

You do not have a journal yet? Start one today. If you are intent on forcing bulbs, you will need to keep meticulous notes to improve your successes.

OCTOBER
BULBS, CORMS, RHIZOMES, & TUBERS

PLANNING

Tender bulbs, corms, and tubers must be carefully stored for the winter.

Plan ahead, and prepare a place suitable for them. It must be cool, dry, and safe from rodents. If the garage is heated and secure, a cabinet or shelves on an inside wall may work. Temperatures should be around 45 degrees Fahrenheit.

PLANTING

October is a great time to plant spring-flowering bulbs. Sunny, cool days make working outdoors a joy. If you did not plant them last month, there is still time. The earlier they are planted, the better the chances that they will develop substantial root systems before soil temperatures get too low.

If soils are wet, do not destroy the structure by working them excessively. Instead of tilling or spading the soil, plant the bulbs with a trowel or bulb planter.

If you have not already done so, pot bulbs for forcing. Bulbs started now will be ready to force in February.

CARE

Dig the corms of the **glads**: Dry the **gladiolus** corms. Peel the old mummy from the bottoms of the new corms. Separate the large ones from the cormels. The cormels may be lined out next year and will grow into flowering-sized corms in 1 or 2 seasons. Store them in a cool place in onion bags or boxes of dry peat moss.

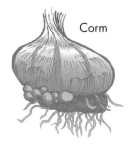

Corm

Dig clumps of other plants: Dry **dahlia** clumps, and knock off the soil. Store the entire clump. Or divide it, and store the largest tubers. When dividing, include a sliver of stem on each tuber. That is where the bud is located. Without a dormant bud, the tuber will not grow the next season. Use care in handling the tubers so as not to break off their buds. Store them in boxes of dry peat.

Shake **begonia** tubers free of soil. Remove the old, dried stems. The first freeze will kill the tops, after which the tubers must be dug up if the plants are to be saved. Allow the soil to dry, and shake the tubers loose. Store

them in boxes of dry peat around 45 degrees Fahrenheit.

WATERING

If fall is dry, provide sufficient water to the newly planted spring-flowering bulbs. Be careful not to drown them.

Check bulbs being forced. Pots stored in beds or cold frames will dry out much more quickly than the ground will. Pots stored in a refrigerator in plastic bags usually do not dry out, but check them anyway to be safe.

PESTS

Weeds, especially weed grasses, may be in the bulb plantings. At this time of year, turfgrasses will spread into beds.

Edge the garden to discourage the grasses. Hoe out clumps before they become established.

Mice and squirrels will go after shallowly planted bulbs, destroying the garden.

If you see evidence of animals digging in the bulb garden, cover it with chicken wire. If you are storing potted bulbs in the garage for forcing, make sure no mice are getting in. They can destroy the plants before you notice the destruction.

NOVEMBER
BULBS, CORMS, RHIZOMES, & TUBERS

 PLANNING

If you are just now planting spring-flowering bulbs, plan to do it earlier next year.

 PLANTING

It is not too late to plant bulbs now, but they would have been better off if they had been planted 1 or 2 months ago. Planting now is preferable to not planting them at all.

This is the last chance to pot bulbs for forcing in spring. Any later and they will bloom about the same time as the outdoor plantings.

 CARE

Once the ground has started to freeze, apply a light mulch to the later-planted bulbs. This may prevent the ground from freezing and allow the bulbs to root better. Earliest plantings will not profit from mulching.

 WATERING

Check the moisture in the bulb beds. If the ground is dry, water it. This may be the last chance before winter sets in.

Check bulbs potted for forcing. Outdoors, they may need water. In plastic bags indoors, they tend to stay wet. If the plastic bags are sweating, open them for a day or so to dry out. If they stay sopping wet, the bulbs will rot.

Examine summer bulbs being stored for the winter. They should be dry, but not so dry as to shrivel. Mist to moisten them, but be careful. If they are wet, they will mildew or rot.

 PESTS

No insect problems should be anticipated this late in the season in the garden, the forcing pots, or the bulbs being stored for the winter.

Molds may appear in the potted bulbs being stored in plastic bags.

If you see any signs of rot, prune off rotted portions.

If any are noticed, open the bags for 1 or 2 days to dry them out.

If potted plants are being held in beds or cold frames, mice can become troublesome. A garage can have openings through which mice might enter. Squirrels can be bothersome as well if the pots are exposed.

Use brodifacoum (D-con), traps, chicken wire, or whatever you can devise to control them.

HELPFUL HINTS

Start an **amaryllis** at the beginning of this month, and it should be in bloom for the holidays. Bright red or white would be appropriate. If you do not have plants stored, you will find them in many garden stores specially packaged as holiday gifts. Buy some for friends and a few for yourself.

DECEMBER
BULBS, CORMS, RHIZOMES, & TUBERS

CARE

Winter can start with a vengeance. If you are forcing bulbs in an outdoor cold frame or bed, properly protect it. The best protection is a 6-inch blanket of snow. Barring that, you will need to cover the bed with several inches of sand, several inches of soil, and straw.

For bulbs being held indoors and receiving cold treatment, maintain temperatures at 32 to 40 degrees Fahrenheit. Do not let the plants freeze or the treatment stops.

Every month check tender bulbs being stored for the winter. As the outside temperatures drop, the indoor humidity drops, too. If the bulbs are beginning to shrivel, moisten them. Misting is enough. If the bulbs have been drying out, examine them more often, maybe every 10 days.

When handling the **tuberous begonias** and **dahlias**, do not damage the eyes. They are very fragile when they are dry.

PESTS

If potted bulbs in plastic bags are too wet, they will mold.

Open the bags to dry them if necessary.

HELPFUL HINTS

Garden catalogs are arriving, and many list summer-flowering bulbs. These are exciting plants to grow. Some are completely hardy. **Lilies** are fantastic plants. Many new varieties are developed each year, and they are hardy. Others such as **dahlias** and **glads** require winter care. Once you are set up to handle these plants, try as many of them as you can. One plant of each set out in rows will give you an idea of the ones that will do well in your garden. It will give you a chance to see how difficult they are to handle for the winter, too.

The planting chart at the beginning of this chapter lists various bulbs, many of which are rarely planted. They are rarely planted not because they are so difficult to grow, but because most of us get stuck in our own little comfortable worlds. Make a resolution to try different plants every year.

Lily 'Connecticut King'

Mice may get into outdoor bulb beds or frames. They appreciate nice, warm winter quarters, exactly what you have prepared for your bulbs.

Use brodifacoum (D-con), traps, or hardware cloth to keep them out.

HERBS & VEGETABLES

Herbs and vegetables are grown for fresh produce during the summer, for produce to freeze or can, and for culinary herbs and some spices. Home-grown produce is fresher and can offer more variety than is available from the market.

With careful planning and some skill, you can take produce from the garden for 8 to 10 months of the year. If plants taken in for the winter are included, something from the garden is available throughout the year. Starting in spring, things that overwinter can be harvested. These might include parsnips or carrots with some winter pro-

tection. Early planting can produce radishes or green onions about the time spring bulbs bloom.

Perennial vegetables and herbs start early and continue producing for weeks. Once established, asparagus, rhubarb, thyme, sage, chives, and others become permanent residents in the garden. They may be harvested as soon as they begin to grow.

Most herbs and vegetables are easily started from seeds sown directly in the garden. A cool or wet season will mean a late start and a possible reduction in the yields. Garden centers

provide fairly good selections of vegetable plants in spring, but selection is still limited.

Starting transplants indoors under lights and using cold frames or a portable greenhouse for overflow lengthen the growing season and add to your gardening enjoyment. Selection of varieties is limited only by the number of catalogs from which you select seeds. Setting larger, well-developed plants into the garden speeds up the harvest.

Timing is very important because plants started too early will be overgrown and leggy. Some vegetable varieties will stand a freeze and can be set out quite early. Others can stand some cold weather without injury. Others are strictly warm-weather plants. They may not freeze if set out early, but they do not grow and could rot off. The planting chart starting on page 266 indicates which plants fit in each category.

Here are general rules for planting:

• Hardy vegetables can be planted as soon as the ground can be worked in spring.

• Semihardy varieties can be planted 2 or 3 weeks before the average date of last frost (frost-free date).

• Tender kinds should be planted at the frost-free date.

• Very tender vegetables should be planted no sooner than 3 weeks after the frost-free date.

The frost-free dates vary from one end of the state to the other by a month. The planting dates suggested in the calendars are appropriate for Zone 5b in the central part of the state. The dates in the southern part will be as much as 2 weeks earlier, those in the north up to 2 weeks later.

PLANNING THE VEGETABLE GARDEN

The first item in planning a garden is determining the size. If this is your first garden, smaller is better than bigger. Planting a garden is the easy part. Keeping it watered, controlling weeds and other pests, tending, and harvesting are infinitely more work.

The size depends on the space you have available, the amount of produce you need, and the time you have to devote to it. Make your garden just big enough that it is interesting and fun. A 10-by-10-foot garden can grow a lot of vegetables if it is efficiently planned and handled. Once you gain experience, you may be able to handle more space.

Locate the garden away from roots of trees and shrubs and away from family recreation areas. If possible, include the vegetable garden in the total plan for your home landscape.

• Draw a map of the garden on graph paper, to scale if possible.

• Decide whether you will grow in raised beds or in rows.

In either case, try to run them east and west to take advantage of the best light exposure.

• Indicate on the map where each variety will go.

Place the taller plants on the north side so that they do not shade out smaller ones.

STARTING HERBS AND VEGETABLES FROM SEEDS

Most vegetables can be seeded directly in the garden. Some that do not take transplanting very well should be direct seeded. Others start so easily and quickly that there is no advantage to starting them indoors.

To start seeds indoors, you will need a place with excellent light. A greenhouse is best. Barring that, a stand with fluorescent lights will work very well. You can buy one or build one. Follow these steps to build a plant stand:

1. Make a fixture that will accommodate four standard 10-inch-by-20-inch flats. Plant lights are not necessary; cool white fluorescent tubes work well. Attach two 2-tube 40-watt fluorescent shop lights side by

side to a piece of ³/₄-inch plywood or two 1-by-4s.

2. Suspend the lights so that they may be raised and lowered as necessary. Hang chains on hooks from the ceiling, or construct a system of pulleys and weights using old sash weights or bricks for counterbalances.

3. Use a work bench or place boards over saw horses for the stand. It should be 4 feet long and 20 inches wide. See the diagram of a plant stand on page 24.

Seed is most easily sown in the 20-row, seed-starting inserts sold to fit the 10-inch-by-20-inch flats.

1. Use one of the commercial artificial soil mixes composed of shredded brown peat and Styrofoam beads or perlite, such as Fafard, Jiffy Mix, Pro Mix, or any other brand. (The black "potting soil" is not satisfactory.)

2. Moisten the soil mix, sow the seeds, and cover the container with clear plastic wrap to keep it from drying out.

3. Label the rows so that you can tell what you planted.

4. Set the flats on the plant stand, and lower the lights to 1 inch or so above the surface. This will provide all the heat and light needed.

TRANSPLANTING SEEDLINGS

When they are big enough to handle, transplant the seedlings into plastic cell-packs, the kind commercial growers use (these fit into flats, too), or into any other convenient container. Keep the lights just above the plant tops. Fertilize the plants with liquid fertilizer after they start to grow.

Keep the plants under the lights or move them into a cold frame or greenhouse until it is safe to set them in the garden.

SOIL PREPARATION

Prepare the soil before planting:

• Kill all the weeds that have started in the garden over the winter.

Hoe them out, or kill them with herbicides. On perennial grasses such as quackgrass and Kentucky bluegrass, use glyphosate, which kills underground parts as well as tops. Glyphosate is deactivated as soon as it hits the ground or is absorbed by the weeds, so there is no danger to plants later. Keep it off perennial garden plants.

• Add any organic matter you can acquire, such as compost, old plant tops, or leaves.

• Spread a complete fertilizer such as 1 pound of 10-10-10 per 100 square feet of garden.

• Spade or till to a depth of 6 inches, and break up any lumps or clods.

Set the plants at the proper spacing and at the same depth they grew in the transplant containers.

PEST CONTROL

Weeds are a continual garden problem.

Hoe out weeds as soon you see them. They are easy to remove when they are small. Apply herbicides to weed-free soil. Follow directions on the label. Herbicides will prevent germination of new seeds, so do not apply them where seeds will be sown later.

Insects will find your garden.

If the infestation is limited to a few insects on 1 plant tip, pick them off. If the whole garden is infested, spraying or dusting may be needed. Usually, infestations are limited to 1 or 2 kinds of plants, not the whole garden. Some kinds will need pest control every year.

Gardens may be subject to various diseases.

Prevent diseases by using resistant varieties, by keeping the leaves dry, and by using fungicides where necessary.

JANUARY
HERBS & VEGETABLES

PLANNING

January is the time to make decisions about what you want to grow in your herb and vegetable garden.

The seed catalogs provide helpful information and enticing color photographs, but the plants that you choose should fit your family's needs. If you or the family will not eat it, you should not bother to grow it—no matter how good it looks. For example, some kids just do not like **broccoli** or **eggplant**.

Review your plants from last year, and ask yourself several questions as you plan your garden:

• What plants did well?

• What plants did not do so well or were not used?

• Do I want them for fresh eating or for processing?

The answers will determine not only what to grow, but the varieties, how much, and when to plant them. Processing varieties generally bear all at the same time.

• What varieties are suitable for my locality?

Your local Extension Service office can provide a list of recommended varieties.

Next, draw your garden layout to scale so that you can decide how much room to give each kind of herb or vegetable.

1. Orient the drawing so that you know which way is north. Run rows or beds east to west for better exposure to light. Locate taller plants to the north to keep them from shading the lower ones.

2. Choose rows or beds for your plantings. Rows are best for large gardens where mechanical equipment such as a tractor or a plow will be used. Beds are better suited for backyard gardens where most of the work will be done by hand. You can make your beds 3½ to 4 feet wide

and as long as the garden. You can work them from the sides and never walk on the beds, which reduces compaction and makes spading much easier.

3. Consider successive plantings. Where a crop has been harvested, decide what will be planted next. Use every inch of the garden to maximum advantage, especially in beds.

Finalize your list, and order seeds or plants. The earlier you place your order, the better. Early orders are more likely to be filled with the varieties you want.

PLANTING

If the weather conditions permit you to get into the garden, dig, pot, and force **chives** for

Sketch your vegetable garden plan—to scale, if possible—in order to help you determine its size.

Vegetable Garden Five 4x25' Beds	
Tomatoes	
Potatoes	Onions followed by Fall Broccoli
Peppers	Broccoli
Summer Squash	Beans
Peas, Radishes, Carrots & Beets	Lettuce & Chard

N ↑

use. Propagate the plants that you brought in for the winter and are growing under lights. Take cuttings from **rosemary** or **thyme**.

CARE

Indoor plants may experience problems. If the plants under lights are getting spindly, lower the lights to the tops of the shoots. Insufficient light causes the plants to stretch. Protect plants on the windowsill from freezing if the weather is severe. Do not leave them between the window and the shade when it is drawn.

WATERING

Indoors, water with care so that plants are not too wet, but never let them wilt. Water the plants in the sink, and set them back in their places after they stop draining.

FERTILIZING

These plants do not need fertilizer in winter. Overly vigorous plants are not as flavorful as ones that are slightly "hungry."

PESTS

Whiteflies, aphids, and mites can severely attack herbs indoors.

Use insecticidal soap to kill these pests, and do not forget to spray the undersides of the leaves. When the pests are dead, remove infested leaves.

Watch for fungus gnats.

The larvae live in potting soil. Use insecticidal soap or *Bacillus thuringiensis israelensis* to control them. Check the label to make sure they are appropriate for the plants you are growing.

Mildew can be a problem on herbs indoors.

Keep moisture off the leaves. Sanitation is the best defense against diseases. Remove any diseased plants before they can infect others.

Cats occasionally take a liking to certain herbs.

Try setting out a plant for the cat so that you will have some left for yourself. Or you may have to make a cage of chicken wire to protect the plants.

GROOMING

Keep the plants shaped by clipping them as needed. Harvesting for culinary use should help.

HELPFUL HINTS

It will soon be time to sow seeds under lights. Is there room under your lights for more plants? If not, consider what you can do to make more space.

• Evaluate your gardening tools.

1. Do an inventory. Make a list of new tools you need to purchase.

2. Sharpen the shovels and hoe to make them easier to use. Dull tools take more effort. To prevent rust, wash the mud from the tools after each use, and wipe them with an oily rag.

• Record the following information in your journal: where seed and plants were ordered, when you ordered them, and the varieties. Get in the habit of recording any important thoughts in the journal as they occur, or a few days later you will be unable to remember your brilliant ideas.

FEBRUARY

HERBS & VEGETABLES

PLANNING

Growing-things begin to perk up as the days lengthen in February. Gardeners perk up, too, and the urge to begin planting becomes hard to resist.

By the end of this month, you can seed some things indoors, and if the ground is exposed, you can plant some things outside.

To be ready, you will need these materials:

• Containers for starting seeds and for transplanting

Visit your local garden center, and stock up on 10-inch-by-20-inch plastic flats and miscellaneous containers for transplanting. If you intend to grow vine crops from seeds indoors, purchase peat pots as well.

• At least one seedling starter tray

A starter tray has 20 rows of depressions or grooves to fill with artificial planting mix, and it fits into a standard 10-inch-by-20-inch flat. Seeds are sown in the depressions.

• Artificial potting soil for starter tray(s)

A commercial mixture such as Fafard, Jiffy Mix, or Pro Mix is suitable. Do not use the moist black potting soil. Moisten the soil in a bucket, and fill the depressions in the starter tray.

A lack of sufficient light causes most of the difficulties when growing plants indoors. The plants become tall and spindly, and they fall over before you can plant them. You can solve that problem by buying or building an artificial light plant stand and growing your plants under lights. See the diagram on page 24.

To build a plant stand, follow these steps:

1. Make a fixture that will accommodate four standard 10-inch-by-20-inch flats. Plant lights are not necessary; cool white fluorescent tubes work well. Attach

Gather materials before filling seed trays.

two 2-tube 40-watt fluorescent shop lights side by side to a piece of 3/4-inch plywood or two 1-by-4s.

2. Suspend the lights so that they may be raised and lowered as necessary. Hang chains on hooks from the ceiling, or construct a system of pulleys and weights using old sash weights or bricks for counterbalances.

3. Use a work bench or place boards over saw horses for the stand. It should be 4 feet long and 20 inches wide.

Maintain temperatures on the plant stand in the range of 60 to 70 degrees Fahrenheit.

CARE

Herbs spending the winter indoors should be showing signs of renewed growth. The longer days and additional light make a big difference.

Plants that have been under artificial lights should have been growing all winter and providing fresh herbs for your kitchen. If you cannot use them all, freeze them in ice cubes. Then you can thaw them or pop the ice cubes into whatever is being cooked.

WATERING

Watering plants indoors is an art. It is better to keep the plants a little too dry than too wet. Dispose of drainage water that runs out of the pots. Watering from the bottom or letting the water be reabsorbed will cause the soluble salts in the pot to rise to dangerous levels. Any white crust forming along the soil surface, especially at the edge next to the pot rim, is a warning sign. Repot plants in fresh soil, or leach salts out of the pot by flushing with plenty of fresh water.

FERTILIZING

As soon as increased growth begins, fertilize the plants with a complete liquid fertilizer such as Miracle-Gro or Peters. Use the fertilizer at 1/2 the rate recommended on the package.

PESTS

Whiteflies will make the foliage on your herbs unusable. If infected plants are moved into the garden in the spring, the whiteflies will spread to your other plants.

Larvae of these insects can be seen with a hand lens. They look like tiny pills stuck along the middle veins of the leaves. Control them with insecticidal soap applied to the undersides of the leaves.

Keep water off the leaves to avoid diseases.

Remove any diseased leaves if they appear.

GROOMING

Trim the plants indoors to shape them and to stimulate new growth. Root clippings to start new plants. They start readily when placed in water or in moist sand.

HELPFUL HINTS

• Next month will be a busy one. If you have not already done so, take time now to collect all the things you need for starting seeds and for transplanting.

• Update your journal. List the things that you have bought—seeds, supplies, potting soil, tools—along with the source, cost, and any other relevant information that will help when you need to replace items, buy more of the same things, or make a complaint about an item. More than once, I have wished that I had kept such a list. You cannot always rely on memory for these details.

MARCH

HERBS & VEGETABLES

PLANNING

Signs of spring are all around. Your plant stand will soon be full, and you will have more things to plant next month. Where will you put all the plants?

A cold frame may be the solution. You can buy one from a garden catalog, which offers simple and fancy cold frames, or you can make one from scrap lumber. I use a portable one that I can set up in the part of the garden that I will plant last. Here are its specifications:

- It is made of plywood.
- It is the size of an old storm window, 30 by 60 inches inside, and holds nine 10-inch-by-20-inch flats.
- The corners are made of four pieces of 2-by-4s.
- The back is 15 inches high, the front 10 inches.
- The sash slides back to permit me to work on the plants or to let in air. (I may put hinges on it this year.)

Planting dates vary throughout the state. The suggestions offered here reflect dates for the central part of the state in Zone 5b. Frost-free dates in the southern part of the state may be as much as 2 weeks earlier than the dates suggested here. In the far northwest part of the state, the dates are 2 weeks later.

Check with your local Extension office for the frost-free date in your area.

PLANTING

Many main crop vegetables can be sown indoors this month:

- On March 1, sow seeds of **broccoli**, **cilantro-coriander**, **sage**, **cabbage**, **chives**, **dill**, **cauliflower**, **fennel**, **head lettuce**, **spinach**, **thyme**, **French sorrel**, and **winter savory**.
- On March 10, sow seeds of **Chinese cabbage**.

- On March 15, sow early **tomatoes**, **Swiss chard**, **endive**, **escarole**, and **leaf lettuce**.

Under lights, use seed-starter trays filled with moist artificial soil mix. Carefully sow seed in the rows. Label each row so that you will know what is coming up, and include the variety if you are growing more than one. Moisten gently, and cover the trays with plastic wrap to keep them from drying out. Remember, some seeds such as **lettuce** need light to germinate. Set the trays under the lights, and lower the lights to 2 inches above the trays.

If the plant stand is in a cold or drafty place, throw a cover over the whole setup to keep in the heat from the lights. Do not put the cover directly on the light fixture or it may get hot enough to burn.

Record in your journal the source of the seeds, the varieties, the planting date, and when the first seedlings appear. Some seeds will germinate in less than a week.

A few herbs and vegetables can be sown directly into the garden as soon as the soil can be worked. Do not destroy the soil by working it when it is too wet.

A cold frame can be made at home.

- Plant perennial vegetables, **rhubarb**, and **asparagus**.
- Plant or sow plants or seeds of **spinach**, **chives**, **dill**, **fennel**, **oregano**, **mint**, **tarragon**, **sweet Cicely**, **sweet woodruff**, and **thyme**.
- Plant **peas**.

In the garden, plant according to the plan you came up with in January. Keep the perennials that will stay in one place for several years to one side or the end of the garden. There they will not be disturbed when you till or spade the rest of the garden each year.

CARE

As soon as the seedlings are up, remove the plastic wrap over them. Take the cover off the setup, and lower the temperature to about 60 degrees Fahrenheit.

The seedlings will be ready to transplant in 1 or 2 weeks. Transplant them as soon as they are large enough to handle. Lift them out of the seed-starter tray with the end of a small wooden label. Take care not to squeeze the stems or to break off the roots.

Separate seedlings by gently pulling them apart. If the seedlings are left in the seed flat too long, they will become a jumbled mess and difficult to separate.

Fill the containers with artificial mix, and firm it so that it does not settle. Use the point of a pencil or a small label as a dibble to make holes in the mix. Set a seedling in each hole, using the dibble to push all the roots into the hole. Firm the seedling with your finger and thumb on each side.

WATERING

Do not let the seedlings dry out, but do not drown them, either. Light watering with a small watering can will be sufficient.

FERTILIZING

If the seedlings are in the seed-starter tray too long, they will need fertilizer. Fertilize transplants with a dilute liquid mixed at $1/2$ the normal rate. Apply fertilizer carefully, and then rinse off the leaves.

PESTS

Infestations by aphids, mites, and whiteflies pose a danger to plants.

Use insecticidal soap to get rid of the pests.

Damping off is common in seed flats.

Keeping the soil too wet is often the cause. In starter trays, the rows limit the spread of the disease.

HELPFUL HINTS

- March can be cold and miserable or sunny and pleasant. Take advantage of any nice days to do outside work. But don't rush the season. Working wet soils will ruin the structure.

- If you spaded the garden last fall and left it rough, rake out a small area to plant a few **onion** sets for **green onions**, and a row or two of **radishes**. These will provide some fresh produce in just a few weeks.

APRIL

HERBS & VEGETABLES

PLANNING

Early crops such as **radishes**, **green onions**, **lettuce**, and **spinach**, will leave voids in the vegetable garden after you harvest them.

Plan to fill the voids with successive plantings of **snap beans**, **carrots**, **beets**, or started plants of **tomatoes**, **cucumbers**, or **bush squash**.

To fill in places in the garden where plants are missing, use plants that you had started in peat pots. **Leaf lettuce**, herbs, or whatever you have will work. You may not achieve a uniform

look, but it is more important to maximize use of the space.

To get ready to plant **tomatoes**, make tomato cages by following these steps:

1. Use concrete reinforcing wire, which comes in 5-foot widths.

2. Cut pieces 5 feet long and 2½ feet wide.

3. Roll them into cylinders 2½ feet tall.

4. Leave the wires sticking out at the bottom so that you can stick the cages in the ground.

PLANTING

Transplant seedlings started last month under lights to make room for important, main crop varieties.

Plant the following vegetables under lights:

• Early this month, sow **eggplants**, **peppers**, and additional **tomatoes**.

• As soon as the **eggplants**, **peppers**, and **tomatoes** are up and transplanted to cell-packs, sow **muskmelons**, **pumpkins**, **squash**, and **watermelons** in peat pots.

Muskmelons, **pumpkins**, **watermelons**, and **squash** will not transplant well. Sow them in containers that can be planted without disturbing the root systems. Be very careful in handling them.

You have many choices of plants to seed directly in the garden by the end of the month: **radishes**, **carrots**, **Swiss chard**, **beets**, **lettuce**, **mustard**, **rutabagas**, **turnips**, and the first **sweet corn**. Make successive plantings of **sweet corn** every 10 days.

Plant **onion** sets and **potato** seed pieces. The common knowledge that **potatoes** should be planted on Good Friday might get you into trouble if Easter is in March. Have you tried **straw potatoes**? Set the seeds on the ground, and cover the bed with 6 inches of straw. The **potatoes** will develop above ground. You can pick them up instead of digging them.

Make room in your cold frame or on your plant stand under the lights by planting into the garden the **broccoli**, **cabbage**, **cauliflower**, **lettuce**, **endive**, **escarole**, **spinach**, and **parsley** you started earlier.

Transplant seedlings as soon as they are large enough to handle. Move them into the cold frame to harden them off.

Support tomato plants by staking or using wire cages.

CARE

The first **asparagus** and **rhubarb** will be up; pick them when they are young and tender. Do not let them go to waste. Remove any flower stalks from the **rhubarb**.

If the soil is dry enough where the **tomatoes**, **peppers**, **squash**, and **cucumbers** will go, spade it over, rake it out, and lay plastic mulch.

WATERING

Do not overwater the seedlings or the transplants. The first watering after transplanting settles the soil around the roots and should be sufficient to keep the plants from wilting for a week or so. The plants may stay wilted from transplanting for 1 or 2 days. When the soil dries to the touch, water again. These plants can tolerate a little wilting to harden them off.

FERTILIZING

Add transplant starter fertilizer to the first watering to help plants get established. Starter fertilizers have analyses very high in soluble phosphorus; 10-52-17 and 10-30-10 are common, and even 20-20-20 will work. Mix fertilizer according to directions on the label.

PESTS

Soil-borne insects can damage transplants in the garden.

Root crops—**carrots**, **onions**, **radishes**, and **turnips**—can be severely damaged, as can roots of **broccoli** and other coles. After transplanting, cover the row with screening or floating row covers to discourage these pests.

Most diseases at this time of the season are due to excessively wet soils.

Be careful when you water. If the garden is not well drained, plan to do something to correct that condition before the next season.

Weeds can be controlled with a sharp hoe or herbicides.

Apply herbicides to reduce weed problems after the plants are up and growing. Most of these materials are labeled for only a few vegetable crops. Check the label and use them only on the crops listed. They must be applied to weed-free ground.

Rabbits can cause a lot of damage in the garden.

A fence is the only reliable prevention. Using chicken wire that is buried 6 inches at the bottom and that is 18 inches high works! See the diagram on page 35. An attractive and practical rabbit fence is produced by Snapdragon Industries, New Hampton, New Hampshire. To view, visit **www.ezrabbitfencing.com**.

HELPFUL HINTS

If you have not started a journal, it is time to do so. Record the planting dates, varieties, and other pertinent information. Yes, I know that keeping records can be a drag. But they can be very helpful, and they are interesting years later when memory has faded. Your journal does not have to be very formal or fancy. Mine is a spiral notebook that is a little muddy now, but I can look up things that happened years ago and avoid problems.

Now, where did I leave the notebook? I think it was in the garage.

MAY

HERBS & VEGETABLES

PLANNING

As your garden develops, be aware of how much room various plants need.

Even though your planting chart suggests the spacing for your plants, how things actually grow in your garden should dictate how things are planted.

Write your observations in your journal so that you can make adjustments next year.

PLANTING

All seedlings should be transplanted by now. Soon it will be time to turn off the lights for the season.

At the beginning of the month, plant the following:

• Set out the **tomato** plants.

There is still a possibility of frost for a couple of weeks.

• Make the first seeding of **snap beans**.

For continuous production, sow seeds every 15 days.

• Sow more **beets**, **carrots**, **lettuce**, and **radishes**.

Carrots and **radishes** can be sown in the same row. By the time the **carrots** are ready to be thinned, the **radishes** are ready for pulling.

• Seed more **sweet corn**.

These plants take a lot of room, and the yield is only 1 ear

from each plant. If the **corn** is taking too much room in your garden, consider renting space in a community garden.

After the middle of the month, set in the ground plants of warm-weather crops:

• **Tomatoes**
• **Peppers**
• **Eggplants**
• **Cucumbers**
• **Squash**

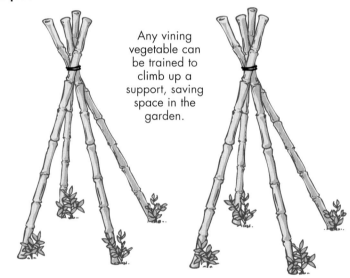

Any vining vegetable can be trained to climb up a support, saving space in the garden.

In beds covered with black plastic mulch, cut holes in the plastic where the plants will go, and plant them through it. If you do not use the plastic, keep weeds under control while the plants are small.

At the end of the month, plant **muskmelons** and **watermelons**

There is no need to get them in early because the cool soils will keep them from developing anyway.

Where early plantings are harvested, replant. Record the dates the things were removed so that next year you can better plan what will go there.

CARE

Be prepared for a late frost with old bed sheets or blankets to cover tender plants for a night or

so. Uncover them if the sun is out the next day.

Thin out the **carrots**, **beets**, and direct-seeded **lettuce**. The extra seedlings can go into the soup kettle.

Many vegetables can be grown vertically in the garden. Any of the vines, such as **cucumbers**, **squash**, **pole beans**, and **peas**, will grow vertically if supported. Try to think of other plants that will take less space if they grow on supports.

WATERING

Set a rain gauge or a coffee can in the garden to measure amounts of water. The plants will need about 1 inch of water per week. If the rainfall is insufficient, supplement it. There is no need to water until the plants begin to wilt, but once that happens, you will need to apply a measured inch of water.

FERTILIZING

Transplants benefit from starter fertilizer. Apply fertilizer in the water the plants receive after planting.

PESTS

Cutworms will destroy plantings very quickly.

Peppers, **squash**, and some herbs are especially attractive to them. Cut collars of aluminum foil to wrap the stems. Some gardeners use small tin cans with the bottoms cut out to slip over the plants.

Cucumber beetles can attack **cucumbers** and **muskmelons**. Carbaryl insecticide will combat these beetles. Spray as soon as the plants are up or are planted in the garden, or cover with floating row covers. These beetles carry bacterial wilt that will kill the plants about the time they begin to produce.

Watch for other signs of insect damage, and treat accordingly.

Insecticidal soap is effective against aphids. Carbaryl controls earwigs. Baits work well for slugs. If plants disappear during the night, carry a powerful flashlight with you as you go on a midnight safari to see what is happening. Depending upon your findings, you may have to be creative to discover the proper treatment methods.

Root rot and damping off are the most serious diseases this early in the season.

Avoid keeping the plants too wet, especially at night.

Continual weed control is important.

More gardeners give up because the weeds take over than for any other reason. This is a good reason for keeping the garden small enough that you can handle it. If it is too big, the weeds will get ahead of you, and you will be discouraged.

Rabbits can devastate a garden. A fence made of chicken wire will keep them out. See the diagram on page 35.

Squirrels dig for no particular reason but can uproot small plants in the process. Neighborhood cats may find your garden the perfect litter box.

Cover the preferred beds with chicken wire so that the cats cannot walk on them. Support the wire above the plants with sticks or bent coat hangers. Remove the wire when the plants are big enough to survive on their own. By then the cats may have found someone else's garden.

GROOMING

Prune staked **tomato** plants to a single stem as they grow. Most other vegetable plants require no pruning.

Cut back more vigorous herb plants to stimulate new fresh shoots for harvesting.

HELPFUL HINTS

Harvest the first **radishes**, **lettuce**, and **green onions**. Keep picking the **rhubarb** and **asparagus** so that they will keep producing. When the **asparagus** spears diminish in size, stop picking and let the plants grow. **Rhubarb** will produce all summer if it has enough water and fertilizer.

JUNE
HERBS & VEGETABLES

 PLANNING

Get ready for the fall garden.

Even though the summer garden has barely gotten under way, June is not too soon to begin planning for fall. Decide what you will plant, how much room it will take, and which parts of the garden will be vacated by then.

When you have decided what to plant, check with the garden center or your other sources for the availability of seeds. Be sure that the indoor light setup is in good working condition. Flats, containers, and the seeding tray from the spring seedings will need to be cleaned up, so do the cleanup now.

 PLANTING

Plant **pumpkins** in June to be ready for Halloween. Use plants that you have started, or direct seed in the garden. Remember, these become huge plants unless you are growing the bush types. Leave them room. They can be grown up a strong trellis, but the fruit will need support. One way to support **pumpkins** is to create parachutes of rags tied at the corners and fastened to the trellis. Position the developing fruit straight in the parachute so that it develops perfectly for a prize jack-o'-lantern.

Plant more **sweet corn**, **beans**, and late **cucumbers**. If you are growing early-determinate-type **tomatoes**, plant mid-season varieties now. They will produce when the early ones are finished.

Replant the **pea** patch with something else as soon as you have picked all of them.

 CARE

While the weather is cool, harvest the following:
- **Peas**
- **Cabbage**
- **Broccoli**

Cut **cabbage** and **broccoli** when they are young and fresh. Delay will allow **cabbage** to crack and **broccoli** to go to flower.

Pull **green bunching onions** as you need them.

Stop picking **asparagus** as the weather warms up.

Cucumber 'Early Pride'

Tie staked **tomatoes**. Tuck in shoots of caged **tomatoes** so that they stay in the cages.

Blanch **cauliflower** by tying up leaves to cover the curds.

 WATERING

As the weather warms up, the plants will need more water. If rain is insufficient, apply 1 inch of water. Water early in the day so that the plants can dry before nightfall.

For extensive gardens, consider a drip watering system or a leaky pipe. Either method places the water where it is needed and reduces waste.

Mulching conserves water. Hoe out any weeds, and apply a 3-inch layer of mulch beneath plants. The mulch will keep weeds down, too.

 FERTILIZING

Actively growing plants need fertilizer. Apply a complete fertilizer such as 10-10-10, 1 pound per 100 square feet of garden. Keep it off the plants to avoid burning them. Water it in immediately. Fertilizer does no good until it is in solution in the soil. Fertilize **asparagus**, and let the plants grow so that you will have a good crop next year. Use 10-10-10 fertilizer, 2 pounds per 100 square feet of bed.

 PESTS

Cabbage worms will find your **cabbage**, **broccoli**, **cauliflower**, and **collards**.

Control the worms with *Bacillus thuringiensis kurstaki*. It is sold under many brand names.

Aphids, whiteflies, and mites can attack your garden.

Use insecticidal soap to combat these pests.

Squash vine borers will destroy the plants at the soil line.

Spray the bases of the stems with carbaryl late in the evening to avoid injury to bees. Or, cover with floating row covers. (You will need to pollinate the flowers if you do this, however.)

Foliar diseases can damage leaves and reduce quality and production.

Dust or spray with maneb, copper, or chlorothanil. Check with your Extension Service office for the latest control recommendations.

Blossom end rot of **tomatoes**, **peppers**, or **squash** is a physiological condition.

Uneven watering or excessive fertilizing, among other things, can cause the problem. It is self-eliminating. Usually only the first fruits have blossom end rot, but subsequent ones are free of it.

Continue to hoe out weeds as they appear and/or use a herbicide.

Do not let weeds get ahead of you. The herbicide dacthal may be helpful because it prevents weed seeds from starting. It is safe to use on many vegetables, but not **beets**. Check the label for specific instructions.

Rabbits will harvest your produce before you do if you let them. They leave certain things alone, but will eat **beans** as they come up. They like **lettuce**, **carrot** tops, and many herbs.

A fence is the only sure protection. An aggressive tomcat works to defend your plants against rabbits, but he can do other damage to your garden.

HELPFUL HINTS

• Watch the garden carefully for signs of trouble. As soon as you notice anything amiss, correct it. If you cannot figure out what is wrong, call your local Extension Service, and describe the problem. Most Extension Service offices have Master Gardeners who will answer garden questions. Botanical gardens, arboreta, and garden centers also have skilled staff members to help diagnose problems in the garden.

• Slugs and earwigs may hide under mulch during the day and attack your plants at night. If they have been threats to your garden, do not use mulch.

JULY
HERBS & VEGETABLES

PLANNING

Pick up the portable greenhouse and cold frames, and move them to storage for the summer. You may need the greenhouse later.

As plant tops are removed, compost them. Dig them back into the part of the garden where they grew if there is not too much bulk. A compost heap or enclosed composter can reduce the bulk quickly. For small amounts, use black plastic bags as composters:

1. Fill bags with chopped tops.

2. Add a shovelful of soil and some moisture (not too much).

3. Close the bags, and toss them behind the garage or another out-of-the-way place.

4. Roll them over every week to mix the soil. After a few weeks the bags will seem empty. That is when the compost is ready.

PLANNING

Sow seeds for more **beets**, **beans**, and **sweet corn**. Seed a second crop of **squash** for fall harvest. By the middle of the month, sow **Chinese cabbage**, **mustard**, **spinach**, **collards**, **turnips**, and **rutabagas**.

For the fall garden, it is time to start transplants indoors under lights. Sow **cabbage**, **cauliflower**, **broccoli**, **peppers**, and **tomatoes**. These seedlings will be ready by the end of the month and can be set out then.

CARE

Serious harvesting gets under way this month:

- **Broccoli**

Continue to pick **broccoli** so that it does not go to flower.

- **Cucumbers**

Pick **cucumbers** when they are mature size.

- **Summer squash**

Pick them immature while they are still small and tender. Some gardeners like huge **zucchinis** for stuffing. Production slows down if extra large **squash** are left on the plant.

- **Sweet corn**

Harvest the first **sweet corn** about 3 weeks after tasseling. Pick it before the raccoons or squirrels do.

- **Tomatoes**

Do not count on them. If the season is on time, the first **tomatoes** should be ready, but sometimes only the earliest varieties are ready by July 4.

- **Straw potatoes**

Lift the straw and steal a few **potatoes**. Replace the straw so that the rest are in the dark. Fluff up the straw while you are at it. **Potatoes** that grow in the light will be green and cannot be eaten.

'Early Golden Summer' crookneck squash

• Dry **onions**

Lift the **onions** when the tops start to turn yellow. Let them dry a couple of days, then collect them. Dry them indoors for a week or so. Remove the tops when they have completely dried. Store the ones with thin necks, and use the thick-necked ones immediately.

Most of the herbs are in full production now. Use them fresh if possible. If you cannot use them immediately, dry them:

1. Cut tender sprigs 10 to 12 inches long.

2. Bunch them loosely, and hang them in a dry location or place them on a screen to dry.

3. Once they are dry, store them in air-tight containers.

WATERING

Provide 1 inch of water a week to the garden. Keeping the soil evenly moist will prevent cracking **tomatoes** and blossom end rot on **squash**. If plants are wilted, they will not be productive.

FERTILIZING

Side-dress **peppers**, **sweet corn**, and **snap beans** with a 10-10-10 fertilizer, 1 pound per 100 feet of row.

HELPFUL HINTS

As the produce begins to come in, there are times when you will have too much. Do not let it go to waste.
• Freeze it.
• Can it.
• Give it to neighbors.
• Participate in the food pantries and soup kitchens in your neighborhood.

Or, Plant a Row for the Hungry. For more information, visit **www.gardenwriters.org**.

Check with your church or local authorities for the locations.

PESTS

Aphids can appear out of nowhere overnight. Use insecticidal soap to reduce numbers of aphids.

Whiteflies will show up now. The adults are of no concern. The damage is due to scalelike larvae on the undersides of the leaves. Use insecticidal soap to control them.

Squash vine borers will destroy the plants. Check the stems at the soil line for damage. Spray with carbaryl weekly, late in the day to avoid killing bees.

All cole crops are susceptible to cabbage worms. Have you seen any white butterflies in the garden? Spray with *Bacillus thuringiensis kurstaki*. It kills butterfly larvae, but nothing else.

Yellow jackets and earwigs will take bites out of ripe **tomatoes** or **squash**.

Pick the vegetables before they are damaged.

Corn borers get into **peppers**. Use carbaryl. Pick the **peppers** when a mature size.

Powdery mildew on **squash** and leaf spots on other things show up when there is evening dew. Use chlorothalonil, copper, maneb, or sulfur. Check the labels for recommendations.

Weeds left now will make seeds for more trouble next year. Gardens kept weed free for a few seasons stay much cleaner as the numbers of residual seeds diminish. Keep hoeing.

Squirrels have a bad habit of taking a bite out of a **cucumber** or **tomato** and then deciding they do not like it. They keep trying and ruin a lot of fruit in the process.

Keep the fruit picked so that they have nothing to sample. I am forced to pick **tomatoes** when they start to turn pink, or the squirrels destroy them.

AUGUST

HERBS & VEGETABLES

PLANNING

The **tomatoes** are too close together, and they keep falling out of the cages. The **straw potatoes** were on the north side of the **tomatoes**, and they did not get any sun. When I was ready to plant the second crop of **broccoli**, the **beets** were still too small to dig.

Does this sound familiar? We gardeners have challenges, and each year we make some progress. Part of what keeps us gardening is the expectation that every year will be better than the last one. It is the same thing that keeps golfers trying to break par or sailors trying to win the next race.

Records can help you improve each season, but only if you do a good job of keeping them. Write down the problems you encountered this year. Next winter, look over them as you make future plans so that you do not repeat them.

Record the harvest dates for the produce. Note the variety and the planting date. It might help to indicate what kind of season you are having . . . hot and dry, cold, wet . . . so that adjustments can be made if necessary in the future.

Radishes

Good planning is based on good information. Each season is a learning experience and adds to your knowledge base.

PLANTING

Plant the **tomatoes**, **peppers**, **broccoli**, **cabbage**, and **cauliflower** started under lights last month. These plants will be harvested in fall. Some cold-tolerant ones will continue to produce well after the first freeze. I have picked **cauliflower** and **broccoli** in December on occasion. Do not be in too much of a hurry to pull these plants out. After the first cutting, the side shoots will get better and better as the temperatures cool down.

In the southern part of the state, the season is extended a month or longer than up north. There is still time to sow **beans**, **beets**, **spinach**, **cabbage**, **broccoli**, and **turnips** for fall. If the weather is hot and dry, lay a board over the rows as soon as they are seeded; it will keep the soil cool and moist. Check twice a day to be sure the seeds have not germinated, and remove the board as soon as they start.

Up north, sow greens of all kinds, **lettuce**, and **radishes**.

CARE

Cages for **tomatoes** work only if you keep the plants in the cages. Once the plants have a full load of fruit, clip back overly long shoots to keep them inbounds. Semideterminant varieties stay shorter than the indeterminate kinds.

As areas of the garden are vacated, chop the residue with a sharp spade, and turn it into the bed or row where it grew. Your garden drawing will show what grew where so that any rotation for disease control can be based on where the residue was buried. Rotate **tomatoes** to a different spot

every few years. Cole crops benefit from rotation, too.

WATERING

If it does not rain for a week to 10 days, apply 1 inch of water to the garden. Water early in the day so that plants dry before dark. Use soakers or leaky pipe to keep the foliage dry.

FERTILIZING

Where second crops are planted in the same place as crops already harvested, fertilize them. Side-dress with 10-10-10, 1 to 2 pounds per 100 feet of row.

PESTS

It is easy to get behind with insect control when the weather is hot. The problems show up overnight, it seems. Check regularly for aphids, mites, whiteflies, leaf beetles, and soil insects. If the **radishes**, **potatoes**, or **carrots** have spots chewed into them, maggots can be blamed.

After seeding or planting, cover the row with screening or floating row covers to discourage these pests.

These same insects can severely injure the root systems of **broccoli**, **cabbage**, and other plants. Bean maggots can ruin a planting, eating the seedlings as they emerge from the seed.

Some herbs are especially susceptible to mites. Both spider mites and the tiny cyclamen mites will affect them. **Parsley** leaves that curl may have mites. Leaves of other plants with mites will have a dirty look to them, and close examination will reveal webs and the mites themselves on the undersides.

Use insecticidal soap, the only treatment recommended for these edible plants.

As the season progresses and nights are increasingly cool, mildew will become troublesome. If the plants are nearing the end of their usefulness, there is no need to treat them. Newly planted **squash**, for instance, is worth treating.

Use chlorothalonil or sulfur. Treat rotting foliage of **broccoli** and other coles with copper.

Tomatoes with heavy fruit loads are susceptible to leaf spot diseases. Use maneb to control them.

By now some plants have given up in the garden. **Tomatoes** that turned brown and died may have had a wilt disease.

Buy VF resistant varieties.

Cucumbers that dried up just as they started to produce probably had bacterial wilt. It is the one carried by the cucumber beetles.

Did you spray with carbaryl or cover with floating covers as soon as the seedlings were up?

Weeds may continue to be a problem. Keep hoeing!

Raccoons will get into the garden, especially for **sweet corn**. There may be no way to stop them.

Plan to pick the **corn** a day early, and you may get it before they do.

HELPFUL HINTS

• **Sweet corn** should be in maximum production now. Even though you made plantings 7 or 10 days apart, the heat units at this time of year accumulate so fast that everything comes in at one time. Freeze what you cannot eat.

• As soon as the tops of the **potatoes** go down, dig them. Allow them to dry off, but do not wash them until used or they will rot. Store them in a cool, dark, dry place. Light will turn them green and ruin them.

• Dig **garlic** when the leaves start to turn yellow. If it is left in the ground too long, the delicate paper covering will begin to rot, destroying the appearance.

Dry it carefully, and store it by braiding the dry leaves and hanging it in a cool, dry place.

SEPTEMBER
HERBS & VEGETABLES

PLANNING

One of the biggest problems in the garden is having room for all the transplants until they can be planted out. If you are serious about getting the most from your garden, you will encounter this problem every year.

Most of us will never invest in a heated greenhouse, but even gardeners who have them run out of space. Portable cold frames and greenhouses can ease the problem of lack of space.

Garlic

Living on a city lot, I do not have room for many structures. But until the garden is completely planted up, I can use the portable cold frame (described fully on page 76). It goes in the garden in the bed that will be planted with either **tomatoes** or **summer squash**—the last bed to be planted in spring.

Another helpful structure is a portable greenhouse. I have a plastic-covered, portable greenhouse that is 6 feet square with enough head room to allow me to stand up. It has 2 shelves and can hold 25 to 30 flats. Because of its height, it holds enough heat to keep it from freezing even when temperatures fall as low as 26 degrees Fahrenheit. It, too, goes in an unoccupied part of the garden until it is no longer needed.

PLANTING

In the southern part of the state, there is still time to sow more **greens**, **lettuce**, and **radishes**.

For gardeners interested in French or Italian cuisine, there is no more important item than fresh **garlic**. Many gardeners try, but few have success growing this plant. The secret is planting in the fall:

Save toes from a head of **garlic**. Plant them in late September. Set them straight with the points up. Planting them this way will allow them to develop straight necks. Harvest next August.

This crop takes a long time to mature.

CARE

As soon as plants finish producing and begin to die down, pull them out.

I prefer to chop them up and dig them in the bed where they were growing. Then I dig over the beds to cover the plant debris and leave it rough until spring.

Each year, I empty one bed to two spades deep. I pile up the soil on the adjoining bed. I toss plant debris into this pit all winter. In spring I chop it up and spade it into the bottom of the pit. Then I mix the rest of the soil with other organic material and refill the bed. The production from these deeply prepared beds is excellent.

HELPFUL HINTS

• If the garden is short of organic matter, try a green manure crop. Something that grows fast and is easily discouraged next year is best. **Oats** or **annual rye** are easy to find and will not persist at planting time.

• The fall garden should be coming into its own. Continually harvest it so that it continues to produce. **Broccoli** will survive a freeze. Save more tender things by covering them with an old bed sheet or blanket.

WATERING

Unless the fall is unusually dry, watering will not be necessary.

FERTILIZING

If beds are to be turned over for the winter, apply a complete fertilizer before spading. Use 1 pound of 10-10-10 or the equivalent per 100 square feet of garden.

PESTS

Thorough composting or deeply burying insect-infested plants will kill the overwintering forms.

Most diseases live over the winter in the soil or air.

Use resistant varieties and keep the plants growing vigorously to prevent most diseases. Bury or compost the diseased plant material to eliminate most of the carryover.

Once the garden is empty, perennial weeds such as bluegrass or quackgrass may remain.

Treat them with glyphosate to eliminate even the underground parts.

Rodents may be a problem.

Turn the compost heap regularly to discourage them. If you notice any, set out appropriate rodenticides such as brodifacoum (D-con). If the problem continues, consider an enclosed composter.

Rabbits may be a threat to your garden.

Keep the rabbit fence up all winter. Rabbits will be less likely to try to get in next year when the garden is full.

OCTOBER

HERBS & VEGETABLES

PLANNING

Organic matter is the solution to some of the most difficult soil problems—compaction, cracking, and drainage.

Getting enough organic matter is sometimes difficult, but at this time of the season it should be no trouble at all.

• Dig the leaves from the trees, the grass clippings, and plant tops into the garden.

• Pile the material on the beds or spread it over the garden.

• Chop it with a sharp spade, and spade it in.

• Leave the surface rough so that it gets the full brunt of winter freezing and thawing, wetting and drying. The weathering will mellow the soil, and the fiber will open the soil.

By spring, the soil will be in excellent shape. Although the coarse organic matter will not have decomposed very much, it will disappear over the summer, and more can be added next year.

If you are using raised beds, they will improve over the years, eventually becoming higher than the unmodified aisles. Try to dig in an aisle and you will quickly see the difference.

PLANTING

Plant some herbs, such as **salad burnet**, in October. It could be planted in early spring as well.

If you cannot find sufficient organic matter for your garden, plant **rye** or **oats** as a green manure. Plow it down next spring and it will help some.

CARE

The last **sweet corn** will be picked shortly. Expect earworms in any late **corn**. Carbaryl would have helped. Make a note of that.

Before the first freeze, pick the last **summer squash**, **peppers**, and **cucumbers**. Freeze **peppers** either chopped or stuffed. Dry and store **hot peppers**. Have you seen the braided **peppers**? Try it yourself. A little twine or wire through the stems helps.

Pick the green **tomatoes**:

• Wrap each in a piece of newspaper, and store them in a dry place indoors.

• Check every few days, and remove those that have ripened.

When kept around 60 degrees Fahrenheit, they will ripen very slowly over several weeks.

• Keep only unblemished **tomatoes**; damaged fruits will rot before they ripen.

Pumpkins and **winter squash** can stand a frost, but not a freeze. When the **pumpkins** turn fully orange, cut the stems with a knife. Cure **pumpkins** in a warm, dry place. Store them cool and dry at 55 degrees Fahrenheit and they will last all winter.

Harvest **broccoli** and **Chinese cabbage** as soon as they are ready. The **broccoli** will make side shoots after the main head is cut. Keep it going until it freezes solid.

Carrots and **parsnips** will keep going until the ground freezes and you cannot dig them. Mulch them heavily to keep the soil from freezing as long as you can. The **parsnips** will survive until spring, but the **carrots** may not. Cold weather increases the sugar storage in these roots, making them sweeter.

Pumpkins

FERTILIZING

Add fertilizer to the organic matter if it contains much dry matter such as leaves. Use a high-nitrogen fertilizer, adding about 1 pound per 100 square feet of garden.

PESTS

Squash vine borers and corn borers overwinter in plant debris.

Compost it or bury it deeply in the garden.

Winter annual weeds such as chickweed and annual bluegrass can grow all winter, even blooming under the snow, making seeds for next fall.

Hoe them out now.

Other annual weeds are just about finished. Perennials such as dandelions will just keep going.

Dig the late **Irish potatoes** and the **sweet potatoes** before a hard freeze. Be careful not to skewer them when digging; handle them carefully to avoid bruising them.

Even after a frost, with Indian summer temperatures, **tomatoes** and some other warm- weather vegetables will continue to produce. Ripening may be a prob-lem, though. It takes day temperatures of about 65 degrees Fahrenheit for **tomatoes** to ripen. When it is cooler than that, pick the **tomatoes**, and bring them indoors to ripen. Pick only damage-free **tomatoes** because imperfect ones will rot before they ripen.

HELPFUL HINTS

Dig up **parsley**, **chives**, **rosemary**, **thyme**, **basil**, **oregano**, **sage**, and any other herb you may need for the winter. Shake off as much soil as you can, and pot them using artificial potting soil. Garden soil will not work in pots. Herbs can grow under the lights until you need them for planting. Or set them in a cool, bright window. Clip off sprigs as you need them. If the **parsley** was frozen, it may bolt. Frozen **chives** will go to sleep for the winter.

NOVEMBER

HERBS & VEGETABLES

 PLANNING

Take a cruise through the garden while events of the season are still fresh in your mind, and make notes in your journal.

You might be a little philosophical, recording impressions and memories. Gardening is more than just growing things. It is communing with nature, spending solitary time with your thoughts. It is enjoying the company of family members or friends who enjoy gardening, too.

I like to remember specific things that happened in the garden or because of my gardening interests. Sometimes it is an event, a trip to the farmers' market, visiting with a commercial grower and really being able to relate to his or her problems. Unless you have fought the bugs, weather, or pestilence, it is hard to understand the difficulties faced by the people who rely on the crops for their livelihood.

 CARE

The garden has just about finished producing vegetables. You need to take care of a few more tasks:

- Pull out the last of the old plants.
- Cut back the tops of the **asparagus** and **rhubarb**.
- Rake out all the old leaves and other trash that collected in the **rhubarb** and **asparagus** beds over the summer.

Put them in the compost heap or the pit you dug in the fall.

- Cover the **rhubarb** and **asparagus** with a heavy application of compost.
- Apply a heavy layer of mulch over the **horseradish**, **parsnips**, and **carrots**.

Try to keep them from freezing as long as possible so that you can harvest some for Thanksgiving and Christmas.

 FERTILIZING

Soil test labs are not as busy during the winter as during the spring, and the results will be back in plenty of time to apply fertilizer in the spring. Follow these steps to collect soil samples for testing:

1. Collect soil from each area that may be different. A sample from each bed may be sufficient.

2. In a bucket, collect several trowels of soil representative of each area being sampled. Mix them together, and take 1 cupful for testing. This makes 1 sample.

3. Repeat for each area to be tested.

4. Air-dry the samples on a piece of newspaper overnight, then package each in a brown paper bag.

5. Mark the bags so that you know which spots the samples

Carrots

came from, and send them to a soil testing lab. Extension Service offices and many garden ceters can arrange to have your soil tested. The report you receive will indicate any deficiencies and necessary corrections.

PESTS

Weeds may still be growing.

Keep weeding. It is too late to do anything about the grasses. Wait until spring to treat them with glyphosate. Remove weeds with seedheads from the garden, or bury them deeply in the pit where the seeds will not grow.

Monitor the presence of rodents. They may try to take up winter residence in the compost or mulch.

Use brodifacoum (D-con) in a box to keep it dry and away from other animals.

CARE FOR YOUR GARDEN TOOLS

• Collect all the garden tools before the snow flies.

It is easy to leave them leaning next to the fence in the garden or where they can be buried by the snow.

• Make an inventory of the tools.

Are some missing? If so, plan to replace them. Are there some you wish you had?

• Make a list, and leave it where someone looking for an appropriate Christmas or birthday gift can "accidentally" find it.

• Scrub all the mud off the tools, and wipe them with an oily rag.

• Check all the tools for wear.

• Check handles for any cracks that could cause splinters. Sand them down, or replace them.

• Sharpen all shovels and hoes.

• Hang the tools on a rack where they can be found immediately when you need them.

Have you ever driven over a rake handle because it fell down under the car and you did not notice it? I speak from experience. Leaning tools against the wall is not the best way to store them.

Collect several trowels of soil representative of each area being sampled.

DECEMBER

HERBS & VEGETABLES

PLANNING

Winter has arrived, and the garden will soon be covered with a protective blanket of snow.

I am thankful for winter. As enjoyable as gardening may be, there are still times when it is pleasant to sit and contemplate.

Another blessing of winter is its cleansing effect. In parts of the country where there is no winter, the weeds keep growing, the bugs keep eating, and the diseases get worse. Here winter puts a stop to all that. The freezing and thawing, and the wetting and drying mellow our soils so that in spring they are wonderfully friable. No matter how much we work our soils, nothing will improve them as much as a good old Midwest winter.

The garden catalogs arrive earlier each year. They used to come after Christmas, but now they come in early December. While there is a lull in the holiday activities, take some time to look through them. And make notes in your journal. Do not be swayed by all the gorgeous photos and descriptions, but pick out some things you want to try next year.

CARE

The herbs brought in for the winter notice the lack of light at this time of year. They notice the low humidity as the cold outside air is heated. A place that often seems to be satisfactory for these plants is a kitchen window over the sink if there is adequate light. The humidity is usually high in the kitchen, and the plants are handy for taking a snip when it is needed.

If the plants are showing signs of distress, find a place where they have as much light as possible and cool temperatures. An unused room where the heat can be turned off or a corner in the basement may be suitable. Of course, the light then becomes a problem. Maybe now is the time to build an indoor light stand.

WATERING

Go easy with water on plants in pots. If you did not repot them using an artificial soil mix, they will stay too wet and may not survive. It is not too late to repot them.

PESTS

Whiteflies and mites are common pests of herbs brought in for the winter.

Combat them with insecticidal soap, the only material that can be safely used to control these pests on herbs.

Fungus gnats are small black insects that fly around the plants, but do no damage. The larvae feed on organic matter in the soil and rarely on plant roots.

If these insects become pests, drench them with insecticidal soap or *Bacillus thuringiensis israelensis* to eliminate the larvae.

GARDENING GIFTS

Most gardeners appreciate gardening gifts. Tools of various kinds, such as the ergonomic ones that reduce the normal bending and stooping, and small hand tools, aprons, gloves, and other things that wear out are all welcome. Garden books are full of ideas to make gardening more fun and more productive. They make good gifts, too. Sometimes looking at the pretty pictures will occupy a cold winter evening in front of the fireplace. Subscriptions to gardening magazines are gifts that last all year.

LAWNS

More time and resources are expended on lawns than on any other aspect of the home garden. On a typical Saturday morning, the din of lawn mowers can be heard throughout suburbia. By Saturday afternoon, the curbs are lined with brown paper bags of clippings. On our radio shows, fully half of the calls are for lawn-care information.

Much of the dissatisfaction with lawns comes from not doing the right things at the right time. It is important, for instance, to apply preemergent weed-control products before the weeds germinate. There is a preferred time to seed a new lawn or to repair a damaged lawn.

Turfgrasses grown in most of our state are cool-season cultivars. Since they do better in the moderate weather of spring and fall, undertaking major cultural operations is more effective then.

You have several choices of grasses:

• Kentucky bluegrass is the most favored species used.

• Turf-type perennial ryegrass is quick to germinate.

• Creeping red fescue tolerates shade better than Kentucky bluegrass or rye.

• Tall fescue is a coarse pasture grass that will tolerate abuse, poor growing conditions, drought, or inundation.

CHAPTER FOUR

• Meyer zoysia grass is a warm-weather grass that will grow throughout the state.

• The creeping bentgrasses are temperate-zone grasses that prefer weather at 80 degrees Fahrenheit and require an extra amount of care.

• Colonial bentgrass often becomes a weed in bluegrass lawns.

Turfgrasses are complex little plants, not just tufts of green sticking out of the ground. Grass plants grow from a crown that is just below the soil surface. Leaves grow from the top of the crown, roots from the bottom. If allowed to grow unmowed, the crown elongates into a culm with a flower at the top and eventually seeds.

Some grass plants produce horizontal stems from the crowns. Below ground, they are called rhizomes; above ground, they are called stolons. The better kinds of turfgrasses spread by means of these stems, improving the density of the grass and repairing any damaged areas.

STARTING A LAWN

Many lawn problems can be prevented by properly starting a lawn. Adequate soil preparation, care in seeding or sodding, and conscientious aftercare are necessary.

To start a new lawn, whether seeding or sodding, follow these steps:

1. Prepare the soil by killing all vegetation (weeds and existing grass) with glyphosate. Follow directions on the label.

2. Till the soil to a depth of 4 to 6 inches.

3. Rake to establish the final grade and to remove rocks, clods, or other debris.

4. Roll with a light roller to firm the seedbed.

To seed a lawn, follow these steps:

1. Use a blend of 3 to 5 varieties of Kentucky bluegrass and 20 percent turf-type

Perennial ryegrass

perennial rye. For shady areas add 25 percent creeping red fescue.

2. Divide the appropriate amount of seed in two.

3. Spread with a drop-type spreader in one direction with half the seed, and then at 90 degrees with the other half.

4. Press the seed into the soil with the back of a leaf rake dragged back and forth across the seeded area, and roll to firm the seed.

5. Water to keep the seed moist, or rely on rainfall to moisten the planting.

To sod a lawn, follow these steps:

1. Select sod grown on a soil as nearly like that in your yard as you can find. The sod must be fresh, green not yellowing, with not more than $1/4$ inch of thatch.

2. Moisten the soil.

3. Apply a starter fertilizer to provide $1/2$ pound of nitrogen per 1000 square feet of the lawn.

4. Lay the sod carefully so that the seams are butted firmly together; stagger the ends.

5. Roll to firm the sod in good contact with the soil.

6. Water daily to keep the sod wet until it knits.

Renovate existing lawns that have been invaded by weedy grasses but are otherwise satisfactory by killing the existing grass with glyphosate and slit-seeding with the seed mix described above.

CARE FOR YOUR LAWN

Keep the lawn at a mowing height of 2 to $2^{1}/_{2}$ inches. Mow often enough to remove only $1/3$ to $1/2$ of the grass blade each time. At times of the season when the grass is growing rapidly, mowing may be necessary more than once a week. Avoid catching clippings unless they will go into the compost pile. They contain the fertilizer materials you applied earlier. Recycle them to benefit the lawn and to save yourself unnecessary work. Clippings do not cause thatch.

Apply 1 inch of water when the grass wilts. Do not water continuously. Wet soils prevent good root development. Unless the grass wilts, it has sufficient water anyway, and adding more is being wasteful.

Apply fertilizer when the grass begins to go off color. In cool weather apply fertilizer to provide 1 pound of nitrogen per 1,000 square feet. Use $1/2$ that rate in hot weather.

Cultivate the lawn to keep thatch under control and to reduce compaction. Core cultivators punch holes in the turf and soil, remove the cores, and open the soil so that roots can develop. Be sure that the machine you use makes a hole every 2 inches, 36 holes per square foot throughout the lawn, and at least 3 inches deep. Any less than that is insufficient. Check the spacing and depth before considering the job completed.

Insects and diseases can affect the lawn. Keeping the grass healthy will prevent most problems.

Control insects such as sod webworms, grubs, chinch bugs, or green- bugs with insecticides. Plant resistant grass varieties and control the thatch and compaction to minimize chances of disease.

JANUARY
LAWNS

PLANNING

Plan the year's lawn-care activities in January. Will you do the mowing, fertilizing, or pest control yourself, or will you contract all or part of it? Lawn-care companies and landscape contractors will be formalizing contracts in a couple of months. Contact a few for prices now. Read the contracts carefully; know what they are proposing. Before picking the lowest price, check with other customers to see how well satisfied they are with the service.

In the southern part of the state, the mowing season starts as early as March. In the north, it starts in April.

PLANTING

Anytime the ground is bare, seed can be spread on the lawn. Scatter the seed by hand over bare or thin areas of the lawn. Freezing and thawing will work the seed into the soil. The seed will germinate when soils warm sufficiently, usually in late March

or April. This is usually before the soil is dry enough to work in spring.

If the melting snow washes the seed away, reseed the spots later.

In the far southern part of the state, lay sod if the ground is not frozen and if temperatures are high enough so that water can be applied. Should the ground freeze later, there is danger that the sod will desiccate if it is unprotected. Snow cover is the best protection.

CARE

Winter damage to turf can occur in several ways. Try to avoid these problems.

- Salt and other deicing materials, even fertilizers used to melt ice, will burn the grass.
- Plowing or snow shoveling can result in mechanical damage.
- Grass exposed during a thaw can be damaged by walking on it, while it is frozen, breaking leaves.

- Snow compacted by cross-country skiers or snowmobiles will damage the grass beneath it. Sometimes these paths are worn through the snow and wear out the grass, too.

Where damage is expected, plan to repair it in spring by seeding or sodding.

WATERING

During a winter with little snow-fall, soils may dry to the point that the grass desiccates. If temperatures are mild enough and the soil is not frozen, try to water the grass to keep it from dying. One-fourth inch of water is sufficient to hydrate the crowns.

FERTILIZING

Fertilizer that is spread over the snow will soak in as the snow melts. Be sure the area is flat enough so that the melting snow and the dissolved fertilizer will not run off.

HELPFUL HINTS

Occasionally, winters are very mild and open. Mild winters and winters with continuous snow cover are easy on lawns. Sometimes the grass makes it all the way through the winter without turning brown. Usually, overwintering leaves are killed by the weather. As long as the crowns remain alive, the grass will recover in spring.

FEBRUARY

LAWNS

PLANNING

You need to be ready for the season, which will arrive in just a few short weeks. Service the mower yourself, or take it to a lawn mower repair shop. These people are not nearly as busy now as they will be in a month or so. Check the condition of the blower and edger, too.

PLANTING

In Zone 6b or even in Zone 6a, if the weather has been mild and the soil has dried a bit, cut out the areas damaged by the winter—those killed by the salt and the places where the plow tore up grass. Steal pieces of sod from the edges of the lawn next to the flower border or garden, and patch them into the lawn. Step on the patches to firm them in place.

Sow seed in bare or thin places in the lawn. There is no need to work the spots up but scratch the surface a bit to give the seed a place to lodge.

CARE

In the northern part of the state, winter will hang around for a while. You can seed the lawn if there is a break in the weather, but don't rush the season.

WATERING

If the season is early and the ground has dried out, the grass can desiccate in warm, drying winds. If this happens, watering may be helpful. Be sure to drain the hose so it doesn't freeze.

FERTILIZING

If you did not get around to fertilizing the lawn last fall, spread fertilizer on the snow. Make sure it is not washed away when the snow melts.

PESTS

Snow mold will develop where the water stands as snow melts.

Apply thiophanate-methyl or chlorothalonil fungicides. These materials can be applied any time the ground is bare, either before it snows or during a thaw. Next summer, recontour the lawn, filling in low spots so that water does not stand.

Perennial weeds and winter annuals are green and growing now, but it is too early to use herbicides. If you must do something outside, dig a few weeds with the dandelion digger.

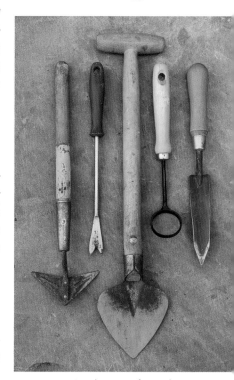

A selection of weeding tools (a dandelion digger is second from the left).

HELPFUL HINTS

Spend some time this winter reading about turfgrass management. Most libraries have helpful books on this subject. Libraries at botanical gardens and arboreta certainly can provide you with resources for your studies. Some offer short courses on turf care during the winter, and you may choose to enroll in them.

MARCH

LAWNS

 PLANNING

Some years, the grass is green and growing in March in the northern part of the state. Whether it is still green or not, it will need mowing soon enough.

While you anxiously wait for things to happen, get the mower ready for the season. You can take it to the mower repair shop, or with a little effort, you can do it yourself.

Follow these steps to service your mower:

1. Remove the spark plug, and throw it away. Stuff a clean cloth in the hole so that no dirt gets in it.

2. Wipe off the accumulated gunk from last season. A little kerosene or solvent helps. Do not use gasoline.

3. Remove the shroud.

4. Clean all the clippings from between the cooling fins on the engine and the flywheel fan.

5. Check the gas tank. If the gas tank was not emptied last fall (shame on you!), it will spill all over when you do the next step. Open the fuel line, and drain fuel into a coffee can for disposal.

6. Tip the mower, and remove the blade. Sharpen it, or buy a new one.

7. Replace the fuel filter.

8. Remove the air cleaner and the filter. Clean out the accumulated clippings and mud. Try to avoid getting any of this into the air intake. Wash the filter in solvent, or replace it.

9. Drain the oil from the crankcase of a four-cycle engine. (Two-cycle engines have no crankcase oil.) Refill it with the proper grade and amount of fresh oil.

10. Replace the blade.

11. Install a new spark plug.

12. Fill the tank with fresh gasoline, mixed with the proper amount of oil if required.

13. Start the mower. You may need to prime it the first time with a teaspoon of fuel in the spark plug hole. Be careful! Ether in an aerosol works too, but it is hard on engines, so use it sparingly.

 PLANTING

Start turfgrass repair this month.

Some garden centers have sod very early in the season for this purpose. Buy sod that was grown on the same kind of soil you have in your yard. Dig out bad areas in the lawn to the same depth as the sod. Loosen the soil. Cut pieces of sod, and set them in the prepared spots. Step them down to firm them against the soil, and soak them thoroughly.

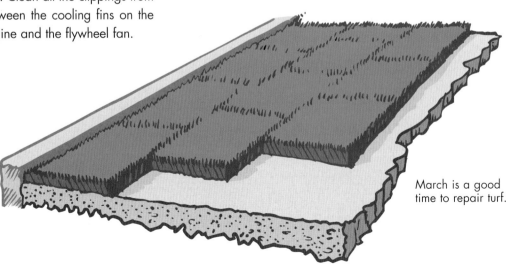

March is a good time to repair turf.

To seed, dig out the bad spots. Replace the soil with soil from the garden or border of the lawn. Seed with a blend of **Kentucky bluegrasses** and **perennial ryegrass**. Firm by tamping the seed with the back of a shovel. Cover with 2 or 3 inches of straw. Spring rain should provide enough water.

CARE

Rake out the lawn if the ground is sufficiently dry so that you do not leave footprints. Raking removes the accumulated trash, old grass matted by snow mold, and leftover leaves. It also pulls up the grass. Air and light can get to the soil, warming it so that the grass can breathe and begin growing.

WATERING

Water to keep new sod moist if there is no rain. Usually, the soils stay moist in the spring, and watering is not needed.

FERTILIZING

If fertilizer was applied last fall, none is needed yet this spring. If none was put down last fall, apply a turf fertilizer now. Apply any of the brands at the normal rate as directed on the package.

PESTS

Snow mold, leaf spot, and low-temperature rhizoctonia can affect the lawn as it begins to grow in spring.

Consider overseeding with improved cultivars of **Kentucky bluegrass** if these diseases appear every spring. The newer ones have better disease resistance. Usually, these diseases disappear when the weather improves.

In the southern part of the state, **forsythia** may be in bloom, and it is time to apply crabgrass preventer.

If you apply fertilizer, make sure it contains preemergent crabgrass herbicide unless you plan to reseed. The herbicide will prevent germination of good grasses, too. It is too early to apply this material for crabgrass in the northern parts of the state.

Knotweed may have been troublesome in the past.

Apply crabgrass preventer now to stop the knotweed. The material may need to be reapplied later for crabgrass.

Squirrels will dig in the lawn looking for things they buried last year. Sometimes they just dig! They are, well, squirrelly!

Just fill in the holes with the soil they shoved out.

MOWING

Mow now if the grass is tall enough. The first mowing can be about 1 inch shorter than normal to remove all the winter-damaged blades of grass. You may choose to collect these clippings. Dispose of them in the compost pile or in the vegetable garden.

Immediately set the mower back to the normal mowing height, 2 to $2\frac{1}{2}$ inches.

HELPFUL HINTS

Try to avoid working in the lawn if the soil is too wet. When a handful of soil from the border next to the lawn can be squeezed into a ball and then crumbled, it is dry enough to work. Wet soil is easily compacted, destroying the structure needed for good aeration and root development.

APRIL
LAWNS

PLANNING

The start of daylight-saving time makes me want to be outside.

One of the first items on the agenda is getting the lawn in shape for the summer. It is hard to tell just when the conditions will be right, but I usually expect to start on Good Friday. If Easter is very early, or if winter is prolonged, that may not be a very good time. If Easter is late, that date works well.

Plan for the following:
- Raking
- Mowing
- Fertilizing
- Controlling weeds
- Making repairs

Have all of the equipment and supplies on hand because if you are unprepared when the perfect day arrives, you may spend the entire time getting ready and miss the opportunity.

PLANTING

With the exception of an unusual, late-season snowfall, winter is over, and lawn care can be started in all parts of the state this month.

If you are growing **zoysia grass**, it will be sleeping for some time yet. Professional baseball fields are already in shape by the beginning of April for the first home game.

Start by raking and cultivating the lawn. Rake by hand or power rake to remove all the accumulated winter debris, thatch, old grass, and dead leaves. Raking stands the grass blades up and aerates the soil.

If the soil is compacted or if a heavy thatch layer has developed, core-aerate the lawn. The machine should leave a hole every 2 inches, 36 holes per square foot. Check the spacing of the holes before considering the job finished. Some machines will need to be run over the yard many times to achieve the necessary numbers of holes.

The grass will fill in small spots by itself as soon as it begins to grow. One grass plant every 2 inches is all that is necessary. Larger areas require turfgrass repairs:

1. Repair bad spots by scratching them up with a garden rake or cultivator. Seed with a blend of **Kentucky bluegrass** and **perennial rye**. Press the seed into the soil with the back of a grass rake, and firm it down by tamping it with the back of a shovel.

2. Dig out larger areas killed by salt, and use soil from elsewhere in the yard to fill them in. Seed or sod. Buy sod that was grown on the same kind of soil you have in your yard.

3. Slit-seed the entire yard if the lawn is generally sparse or thin. Use a machine that cuts slits through the duff into the soil and deposits seed in the slits. A press wheel firms the soil over the seed.

4. Broadcast additional seed so that as much as possible gets into the core holes in a lawn that was core-aerated.

CARE

Following the raking and repair, mow the grass short once. Mowing now will remove winter-damaged grass and will expose the newly developing leaves so that the grass turns green more quickly. Then set the mower back to the recommended 2- to 2$\frac{1}{2}$-inch mowing height.

Be patient with your lawn. It will take just about the whole month for it to recover from the rigors of winter. Grass seed germinates about April 15 in Zone 5b.

WATERING

Soak newly laid sod until it begins to knit. Unless spring rains are not forthcoming, routine watering will not be necessary this month. Excessively wet soils this month will interfere with root development. Wet soils are also easily compacted. Try to avoid walking or working in the grass when the ground is wet.

FERTILIZING

Apply a complete lawn fertilizer at the regular rate. This will provide 1 pound of nitrogen per 1,000 square feet of lawn. If you are using one of the 4-Step programs and have sown seed, do not apply any with crabgrass preventer. It will prevent the germination of the desirable grasses. Some newer 4-step crabgrass preventers are safe. Check the label.

PESTS

Insects are rarely present in damaging numbers this early in the season. Watch for greenbugs that may be blown in on warm fronts from the South. These tiny aphids ride thunderstorms, arriving here sometime in spring.

Most diseases are associated with the kind of weather present as the grass begins to grow. Mildew and rust are common in the cool, wet weather of spring.

Mildew shows up in the shade. It usually does not require treatment. Rust is worse on hungry lawns. Fertilizing to stimulate vigorous growth and regular mowing eliminate it.

Dandelions may be a problem. Carry a dandelion digger as you mow the lawn, and dig out any weeds that you see.

Broadleaf weeds may plague your lawn. Eliminate broadleaf weeds with herbicides applied as they are vigorously growing.

It may be tough to eliminate some weeds.

Call in a professional to combat violets or creeping Charlie.

Don't let crabgrass get started.

Apply crabgrass preventer when the **forsythias** have just finished flowering. Remember, do not apply these materials if you seeded or plan to seed.

The paths left by voles under the snow should be disappearing by now. Rabbits will continue to forage in the grass until other plants are up and growing.

MOWING

Proper mowing is important for a quality lawn. The grass will dictate how often mowing is needed. If the grass is well fertilized and vigorous, it may need to be mowed more than once a week. Mow often enough that no more than $1/3$ to $1/2$ of the length of the grass blade is removed at a time. Keeping the grass at $2^1/2$ inches tall means mowing by the time it reaches 4 inches.

HELPFUL HINTS

Getting the grass started now will give it a good chance to be healthy and dense before crabgrass begins to grow in late May. Making turf repairs as early as possible helps the lawn.

Repair small areas in the lawn by scratching them up with a garden cultivator, scattering seed, and raking it in.

MAY

LAWNS

PLANNING

The cool-season grasses are at their finest now.

As temperatures increase, the grasses encounter stresses and begin to slow down. Flowering begins this month, putting added stress on the plants. Try to keep the grass as healthy as possible with proper mowing and cautious watering.

PLANTING

There is still time to make lawn repairs before temperatures are too high. The disadvantage is the weed pressure in seeded lawns. Most of the weed seeds including crabgrass and foxtail normally germinate now, so you may have to contend with a weedy lawn for the remainder of the summer.

Sodding now eliminates problems from weed seeds. Lawn renovation or new installations are best done in fall, but with some care they can be done in May. To sod your lawn, follow these steps:

1. Kill all existing weeds and grasses with glyphosate before stripping off the old grass or working up the lawn.

2. Prepare the same as for seeding with well-tilled soil, no clods or rocks.

3. Moisten the soil.

4. Apply starter fertilizer before laying the sod.

5. Use freshly cut sod with good green color and no weeds or diseases. Avoid any sod that is yellowing or heating. The soil on which the sod was grown should be the same kind as in your yard.

6. Make sure the seams are butted firmly together and the sod is in good contact with the soil.

7. Roll the sod after it is put down.

CARE

Zoysia is awakening from its winter slumber. This hot-weather grass is dormant until soil temperatures are consistently warm. It is a stoloniferous grass, meaning the horizontal stems are aboveground. (Rhizomatous grasses make horizontal stems belowground.)

Slice, core, and top-dress **zoysia grass** to keep it from becoming puffy.

WATERING

Grasses do not need water until they begin to wilt. In some years,

watering is unnecessary most of the season. When grass wilts, footprints do not spring back after you walk on the lawn.

If the grass begins to wilt, apply a measured 1 inch of water. Set a coffee can under the sprinkler to measure. Run the water until 1 inch is in the can.

On slopes, the water may run off before 1 inch is in the can. Turn off the water until it soaks in, and then resume watering.

Once the grass has received an inch, turn the water off until the grass wilts again. Automatic sprinkler systems often do more harm than good because they run according to their schedule instead of the grass's schedule.

FERTILIZING

Fertilize with a complete lawn fertilizer if you did not do so in April. Incorporate crabgrass preventer if the grass is sparse and thin unless you seeded this spring. Crabgrass will germinate in the middle of this month, so time is short. If crabgrass is already present in the lawn, it is too late.

PESTS

Grubs have moved back to the surface from their wintering quarters well down in the ground. They do little feeding now, and damage is unlikely.

If true white grubs have been troublesome in the past, however, apply trichlorfon now.

Billbugs may have caused damage in the past.

Treat those areas with trichlorfon by Memorial Day.

Cutworms will damage small areas of the turf.

Spot-treat the areas with carbaryl.

Cool, wet weather may result in rust or leaf spot diseases.

Keep the lawn growing and mowed properly until the weather is more favorable. Applying fungicides is rarely worth the expense or effort.

It is time to attack weeds as soon as any newly seeded grass has been mowed twice.

Apply herbicides to eliminate broadleaf weeds such as dandelions, plantain, or knotweed. For creeping Charlie or violets, call a lawn-care company or landscape contractor to treat the problem. The materials they use are not available in consumer-type packages.

Damage from female dogs shows up as dark-green spots in the lawn where the grass grows much faster than the surrounding grass. Or it may appear as dead spots with vigorous, green halos.

Soak the spots with volumes of water to wash them out. Train the dog to use a spot where there is no grass. Male dogs hit tree trunks and fire hydrants, not the grass.

MOWING

Continue mowing at the regular heights: cool-season grasses, except **bentgrass**, at 2 to 2½ inches; warm-season grasses at 1 inch. Mow warm-season grasses to remove only ⅓ of the blade at a time, which means mowing every 3 to 4 days.

Mow bents at ½ inch or less. Where **bentgrass** has contaminated a **bluegrass** lawn, the incompatibility in cutting heights makes the **bent** unsightly. The grass falls over, exposing the long brown culms (stems).

Time your sprinkler's water flow so you will know how long it takes to apply the amount of water needed.

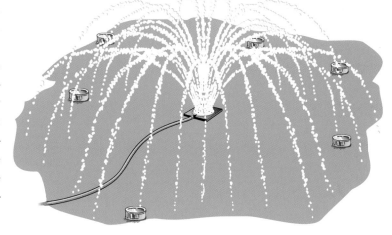

HELPFUL HINTS

Cool-season grasses flower about this time of the season. Many people think the grass is going to seed. The flower stalks are less apparent in well-fertilized, vigorous lawns. Keeping the grass mowed will cut these heads off as they develop.

Later in the summer, culms of these individual plants that flowered will turn brown and die out, which is a normal occurrence. If the grass is healthy, new plants will take over, and the grass will fill in without additional assistance.

JUNE
LAWNS

PLANNING

Often, the Midwest spring is cool and wet. The grass is lush, and roots are shallow. When summer arrives, there is an abrupt change to hot weather. Our cool-season grasses prefer moderate temperatures. They just survive in hot weather.

The culms that flowered last month are turning brown now. Although the lawn may look bad, it is no cause for concern. Many people call me because they are afraid the grass is dying when they see the brown grass. The stiff, dry stems and brown leaves will soon disintegrate, and the lawn will be green again.

As you mow the lawn, notice any crabgrass, other weeds, diseases, or other problems that may need attention later. Postpone lawn repairs until later in the season when the weather moderates.

PLANTING

Sod may be installed during hot weather as long as there is sufficient water to keep it wet.

To sod the lawn, follow these steps:

1. Kill all existing weeds and grasses with glyphosate before stripping off the old grass or working up the lawn.

2. Prepare the soil as if you were going to seed it; till the soil, leaving no clods or rocks.

3. Moisten the soil.

4. Apply starter fertilizer before laying the sod. Use freshly cut sod with good green color and no weeds or diseases. Avoid any sod that is yellowing or heating. The soil on which the sod was grown must be the same kind as in your yard.

5. Lay the sod carefully so that seams are butted firmly together and the sod is in good contact with the soil.

6. Roll the sod after it is put down.

CARE

Give the grass whatever it needs to survive, but do not force it to grow. If it has any basic problems such as layering, thatch buildup, compact soil, or poor drainage, nurse it through, and plan to correct the problems when the weather is more favorable.

If a period of cool weather is expected and if water is available, core-aerate during the summer. Coring opens the soil and removes the layers or thatch and resultant interfaces. The coring must produce a hole every 2 inches, 36 holes per square foot, and must penetrate through the layers.

WATERING

Cool-season turfgrasses can stand drought. They go dormant and turn brown. If water is not available from lack of rain or watering restrictions, do not panic. The grass will not die immediately. If the drought is extended, 3 or 4 weeks without water, crowns of the grass plants may begin to desiccate and eventually to die.

After 3 weeks of drought, try to apply 1/4 inch of water to rehydrate the crowns. Watering in this way will not turn the grass green, but it will keep it from dying. When rains return, the grass will become green again.

Set a coffee can under the sprinkler to measure the amount applied. When there is 1/4 inch of water in the can, turn off the water.

Even during drought, grass does not need to be watered unless it wilts. Watering every 5 to 7 days should be enough. No lawn needs watering every day. Overwatering in hot weather causes other problems.

FERTILIZING

Do not force cool-season turf-grasses to grow in hot weather. If the grass begins to fade because of insufficient nitrogen, apply a turfgrass fertilizer at 1/2 the normal rate. Water it in to avoid burning the foliage.

Fertilize hot-weather grasses such as **zoysia** monthly during the summer. Apply fertilizer at the regular rate to supply 1 pound of nitrogen per 1,000 square feet of lawn.

PESTS

Ants build nests in lawns. They make hills of soil as they excavate. The grass in the spot dries up and turns brown.

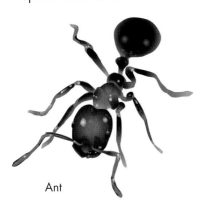

Ant

Treat the hills with cyfluthrin-type insecticide, soaking them thoroughly. Sometimes the ants will just move the hills. Treat them again. Eventually, the ants will be killed or will move to the neighbor's yard.

Adult annual white grubs may emerge at the end of the month. They are 3/4-inch-long beetles attracted to lights at night. They are tan colored with black faces.

Make note of the date and the numbers of them that appear.

As the grass is stressed, the warm-weather diseases may begin.

Prevent leaf spot and melting out by planting resistant varieties of grass.

The summer ring and patch diseases are common in lawns with poor soil conditions, excess thatch, or layering.

Correcting each of the problems prevents the diseases.

Yellow patch rhizoctonia often is associated with soggy soils, commonly where sprinkler systems are improperly scheduled.

Following recommended watering schedules eliminates the problem.

If the lawn is thin or damaged, crabgrass may show up now.

Applying preemergent herbicides earlier in the season will prevent crabgrass. Once the weed is growing, the preventers will not work.

If the grass is allowed to go dormant in dry weather, weedy perennial grasses—quackgrass, tall fescue, and nimblewill— will show up because they tolerate drought better than finer grasses.

Using any chemicals to eliminate these weeds will damage the desirable grasses. Spot-treating with glyphosate or killing off the entire lawn and starting over are options. Late summer is the preferred time to take these measures. Glyphosate kills nearly everything green it contacts.

MOWING

Mow the grass at the highest level when the temperatures are high. The foliage shades the ground, reducing evaporation and the stress on roots.

If a period of mild, wet weather is expected, hide the old brown grass and dead culms by setting the mower 1 inch lower than usual and mowing once. Set the mower back to its regular height immediately. When the new, green leaves have grown back to the normal height, the brown will be out of sight.

JULY
LAWNS

PLANNING

The lawn will not go on vacation just because you take one.

If you intend to be gone for two weeks, it will need mowing and edging, and it may need watering. Before you leave, find someone to take care of it. If you are lucky enough to have kids in the neighborhood who do lawns, have them mow and water once before you leave so that they are familiar with what you expect.

Landscape contractors will mow and edge, but they are reluctant to do watering because of the time involved. Maybe a neighbor could water if necessary. In any case, do not leave your lawn to fend for itself while you are gone.

PLANTING

Do sodding now if there are no watering restrictions.

To sod your lawn, follow these steps:

1. Kill all existing weeds and grasses with glyphosate before stripping off the old grass or working up the lawn.

2. Prepare the soil.

3. Moisten the soil.

4. Apply starter fertilizer before laying the sod.

5. Use freshly cut sod with good green color and no weeds or diseases. Avoid any sod that is yellowing or heating. In hot weather, sod cut one day, stacked on a pallet, and held till the next day will begin to heat. That kills the roots and rots the leaves. Reject any sod that has begun to heat. The soil on which the sod was grown must be the same kind as in your yard.

6. Lay the sod with the seams butted firmly together and in good contact with the soil.

7. Roll the sod after it is put down so that it is in good contact with the ground.

CARE

In hot weather, the **Kentucky bluegrass** and **perennial ryegrass** just survive. Anything that can affect a lawn will show up when the grass is at its weakest. Try to nurse it along. Do not do anything drastic at this time of the season.

Zoysia grass thrives in hot weather. It is in its element. In the northern part of the state, home owners who struggle with the dormant **zoysia** through the spring and fall can appreciate their beautiful lawns now. Mowing and watering will keep this grass at its best.

WATERING

Apply water when the grass wilts. If it does not wilt, it does not need water. Wilting appears as a purplish color to the grass when viewed at a low angle. Footsteps do not spring back when you walk through wilted grass.

Water on a rising temperature so that the surface of the grass dries before dark. If restrictions dictate watering at night, water as late as possible. While the

Magnified cross-section of zoysia grass.

sprinkler is running, the spores of any disease are rinsed off the grass. Once the water is turned off, spores that land on the grass can grow.

Timers that turn the water on for a few minutes every day are designed not for the grass, but for the convenience of home owners. To use a timer to its best advantage for the grass, follow these steps:

1. Set the timer for the time of day you want the water to run.

2. Determine how long it takes for the system to deliver 1 inch of water, and set the duration accordingly.

3. Activate the timer to run and the system to water the grass when you see the grass wilting.

4. Turn the system off until the next time the grass wilts.

FERTILIZING

Zoysia grass does its best in the heat of summer. Fertilize it with a high-nitrogen lawn fertilizer at the full rate. Fertilize **bluegrasses** and **ryes** only if they begin to go off color and are being watered on demand. Apply lawn fertilizer at $1/2$ the regular rate in hot weather.

PESTS

If Junebugs were numerous, both the little tan ones and the big brown ones, be prepared for grubs. These beetles lay eggs in the greenest, healthiest grass they can find. Grubs are the larvae of these beetles.

Apply halofenozide or imidacloprid insecticde now to prevent damage. Soak it in with $1/2$ inch of water. These materials take 30 days to become effective.

Sod webworm adults fly in late June to July laying eggs. These larvae do damage in late July.

Treat the grass with carbaryl, deltamethrin, or trichlorfon insecticide now if you saw the little moths flitting ahead of your mower. These materials will control billbugs and chinch bugs, too. Do not water these chemicals in. They must stay on the leaves where the insects feed.

Summer ring and patch diseases, once called *Fusarium*, cause circles, rings, donuts, or serpentine patterns of dead grass. They are stress diseases and don't respond to chemical treatment.

Eliminate thatch, layering, compaction, or poor drainage to solve the problem. Thiophanate-methyl fungicide may provide some improvement until the conditions can be changed for the better. Core-aeration to produce

a hole every 2 inches through the thatch and layers will eventually correct the conditions. Repeated coring may be needed. Do not let anyone sell you on a coring job that does not result in the necessary numbers of holes, 36 per square foot.

Dandelions and plantain may appear. Carry a dandelion digger with you as you mow, and dig the weeds out when you see them. Unless the entire lawn is weedy, spraying is not necessary.

If crabgrass took over, at least the lawn is green. Do not do anything about it now. Wait until it dies out naturally, and renovate the lawn. A good lawn will reduce the chances of the growth of crabgrass next year.

MOWING

Zoysia should be mowed at 1 inch at least twice a week at this time of the season. You will notice that your mower will become dull because **zoysia** is tough grass. Keep your mower sharpened whether you are growing **zoysia** or the cool-season grasses. A sharp mower makes a clean cut. Frayed leaves invite diseases and look shabby. You can tell which lawns have been mowed by a dull mower because the frayed leaves produce a kind of haze over them.

AUGUST

LAWNS

PLANNING

If you have kept track of the problems in your lawn, now is the time to plan how to correct them. Late August or September is the time to repair or renovate lawns.

I have not mentioned journaling as a lawn-care practice. Since most lawn maintenance is routine, there is little need to keep records. But now you need to think about the things that need repair. Did the melting snow cause puddles where the grass had snow mold? Was crabgrass a problem? Were perennial grasses taking over the lawn? Correct thatch problems and especially layering from dissimilar sod and soil, thin topsoil from the time of construction, and buried debris in late summer.

PLANTING

In Zone 5b, prime time for seeding lawns is August 15. In other parts of the state, it may be earlier or later.

To completely renovate a lawn with grassy weeds and a poor stand of grass, seed or sod the lawn. To seed, follow these steps:

1. Treat the lawn with glyphosate on August 10, or 5 days before the seeding date.

2. Dig out any buried trash. (If the lawn is free of buried debris, there is no need to dig up the lawn.)

3. Proceed with planting after 1 or 2 days; the glyphosate will have been absorbed by the weeds and grass by then.

4. Core-aerate thoroughly, 36 holes per square foot, if thatch or layering is a problem. Be sure the cores go through all the layers into the underlying soil.

5. Slit-seed the lawn in 2 directions at 45 degrees from each other. Use a blend of 3 to 5 cultivars of **Kentucky bluegrass**, and 25 percent **turf-type perennial ryegrass**. If the grass is in the shade, use A-34 **Kentucky bluegrass**, **turf-type perennial rye**, and 25 percent **creeping red fescue**.

6. Broadcast-seed with the same seed to get as much in the core holes as possible.

With adequate rainfall or watering, the new grass will be up and growing before the old grass has died.

To sod, follow these steps:

1. Following treatment with glyphosate, strip off the old grass with a sod cutter. Put it in the compost heap or in the garden.

2. Loosen the soil by raking or cultivating to make a fine seedbed.

3. Core-aerate if layering is a problem.

4. Moisten the soil.

5. Apply starter fertilizer prior to laying the sod.

6. Use freshly cut sod with good green color and no weeds or diseases. Avoid any sod that is yellowing or heating. The soil on which the sod was grown must be the same kind as in your yard.

7. Lay the sod so that the seams are butted firmly together and the sod is in good contact with the soil.

8. Roll the sod after it is put down.

9. Water!

CARE

As temperatures moderate, the grass will resume growth. Mow as needed to keep the grass at the correct height.

WATERING

New sod will require watering several times a day for 1 or 2 weeks until it begins to knit together. Then reduce the frequency. Do not let the sod dry out, or it will turn brown and dry up.

New seed can rely on natural rainfall, but there is a risk that rains will not come for several weeks. Keep the lawn moist by sprinkling until the grass is up.

Established grass should receive 1 measured inch of water when it has begun to wilt. Use a coffee can under the sprinkler to measure the amount. When there is 1 inch in the can, turn off the water.

FERTILIZING

Apply fertilizer at the end of the month. Use a high-nitrogen fertilizer at the regular rate, applying 1 pound of nitrogen per 1,000 square feet of lawn. If no lawn repairs were needed, use a weed-and-feed product to eliminate broadleaf weeds.

PESTS

If no grub-proofing materials were applied, watch for grub damage to show up. Skunks or raccoons excavating the lawn are a good indication that grubs are present. Roll back damaged turfgrass to see the grubs.

White grub

Treat the lawn with carbaryl, deltamethrin or trichlorfon insecticide now, and apply 1/2 inch of water immediately. Apply carbaryl for controlling green Junebug grubs.

Rust will show up if the weather is cool and wet.

Stimulate the grass with fertilizer, and keep it mowed to remove the rust before it matures.

Mildew will appear in shaded places.

Overseed with A-34 **Kentucky bluegrass**, which is resistant to mildew.

Fall is the best time to treat broadleaf weeds. Actively growing, they are easily eliminated.

Raccoons or skunks digging in the lawn are seeking insects. Rabbits graze on the grass, clipping it short. Squirrels dig holes to bury nuts and seeds.

MOWING

Keep the grass mowed at the normal height. There is no need to collect clippings if the grass is not allowed to get too tall. Mulching-mowers chop the clippings tiny enough that they filter back into the grass and are recycled. Put collected clippings in the garden or on the compost pile. Do not throw them away.

HELPFUL HINTS

Cool-season turfgrasses grow in the fall until freeze-up, and in spring until it gets hot. In summer, they suffer. In winter, they are dormant. Do power raking or renovation by early fall. Good weather all fall and again in spring allows the grass time for full recovery before summer. The lawn should be dense enough by then to resist crabgrass invasion and to tolerate the hot weather.

Hot-weather grasses are dormant until it gets warm. Repair them in spring.

September

LAWNS

PLANNING

Labor Day is the start of a new season. I know fall does not begin until the end of the month, but with schools starting, vacations over, and the weather cooling off, the pace quickens. A lot of season's-end activities begin, and all of us get back into our normal routines. Actually, the meteorological fall does begin on September 1.

If turfgrass repairs were not completed last month, plan to do them as quickly as possible. Time is indeed short. New seed should have at least two months before freeze-up to be strong enough to survive.

PLANTING

The grasses recommended for fine lawns in the Midwest include the **Kentucky bluegrasses, perennial ryegrass**, and **fine fescues**. Blends of these grasses provide the best chance of having a sturdy, disease-resistant lawn. Selecting cultivars that tolerate your conditions is important but difficult because every yard is different.

Select **Kentucky bluegrasses** for disease resistance and site tolerance. Since the first cultivar, Merion, was discovered about 50 years ago, tremendous improvements have been made in **Kentucky bluegrass**.

Today I recommend sowing at least 3 to 5 different cultivars in a blend to give you a better chance that the **bluegrasses** will be able to stand the conditions in your yard. There will be less chance that the lawn will be lost from diseases as well.

Add seed of 1 or 2 **turf-type perennial ryegrass** cultivars to increase disease resistance. Seed suppliers in your area usually provide blends selected for your conditions.

Fine fescues have undergone quite an improvement over the years. Many have been hybridized at Pennsylvania State University. Incorporate **fine fescues** where light is limited or where the soils are poor.

Buy seed and supplies from a reputable source. Unusually cheap seed from a grocery store or discount outlet may be old or may not be varieties that will do well in your location. Do not risk all the effort you expend in preparing for seeding on seed of unknown quality.

CARE

Autumn is the beginning of the season for the cool-weather grasses. They grow a lot in the cool weather of fall, and again in the spring until it turns hot. Since this long period of growth allows the grass to recover from any injury, it is time to core-aerate, power rake, reseed, or sod.

• Core-aerating punches holes in the turf, through any layers, removing them and breaking up the compaction.

The process must leave a hole every 2 inches, 36 holes per square foot.

• Power raking can remove the layer of thatch that is conducive to poor growth and to disease susceptibility.

If the thatch layer is $1/4$ to $1/2$ inch thick, power raking is an acceptable process. If the thatch exceeds $1/2$ inch in thickness, power raking will remove the lawn. Core-aerate in that case. Repeated core aerating may be needed.

Fine fescue

• Seeding is still advisable at this time of year.

Soils are still warm, and seed will germinate very quickly with sufficient water. Prepare the seedbed carefully.

• Sodding may occur throughout the fall.

The section on planting on page 96 offers details on seeding and sodding.

WATERING

If fall is dry, continue the watering program initiated for the summer. Apply 1 measured inch of water when the grass wilts. Do not water until the grass wilts again, and then apply another inch of water. If the grass does not wilt, no water is needed.

Do not get in the habit of sprinkling the lawn. Sprinkling does not provide sufficient water, and it encourages shallow rooting.

New seed and new sod need special attention and frequent watering until they are well established.

FERTILIZING

Many turfgrass books recommend application of lime to lawns. There is excess lime in the soils throughout most of the Midwest, however. The soil can be very alkaline. Acidic soils are preferred, so lime complicates the problem. Do not lime lawns unless soil tests indicate the need. Alkaline soils may benefit from applications of sulfur to lower the pH.

Fertilize cool-weather grasses at $1/2$ rate in hot weather, full rate in cool. Around Labor Day, make a full application of lawn fertilizer, which will provide 1 pound of nitrogen per 1,000 square feet of lawn. If slow-release fertilizer such as sulfur-coated urea is used, apply it at double the normal rate.

Fertilize hot-weather grasses at full rate monthly throughout the summer. In fall when temperatures cool off, the plants become dormant and need no fertilizer. There will be at least another month of warm weather in the southern part of the state; fertilize **zoysia grass** lawns one more time.

Zoysia in the north is beginning to slow down and will be dormant in a few weeks.

PESTS

Grubs are very active in September. If no grub-proofing materials were applied earlier, do so now where the grass is being damaged. Skunks and raccoons mine lawns infested by grubs.

Use carbaryl or trichlorfon. Apply $1/2$ inch of water immediately following application.

In moist, lighter sandy soils, a parasitic nematode is very effective in keeping grub populations under control.

Use *Steinernema carpocapsae*, a parasite of grubs and other larvae. Keep the soil moist following application.

Leaf spot, rust, and mildew diseases are common in the fall if weather is cool and moist.

Control these diseases by planting resistant grass varieties and keeping them growing.

New broadleaf weeds have germinated and can be eliminated at the same time as the older established ones.

Apply a herbicide. Herbicides are most effective in the fall. Hire a lawn-care company to treat tough weeds such as creeping Charlie or violets.

Clover in a lawn is a sign that the fertility level is low. It is a legume and produces its own nitrogen.

Fertilize the grass so that it can compete with the clover, and the clover will disappear.

Skunks and raccoons are attracted to the insects in the lawn.

Get rid of the insects and the animals will leave.

OCTOBER

LAWNS

PLANNING

What will you do with all those leaves? If local ordinances permit the burning of leaves in your neighborhood, burning them is a way of reducing their bulk. For most of us leaf burning is just a memory. But we can still enjoy the smell of burning leaves as we drive through rural areas in the fall.

The leaves cannot stay on the lawn or they will smother the grass. Figure out something to do with them.

If there are not too many or if the leaves are tiny, shred them with your mower and leave them where they fell. They will filter into the lawn where microorganisms will decompose them, recycling the nutrients. This is beneficial to the trees and to the lawn.

Remove larger leaves or great volumes of them from the lawn by raking, vacuuming, or picking them up with a power mower and bagger.

PLANTING

There is still time to reseed damaged places in the lawn. By the middle of the month in the northern part of the state to the end of the month in the southern, it will be risky to seed. The plants will germinate but may not be big enough to survive the winter.

Lay sod as long as the soil is not too wet and until freeze-up. The weather is mild and usually moist, so sod has every chance to knit and grow. If rainfall is consistent and regular, watering may not be necessary once the sod has been thoroughly soaked. This is the best time for sodding.

CARE

Layers of thatch or shallow layers of topsoil over heavy clay will cause shallow rooting of turfgrass, making the lawn susceptible to ring and patch diseases. These diseases are stress related and attack grass that has poor growing conditions. Layering is the most common cause of poor lawns.

Thatch can build up.

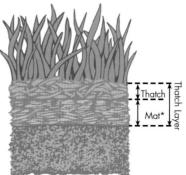

*Old thatch and soil

Core-aeration now will help eliminate layering and open the soil so that healthy roots can develop.

• Core-aeration removes tiny cores from the turf, discarding them on the surface.

Breaking up these cores permits the soil on them to filter into the turf and the duff to blow away.

• The coring machine must be able to penetrate all the way through the layers, commonly 2 to 3 inches deep. It must produce a hole every 2 inches, 36 holes per square foot of lawn.

Roots develop rapidly in the holes at this time of the season, improving the health of the lawn immediately.

• Coring may be repeated until the layers are removed, one core at a time. Seeding into the core holes will increase the density of the lawn and develop roots beyond the layers where they will improve the condition of the soil.

WATERING

If fall is dry, water every time the grass wilts. If there is no wilting, the grass does not need water. Apply 1 measured inch every time you water. Use a coffee can as a rain gauge. Turn off the water when 1 inch has accumulated in the can.

FERTILIZING

In late October, apply fertilizer to provide another pound of nitrogen per 1,000 square feet of lawn. Use a high-nitrogen lawn fertilizer at the regular rate.

Often grass growing in the shade begins to thin out and pulls out easily. The natural inclination is to fertilize it to improve the vigor. Actually, the opposite is true.

• Grass in the shade needs much less nitrogen fertilizer than grass in full sun.

• Shaded grass produces far less carbohydrate through photosynthesis.

There is less for the plant to use making leaves and roots. Nitrogen tells the plant to make leaves. If there is not enough carbohydrate to go around, the roots suffer while the plant makes leaves.

• Grass in shade is always thinner and lighter colored than grass in full sun.

In the shade, fertilize the grass at $1/2$ the rate of the sunny grass. The grass will find a balance between the roots and the top.

PESTS

Grub activity slows down as the soil cools off. The grubs burrow down into the soil for the winter.

If grub-proofing materials were not applied earlier, it is too late now. These grubs will surface next spring and will emerge as adult beetles in early summer.

Cool-weather diseases show up as the weather becomes more fall-like. Mildew will appear in shaded areas. Rust develops in slowly growing grass that needs fertilizer. Resistant **bluegrass** cultivars should be overseeded into areas where these diseases develop.

Fungicides are not usually recommended for home lawns. Chlorothalonil may be helpful if there is danger that the lawn will be destroyed before improvements can be made. Fertilize rusty lawns to improve the growth, and keep them mowed so that the disease does not mature on the leaves. Frequent mowing will remove the disease before it can fully develop.

Broadleaf weeds are most easily killed at this time of the season.

A weed-and-feed product or turfgrass herbicides can be applied now. Follow directions on the package. Keep these materials off desirable plants.

Once the grubs burrow well into the soil, the animals that were feeding on them will find other things to eat.

Squirrels are burying nuts and other things now. They dig several holes before finding just the right place.

Fill in the discarded holes, which will recover quickly.

MOWING

As long as the grass is growing, mow it. Cut frequently enough that only $1/3$ of the blade is removed at a time. Regular mowing will keep the accumulation of leaves to a minimum, whether you collect them or chop them into the grass.

November

LAWNS

PLANNING

Thanksgiving usually sees one of the first snowfalls of the winter season, at least in the northern part of the state. With snow on the ground, air temperatures can plummet. But the ground is protected and stays much warmer.

The grass will stay green and will continue growing as long as the ground is not frozen. Much of the growth takes place below ground where you do not see it. Roots and rhizomes continue to grow. Tillers, the secondary shoots that develop in the same crown of the plant, initiate as well. Even under the snow, grasses continue to develop as long as the ground remains unfrozen.

PLANTING

Sod can be laid as long as the ground is not frozen and there is a water supply to soak it in. If the weather turns cold before the sod knits, keeping it watered may be difficult, and some desiccation may take place. Good snow cover is the best protection.

After a period of time when seeding is not advisable, there is a short time when you may do dormant seeding. Dormant-seeding gets the seed in the ground too late for it to germinate until next year. There is no chance that it will be lost through winter damage, and it will be up and growing before the soils are dry enough to work in spring.

CARE

Keep raking the lawn to remove late-falling leaves. Wet leaves that stay on the lawn all winter will kill the grass.

WATERING

Watering will be necessary only to establish new sod or to provide moisture in the southern part of the state where weather is still warm and dry. Roll up and drain the hose. Drain the irrigation system, and note any repairs that will need to be made before next summer.

FERTILIZING

Dormant fertilizer, or late-fall fertilizing, is often recommended, especially for turfgrasses that will receive heavy wear during the winter. It also may reduce the incidence of snow mold. These fertilizers have analyses with low nitrogen, high phosphorus, and high potassium. This mix is intended to harden the grass so that it can tolerate the adverse conditions. If grass is lush and soft going into winter, these fertilizers may be helpful. Apply them according to recommendations on the package. Usually, the application will provide 1 pound or less of nitrogen per 1,000 square feet of lawn.

PESTS

Insect pests are of no concern at this time of the season.

Snow mold may have been troublesome in the past.

Apply thiophanate-methyl or chlorothalonil-type fungicides after the last mowing this fall.

As long as the weeds are growing, herbicides will be effective.

Apply turf herbicide to dandelions, plantain, chickweed, or other broadleaf weeds.

MOWING

Keep mowing as long as the grass is growing. Keep chopping or removing leaves at the same time. Reduce the mowing height for the final mowing in order to reduce the amount of dead grass in spring and possibly reduce the amount of snow mold.

DECEMBER

LAWNS

PLANNING

Before winter gets a good start, take a trip around your yard. If there were lawn problems that you never quite corrected, plan to investigate them this winter.

PLANTING

Sod can still be laid as long as the soil is not frozen and there is a source of water. Keep in mind, however, that sudden freezing weather with no snow cover may be very hard on the new sod, desiccating it if there is no way to water it.

Dormant seeding can be done this month without fear of failure. Since the seed will be well moistened, it will germinate when the soil temperature is high enough.

CARE

Warm-season **zoysia grass** is dormant and completely brown now. See how much contamination by weeds or cool-season grasses has taken place. These weeds can be killed with glyphosate in spring before the dormant grass turns green.

WATERING

Usually, watering will be needed only where new sod has been laid. If the winter turns out to be very mild and dry—an El Niño year can be like that—grass sown in the fall may be shallowly rooted and can stand watering. Watering may be the difference between having the lawn survive the winter and having to redo it in spring.

FERTILIZING

Apply late-season fertilizer if it was not applied in November. Late-season or dormant fertilizers are much higher in phosphorus and potassium than normal lawn fertilizers. Apply it at the rate suggested on the package.

PESTS

Insects that would damage the lawn are long gone. Those that survive the winter are dormant; the others have been killed by the cold weather by now.

Snow mold may have been troublesome in the past. If so, apply fungicide now before the ground is snow covered. Thiophanate-methyl or chlorothalonil-type fungicides will prevent the disease. Repeat this treatment during the January thaw.

MOWING

There is no need to mow the grass in December.

HELPFUL HINTS

Soon, snow-salting and removal will occupy your outdoor time. These activities can severely damage lawns. Try to avoid salting as much as possible. Use ice-melting substitutes or calcium chloride instead of salt. Fertilizer will melt ice, but it will burn, too. Urea is used for melting snow at airports. It works, but it is a hot nitrogen fertilizer. Shovel as much of the snow as possible first. Apply the deicing material down the middle of the walk, getting as little of it as you can on the grass. Shovel the salty snow into the street, driveway, parking lot, or anywhere but on the grass. It may take planning to find a place to get rid of salty snow, but it will mean a lot less damage to the grass.

PERENNIALS

Growing perennials is a challenge. Once the "gardening bug" bites, most of us turn from annuals to perennials for gardening excitement. I look forward to getting up each morning and going out to the garden to see what is new. And something new is always going on in the perennial garden.

Perennials are plants that germinate from seeds, grow the first year or so without flowering, survive the winter, and come back every year. Perennial flowering plants usually bloom every year once they start.

Herbaceous perennials die to the ground each fall. They regrow from roots, bulbs, tubers, or other underground parts that survive the winter. Peonies, iris, bleeding hearts, and grasses are typical examples. Woody plants that develop structures to survive winter—trees, shrubs, tree peonies, and rose bushes—are all perennials by definition, too.

Perennial flowering plants are gaining in popularity. One reason is that gardeners do not have to plant them each year. Another is that they provide gorgeous and interesting blooms. Most perennials have a short blooming period, a couple of weeks at most, and something needs to be done to fill the voids in the garden. This is where planning is essential. Because the plants will be in the same location for several years, a lot of preparation is needed.

Some gardeners have the idea that they can "spend some money on a few perennials, plant them once, and they will flower forever after-

ward." It sounds good, but the reality is that perennials require a lot of care:

The plants will need to be divided. Times when it is best to lift and divide these plants vary. Some perennials can be planted in fall, others in spring. Some may not fit into the garden very well.

Pest control is also very important. Timing for the most efficient use of control measures is critical.

PLANNING THE PERENNIAL GARDEN

Perennials come in all sizes, shapes, and colors. Garden books and catalogs describe these plants in detail, but to know exactly what to expect from these plants in your yard, start with a trial garden. Line out the plants that interest you in rows in your garden. Label them so that you get to know them by sight.

Once you know what to expect from the plants, you can properly place them in the garden. Consider these elements:

- How big will they grow?
- When do they flower?
- What is the bloom color?
- Do they flower then die?
- Are there any features of special interest to you?

Draw your garden plan to scale on graph paper. Then when planting it you will be sure to leave enough space for each variety. Place the taller plants at the rear of the garden, lower ones at the front. Plants such as poppies that bloom early and then die out need to be placed so that the hole they leave will be hidden by something that develops and blooms later.

SOIL PREPARATION

Take your time preparing your perennial garden.

Your perennial garden will be in place for a number of years, so careful preparation is worth the effort:

1. Control weeds before you plant. Weed problems cause most perennial garden failures. Once you have selected the spot for your garden, kill off the perennial weeds and grasses with glyphosate herbicide. Then either cover it with black plastic to "cook" anything that tries to grow or allow the plot to go fallow to prevent any weed growth for a full season.

2. Spade over the area after it is completely weed free. Perennials are deeply rooted plants. Rototilling 4 or 5 inches deep is fine for annuals, but double-digging—turning the soil two spades deep, 12 to 15 inches—is recommended for perennials. Do a little at a time, not all at once, if you prefer. Keep in mind, more weeds will germinate from exposed seeds. Eliminate them immediately. Preemergent herbicides may be helpful.

3. Incorporate organic matter. Collect shredded leaves, grass clippings, and kitchen scraps. Compost it, or dig it directly into the garden. Up to 40 percent organic matter is recommended in perennial garden soils; continue to add organic matter each season.

PLANTING

Now you are ready to plant:

1. Space the plants according to how they grew in your trial plot.

2. Set the plants at the depth they were growing.

3. Water them in carefully.

4. Label them so that you know what they are.

There is no need to plant the entire garden at one time. Temporarily fill in voids with annuals.

Perennial gardens are dynamic, always changing. Some plants you thought were perfect will be disappointments; plants you thought unsuitable will become interesting to you. When growing perennials, you will never stop learning new things. Visit other gardens. Take notes. Talk to other gardeners. You will find a perennial garden is not a finished product, it is an adventure.

JANUARY

PERENNIALS

PLANNING

Perennial gardens do not just happen. In fact, they require the most planning of all gardens.

By January, garden catalogs have arrived in profusion, filled with glowing photos and descriptions. Even though you should take these "promises" with a grain of salt, there is a wealth of good information to be gleaned from the catalogs. For one thing, they can get you started on your plant lists.

When planning your garden, you should remember several things about perennials:

• Not all perennials bloom at the same time, and most bloom for only a short time during the season.

Develop a blooming sequence chart.

• Colors are important in the perennial garden.

On your blooming sequence chart, note the colors of the plants that will bloom at the same time.

• Height and spread of the plants and the rate at which they spread will determine where they will fit in the garden.

Taller plants are usually best when placed at the back and ends of the garden, but the exposure of the plants may affect this plan. (For example, a north-fac-ing garden with tall plants at the back will result in all the shorter ones being shaded by the taller ones to the south.)

• Some perennials die down after they flower, leaving a hole in the garden.

Identify the plants that do this, and decide how to handle the void. Sometimes earlier-blooming plants can be hidden behind ones that develop later and fill in the void.

Make a plant list. The catalogs are fine as guides, but check catalog descriptions against the garden books available at your library, botanic garden, or neighborhood garden center. Your location will influence the way a plant grows. Some things listed in the catalog may not grow in your locality, or they may grow taller or shorter, or bloom earlier or later.

Plant a trial garden. A trial garden is one way to find out how things will grow in your location. Line the plants out in rows for a season or two in your trial area to see how they do in your yard. Once you know, set them in the perennial garden where they will fit best.

Draw the proposed garden to scale on graph paper. Identify the placement of the things you want to plant.

Once the garden is designed, make a final list of the kinds and numbers of plants you will need. Order plants from the catalogs, or buy them from garden centers in spring.

PLANTING

Start some perennials from seeds sown indoors under lights. If you are interested in starting your plants indoors, order your seeds now.

Techniques for growing perennials from seeds are similar to those used for growing annuals or vegetables. Perennial growers are seeding in greenhouses now. If you are familiar with one of the greenhouses that grows perennials, pay a visit to see how they do it. Professional growers rely on sunlight instead of the lights you will use, but the process is the same.

Growing plants under lights is discussed on page 24.

CARE

Perennials usually take care of themselves throughout the winter. If there is a January thaw, however, and plants are exposed to freezing and thawing, the shallowly rooted ones may be heaved out of the ground.

Reduce heaving by keeping the plants frozen using straw, evergreen boughs, or other light, airy materials as mulch.

If the ground is still unfrozen, gently firm heaved plants back into the soil before replacing the mulch.

WATERING

In the southern part of the state where winter may be open and mild, shallowly rooted plants can desiccate.

The sun or freeze-drying can dry out the upper few inches of soil in a few days. Watering can save the plants. Mulch after watering to protect them from the sun and wind.

PESTS

Perennials planted in wet spots may suffer from winter damage. Rotting of the roots and crowns can take place over the winter and the plants fail to grow in spring.

Plan to improve drainage next summer. Fungicides applied in fall may also be helpful.

Use covered bait traps so that pets and larger animals cannot get to the bait.

Mice (voles) and rabbits can damage perennial plantings over winter.

Place brodifacoum (D-con) in covered bait stations so that other animals cannot get to it. This will reduce the vole damage. Fencing is the only way to keep rabbits out. Chicken wire laid over the garden will protect it. Remove it before the plants grow through it in spring.

GROOMING

Perennial tops that were not cut down will be flattened by the snow.

If there is a warm, sunny day during the January thaw, remove the flattened tops, and add them to the compost pile.

HELPFUL HINTS

Winter is not a time to do much gardening, but you can do a few things to keep you occupied. Any days that can be spent outside will give you a chance to inspect your plantings.

Keeping a journal is a way of keeping track of what you see. If you do not have a garden journal, start one now, before the season begins. It does not need to be complicated—a spiral notebook will do. Every time you make an entry, head it with the date, including the year. Make notes in your journal each time you see or do something significant in the garden.

Record the bad as well as the good. Unless your memory is exceptional, you are likely to repeat the mistakes. Several times I have asked myself why I planted something again, when the last time I grew it, it was a flop. I have repeated some of my mistakes, and most other gardeners have, too. That is the main reason I finally started journaling.

FEBRUARY

PERENNIALS

PLANNING

Planning is a vital part of perennial gardening. Growing perennials is not an end in itself—it is a journey.

Since it is a dynamic entity, the perennial garden is in a constant state of change. Each year, you will decide to make changes, adding plants, eliminating plants that are not working out, and expanding. Constant expansion is a hazard of working with perennials! You will always find another plant that you want to try as new ones enter the market every year, and even plants that once were uninviting may suddenly become interesting.

When planning the perennial garden, make several lists:
- Plants to be removed
- New plants to try this year
- Plants to be divided or transplanted

Divide plants or transplant them as soon as the weather will allow.

PLANTING

Starting perennials is a challenge to any gardener. Perennial seeds have particular requirements for germination. The seedlings grow slowly, and do not flower the first season.

To start perennials indoors, you will need a greenhouse or a lighting system to provide heat and light. Although you may not have room for a greenhouse, you can probably find a place to set up lights:

- Fluorescent lights on a stand work well for indoor lighting. See the diagram on page 24.

The stand can be a work bench or boards placed over saw horses. It should be at least 4 feet long and 2 feet wide. This space will accommodate 4 standard 10-inch-by-20-inch flats.

- A pair of shop light fixtures, each holding two 40-watt, cool white tubes, will provide sufficient heat and light.

Attach shop lights to chains, or to ropes, pulleys, and weights, so you can adjust their height above the plants.

For the soil, use one of the commercial artificial soil mixes composed of shredded brown peat and Styrofoam beads or perlite, such as Fafard, Jiffy Mix, Pro Mix, or any other brand. (The light black potting soil, which is technically muck, is not satisfactory.)

Some perennial seeds need to be exposed to freezing temperatures before they will germinate. Do research on the kinds of seeds you are trying to grow before starting. (Part of the fun of doing these projects is learning something new.) The ones that are most often started in fall outside are the ones that will require cold treatment. Flats seeded with these kinds can be set outside for 30 to 45 days before they are put under indoor lights.

Many perennials that started from seeds outdoors in late summer can be started under lights indoors. Consider the following plants:

- **Purple coneflower**
- **Rudbeckia**
- **Shasta daisy**
- **Bleeding heart**[+]
- **Yarrow**
- **Delphinium**[+]
- **Heuchera**
- **Phlox**[+]
- **Columbine**
- **Blue star**
- **Gaillardia**
- *Salvia* x *superba*

[+] Needs cold treatment before germinating.

Most commercial producers start perennials from seeds so that they can produce the numbers needed in their operations. Seeds for types that can be propagated this way are available from various suppliers. If you are growing a particular cultivar, buy seeds. The open-pollinated seeds you can collect from these plants will not "come true," which means the offspring will seldom be like the parents.

Seeds are most easily sown in the 20-row, seed-starting inserts sold to fit the 10-inch-by-20-inch flats.

Once you have acquired your inserts and flats, soil mix, seeds, and lights, it is time to set up your indoor seed-starting system:

1. Check the seed pack for the proper temperatures and light requirements necessary for the seeds to germinate. (For example, you will not cover seeds that need light.)

2. Moisten the soil mix.

3. Sow the seeds, and label the rows so that you can tell what you planted.

Mist seedlings as needed; check twice daily.

4. Cover the flats with clear plastic wrap to keep the soil from drying out.

5. Set the flats on the plant stand, and lower the lights to 1 inch or so above the surface to provide heat and light. Because the lights should be on 18 hours out of every 24, you may want to use a timer to turn them on and off.

CARE

As seedlings germinate, remove the plastic wrap cover, and reduce the temperatures to about 60 degrees Fahrenheit.

As soon as the seedlings are large enough to handle, transplant them to cell-packs.

WATERING

Seed flats dry out very quickly. Examine them twice daily, and water as needed.

FERTILIZING

If the seedlings are kept in the seed flats for more than a week, fertilize them with soluble Peters or Miracle-Gro 20-20-20 at $1/4$ the normal rate. Remember that these are very tender plants that can be injured by excess fertilizer.

PESTS

Mites are always potential pests on plants under lights. Watch carefully for them.

Use insecticidal soap, which is the safest material to use on seedlings.

Keeping the seedlings too wet risks damping off.

To contain this disease, water seedlings carefully.

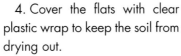

HELPFUL HINTS

Look for a book that provides detailed information about the germination requirements of perennial plants. Steve Still's *Manual of Herbaceous Ornamental Plants* is excellent.

MARCH

PERENNIALS

PLANNING

On the first warm day when you have the urge to get out and do something, begin to lay out your perennial garden. If you have a garden already, plan the changes you will make this year.

The labels in the garden may have been uprooted by the winter weather. Before they are scattered so that you cannot tell where they came from, reset the labels.

If you are not sure where the labels belong, check your planting plan. You still do not have a plan?

• Make a planting plan this year in your journal.

• Note the varieties of the plants as well as the common names.

• Indicate where the plants came from, too, so they can be duplicated later if there is a need.

PLANTING

As soon as the ground is dry enough to work, prepare the soil for planting. When a handful of soil can be squeezed into a ball and then crumbled, it is dry enough.

In the perennial garden, work the soil well by double digging and adding as much as 40 percent organic matter by volume. The plants will be in the same place for several years, so take time to do the job right. There is no need to spade the entire garden at once. Do the parts that are to be planted immediately.

Perennials are some of the first plants available from garden centers and nurseries in spring. Plant the hardiest ones now. If you have not grown them in your garden before, plant them in your test garden to see how they do before setting them into the perennial garden.

Transplant seedlings started under lights as soon as they can be handled. You will need transplanting soil and various containers into which to transplant the seedlings. The artificial mixes with brown peat moss and perlite are excellent. (Do not buy the moist, black potting soil for this use.) You can make your own soil mix with 1/3 each garden soil, #2 torpedo sand, and brown peat moss.

Now you are ready to transplant seedlings:

1. Lift them out of the seedling tray with the end of a small wooden label. Be careful not to squeeze the stems or to break off the roots.

2. Separate seedlings by gently pulling them apart. If the seedlings are left in the seed flat too long, they will become a jumbled mess and difficult to get apart.

3. Fill the containers with artificial soil mix, and firm it so that it does not settle.

4. Use the point of a pencil or a small label as a dibble to make holes in the mix.

5. Set a seedling in each hole using the dibble to push all the roots into the hole.

6. Firm the seedling down with your finger and thumb on each side.

Use something with a pointed end to serve as a dibble.

CARE

In the garden, protect newly planted perennials from any unusually severe weather by covering them. Until they have hardened off, they may be susceptible to cold injury.

Keep transplanted seedlings growing under the lights at 60 degrees Fahrenheit, or move them into the cold frame. If unusually low temperatures are expected, these plants may need protection until they are fully hardened off. The hardening-off process gradually acclimates the plants to low temperatures. Fully hardened-off perennial plants can tolerate freezing.

WATERING

Soak in newly set plants thoroughly to settle the soil. Transplants need only enough water to keep them from wilting.

FERTILIZING

Fertilize the existing perennial garden with a complete fertilizer to provide 1 pound of nitrogen per 1,000 square feet of garden. This is equivalent to 1 pound of 10-10-10 per 10-foot-by-10-foot square. A 1-pound coffee can holds about 2 pounds of fertilizer. If the analysis you are using is different, you will need to recalculate the amounts. Water the fertilizer in, and wash it out of the crowns of the plants so that it does not burn them.

PESTS

It is too cold for most insects to do any damage yet. As soon as the weather warms up, they will become active.

Several perennials are susceptible to root and crown rots and to other spring diseases. Drench the garden with a thiophanate-methyl fungicide. Use maneb on **peonies** that have had phytophthora blight in the past. Spray to cover shoots as they emerge. PCNB will prevent sclerotinia on **delphiniums**.

Perennial broadleaf and grassy weeds may grow all winter. While the perennials are dormant, they are easy to see.

If weeds can be treated before the perennials begin to grow, kill them with glyphosate. Be very careful not to get this material on the green parts of desirable plants. A simple method is to cover your hand with a rubber glove and then a cotton glove saturated with glyphosate. Carefully wipe the foliage of the weeds without getting any on the perennial flowers. Pull weeds that cannot be hoed or treated without danger to the valuable plants.

Rabbits will find the new green shoots of some perennials perfect for a spring snack. After a tough winter, they are looking for a change of diet. The rabbit repellents such as moth crystals or dried blood are effective only until the animals discover they will not be harmed by them.

Use thiram rabbit repellent or a mixture of a bottle of Tabasco sauce and a gallon of water to spray them. The spray will need to be reapplied. Add soap or spreader-sticker so that the mixture does not wash off. Antitranspirants mixed with the repellents will not wash off, either.

GROOMING

If the plants were not cut back last fall, do so now before they begin to grow. Remove tops to reduce diseases. Put the tops in the compost pile, or dig them into the vegetable garden.

Pull back mulch this month, but keep it handy. You may have to put it back if the weather turns nasty. The weather forecasts are reliable, if not overly aggressive. If they say it will be bad, protect the plants. If conditions turn out not to have been as bad as predicted, the plants will be safe.

APRIL

PERENNIALS

 PLANNING

The first really good weather comes this month. As much as we wish spring would start in March, it is usually April before the ground is dry enough and warm enough to do much gardening.

Once daylight-saving time begins, we have the light to work outside in the evening. What a wonderful time of year it is! Any gardener worth his or her salt wants to be outside as much as possible.

If your plans for your perennial garden are not complete, work on your plans.

I talk often about the importance of planning, but I must admit, it is not one of my virtues. And frankly, our garden just sort of happens. It seems to have turned into one big experiment. There are so many plants to try each season that the entire garden ends up as a test plot. (The front yard does look nice, though.)

Even though the garden is not well organized, we do learn a lot from it. The flowers are always a joy, and we thoroughly appreciate the cut flowers that seemingly appear just as we need them. Someday I will surprise my long-suffering spouse and plant a real garden.

 PLANTING

By the end of the month, the worst of the cold will be over. Garden centers have big displays of perennials to select from. It is time to plant. You can move transplants that have been held in the cold frame into their permanent locations, too. Perennials come in all sizes for planting:

• The larger the size, the sooner you will have flowers.

The larger ones may outgrow their situations sooner, however. It is important to space the plants correctly.

• Tiny plants from a quart-size container will look funny spaced at 36 inches.

If that is the size they will be in a year or so, that is how they should be planted. Sometimes it is better to plant them in a nurse bed to grow until they have attained some size.

To plant each perennial, follow these steps:

1. Prepare the soil to at least 12 inches deep by spading and incorporating 4 to 6 inches of organic matter.

2. Dig a hole twice as wide as the soilball and as deep.

3. If the plant is growing in an artificial soil, shake some off, and mix it with the soil going back into the planting hole.

 CARE

Remove the mulch from the beds. If the soil is wet, avoid working in it until it dries. Firm in plants heaved out of the ground as soon as possible. If the roots are exposed, they will be dried and killed.

Remove the old tops, and rake out leaves where plants have had foliar diseases in the past. **Peonies** and **delphiniums** are susceptible to these diseases, which can kill plant tops.

Before the plants get too tall, set stakes for support. If the plants start to fall over, it is difficult to straighten them, and they look bundled up for the rest of the season. Cage the **peonies**.

 WATERING

After planting, thoroughly soak the soil around the plants to settle it.

The established plants will not need water unless the weather is unusually dry, rare at this time of the season.

If water collects around the plants, correct the problem, or root and crown rot can develop.

FERTILIZING

If fertilizing was not done earlier, fertilize the plants with a complete fertilizer to provide 1 pound of nitrogen per 1,000 square feet of garden. This is the equivalent of 1 pound of 10-10-10 per 100 square feet, for instance. A 1-pound coffee can holds about 2 pounds of fertilizer.

PESTS

Aphids will emerge about the time plants begin to turn green. Watch closely for them. If the weather is warm, mites may appear. Use insecticidal soap.

Slugs that survived the winter are out looking for something to eat. They will find **hostas** and a few other perennials.

Spread metaldehyde baits now to eliminate them. Tiny slugs will hatch from eggs as soon as the weather warms. They are easily eliminated with baits before they get too large. Once adult-size, they do a lot of damage and are harder to kill.

As the perennials emerge from winter dormancy, root and crown rot may be problems.

Treat them with fungicide. Thiophanate-methyl fungicide drench is the most widely recommended material. Use PCNB on **delphiniums** for sclerotinia; use maneb on **peonies**. Only 1 treatment per season is needed. If the garden was treated earlier, there is no need to treat it again.

As the plants begin to develop leaves, they may get foliar diseases. Spray them with thiophanate-methyl fungicide to prevent foliar diseases. Follow package directions.

Weeds may appear in the garden. Hoe or pull weeds. It is too late to use glyphosate. Use preemergent herbicides to prevent germination of weed seeds. Use DCPA and trifluralin on many perennials; read the label

HELPFUL HINTS

April can be frustratingly cold and dreary. A warm, sunny day here and there simply teases us. Take your time, but do what you can to start the garden. Next month, things will warm up, and plants will develop quickly. Remember to vent the cold frame or greenhouse whenever the sun shines.

Make notes in your journal. Look at your list of things to do. Do you have the supplies you will need? Have you visited the garden center yet?

to be sure they are safe on the plants you are growing.

Rabbits can be pests.

Protect plants from rabbits with repellents or with fencing. A bottle of Tabasco sauce mixed in a gallon of water and sprayed on the plants will usually dissuade rabbits.

GROOMING

Most perennials do not require pruning. A few will profit from pinching to make them bushier. Pinch **hardy mums** to remove the growing tip when the stems reach 6 inches long.

Pinch back mums to develop bushier plants with more flowers.

MAY
PERENNIALS

PLANNING

May is a wonderful month in the perennial garden. Lots of things are in bloom. The weather is warm, and later in the month, it will be summer-like. There is much to be done in the perennial garden.

You are ready to plant if your plans are complete for your garden. Even if your plans are still in the works, you can use them. Because the perennial garden is never finished, semicomplete plans will tell you where at least some of the plants will go. Follow the plans so that you allow sufficient room for all the plants. If you planned correctly, this will not be a problem. Lay out the garden, indicating where the plants will go. Then work the soil.

If you are changing an established garden, upgrade the plan accordingly. Make entries in your journal indicating the source, variety, cultivar, and date for each new plant.

PLANTING

Because perennials will occupy the same spot for a number of seasons, prepare the soil well.

In a new garden, turn it over two spades deep if possible. Incorporate up to 40 percent organic matter and bone meal or superphosphate throughout the soil depth. After spading and working the soil to break up lumps, you are ready to plant:

1. Dig a planting hole for each plant. It should be twice as wide as and the same depth as the rootball on the plant.

2. Shake as much artificial soil mix off the roots as you can, and mix the artificial soil with the soil going back into the planting hole.

3. Set the plant at the depth it was growing, spread the roots, and fill the hole.

4. Firm the soil gently.

Use your hands to gently firm the soil around bare-root plants.

Plant rooted cuttings or seedlings by hand without digging a hole. With your hand or a trowel, open a hole in the soil, set the plant, and push the soil back around the plant. Firm the soil straight down with 4 fingers. Do not squeeze soil against the stem or it will be damaged.

Old plants in an established garden require special attention:

1. Lift the old plants carefully. Put them where the roots will not be dried out, and cover them with wet burlap if necessary.

2. Spade the spot as deeply as you can, incorporating organic matter and superphosphate or bone meal. Space will be limited, and working the soil may be difficult to do.

3. If you are double digging, lay a piece of plywood over part of the garden on which you can pile soil as you spade the second depth.

4. Divide old plants for replanting (see pages 67, 134, and 136).

5. Set them in their new locations at the same depth they grew.

CARE

Provide support for tall plants— **delphiniums**, **bearded iris**, **joe-pye weed** and **peonies**—if necessary. Install stakes or cages while the plants can be controlled. Once they are falling over, getting them under control will make them look bundled up all season.

Examine the plants every day. While you are looking, pinch off the broken stem. Tie up the loose branch or tuck it into the cage. This is plant tending, which keeps the garden tidy without a lot of effort. Look for pest problems, then take the proper steps to correct them.

 WATERING

Soak in newly set plants immediately. Use a slowly running hose or a wand with a watering rose on the end. Unless the weather is unusually dry, the perennial garden will not need to be watered this month. If drought does occur and the plants wilt, apply 1 inch of water early in the day so that the plants dry before temperatures drop in the afternoon.

 FERTILIZING

As the plants are vigorously growing in spring, apply a complete balanced fertilizer such as 10-10-10 or 12-12-12 to provide 1 pound of nitrogen per 1,000 square feet. This application should be sufficient for the season.

 PESTS

As the weather warms up, bug problems will show up, too. Aphids and spider mites are usually the first to appear.

Use insecticidal soap to control both pests. Be sure to spray the undersides of the leaves. Wipe off a few aphids on a shoot tip. Pinch off a single shoot severely infested with aphids before they spread instead of spraying the entire planting.

If the weather is wet, foliar diseases can develop quite quickly.

Control most foliar diseases with a thiophanate-methyl fungicide. Read the label to make sure the material is safe to use on your plants.

Where drainage is a problem, root and crown diseases can develop. Correct the problem, and drench with thiophanate-methyl fungicide.

Weeds may appear in the garden. Hoe or pull weeds. It is too late to use glyphosate. Use preemergent herbicides to prevent germination of weed seeds. Use DCPA and trifluralin on many perennials; read the label to be sure they are safe on the plants you are growing.

Rabbits may be a threat to your plants.

Protect the plants from rabbits with repellents or with fencing.

Spraying the plants with a mixture of a bottle of Tabasco sauce and a gallon of water will usually repel the rabbits. Fencing must be 18 inches high and the lower 6 inches or so buried so that they cannot dig under it. Turn the buried 6 inches outward so that the rabbits encounter it before they dig very far. See the diagram on page 36. An attractive and functional rabbit fence is produced by Snapdragon Industries, New Hampton, NH, **www. ezrabbitfencing.com**.

GROOMING

Pinch some perennials, such as **hardy mums** and **dwarf dahlias**, so they will bush out. Do not shear these plants. Roll out the tip of each shoot. Usually, there is a spot on the shoot just above the uppermost mature leaf where the shoot snaps off easily. This is the correct place to pinch. Each time the shoots reach 6 inches in length, pinch them off. The result will be a bushier plant with many more blooms.

Disbud **peonies** for larger flowers. Preserve the tip bud, but roll out the side buds as soon as they appear. If you wait too long, they will be tough and hard to remove.

Cut off damaged or broken stems. Remove old leaves and blooms.

JUNE
PERENNIALS

PLANNING

Lots of things are going on in the perennial garden now.

Update your journal:

• Make note of the plants that are growing well.

• Identify anything that needs to be changed.

The plant that is crowding out everything else, the ones that flowered poorly, and the ones that cannot be seen behind the taller plants (the catalog said they were 18 inches tall) need to be listed for changes next year.

• In the trial garden, evaluate the plants so that they can be located properly in the perennial garden.

The size, height, flower color, bloom time, and whether the foliage dies down after blooms fade deserve notations.

• List the plants that will not work in your garden.

Noting these failures is important because you will avoid trying them again.

PLANTING

By the first of this month, plant in the perennial garden all of the seedlings that you started indoors under lights. If they are too small to go into the perennial garden, grow them in the trial garden or in a nursery bed until they are large enough.

Fill voids that occur now in the garden:

• Fill them with plants from garden centers or plant nurseries.

Most of these firms will have perennials in containers all summer.

• Make sure that the plants you buy are free of insects or diseases, that they are healthy green, and if in flower, that the blooms are typical.

• Check the label to determine that the cultivar will work in your garden.

Some discount outlets offer perennial plants of unidentified cultivars or without any identification at all. Buying these plants is risky because they may not perform the way you expect them to. Many perennials are hybridized for form and flowers. **Purple coneflower**, for instance, can be white, pink, purple, tall, short, or bushy; the open-pollinated plants are tall and purple. Open-pollinated **phlox** are tall and weak, and flower poorly.

Plant a row of **hardy mum** cuttings or small plants in the trial garden for transplanting into the border in fall.

CARE

Perennial gardens can get out of hand very quickly. Tending, tying, staking, and grooming are necessary to keep the plantings looking nice.

WATERING

If the weather is dry, water plants when they wilt. Apply 1 inch of water early in the day so that the plants dry before temperatures drop in late afternoon.

Certain plants wilt during the day and perk up as soon as the sun begins to go down. These plants may not need water. The wilting is a protection so that they do not lose water faster than they can replace it. Syringing water over the tops of these plants will cool them. If the soil is not dry, do not water the plants, or the roots may drown.

FERTILIZING

Newly planted perennials may benefit from soluble fertilizer. Mix Peters or Miracle-Gro using the directions on the package. Apply 1 pint or quart to each plant. Do not get fertilizer on the foliage.

PESTS

There are numerous pests that can damage your plants.

Control aphids, mites, thrips, and whiteflies with insecticidal soap. Cover the lower surfaces of the leaves.

Use carbaryl to control earwigs.

Treat plant bugs and stem borers with acephate from a hose-end sprayer.

Did you treat the **iris** with permethrin or acephate in May?

If not, spray now to the point of runoff to eliminate borers before they eliminate your **iris**.

Slugs are larger now and harder to kill.

Get rid of slugs before they destroy the **hosta**. Apply slug baits at the edge of the garden so that the pests are drawn out. Setting out stale beer in a pan will work, too, but be sure to collect them early every morning before they sober up and go home.

If things are happening to your plants at night, take a flashlight on a midnight safari. You may be surprised at how much goes on at night.

If weather is wet, foliar diseases or mildew may show up.

Protect the leaves with a thiophanate-methyl fungicide.

Weeds may still be a problem.

Keep hoeing and pulling weeds. If you can get the garden free of weeds, apply a preemergent herbicide. DCPA and trifluralin can be used on many perennials. Read the label to make sure they are safe on the plants you are growing.

GROOMING

As soon as the blooms fade, cut them off. Some perennials will rebloom if old flowers are removed. For others, there is no need to burden the plants with a seed load unless you are collecting the seeds. Let the energy go into the plants.

Hosta

HELPFUL HINTS

Grooming plants should be a habit. Anytime you are in the garden, have your pocket knife with you. When you see a yellow leaf or broken stem, cut it out. Tuck in the stems that fall over, or tie them up.

Pull out weeds as you see them. I carry my hoe as I walk the garden each evening. A few weeds here, a few more there, and the job is done. The only time weeding becomes a chore is following a trip away when they might get away from me. But if the garden is clean when we leave, it is not an insurmountable job.

JULY
PERENNIALS

PLANNING

When the weather is hot, mornings are usually cool and fresh. Sometimes there is heavy dew, and it is wise to stay out of the garden until things dry off a bit. Certain diseases are easily spread if the plants are disturbed when they are wet.

Sometimes I make entries in my journal in the morning, but usually, I just look and enjoy what God has done. Special rewards are those mornings when the air hangs with the fragrance of the flowers, the birds are singing, and the sun is cheery yellow as it rises into a clear, blue sky.

PLANTING

You may need to do just a bit of planting:

• Where there are empty spaces, and where you know what is to be planted, buy potted plants from your favorite garden center or nursery.

These plants may even be in bloom, so you will know exactly what you are getting.

• Take the time to plant them correctly.

See the suggestions in the "Planting" section on page 126.

• Where the **Virginia bluebells**, **bleeding heart**, or **poppies** have left holes in the garden, plant a few annuals or set a few potted plants.

Do not injure the dormant root systems.

CARE

I rarely interrupt the morning garden visit with any real work. I do the serious work in the cool of the evening. After supper when things have slowed down for the day, it is time to "walk the rows," hoe in hand and sharp knife in the pocket. This is plant tending.

While the mornings are times for pure enjoyment, the evenings are times to see the problems, seek out the causes, and initiate the corrections. A little pruning here, a touch of insecticide there, and maybe a few weeds dispatched down the row.

WATERING

July can be dry as well as hot. Water each time the plants wilt.

Apply 1 measured inch early in the day so that the plants dry before nightfall. Set coffee cans around the garden to measure the amount of water. When 1

inch is in each can, turn off the water. I like to use a Rainbird oscillating sprinkler, which seems to provide the most even coverage in the shortest time compared to other sprinklers. It is on a stand and gets over the tops of the tallest plants.

Mulching can reduce water loss and keep weeds down. It is difficult to do in the perennial garden, however, because the plants are so close together. Be aware that a snail or earwig problem will be worsened by mulching.

Arrange for someone to water the garden while you are on vacation.

FERTILIZING

Plants not yet in bloom can stand another shot of fertilizer. Apply a high-phosphorus analysis such as 10-30-10 or 10-15-10, 1 pound per 100 square feet. A 1-pound coffee can holds 2 pounds of fertilizer.

PESTS

Various insects may be troublesome in your garden.

Control aphids, mites, thrips, and whiteflies with insecticidal soap. Cover the lower surfaces of the leaves. Use carbaryl to control earwigs, Japanese beetles, and June bugs (adult white grubs).

Treat plant bugs and stem borers with acephate from a hose-end sprayer. Apply slug baits at the edge of the garden to draw the pests out. Using stale beer in a pan will work, too, but be sure to collect slugs early every morning before they sober up and go home.

One of the major garden pests is the mosquito. Not that it attacks the plants directly, but there are times of the year when gardening can be almost impossible because of the mosquitoes attacking you, the gardener.

Try to eliminate standing water—in gutters, the coffee cans used for rain gauges, whatever holds water. Most of the mosquito problems are locally generated. Wear mosquito repellent. If you are sensitive to DEET, apply it only to clothing. Citronella and Skin So-Soft work but not quite as effectively. Find a friend who attracts mosquitoes to work with you. When I am around, no one else gets bitten by them. Mosquitoes love me!

During wet weather, foliar diseases or mildew may show up.

Protect the leaves with a thiophanate-methyl fungicide.

Weeds may still be a problem. Keep hoeing and pulling weeds. If you can get the garden free of weeds, apply a preemergent herbicide. DCPA and trifluralin can be used on many perennials. Read the label to make sure they are safe on the plants you are growing.

GROOMING

As soon as the blooms fade, cut them off. Cut back plants such as **yarrow** (*Achillea*) and **columbine** that have finished flowering, and they may bloom again.

Do not pinch the **mums** and **dahlias** after the first of this month or they will be late flowering.

Columbine

HELPFUL HINTS

Evaluate the plants in your test garden:
- Did you enter them in your journal when you planted them?
- Can you still tell what is what?

Labels get lost, so the only way to be sure what you have is to keep a record.
- How will the plants you are testing fit into your garden?

You may need to measure them to be certain how big they are.
- What are the flower colors and the dates the plants bloomed?
- Are any insect or disease problems showing up?

Note them in your journal, too.

AUGUST
PERENNIALS

PLANNING

The dog days of August have arrived. Some of us are tiring of mowing the grass. It seems like a waste of time. But lawns are essential to most landscapes, particularly for activities while the kids are small.

While you are mindlessly mowing, imagine where the perennial garden could be expanded or where an addition would reduce your time spent mowing. Lawns need not be expansive. They can be small and intimate, surrounded by flowers.

Think about it. Make sketches. There is time. Part of the joy of gardening is daydreaming.

The seasons pass too quickly. Many plants have finished flowering. The warm colors of summer predominate at this time of the season. By the middle of the month a few cool nights with heavy dew remind us that seasons are short indeed.

PLANTING

When the foliage of **iris**, **bleeding heart**, and other early-blooming plants turns yellow, lift and divide the plants. Cut out borers and rotted rhizomes. Divide the rhizomes so that each piece has a healthy fan of leaves. Replant with the rhizome at the soil surface or slightly below the soil surface.

Collect seeds of some perennials as soon as they ripen, and sow them:

1. Select a spot where the plants can be protected and not inadvertently hoed out of the garden, or prepare germinating trays under lights indoors.

2. Sow **columbine**, **delphinium**, **baptisia**, and **heuchera** seeds.

3. Label the rows carefully, and note the location of each kind in your journal.

Sometimes it is hard to identify seedlings, and they look just like weeds.

Some seeds will germinate immediately. Others will require cold weather to break the dormancy. They will germinate in spring.

Lift and divide iris to expand your collection.

CARE

Taller plants need help to keep them from falling over.

• Cages

Use cages made of concrete reinforcing wire instead of the flimsy ones available at most garden stores for **peonies**, **coneflowers**, and **bee balm**. The concrete reinforcing wire comes in 5-foot widths. A 5-foot-long section cut in half makes two 2½-foot-high cages. Make some this winter.

• Stakes

Stake other tall plants such as **delphiniums** and **dahlias**.

Keep the plants tucked into the cages or tied to the stakes. Doing this is part of grooming and plant tending.

Many gardeners become bored by midsummer and let the details slip. The results are a

messy garden and disappointment. If this is the case for you, in the future reduce the size of the garden, or select plants that require little care.

WATERING

August can be hot and dry. Water the plants when they wilt. Apply a measured 1 inch of water.

Mulch to keep the soil from drying out. Shredded bark, compost, and even grass clippings are satisfactory mulching materials. Mulches can make slug and earwig problems worse, however.

FERTILIZING

Be cautious fertilizing this late in the season. Perennial plants need to slow down for fall. Unless the plants are obviously deficient with yellowing foliage, do not apply fertilizer.

PESTS

August is the worst month for insects. They are in greater numbers and full sized by now. Numbers build up fast in the warm weather. Examine the garden closely every day, and treat problems immediately.

Control aphids, mites, thrips, and whiteflies with insecticidal soap. Cover the lower surfaces of the leaves. Use carbaryl to control earwigs and Junebugs (adult white grubs).

Pick small numbers of Japanese beetles, which are slow-moving bronze-and-gold insects, off the plants. If large numbers are present, they will strip the plants of foliage before any insecticide works. Use carbaryl or acephate from a hose-end sprayer to control them. Traps attract the beetles from quite a distance, and many escape to feed on your garden. Set them as far away from any garden as possible.

Treat plant bugs and stem borers with acephate applied from a hose-end sprayer.

Some plants attract beneficial insects. For example, **bee balm** attracts honeybees. Once in your yard, they will help pollinate plants in your vegetable garden. Do not use carbaryl on **bee balm**, **butterfly bush**, or other plants grown to attract beneficial insects.

Mildew is a disease of late summer. Cool nights with dew are perfect for the disease.

Protect leaves with a thiophanate-methyl fungicide.

Weeds are making seeds now. Keep weeds hoed out. Any seeds that can be eliminated now are weeds you will not need to hoe out next year. With conscientious weed removal, each season should be increasingly weed free.

Flower seeds will attract birds and other animals. Larger seeds attract mice and squirrels. Some plants such as **coneflowers** attract various kinds of small birds. Finches hanging upside down to get the last seeds from an old flower or wrens jousting to get at the same seedhead are fun to watch. Remove spent blooms to prevent seed production.

GROOMING

As flowers fade, remove them. As the foliage begins to fade, cut it back, too.

HELPFUL HINTS

Many of the late-flowering perennials are wonderful cut flowers. Cut a handful for the dinning room table and another for a friend. As gardeners, we sometimes take for granted the beauty that we see every day. Many people—cliff dwellers, older people who cannot leave their homes—rarely see flowers. A few cut flowers in a simple glass will bring joy into a life. In many countries, no one would think of visiting without bringing flowers. We should start that tradition here.

September

PERENNIALS

PLANNING

Labor Day is the start of a new season. I know that fall does not begin until about the 21st of the month, but with schools starting, vacations over, the weather cooling off, the pace of things quickens. Fall activities begin, and all of us get back into our usual routines.

Fall is planting season.

Before you start digging holes, refer to your plan for your garden. All summer you should have been making observations and notes to fine-tune your garden plans. If you are just starting a perennial garden, the observations made in your trial garden should be very helpful now. I hope that it met all of your best expectations, and that all the plants you have been trying are going into your garden.

Seldom is this the case, however; some plants are likely to be disappointments. Not to worry. Perennial gardening is not an end in itself; doing the gardening is the fun part.

PLANTING

Plant **hardy mums**, which were started in the trial garden last spring, in the border to replace spent annuals. Or buy potted **mums**. They will be colorful and cheery, flowering until frozen out later this fall.

Sow the seeds outdoors that you collected this summer, or start them indoors under lights. The ones that are most often started in fall outside are the ones that will require cold treatment. Flats seeded with these kinds can be set outside for 30 to 45 days before they are put under indoor lights. (The lighting equipment and the process are described on pages 24 to 25.)

If there is room to grow these plants indoors or in a cold frame, they can be set in the garden next spring. Tiny seedlings started outdoors usually survive the winter with some protection from frost heaving.

Start the following perennials seeds:

- **Purple coneflower**
- **Rudbeckia**
- **Baptisia**
- **Shasta daisy**
- **Bleeding heart**[+]
- **Yarrow**
- **Delphinium**[+]
- **Heuchera**
- **Phlox**[+]
- **Columbine**
- **Blue star**
- **Gaillardia**
- **Salvia x superba**

[+] Needs cold treatment before germinating.

Daylilies and almost all other perennials can be divided in the fall. **Peonies** must be divided in fall. There are a few exceptions, kinds that are slow to recover. They suffer from the rigors of winter if planted in the fall. **Butterfly weeds**, **asters**, **ferns**, **coreopsis**, and a few others are better divided and planted in spring.

You can use a sharp knife to divide the roots of perennials.

CARE

Pull out the stakes, and remove the cages as the plants finish for the year. Clean the stakes and cages, and store them where you can locate them next spring.

Accumulate mulching materials for winter protection. Light, airy materials such as clean straw or evergreen boughs are preferred. Do not apply these materials until the ground has frozen, or mice will invade them for the winter.

WATERING

Soak newly planted **mums** and seedlings to settle the soil. Moisten the seed bed carefully. Seed flats should be covered with plastic wrap so that they do not dry out while the seeds are germinating. Once the seedlings are up, remove the plastic. Water them as needed to keep them from wilting.

A late summer drought is fairly common. Water the garden if rains are not forthcoming. Apply 1 inch or so of water each time the plants wilt.

Once plants are dormant, they will need no water.

FERTILIZING

Fertilizing is not necessary this late in the season. Allow perennials to become dormant so that they can tolerate the winter weather.

PESTS

Insect activity slows down as the weather cools off, but whiteflies and aphids are still active.

Control them with insecticidal soap.

Slugs become active when the weather is moist.

Reduce their numbers now to lessen the numbers surviving the winter and decrease the problem next spring.

Mildew and root and crown rot diseases can ruin plantings in fall if the weather is wet.

Protect the leaves, and drench the soil with a thiophanate-methyl fungicide.

Any remaining weeds will produce seeds.

Continue hoeing out weeds. Once the tops of the perennials have dried up, apply herbicide to perennial weeds that have persisted.

Mice will take up residence in the trash left in the garden. If this is near tender roots and crowns, the mice may find them a convenient source of food for the winter.

Remove the trash. If mice are seen, set out brodifacoum (D-con) bait stations.

GROOMING

As long as the plants are blooming, continue to remove faded flowers. Cut down the plants as soon as the foliage begins to ripen. Rake out dead leaves.

Put the debris in the compost pile or on the vegetable garden to be spaded into the soil for winter. All free organic matter improves the soil. Do not let it go to waste.

HELPFUL HINTS

• Fall is a good time to trade divisions and seeds collected during the season. A friend who has a variety you have wanted will be glad to give you a piece. Seeds of some perennials are plentiful. If they are from a variety that comes "true" from seeds, you can get many plants from one seedhead.

• Join a garden club. The fall programs are exceptionally good because everyone has new experiences to share. If you are a new gardener, you can learn more at one of these meetings than you can by a year of trial and error on your own. You can make lifelong friends, too.

OCTOBER

PERENNIALS

PLANNING

Perennials were out of favor for decades. Only in the last few years have they become popular again.

There are a couple of reasons for the renewed popularity. First, the baby boomers matured and became interested in gardening. They are well educated and sophisticated, and were not satisfied with simple kinds of gardening. They needed a challenge.

Second, new, hybrid cultivars have been developed with growth characteristics, extended bloom times, and colors never before available. These hybrids can complicate growing perennials because they do not come "true" from seeds. The seedlings revert to the old types, losing the characteristics of the hybrid. With hybrids, collecting seeds and growing plants are things of the past.

Today, if you are interested in growing the best perennials from seeds, buy the seeds. This means not allowing the perennials in your garden to drop seeds. Volunteer plants that grow will be rogues. **Phlox** is notorious for dropping seeds, and it germinates easily. In 1 or 2 years, all the plants will be inferior seedlings, and the beautiful hybrids will be gone.

Plants are still available at garden centers and plant nurseries, sometimes at quite a bargain. But you need to keep these things in mind:

• Even though it is late in the season, you can set out these plants in the garden.

Protect them during the winter since they will not be well established before its onset.

• There is a risk that they will not survive.

Weigh the price against the chances. If they are things you have decided you want in your garden, buy them. If they are not things you have planned to use, skip them.

PLANTING

Peonies can still be planted this month, but time is short. They need 6 to 8 weeks to develop roots before the ground freezes solid. Set them so that the buds are exactly 1 inch below the soil surface.

By the end of this month, snow may be flying in the northern part of the state. In the south, fall will last a while longer. Move plants that need to be divided or transplanted as soon as possible. Plant new plants immediately so that they can become established before severe weather arrives.

October can be a wet month. The soil may be wetter than it should be for planting. Use care not to muck up the soil any more than necessary. Fortunately, the freezing and thawing over the winter will improve the soil condition by spring.

CARE

Continue pulling out stakes and removing cages as the plants finish for the year. Clean them, and store them where you can locate them next spring.

Accumulate mulching materials for winter protection, such as clean straw or evergreen boughs. Do not apply these materials until the ground has frozen, or mice will invade them for the winter.

WATERING

If the weather is dry, water newly planted perennials.

Usually, the soil is moist enough for established plants. Unless the plants wilt, do not water them.

There are many types of mulch including leaves, straw, pine needles, and even grass clippings.

Weeds may persist. Continue hoeing out weeds to prevent seed production. Once the tops of the perennials have dried up, apply herbicide to any perennial weeds that are still green and growing.

 GROOMING

As the plants finish blooming and foliage begins to ripen, cut them to the ground. Dispose of them in the compost pile, or chop them up and spread them on the vegetable garden to be spaded in later.

Some perennials produce seeds that are attractive to birds. Leave these plants standing as long as there are still seeds on them. You may need to hoe out rogue seedlings next spring.

 FERTILIZING

Do not fertilize this late in the season. Perennials should be allowed to become dormant so that they can tolerate the winter weather.

 PESTS

As the weather cools off, insect activity slows down. Whiteflies and aphids may still be active until the leaves dry up. Control them with insecticidal soap.

Slugs are active as long as the weather is warm. Reduce their numbers now to lessen the numbers surviving the winter and decrease the problem next spring.

Mildew and root and crown rot diseases can ruin plantings in fall if the weather is wet.

Protect the leaves and drench the soil with a thiophanate-methyl fungicide.

NOVEMBER

PERENNIALS

PLANNING

November is a time for finishing up, and most of us are not concerned with planning. But preparations for spring need to be made during the winter:

• Make a list of broken or missing tools, materials that you ran out of, a tool you always wished you had, or something frivolous that someone might get you as a gift.

You might leave a note where someone making a Christmas list could "accidentally" find it.

• Write down the chores for the winter, such as building the plant stand or cold frame.

• Check your journal for plants you will want to try next year.

As the garden catalogs arrive, you can begin making out an order.

PLANTING

If the soil in the perennial garden was not worked sufficiently earlier in the season, it may be preferable to heal in the new plants in the trial garden for the winter. Healing in means planting them in a temporary spot. Here is the way to do it:

1. Dig a trench, and set the plants closely next to each other in a row.

2. Set them deeper than usual, and cover the roots or soil balls with soil.

3. Mulch the plants for the winter.

4. In spring work up the soil in the permanent place in the garden, and relocate the healed-in plants.

CARE

Clean up the garden now. All but a few of the plants have been cut back by now, and the garden can be raked out. Remove the old leaves to reduce the carry-over of diseases and insects. Compost this plant material, or bury it in the vegetable garden.

WATERING

Soak the newly healed-in plants to settle the soil around the roots.

Keep the soil moistened throughout the winter. Dry soil freezes faster than wet soil. With sufficient snow cover, the soil may not freeze all winter.

FERTILIZING

Fertilizer is not needed at this time of the season.

PESTS

Mulch applied now may be inhabited by voles, providing them with easy access to the crowns of your plants. Voles will feed on various kinds of vegetation during the winter. If they can find cover next to your plants, they can be very destructive.

Do not apply mulch around the crowns of the plants until the ground is frozen. If you see voles during the day, set out brodifacoum (D-con) bait stations.

GROOMING

Remove all dead plant tops, except those being left to provide seeds for birds.

DECEMBER

PERENNIALS

PLANNING

Cold and snow will soon put the garden to sleep for the winter.

Finish up the year by taking stock of the joys your garden has provided. Garden catalogs arrive this month, and you can begin to plan next year's garden. For now it may be enough to just relax and look at the pictures. For us avid gardeners, though, the season never ends. We are always looking forward to the next year.

PLANTING

Bring indoors the seeds sown in September and left out for cold treatment. Germinate them under lights.

Catalogs from seed companies that sell perennial seeds may be arriving. Seeds ordered now may arrive in a few days, and you may sow them:

1. Start these seeds on a lighted plant stand (see page 24) or in a greenhouse. Remember, they will need room for transplanting and for growing on this winter.

2. Do not be in a hurry. Seeds of perennials may take their time about starting. Six weeks is not too long for some of them. Some of them need warm temperatures to germinate—70 degrees Fahrenheit is usually satisfactory.

3. As soon as the seeds have germinated, reduce the temperature to about 60 degrees Fahrenheit at night.

4. Transplant them as soon as the seedlings have 2 leaves.

CARE

As soon as the ground has frozen, mulch all the perennials. The mulch can be clean straw, evergreen branches, or any other light, clean material. The object is not to keep the plants warm, but to keep them frozen until spring. If they are mulched when it is still warm, they may begin to rot under the mulch. Do not be too hasty.

It may be a good idea to apply fungicide to the crowns of **delphiniums** before mulching. Use a thiophanate-methyl fungicide or dust with PCNB fungicide.

PESTS

Diseases can be carried over the winter on plant parts and infect the plants in spring.

Remove all the fallen leaves and dead stems from the perennials before applying mulches.

Mice may become pests.

If traces of mice are noticed, set out brodifacoum (D-con) bait stations as the mulch is applied. Be sure the stations are not accessible to other animals and birds. Wooden boxes with holes sufficiently large for the mice, but too small for other creatures, are acceptable.

GROOMING

Cut down the last of the stems that were left to provide seeds for birds as soon as the seeds are gone. These stems are usually flattened by the first snow. It is easier to cut them while they are still standing.

Delphinium

ROSES

Roses seem to be everyone's favorite flowers. For the last 50 years or so, hybrid tea roses have been the most popular kinds. They and their near relatives—the floribundas and grandifloras—have earned the reputation for being difficult.

In spite of the other options available, such as old-fashioned roses and landscape roses (shrub roses), many rose fanciers still consider the classical form and beauty of the hybrid teas the ultimate in roses. They persist in growing these beautiful cantankerous plants.

PLANNING

Roses have many requirements:

• They require full sun.

Shrub roses are not bothered by the diseases common to the hybrid teas, but still need as much sun as possible for maximum flowering.

• A well-drained soil is essential.

If the soil in the area you select for your roses does not drain, you should consider building raised beds or install drain tiles.

• Rose plants take room.

They should be spaced according to their maximum sizes. They do not like to be moved.

Generally, rose hobbyists plant all their hybrid tea types in a rose garden of some type. They do not mix these roses with other things. There is no reason why they cannot be included in the flower garden or shrub border, however.

Shrub roses are usually planted as specimens if they are large or as a part of the landscape design.

CHAPTER SIX

PLANTING

If the soil is a good loam with plenty of organic matter, plant hybrid tea roses directly in it. If the soil is poor, prepare it by following these steps:

1. Turn over the soil to at least 1 spade depth.

2. If you are planting only 1 or 2 roses, spade the couple of square feet where each plant will be set.

3. Incorporate up to 40 percent organic matter such as compost, peat moss, or whatever you can get your hands on, such as shredded leaves, manures, shredded bark, or corn cobs.

Hybrid tea types are grafted plants. The flowering part—the scion—is grafted to a root that is a different kind of rose. The roots are vigorous plants that do not flower.

Plant hybrid teas so that the scion is 2 inches below the soil surface. The graft and part of the scion must be covered for the winter. An unprotected scion exposed to the rigors of a Midwest winter will not survive, and the rootstock, ultimately more hardy, will grow.

Plant shrub and landscape roses like other flower-ing shrubs. They are generally available in containers.

1. Dig each hole for planting shallower than the depth of the ball and at least twice as wide.

2. Remove plants from containers, and slice circling roots.

3. Space plants according to their mature sizes.

4. Set each plant in the hole, keeping it at the same depth or slightly higher than it grew in the nursery if drainage is poor.

5. Replace the soil.

6. Soak the soil to settle it.

Roses will need regular watering the first year after planting.

WATERING

Roses need water, usually about 1 inch per week. Apply water as needed, keeping it off the foliage. A soaker hose or a wand with a breaker on the end will keep the water on the ground instead of on the plants.

A mulch of shredded bark, wood chips, or other coarse organic material will keep soil from compacting, will reduce evaporation, and will reduce chances of heavy rains splashing water and spreading diseases.

FERTILIZING

Fertilize monthly until midsummer using a complete, balanced fertilizer such as 10-10-10, a handful spread evenly under each plant. An alternative is a soluble fertilizer such as Peters or Miracle-Gro. Follow the directions on the label. Do not fertilize after August 1, or the plants may not harden off for the winter.

PEST CONTROL

Control aphids and mites with insecticidal soap. Use carbaryl for Japanese beetles. Control other insects with acephate applied from a hose-end sprayer.

In wet weather, mildew and blackspot diseases can be serious, destroying the leaves of roses. Spray with triforine once a week as long as wet weather persists. Resume treatments if the diseases reappear.

PRUNING

Prune roses in spring to remove dead and weak stems. Follow these steps to prune them properly:

1. Select 2 or 3 strong canes, cutting them back to side buds pointing away from the centers of the plants.

2. When cutting flowers or deadheading, cut to a 5 (a leaf with 5 leaflets) near the middle of the stem. Try to leave two 5-leaflet leaves on the remaining stem. (See the diagram on page 155.)

3. Make the cut $1/4$ inch above the leaf. If you have had trouble with cane borers in your area, dab the cut with a little yellow shellac or wood glue to protect it.

JANUARY
ROSES

PLANNING

Catalogs have been arriving for weeks. It is fun to look through them and see what is new.

The rose catalogs are getting more interesting as well—it is not just the new **hybrid teas** (more of the same old thing) but totally new plants. The **shrub roses** give us something new to plant in our landscapes. The improved **antiques**, **species**, **rugosas**, and **English hybrids** give us new things to look at.

Maybe you are ready to try different plants in your garden. While looking through the catalogs, jot down a couple of things you want to try. Order the plants so that they will arrive at the proper planting time.

English rose 'Graham Thomas'

Most mail-order firms are very good about sending the plants at just about the right time for your locality.

CARE

If you brought roses indoors to be stored for the winter, check that they are not too warm or too wet. Frequently examine potted **miniatures** being grown indoors for pests. Deadhead them to keep the energy going to support the plants.

Outside, check the winter protection to make sure it is still doing the job. If the mulch or cones have blown away, locate them, and set them back over the plants. Notice the extent of the dieback on the canes. It will give you an indication of the severity of the winter damage.

WATERING

Miniatures indoors will suffer from the dry air. Humidifiers help greatly. They need sufficient water, but do not drown them.

PESTS

Mites can be troublesome on indoor roses.

Use insecticidal soap to eliminate them.

Unprotected tops outdoors may be attractive to mice and rabbits if there is heavy snow cover. Mice will gnaw on exposed bark. Rabbits will prune the stems down to the hill of soil protecting the plants.

This does no harm because the plants will be pruned in spring anyway.

HELPFUL HINTS

Other than a foray out into the garden on a nice day, there is not much that can be done in rose gardens this month.

Take care of these tasks:

• Inventory your supplies and materials.

Did you move the sprays and materials indoors where they will not freeze? Did you run out of triforine or acephate?

• Check the condition of your shears.

Having a good pair of shears is important for rose fanciers. If your shears do not produce a good, clean cut, invest in another pair. The bypass types are to be preferred over the anvil types. Anvil types squeeze the stems and do not cut cleanly once they are nicked or dulled.

• Make a list of the things you will need.

In 6 to 8 weeks, you may see buds beginning to swell, and spring will be right around the corner.

FEBRUARY

ROSES

PLANNING

On the first bright, sunny day, walk around the garden, and examine your roses:

• Make sure the mulch or cones have not blown away.

If they have, replace them.

• Check for rodent or deer damage.

Make sure the animals have not pushed the protective soil hill away to get at tender stems.

• Notice the extent of the dieback on the canes.

Pull a little soil away to see how deeply the frost has damaged the canes. If the injury appears severe, be prepared to order replacement plants so that they can be planted as soon as the soil dries enough.

PLANTING

It is too early to plant outside, but the potted **miniatures** being carried over indoors need to be tended. Repot any that have outgrown their pots. Use a light, commercial potting mix, or prepare a mix of $1/3$ garden soil, $1/3$ coarse sand, and $1/3$ coarse brown peat moss. Or, use an artificial soil mix such as Fafard, Jiffy Mix, or Pro Mix.

CARE

Check **climbers** laid down for the winter and **tree roses** that are buried. See that they are properly covered.

Shrub roses and the other hardy types may suffer winter damage, but they are not usually grafted. If they are killed to the ground, they will regrow quickly. **Hybrid tea types** killed to the bud union will grow back wild and will not flower.

PESTS

Remove overwintering leaves and old clippings to reduce the disease problem this summer.

Rabbits and deer will nibble the tops of **hardy shrub** and **groundcover roses**. Mice (voles) may chew on the bark. The thorns do not seem to dissuade these animals at all if they are hungry. A little pruning back is not harmful to the plants. If they are eaten to the ground, they will be slow to bloom or may even skip a year.

Try repellent sprays. If they do not work, the only solution is to use wire cages or fencing.

PRUNING

Limit pruning to removal of broken stems. Postpone heavy pruning until the plants have begun to grow in a month or so.

MARCH

ROSES

PLANNING

Just about the time when snow disappears, little red buds begin to sprout. In the southern parts of the state, it is time to assess the winter damage.

Pull the hills of protective soil back a bit to see whether the canes are still green. The plants with green to the top of the soil hill will probably be fine. The ones with very little green or no green all the way down to the bud are probably finished. Plan to replace them.

Buy roses from garden centers and discount outlets. They begin to stock roses very early in the season. Or place your order with a mail-order firm as quickly as you can.

PLANTING

You can plant bare-root roses as soon as the soil is dry enough to work. The dormant plants will take a freeze, so there is no value in waiting.

1. Spade the area over, incorporating organic matter.

2. Dig the planting holes deep enough so that the plants can be set with the buds just at or below the surface.

3. Remove the plants from the wrappers.

4. Soak them in a bucket for a couple of hours to hydrate the roots.

5. Trim any overly long or damaged roots.

6. Make cones of soil in the bottoms of the planting holes, and set the plants over the cones so that the roots are spread out evenly in the holes.

7. Backfill halfway with soil, and fill the holes with water to settle the soil.

8. Replace the remaining soil, and soak again.

You can plant containerized **shrub roses** now, too.

1. Dig the planting holes.

2. Remove the plants from the containers.

3. Set them at the correct depth in their assigned spots.

4. Backfill with soil, and water as indicated for planting bare-root roses.

Bare-root **hybrid tea-type roses** may be slow to sprout. Hill soil over the plants to keep the buds moist and hasten sprouting.

If plants were held over winter in cold storage, bring them out, and plant them now. Move **miniatures** that have wintered in pots indoors to the outside.

CARE

As the plants begin to grow, remove the winter covering. If the plants are left covered in warm weather, the new shoots will be etiolated (weak and yellow) and will die back when they are eventually exposed. A good indicator for removal of winter protection is flowering of **forsythia** bushes. When they are in full bloom, it is time to uncover roses.

Remove the **tree roses** and **climbers** that were laid down for the winter. Tie up the **climbers** on their supports. Replant the **tree roses**, staking them to keep them from being knocked over.

WATERING

Water newly set plants when they are planted. Unless the weather is quite dry, no further watering is needed until they are growing. Excess water will inhibit new root development.

 FERTILIZING

As soon as the plants begin to grow, fertilize them with Peters or Rapid-Gro. Follow directions for mixing on the package.

 PESTS

Aphids can appear early, as soon as the plants start making leaves. Watch carefully for them.

If you notice aphids, rub them off the plants, being cautious not to injure the tender shoots. Later, or if the plants are badly infested with aphids, use insecticidal soap to control them. Again, use caution. Tender shoots are easily injured.

Canker diseases may develop on stems that were injured during the winter. Stems left covered too long are susceptible.

Apply triforine fungicide to stems showing cankers. Prune out weakened stems with cankers below any evidence of the disease.

Winter annuals and perennial weeds are starting to grow now.

Hoe or pull them out before they get a good start. Once the weeds are removed, apply preemergent herbi- cides to keep them out. DCPA and oxyfluorfen and pendimethalin granules are recommended.

If there is little else to eat, deer will eat roses down to the ground.

Apply a commercial repellent or one concocted of a bottle of Tabasco in a gallon of water to dissuade them. Add a little soap so that the mixture stays on the plants.

 PRUNING

As soon as the **hybrid tea-type roses** begin to grow, the winter damage will be apparent. Prune out the damaged stems to a point just above a healthy, outward-facing bud. Remove all weak stems, leaving just 2 or 3 healthy canes.

Prune out damaged stems.

Prune **climbing rose** plants to fit their supports. Remove thin canes, and pinch back overly vigorous canes to force branching.

Remove only broken or winter-damaged canes from **bush roses** and other hardy types.

HELPFUL HINTS

Getting roses off to a good start is important. **Hybrid tea-type roses** have a short season in this climate. It is essential that you develop a large plant quickly. Only large, healthy plants will produce lots of blooms all summer. Anemic, weak plants will struggle just to survive, and flowers will be few and anemic too.

APRIL

ROSES

PLANNING

Spring is here! Even though we can expect more cold and some snow, these conditions will not last. Daylight-saving time makes it seem that winter is really a thing of the past. There is enough light after supper to do some things outside, even if you just look around.

Make changes in your rose garden. Before you can make intelligent decisions, you need information. Sometimes I cannot remember from one season to the next what happened in the garden and what roses were planted where.

Keep a journal to solve this dilemma. It does not have to be fancy—a spiral notebook will do. At the top of the page, record the year. Then each time there is something of interest you need to remember, write the date and the impressions. Mark for replacement a rose that never seems to make blooms. Or note a plant that makes one flower on a long stem and never branches to make more flowers. If the bloom is spectacular, possibly one is enough. Otherwise, it is taking space and not performing.

I am reluctant to give up on any rose plant. Maybe I can fix it with a little extra fertilizer or pinching. Despite my efforts, however, the dogs show up. Spring, when there are lots of plants available, is a good time to make changes.

Look up the candidates for replacement in your journal, and pull the offending plants before you change your mind.

Then select more productive plants for that spot in the garden.

PLANTING

Bare-root plants are still available in the garden centers. Some discount stores may be running specials. Often these plants are lower grades, but sometimes they are perfectly good plants. Buy them if you know what you are getting—1X or 2X plants are smaller, but can be grown successfully if they are of decent varieties.

To plant bare-root plants, follow these steps:

1. Dig the planting holes deep enough that the plants can be set with the buds just at the surface.

2. Remove bare-root plants from the wrappers.

3. Soak them in a bucket for a few hours to hydrate the roots.

4. Trim long or damaged roots.

5. Make cones of soil in the bottoms of the planting holes, and set the plants over the cones so that the roots are spread out evenly in the holes.

6. Backfill halfway with soil, and fill the holes with water to settle the soil.

7. Replace the remaining soil.

8. Soak again to settle the soil.

Containerized plants are available now. They are usually started in the greenhouse and may be in bloom. Generally, these plants are not much more expensive than packaged bare-root plants.

Soak and feed a bareroot rose before planting.

To plant containerized plants, follow these steps:

1. Dig the planting holes.

2. Remove potted plants from the containers. Set them at the correct depth in their assigned spots.

3. Backfill halfway with soil, and fill the holes with water to settle the soil.

4. Replace the remaining soil.

5. Soak the soil again to settle it.

CARE

Remove all of the soil and mulch used for winter protection:

• Carefully shovel the soil from around and under the plants.

• Mix it with the mulch, and put it back in the bed in the vegetable garden where you got it last fall.

• Hose the remaining soil off the plants.

• Replace the old summer mulch with fresh mulching material.

Shredded bark, wood chips, or other coarse organic material will keep soil from compacting, will reduce evaporation, and will reduce chances of heavy rains splashing water and spreading diseases.

WATERING

The plants need about 1 inch of water per week. Usually, there is sufficient rain at this time of year. Do not water unless the soil is dry. Keeping the plants too wet will drown the roots.

Set up a rain gauge in your garden to more accurately provide water for plants. I use 2 of them. Too often, I am surprised by the difference in rain we get compared to the official reports. If both gauges are the same, they are probably more accurate than the weather bureau.

FERTILIZING

Fertilize with soluble Peters or Rapid-Gro. Follow directions for mixing on the package, and apply 1 or 2 cupfuls per plant. Or use granular 10-10-10 or something similar, 1 handful spread evenly around each plant. Water to soak it in, and wash off fertilizer spilled on the plants.

PESTS

Aphids will show up just about the same time the leaves start.

If just a few are starting, carefully rub them off; be careful not to damage the tender shoots.

If aphids heavily infest a single shoot, pinch it off. Spray general infestations of aphids or mites with insecticidal soap.

Mildew will start right away if the weather is wet. Apply triforine fungicide weekly to keep it in check.

Blackspot usually does not show up this early. If it does, triforine will stop it.

Grasses are the most difficult weeds to keep out of rose plantings. Use the grass herbicide fluazifop-p-butyl to kill grasses without damaging the rose plants. It is available in a ready-to-use spray bottle. Follow directions on the package.

Broadleaf weeds may show up.

Hoe out broadleaf weeds. Apply DCPA or oxfluorfen and pendimethalin to weed-free ground to prevent more weeds. (See the suggested Pest Control Materials beginning on page 281 for trade names of these products.)

PRUNING

Try to keep as many leaves on the plants as possible. Remove stems that die back from canker diseases. Even though canker diseases are often due to winter damage, they may show up now. Clean up stubs left from the pruning last month. No other pruning is necessary yet.

MAY

ROSES

 PLANNING

May is a wonderful month in the garden. For rose gardeners, it is a time of anticipation. If you are fortunate, you will have the first flowers this month. **Miniatures**, **polyanthas**, and **floribundas** can start early. Whichever it is, the first rose is always a welcome sight.

 PLANTING

Containerized roses in full bloom are wonderful Mother's Day gifts. One of my favorite roses is 'Fragrant Memory'. It is pink with good form, and it keeps as a cut flower for up to a week. It makes a great gift because of the name and because it blooms steadily all summer.

Using roses in containers is the easiest way to start these plants in your garden:

1. Select plants that are healthy and free of insects or diseases.

2. Prepare the sites for planting by turning the soil and adding organic matter.

3. Dig each planting hole twice the diameter of the container and deep enough so that the buds of the plant can be set at the soil line.

4. Knock the plants out of the containers, and set them in the holes.

5. Backfill halfway with soil, and fill the holes with water.

6. Replace the remaining soil, and soak the soil to settle it. Any extra soil can be left as a ring around the planting holes to hold water.

 CARE

As spring-blooming kinds finish blooming, leave the old flowers on so that the fruit can develop. These are called hips and will often turn bright red and last into fall or even winter.

Visit your roses every morning and again in the evening. These plants develop quickly. Flowers that were only buds in the morning can open by evening.

While you are enjoying the beauty and fragrance of the flowers of **hybrid tea** types, notice how the plants grow. How does the little bud develop from a cut? Do they all develop the same, no matter where the cut is made?

 WATERING

If the weather is dry, water the roses. Be careful to keep the foliage dry, and avoid splashing water on the lower leaves. Blackspot is transmitted by splashing water.

If you have many roses, invest in a drip watering system or in leaky pipe. Leaky pipe is the term for a hose that sweats water from pores. It can be positioned to wind through the rose planting so that each plant receives water. I usually set the leaky pipe in the spring and leave it in place all season. It can be left over the winter if you wish, since the water drains out and it will not be ruined by freezing. I usually remove it as I clean up the garden in fall.

 FERTILIZING

Fertilize with soluble Peters or Rapid-Gro. Follow directions for mixing on the package, and apply 1 or 2 cupfuls per plant. If you prefer, use granular 10-10-10 or something similar, 1 handful spread evenly around each plant. Water to soak in fertilizer, and wash off any spilled on the plants.

PESTS

Aphids, mites, and thrips will find your roses.

Control them with insecticidal soap or acephate from a hose-end sprayer.

Earwigs will eat the petals from the flowers during the night.

You can use carbaryl to control them, though they will usually have done some damage before they are noticed. Begin treating as soon as any injury is seen to kill the earwigs while they are still small.

Caterpillars may be a problem. Use carbaryl to control them. Or use *Bacillus thuringiensis*, the biological control. It is sold under a number of names.

Cane borers may bore into the ends of stems where flowers were cut.

Dab the ends with yellow shellac or white glue.

Midges are tiny larvae that bore into the stem just below the bud. The stem collapses, and the bud hangs down, ruined.

Clip out damaged buds immediately, and dispose of them in the trash so that the adult cannot emerge. Spray the plants with acephate from a hose-end sprayer.

As soon as the plants begin to grow, the diseases begin as well. All they need is the proper moisture, and diseases quickly mar the leaves and buds.

Set up a regular spray schedule as long as the weather is moist to protect the leaves. Many fungicides will work on most of the rose diseases. Copper compounds, mancozeb, sulfur, thiophanatemethyl, triforine, and chlorothalonil are some of them. Where I shop, the easiest to find are copper, mancozeb, thiophanate-methyl, potassium bicarb, and triforine. Orthenex (triforine) Garden Insect and Disease contains insecticides in addition to the fungicide. Select two or three, and alternate them as you spray. By doing so, the possibility of resistance is reduced. See the Suggested Pest Control Materials beginning on page 281 for a list of trade names.

Weeds need to be controlled.

Hoe or pull weeds as soon as you notice them. Dandelions and, in our garden, violets are very often visitors. The old-fashioned dandelion digger still works the best to get rid of these weeds.

PRUNING

Disbud large-flowered **hybrid tea roses** to produce 1 large bloom for cutting.

As the flowers fade from the **hybrid tea** types (including the **multifloras** and **grandifloras**), remove them for new flowers to begin. These roses produce compound leaves with one, three, or five leaflets. Buds in the axils of leaves with five leaflets, called fives, will develop long stems and normal flowers; threes will produce short stems and sometimes smaller or misshapen flowers.

HELPFUL HINTS

This month, establish the routine for your rose garden. Get into the habit of daily rose care. If the plants are ignored and begin to have troubles, it may take the rest of the season to get them back under control.

JUNE

ROSES

PLANNING

Roses are at their best this month. The spring-blooming types are in their full glory. The **hybrid tea types** are making their first flush of blooms. The **landscape roses**, which bloom fairly well all summer, make their best show now. If there is a best time to evaluate your rose plantings, now is the time. If they do not look good in June, they will not improve later. Enjoy your roses. But at least once while things are at their best, make notes in your journal. List the following:

• Blooming dates for each variety

• Size and condition of the flowers

  • Disease problems

  • Insect pests

  • Sizes of the plants

  • Plants to remove and replace

PLANTING

Remove and replace the plants that are not performing up to your standards. Most garden centers have good selections of potted plants in bloom. They carry most of the better selections and probably have the ones on your list. If the exact ones you need are not available, you might buy one that has looked

particularly good to you in other gardens.

Plant **landscape roses** all summer. They are available in containers from garden centers and retail nurseries. Landscape architects and landscape contractors are using these plants more and more. If you are in the process of installing new landscape plantings, talk to your architect about using roses instead of other shrubs or ground cover plants.

Prepare the sites for planting by turning the soil and adding organic matter. Now you are ready to plant:

1. Dig each planting hole twice the diameter of the container and deep enough that the buds of the plant can be set at the soil line.

2. Knock the plants out of the containers.

3. Set plants in the holes.

4. Backfill halfway with soil, and fill the holes with water.

5. Replace the remaining soil, and soak again. Any extra soil can be left as a ring around the planting holes to hold water.

CARE

Growing **hybrid tea-type roses** takes as much effort as any other kind of outdoor gardening. The plants are almost completely

dependent on you for their well-being.

Without constant tending, pruning, spraying, watering, and fertilizing, they quickly go to ruin. By midsummer they have few leaves and few flowers. After the first winter, few survive as **hybrid teas** and have reverted to rootstocks.

If there is any question as to the value of the more hardy types of roses, that should answer it. Most people are not willing to put up with the demands of these plants. But with care, the continuous production of first-class flowers is unrivaled.

WATERING

Hybrid tea-type roses need about 1 inch of water per week. Water early in the day so that the plants have a chance to dry before nightfall. Keep water off the leaves to reduce disease problems.

Automatic watering systems such as drip or leaky pipe will apply the water to the ground instead of to the plants.

FERTILIZING

Fertilize with soluble Peters or Rapid-Gro. Follow directions for mixing on the package, and apply 1 or 2 cupfuls per plant. If you prefer, use granular 10-10-10 or something similar, 1 handful spread evenly around each plant. Water to soak in fertilizer, and wash off any spilled on the plants.

PESTS

Aphids, mites, and thrips are continuing problems for your roses. Control them with insecticidal soap or acephate from a hose-end sprayer.

Earwigs will eat the petals from the flowers during the night. Use carbaryl to control them, though they usually have done damage before they are noticed.

Caterpillars may be a problem. Use carbaryl to control them. Or use *Bacillus thuringiensis kurstaki*, the biological control. It is sold under a number of names.

Cane borers may bore into the ends of stems where flowers were cut. Dab the ends with yellow shellac or white glue.

Roses may suffer from various diseases. Set up a regular spray schedule to protect leaves from diseases. Many fungicides will work on most rose diseases. (They are listed on page 151 and in the Suggested Pest Control Materials beginning on page 281.)

Select 2 or 3, and alternate them as you spray to reduce the possibility of disease becoming resistant to any of the materials.

Weeds may be a problem.

Keep weeds under control. Hoe or pull them as soon as you notice them. Use your old-fashioned dandelion digger to dig out dandelions, plantain, and violets. It still works the best to get rid of these weeds.

Mulching helps control weeds. Use shredded bark, wood chips, or other coarse organic material. The mulch also will keep soil from compacting, will reduce evaporation, and will reduce chances of heavy rains splashing water and spreading diseases.

 PRUNING

For larger blooms, disbud the side shoots from **hybrid teas** and **grandifloras**.

Roses need constant pruning. Carry your knife or shears anytime you are in the rose garden. Do not leave dead or diseased stems on the plants because the diseases will spread to healthy parts of the plants. Remove bare or spindly stems at the bottoms of the plants. They are places where canker diseases can start.

Remove flowers as soon as they drop their petals. The sooner the cut is made, the sooner a new flower will develop on that stem.

Protect the ends of cut stems with a dab of glue to prevent cane borer damage.

HELPFUL HINTS

Visit a public rose garden this month. Most gardens label the varieties so that you can identify them. Take your notebook with you, and list plants of interest to you. By visiting the display several times during the season, you can get a good idea of how the varieties behave. Although the staff members of the gardens are diligent about pest control and pruning, some varieties may develop problems. These are ones you may want to avoid.

JULY
ROSES

 PLANNING

If you have resisted trying roses because of the difficulty in growing them, try a few of the **shrub** or **landscape roses**. (See the table page 270.) They will not develop the perfect, classical blooms for cutting, but the colors and fragrances are the same. A rose is a rose. . . .

Most **landscape** and **shrub roses** are relatively free of disease problems, and their winter hardiness is a big advantage.

 PLANTING

Container-grown roses can be planted all summer. Follow these steps to plant them:

1. Prepare the ground by spading over and adding organic matter.

2. Dig planting holes twice the width of the containers.

3. Knock the plants out of the containers, and slice roots that have begun to circle the balls.

4. Set the plants at the same height they were growing in the container. Set buds of **hybrid tea types** 2 inches below the soil surface.

 WATERING

Roses are woody plants, but the flowers and leaves are mostly water. Without sufficient water, the plants become hardened off. The flowers become smaller, and flowering decreases. During hot weather, the plants wilt, and unless they can transpire, they cannot cool.

Apply 1 inch of water weekly or when the plants wilt.

 FERTILIZING

Keep your plants growing vigorously. The faster they grow, the more flowers you get. Vigorous plants are more able to resist certain diseases and repair injuries quicker.

Use a granular 10-10-10 fertilizer, one handful per plant. Or mix and apply soluble Peters or Miracle-Gro, about 2 cupfuls per plant.

 PESTS

Bud worms can destroy a flower overnight. Nothing is as disappointing as heading to the garden one morning anticipating a bud bursting open and then discovering that something ate the heart out of it the night before. All that is left is some frass and a little webbing.

Keep the buds covered with carbaryl or *Bacillius thuringiensis kurstaki*.

Earwigs will eat the petals as they open.

Apply carbaryl while the insects are still small.

Japanese beetles arrive this month.

Use carbaryl to control Japanese beetles. If you decide to use traps for these pests, set them as far from your garden as you can. They attract the beetles from the entire neighborhood, but not all of them end up in the trap. The rest stop for dinner in your garden.

Continually watch for aphids, mites, and thrips.

Use insecticidal soap to control them.

During wet weather, fungal diseases need to be controlled.

Apply one of the fungicide materials listed on page 151 and in the Suggested Pest Control Materials beginning on page 281. Alternate these materials so that diseases are less likely to develop resistance. If the weather is wet, make applications every week.

Weeds can still be problems.

Keep weeding. The most disastrous weed in the rose garden is morning glory or field bindweed. There is no chemical that can be sprayed on it without killing the roses. Unwind the vines from the roses, and pull them out. Every time they try to regrow, cut them off immediately.

If the vines can be separated from the roses so that they can be treated without contacting the bushes, wipe them with herbicide—this is called wick application. Put a rubber glove on your hand and a cotton glove over it. Moisten the cotton glove with glyphosate diluted equally with water. Wipe the vines without touching the bushes. The glyphosate will translocate to the roots of the vines, killing them. Remove and discard the gloves; wash your hands and arms thoroughly.

PRUNING

Disbud the side shoots from larger-flowered varieties. They are easy to snap out when they are small; they become tough and must be cut out when they are larger.

One of the most useful grooming aids is your pocket knife. Keep it sharp at all times. Nearly all commercial rose growers use pocket knives to cut the flowers and groom the plants. Shears are rarely used in commercial rose greenhouses except for heavy pruning.

To protect your thumb from cuts and your index finger from thorns, use 2 pieces of old garden hose. Slice them down one side so that you can slip them over your finger and thumb. As you cut flowers or

pinch stems, you can hold the flowers or stems between the thumb and index finger of one hand. You do not have to pick up the flowers, either, because you will not drop them on the ground with this method.

Spring-flowering roses, **shrub roses**, **hybrid perpetuals**, and some **rambling roses** flower on wood produced the previous year. Prune these plants shortly after flowers have dropped to assure time for the plants to develop the buds for the next year's blooms.

Cut an old hose into sections to protect your fingers when pruning.

HELPFUL HINTS

Cut roses to enjoy indoors.
- For the flowers to last the longest, cut them in the morning.

The buds should be just beginning to open at the tips.
- Cut just above a "five" (a five-leaflet leaf) near the center of the stem, leaving at least two fives on the plant.
- Immediately immerse the cut stems in warm water, at 100 degrees Fahrenheit, mixed with floral preservative.
- Place the vase of flowers in the refrigerator for 4 hours to harden them.
- Put the roses on display.

Cut a rose stem just above a five-leaflet leaf.

AUGUST

ROSES

 PLANNING

Midsummer is August 6. It is the halfway point between the summer solstice and the autumnal equinox.

Some people celebrate midsummer on the longest day of the year, about June 21. Other people insist that summer actually starts at the spring halfway point, which is May 5 or 6, and that winter begins on the fall halfway point, November 7. Those dates may be more worthwhile because many tender garden plants can be set out on the May date. The November date is often about the time of the first hard freeze.

However you calculate it, summer is on the downside. As days shorten and evenings become cooler, heavy dew begins to form every night. Diseases become more troublesome as a result. You have lost 1 hour of daylight already.

There is still plenty of warm weather ahead, but you need to make changes now in handling your garden. Begin preparing the rose plants for winter.

 PLANTING

Hybrid tea-type roses can still be planted from containers, but there is a greater chance that they will not be well established by the time cold weather arrives. **Shrub roses** are less tender and can still be planted with fairly good assurance that they will be able to stand the winter.

Provide the plants with water, and mulch them to provide the roots with optimal growing conditions. Use transplant starter fertilizer, low in nitrogen and high in phosphorus, as the plants are watered the first time.

 CARE

Roses need constant tending:
- Remove diseased or damaged twigs each time you are in the garden.
- Notice how the plants are growing.
- Make sure no suckers are starting from the rootstocks.

These shoots will have more than 5 leaflets on each leaf. The leaflets are smaller and have deeper saw teeth.

 WATERING

Keep the plants adequately watered. If the plants wilt, check to see whether the soil is dry or too wet. The plants will wilt either way. If the soil is too wet, pull back the mulch, and cultivate it lightly to air it out.

 FERTILIZING

You may fertilize **hybrid tea types** on the first day of this month, but not after that.

If you persist with fertilizing, you may kill them with kindness. These plants need time to slow down so that they are dormant by the time winter arrives. If they are fertilized with nitrogen, they are obedient enough to keep growing. The soft new growth will not be mature enough to stand the winter, and in growing, it uses up the sugars and starches that should have been stored up by the plant for winter.

PESTS

Mites are always present in the garden, waiting for the chance to attack your roses. Aphids are around, too, and are more visible. Remove both with insecticidal soap.

Onion thrips are abundant at this time of the year. The onions have dried up, and the thrips are looking for a new home. They prefer roses and some perennials.

Use acephate from a hose-end sprayer to remove them because they hide deep in the flowers where they are hard to hit with soap.

Japanese beetles are at their peak now.

Keep the foliage covered with carbaryl or it will become lace. If the beetles are numerous, they will do a lot of damage before the carbaryl does away with them. These beetles are slow moving, but will drop off the plants if disturbed. One sure way to get rid of them, at least for the moment, is to pick them off the plants. They do not bite, so there is no danger. Drop them in a can of kerosene or fuel oil. Traps may attract your neighbor's beetles as well as yours.

The sunny, hot days and cool nights are perfect for mildew and blackspot.

Spray the plants religiously every week to protect new leaves. Triforine works well and is easy to find in stores. (Other effective materials are listed on page 151, and in the Suggested Pest Control Materials beginning on page 281.)

Weeds are making seeds now. Every weed you remove now means fewer weeds next year.

Keep hoeing.

Few animals bother roses, but deer are exceptions. They will eat them down to the wood if they find them. They especially like some of the **landscape roses**. Sparrows will peck at the flower buds to get moisture if they are short of water.

PRUNING

By August, your rose plants may have grown quite tall and lost many of the lower leaves. Blackspot may have taken its toll as well. Cut back long, leafless canes to a reasonable height this month to start over. Try to cut to just below a hook where a shoot grew from an old cut.

Do not cut the entire plant back at one time. As old flowers are deadheaded from these unsightly canes, cut them down. Cooler weather will result in a last flush of new leaves that should supply the plant with energy to survive the winter. Protect these new leaves from blackspot and other problems.

Shrub rose 'The Fairy'

September

ROSES

 PLANNING

As soon as Labor Day is past, the pace of our activities quickens. School is back in session, vacations are over, and normal activities resume after the summer hiatus.

Mornings are not as warm and bright as they were a few weeks ago, and it is harder to get into the garden. We have lost nearly 3 hours of daylight since the first day of summer.

Meterological fall starts September 1, and official fall starts the third week of the month. (The date varies from year to year.)

Although summerlike days are still ahead, the hint of fall is in the air, and the season is dwindling. Plan for the winter.

Hybrid tea-type roses need special care to survive the winter. Decide how you will tackle the problem:

• Will the roses be covered with hills of garden soil?

Decide where you will get it.

• Will rose cones suffice?

Do you have enough on hand?

• Do you have the facilities to remove the plants for winter storage?

It takes controlled cold storage such as a walk-in cooler. In the parts of the state with the most severe winters, that is the only sure way to protect the plants. Some park districts do this every year to protect their huge investments.

 PLANTING

Landscape roses can be planted all fall. It is an excellent time for planting. Most landscape nurseries and contractors are very busy during September and October.

It is too late to plant **hybrid tea-type roses** because there is insufficient time for them to become established before winter. The good possibility that **hybrid tea roses** in general may suffer winter kill makes planting now unwise.

 CARE

If you cut back your plants in August, make every effort to protect the new leaves from insects and diseases. The plants need as many leaves as possible to produce the stored energy they need for winter survival.

 WATERING

If rains are insufficient to keep the plants watered, soak them every 10 days to 2 weeks. Keep water off the leaves.

 FERTILIZING

Do not fertilize roses at this time of the season. If soft growth is forced now, it may not harden off sufficiently before winter.

 PESTS

Aphids, whiteflies, and mites may still be problems. Control them with insecticidal soap.

Earwigs may attack buds.

Protect buds with carbaryl.

Most other insect problems have diminished by now.

New foliage may be subject to fungus. Keep the new foliage protected with fungicides. (See page 151, for a list of recommended fungicides for roses.)

Some weeds get their start now. Seeds of winter annuals, such as chickweed, and some perennials, such as dandelions, germinate now.

Hoe or pull weeds as you notice them.

Voles may decide to live in the mulch.

Pull the mulch away from the bottoms of the plants.

PRUNING

As the weather cools from the heat of summer, the rose flowers are larger and deeper colored. Since you spend less time in the garden at this time of the year, cut some of these blooms for indoor use.

• For the longest vase life, cut the buds as they begin to loosen, but before they open.

• Cut immediately above a leaf with 5 leaflets (called a 5), and try to leave two 5s on the plant.

• Immediately stick the stems in warm water, 100 degrees Fahrenheit, mixed with floral preservative.

• Harden them in the refrigerator for about 4 hours.

• Set them where they can be enjoyed.

After the ground freezes, cover rose plants with 1-foot high mounds of topsoil from elsewhere in your garden.

HELPFUL HINTS

Have you noticed that sometimes after flowers are cut, the stems are longer with several fives? Other times the plant makes a short stem with a few threes before it blooms. Not all five-leaflet leaves are equal. If you will examine the buds at the axils of the fives on a stem, you will notice that the ones at the upper part of the stem have points on them. Lower down, the fives have plump, round buds. The pointed buds make short stems; the rounded ones long, full stems.

Always try to cut to a five with a rounded bud. Sometimes this is not possible, but it is preferred.

OCTOBER

ROSES

PLANNING

October can be a beautiful month with clear, crisp days and cool nights. Though the first freeze can occur early in the month, roses are unaffected and will continue to grow until the leaves fall. This may be into November. Many years we have picked roses in late October.

Keep the plants going as long as possible by protecting the foliage so that it continues photosynthesizing. The carbohydrates produced will keep the plants alive over the winter.

Climbing hybrid tea types and other **ramblers** will need winter protection. Remove them from their supports, and cover them after the leaves fall. Lift **tree roses** to one side, and lay them on their sides to be covered later this fall. Collect materials to cover these plants—soil if you can provide enough, straw, and burlap. You may need antitranspirants to protect the canes from desiccation, too.

PLANTING

Fall is planting time for trees and shrubs, including **shrub roses**. These plants are more like flowering shrubs than like the demanding **hybrid tea-type roses**.

To plant **shrub roses**, follow these steps:

1. Prepare the soil by spading and incorporating organic matter.

2. Dig planting holes twice as wide and as deep as the containers.

3. Knock the plants out of the containers, slice circling roots, and set plants at the same depth that they grew in the containers.

4. Backfill halfway with soil, fill the hole with water, and replace the rest of the soil.

5. Soak the soil to settle it.

If fall is dry, water **shrub roses** every 2 weeks.

CARE

Prepare to cover **hybrid tea types** for the winter. Dig out one of the beds in your vegetable garden, piling the soil on the next bed. Cover it with a tarp to keep it dry so that you can use it to cover your rose plants. Wait until the ground freezes to cover the roses.

It is still possible to plant shrub roses. Measure the planting hole to assure the proper width and depth.

HELPFUL HINTS

• **Hybrid tea** types will need winter protection. The plants will lose their leaves in fall when temperatures go below freezing. Cut the canes back to 15 or 18 inches high. When the ground begins to freeze in late fall, cover the bases of the plants with 1-foot-high piles of topsoil from elsewhere in your garden. After the soil freezes, cover the piles of topsoil with another foot of mulch. Rose cones can be used in milder zones; they hold the soil and mulch in place.

Some rose specialists actually remove the plants and keep them in cold storage for the winter, planting them back in the garden in spring. In especially severe localities, this may be the only way to assure winter survival. The Chicago Park District used this system for many years.

• Make notes in your journal. Mention problems that developed and how you confronted them, varieties that were troublesome, varieties that were not what you expected and need to be replaced. Add other comments that may be helpful for planning.

WATERING

Water newly planted **shrub** and **landscape roses** if there is insufficient rain. October can be very dry.

FERTILIZING

Do not fertilize **hybrid tea types** this late in the season. They will not harden off for winter.

Feed newly planted **landscape** and **shrub roses** with transplant starter fertilizer such as 10-52-17, 10-30-10, or something similar. Mix 1 ounce in 2½ gallons of water, and apply 1 quart per plant.

PESTS

Insects may continue to appear for a while. Usually, cool weather reduces insect problems. A good freeze will put a stop to them.

Control insects with insecticidal soap.

The leaves may need to be protected from blackspot and mildew. Use a fungicide named on page 151, and in the Suggested Pest Control Materials beginning on page 281.

Weeds will continue to grow until frozen.

Hoe or pull weeds as you see them.

PRUNING

Keep deadheading the faded blooms. Or better yet, cut the flowers as they develop and use them indoors. Cut about midway in the stem, leaving half the leaves for the plant.

Wait until the leaves have dropped before doing heavy winter pruning.

NOVEMBER

ROSES

 PLANNING

Winter can arrive anytime after the first of November. Usually, the first significant snowfall occurs before the end of the month, and an Arctic outbreak is not impossible, at least in the northern part of the state.

Complete your preparations for protecting the plants:

• Be sure you have the supplies you will need.

• Stockpile soil if you have not done so already.

• If you intend to use rose cones, check that you have enough of them.

In milder parts of the state, wire cages full of leaves adequately protect the plants. Make them out of chicken wire or hardware cloth. Stockpile leaves to fill them.

 PLANTING

There is still time to plant **landscape roses**. Water them thoroughly, and mulch to keep them from freezing in for as long as possible. They will develop new roots until the ground freezes.

If you are lifting and storing plants for the winter, follow these steps:

1. Cut back the plants to 12 inches tall.

2. Dig each plant carefully.

3. Wash off the mud, and trim the roots to about 12 inches long.

4. Label each plant so you know what it is next spring.

5. Pack the plants in waxed boxes, and store at 35 degrees Fahrenheit in a cooler.

6. During the winter, check roots. They must not dry out. Moisten if necessary.

Move in **miniatures** in containers before the pots freeze. These plants can be kept blooming all winter if they have enough light. Keep the temperature at 60 degrees Fahrenheit. You may want to use a humidifier with them.

 CARE

Do not dally in cleaning up the garden. Rake out the dead leaves, old mulch, and other accumulated debris. Diseases and insects can overwinter on this stuff and get an early start on your plants.

Make it tough for them and relocate them, with the leaves and trash, to the compost pile. An active compost pile will heat enough to kill these pests.

 WATERING

Limit watering to soaking newly planted **landscape roses**. Make sure they do not go into the winter in dry soil.

 FERTILIZING

Do not fertilize **hybrid tea types** this late in the season. They will not harden off for winter.

Feed newly planted **landscape and shrub roses** with transplant starter fertilizer such as 10-52-17, 10-30-10, or something similar. Mix 1 ounce in 2$\frac{1}{2}$ gallons of water, and apply 1 quart per plant.

 PESTS

Removal of fallen leaves will reduce the numbers of overwintering insects and mites in your rose plantings.

Blackspot overwinters on fallen leaves. Rake out leaves, and dispose of them in the compost pile or vegetable garden to reduce the amount of inoculum

Blackspot can overwinter on fallen leaves; rake out leaves and dispose of them.

HELPFUL HINTS

Update your journal:

• List all the insects and diseases that affected your plants this season.

• Note the treatments used to correct the problems and how effective they were.

If certain treatments did not work, try to find out why. Plan to modify the treatment next year.

Inventory all the chemicals left over from the season:

• Assemble them in one place where they will not freeze over the winter. A lockable cage in the basement works. Ours has chicken wire over the doors so air can circulate.

• Make sure all original labels are in place and intact.

• Do not store chemicals in any containers that may be mistaken for food containers.

• The cage should have a hasp and lock, especially if children or other unsuspecting people are apt to encounter it.

• Dispose of empty containers properly. The instructions are on the labels.

for next year. Blackspot may eventually arrive, but it will take longer if it is not waiting right under your plants.

Weeds are easier to see after the leaves have dropped.

Hoe out or pull remaining weeds. Dig out grasses that have started to grow among the canes. This seems to be a place where grass gets started and is very difficult to eliminate.

Voles may be in the garden.

Set out brodifacoum (D-con) bait traps. Construct them so that other animals or birds cannot get into them. Do not cover the roses with leaves until the ground freezes, or the voles may decide to live in the leaves. They will be right next to a good food source if the winter is severe, and may gnaw the bark off the lower parts of the canes.

PRUNING

The canes that have green leaves can be left for a while. There is no need to remove them until the leaves drop. Cut back bare canes to about 18 inches or short enough to fit under cones. Cut up these canes into short pieces, and compost them.

DECEMBER

ROSES

 PLANNING

The season is barely over when garden catalogs begin arriving. They used to come after the holidays, but now they are here during the holidays. They are fun to look at and may give you ideas for next year.

On rare occasions, winter is delayed, and roses are still growing this late in the year. It is not to be expected, however, and all preparations for winter should be completed by now.

Final notes should have been made in your journal so that you may plan changes during the winter.

 PLANTING

Check stored plants to make sure they are not drying out.

Keep temperatures at 35 degrees Fahrenheit.

 CARE

Tender **climbers** and **ramblers** need attention now:

1. Take canes of tender **climbers** and **ramblers** down from their supports.

2. Dig a trench so that you can bury the canes.

3. Lay the canes in the trench, and hold them down with crossed stakes.

4. As soon as the ground freezes, cover them with soil or with straw and burlap.

Tree roses need attention now:

1. Dig a trench next to **tree roses**, long enough and deep enough so that the plants can be buried.

2. Dig under one side of the **tree roses** so that they can be laid on their sides.

Mound soil over hybrid tea rose canes for winter protection.

3. Hold them down with crossed stakes.

4. Cover them with soil or straw and burlap after the ground freezes.

Hybrid tea roses need attention at this time:

1. Cut back the tops of the **hybrid tea types** to 18 inches.

2. After the ground freezes, cover the plants with 12-inch-high mounds of soil or with rose cones.

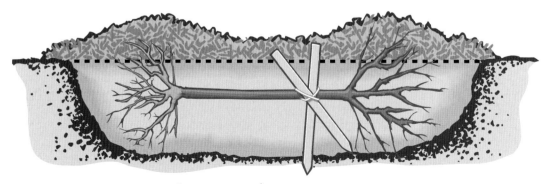

Construct a trench to protect your roses.

3. Or place cages of chicken wire or hardware cloth, 18 inches high and wide, around the plants, and fill them with leaves.

WATERING

Miniatures indoors for the winter will suffer from dry air. Make sure they receive enough water. Use a humidifier if possible during the coldest weather when indoor humidity is at its lowest.

Landscape roses outside may need water if the winter is mild and dry.

FERTILIZING

Do not fertilize roses this month.

PESTS

Mites can be troublesome on indoor roses.

Use insecticidal soap to eliminate them.

Unprotected tops outdoors may be attractive to mice and rabbits if there is heavy snow cover. Mice will gnaw on the bark. Rabbits will prune the stems down to the hill of soil protecting the plants.

This does no harm because the plants will be pruned in spring anyway.

Deer may eat **landscape roses** down to the ground if the weather is severe and forage scarce.

Try a repellent such as a bottle of Tabasco mixed in a gallon of water with dishwashing soap to help it stick to the plants. When applied to the plants being grazed, it may protect them for a while. Reapply it periodically.

PRUNING

Prune only winter-damaged stems at this time of the year.

REFLECTING ON ROSES

December is a time of reflection for most of us hobby rose growers. I recall Decembers when I was producing commercial cut roses. It was a hectic time, trying to get the crop harvested and shipped in the few days before Christmas. There was very little time to enjoy the flowers. But we always had roses in our home after the crop was shipped.

We still enjoy cutflower roses, and we enjoy the potted **miniature roses** that are available for holiday enjoyment. These are often **polyantha** plants that can be grown through the winter and planted out the next spring.

If you have built a plant light stand for growing annual seedlings, use it for **miniature rose** plants, too. Remember: Keep the lights at the tops of the plants, just high enough so that the tips are not burned.

Sometimes I long for the mild winters of Southern California. But before long, I remember that without winter, the watering, fertilizing, bugs, and diseases never stop. I think I'll light a fire in the fireplace and just sit back to enjoy the pictures and the rose bouquet on the coffee table.

SHRUBS

Shrubby plant material is easier to handle than trees. Shrubs do demand proper care, however. Shrubs are the most commonly used (and misused) plants in the landscape.

I often see plantings that have been allowed to overtake their locations, becoming unattractive and detracting from the looks of the garden. Usually, the owners had no idea of ways to handle the problem.

Shrubs do grow (sometimes too much), and they have pest problems that require the proper attention at the right time.

SELECTING SHRUBS

Before planting shrubs, draw a plan of your yard indicating the areas for public viewing, privacy, and utility. Mark things that need to be hidden, such as utility poles, the neighbor's compost heap, or the church's parking lot.

In the front of the house, plantings should emphasize the front entrance, with plants lowest at the entrance and tallest beyond the corners of the house. Decide the sizes of plants needed in each part of your yard. Then select plants that will fit and that you will enjoy seeing in your yard. Mixshapes, textures, and colors. Take your time and have fun.

Select shrubs that will grow without too many difficulties in your location.

• Do not plant shrubs that need acidic conditions if your soil tends to have a lot of lime.

• Select plants that will grow in your climatic zone. Some species are not hardy in all parts of the state.

CHAPTER SEVEN

• To avoid soil incompatibility problems, buy shrubs grown in soil as nearly like that in your yard as you can find. Containerized plants are grown in artificial soil mixes and require special planting care.

PLANTING

Follow the steps for planting shrubs outlined on page 172.

Keep the plant watered the first year. About one inch of water a week should be adequate, but do not drown it. Water plants located under overhanging roofs even in wet weather because they will not benefit from rainfall.

CARE

In order to maintain shrubs, it is essential to prune them. Timing to enhance flowering and fruiting and to stimulate healthy growth is vital. Plants pruned at the wrong time will fail to bloom. I receive calls to the radio program every spring from listeners with flowering shrubs that have not bloomed for years because of improper pruning. Improperly pruned plants may have a difficult time recovering and may suffer loss of stems; entire plants may succumb.

WATERING

Water during dry weather when the plants begin to wilt. Use care. More shrubs are killed by overwatering than by drought.

FERTILIZING

Fertilize shrubs either with soluble fertilizers or with granular materials. One pound of 10-10-10 or an equivalent per 100 square feet of shrub bed is sufficient.

PEST CONTROL

Diseases and insects will attack shrubs. Some kinds, such as alpine currant, are very susceptible to foliar diseases when spring weather is wet. Many times this does not hurt the plants, but it is unsightly. Spraying as the leaves open in spring is helpful, but timing is important. Control foliar diseases such as leaf spots, anthracnoses, or mildew with thiophanatemethyl fungicides.

Shrubs are susceptible to chewing, sucking, or boring insects. Some are annoying. Others, such as crown borers, are severely damaging and need to be controlled. Applying the correct material at the right time is essential:

• Control chewing types with carbaryl or acephate.

• Control sucking kinds with acephate or insecticidal soap.

• Control borers with lindane, permethrin (moth larvae), or imidacloprid (beetle larvae). Check the labels for recommended uses.

• Always apply acephate with a hose-end sprayer.

• See the Suggested Pest control Materials beginning on page 281.

Wildlife can do a great deal of damage to shrubs. Rabbits gnaw the stems and clip the tips of shoots. Voles or meadow mice girdle the stems at the ground. Deer eat some shrubs to the ground. Repellents may be helpful:

• You can buy various proprietary spray materials from garden centers that may prevent feeding by the animals.

Some contain thiram, which is very bitter. Another contains egg products that smell very bad to the animals.

• You can make a concoction of a bottle of Tabasco in a gallon of water that is so hot that one bite is enough.

• Add a spoonful of soap to keep it from washing off after you spray the plants.

• You can try other things, including bags of human hair hung among the plants, bars of fragrant bath soap staked among the plants, or mothballs scattered around the area.

All of these work if the feeding pressure is not too great. If feed is scarce, the animals may ignore the repellents.

The only sure means to prevent damage is to construct mechanical barriers—fences, cages, and collars or something similar around the stems.

JANUARY
SHRUBS

 PLANNING

Shrubs are the most misused plants in the landscape. Much of this is due to poor planning—or no planning at all. New home owners looking for small plants to fill the void around the house stop at a nursery and see the sweet little plants in containers. They take them home and plant them too close together and too close to the house. In a few years, these darling little plants are covering the front walk, and no one can see out the front windows.

Before buying and planting shrubs, draw a design. If you are at a loss about how to proceed, consult a designer at your favorite garden center. Landscape designers are often certified landscape architects. They are capable of helping you design your plantings and doing a plan for you. With some diligence, most home gardeners can do respectable designs as well.

Consider the mature size, the form, and the flowers of the shrubs. Plant them far enough away from the house and walks, and far enough from one another, to allow for their growth. Consider potential pest problems, too.

Consult catalogs or your *Gardener's Guide* for descriptions and other ideas.

 PLANTING

In the milder parts of the state, some planting can be done if the ground is not frozen. Usually, the planting season starts in March after the ground has thawed and has dried enough so that the soil structure is not destroyed when you work it.

 CARE

Ice and snow can bend and break your shrubs. As snow is falling, brush it off the plants before it freezes. Once it is frozen, trying to remove it will do more damage than leaving it alone.

Do not shovel snow on top of your shrubs. It will pack down and break them. Light snow covering low-growing shrubs insulates them from the cold. Often, **boxwood** or the lower parts of **forsythia** protected by snow are the only parts that escape winter damage.

Try to keep salt spray from getting onto the shrubs and from washing into the soil. Salt easily damages evergreen shrubs. Set burlap screens to protect the plants, or install the fabric used by landscape contractors for erosion control. Tack the fabric to 2-by-2-inch stakes driven into the ground.

 WATERING

If there is little snow cover and the soil is allowed to freeze-dry, shrubs may suffer from root damage. A January thaw will give you a chance to water evergreens. The ones under overhangs are especially vulnerable.

 PESTS

Are the rabbit and deer repellents working? Seeing any signs that the animals have begun to feed means the repellents need to be reapplied or changed.

Take advantage of the January thaw to reapply the repellents. Sometimes it is necessary to change the materials. If you have used balls of hair or soap, the animals may have discovered that they will not harm them. Use the thiram spray repellents. Or mix a bottle of Tabasco in a gallon of water; add a little soap so that the mixture sticks to the plants better.

Voles (meadow mice) may have been active.

Walk down the snow around the plants so that voles cannot burrow under it, and set out bait stations of brodifacoum (D-con). Be sure that the bait is

accessible to the voles but not to birds and other animals. Make small wooden boxes with a ³/₄-inch hole or two. Or use a plastic butter or cottage cheese container, and cut a ³/₄-inch notch in the edge. Add the brodifacoum (D-con), and replace the lid. Set the container upside down where the voles have been active. Check regularly, and add brodifacoum (D-con) if needed.

Deer and rodents can inflict severe damage to shrub plantings. Rabbits clip back stems and may gnaw the bark from the bases of the plants. Mice girdle stems at the soil line.

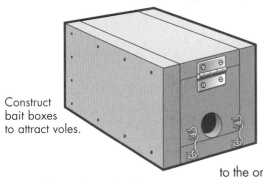

Construct bait boxes to attract voles.

HELPFUL HINTS

During mild spells, examine your plantings. Note anything unusual, and try to find out what is causing it. The sooner damage is noticed and repaired, the more likely the plants will recover. Animal damage can be severe in just a few days if the weather limits the amount of food available to them. Sometimes setting out food for the animals will preserve your plants, but it may entice more animals into your yard. Then you must be ready to keep feeding them.

Repair any damage to screens and structures installed to protect plants. Deer may knock off the cages over **yews**. Wire collars around shrubs should be tall enough to keep rabbits from getting over them.

Deer can eat a **yew** hedge to the ground in a few days if forage is unavailable.

Sometimes it is necessary to resort to the only sure protection— cages or wire collars fitted to the plants.

 PRUNING

Remove any broken branches after storms. Use shears or a saw, and make clean cuts. Any major pruning should be left until next month.

Yew hedge

FEBRUARY

SHRUBS

PLANNING

Have you completed your planting plans for this spring? If not, there is still time to do so. Nursery catalogs for shrubs are not as numerous as those for flowers, but you can find them at libraries, botanic gardens, and some garden centers. They usually have good descriptions and color pictures.

Local nurseries are more likely to carry varieties that will stand the conditions in your yard. After looking at the pretty pictures, look up a plant list from one of the nurseries near you. See if they list the things that interest you. If not, it may be wise to select something else. Many kinds of plants grow naturally over a large part of the country, but locally grown plants are more likely to survive in your yard. They have spent several years in your climate already and survived it.

PLANTING

Do not rush things. Next month is soon enough to worry about planting. Give the snow a chance to melt and soils a chance to dry a bit. Planting in wet soil ruins the structure and makes it harder for the plants to develop new roots.

CARE

Check that the structures you set up to protect your plants are still in place. Until the chances of snow and severe weather are over, they will be needed.

Brush snow off the shrubs as it falls. Once it has frozen, it is hard to remove, and plants can be damaged. Check your plants after every storm. Prop them up if needed, and cut out broken branches.

PESTS

Until there is sufficient other forage for the animals, they will continue to feed where they are familiar with the territory.

These animals will try anything you set out to discourage them. The animals are interested in little but eating at this time of year and have nothing to do but test these materials. They will edge up to them and quickly back away. Then they will keep edging a little closer until they discover that there is no danger. If they find that it will not injure them, they will ignore it. That is why repellents relying on smell do not last.

Reapply repellents that have washed off. Mothballs, fragrant soaps, balls of hair, dried blood, and even coyote urine are temporary solutions at best.

Red twig dogwood

PRUNING

Valentine's Day is the date I try to start pruning shrubs. The sap has not started to rise; it is safely stored in the roots. None is wasted in removing branches. The structure of the plants is much easier to see without the leaves in the way.

All deciduous shrubs can be pruned at this time, but pruning will remove flower buds from spring-flowering kinds. Those can be left until later if you want the flowers. Minor renewal trimming can preserve most of the flower buds, though.

Renew plants with colorful winter bark. Cut out 1/3 of the oldest stems to the ground. **Yellow twig** and **red twig dogwoods** are good examples. The older stems lose color after growing bark. The older stems get cankers and scale insects that are removed in pruning. Any overly long branches remaining need to be headed back to a shorter branch growing in the same direction.

HELPFUL HINTS

Vernal witchhazel blooms this month. If the weather is sunny, even though the temperatures are barely above freezing, the strap-shaped, yellow petals unfold for the day. The fragrant blooms last for several weeks.

Plants are noticing the approach of spring. The color of the bark changes. Buds begin to swell on some of the earliest plants, such as **honeysuckle** and **forsythia**. By the end of the month, the worst of the winter weather is over. The snow is melting, and kids are wading in the puddles on the way home from school. Spring is just 3 weeks away.

You can bring a preview of spring into your home now:

1. Cut a few branches of **forsythia** or other flowering shrubs for forcing.

2. Smash the ends of the stems with a mallet so that they do not heal.

3. Wrap them in wet newspaper or soak them in the tub to loosen the buds.

4. Stand them in vases of water to force them.

5. When they begin to bloom, use them in making arrangements or just brightening your home.

Rejuvenate plants such as overgrown **spireas** or **privet** hedges by cutting them to the ground. They will grow back, with leaves to the bottom, after rejuvenation. If you are worried about the lack of screening while the plants are growing back, cut down the back half this year and the front next year after the back has begun to recover.

Prune **blueberries**, **gooseberries**, and **currants** starting late in the month.

• Remove all weak wood.

• Cut all but half a dozen of the older branches to the ground to force vigorous new shoots.

• Remove weaker shoots in **gooseberries** and **currants**, leaving 4 or 5 each of the 1-year-old, 2-year-old, and 3-year-old stems, a total of about a dozen or so per plant.

MARCH

SHRUBS

PLANNING

Signs of spring are all around. Buds are swelling and birds are singing. Planting time has arrived. But before you head to the nursery, think about what is to be planted and where it will go.

Draw a diagram of your yard.

1. Use graph paper and make the diagram to scale if you can.

2. Identify the areas in which you intend to set plants.

3. Look up in your references each plant that interests you. What is its size at maturity? Are there any special needs, such as full sun, winter protection, or good drainage?

4. Place each plant into your drawing to see if it fits.

Once you have an accurate list of the plants that will fit into your landscape plan, you are ready to visit the nursery.

PLANTING

As soon as the soil is dry enough to work, begin planting. If a handful of soil can be squeezed into a ball and then crumbled, it is ready for planting.

Shrubs are available bare root, balled and burlapped, or containerized. To plant, follow these steps:

1. Dig the holes for planting as deep as and twice as wide as the roots of the plants.

2. Set the plants at the same depth they were growing or higher if the site is wet.

3. Fill the holes halfway with soil, fill the holes with water, and replace the remaining soil.

4. Soak the soil to settle it.

Yews are especially susceptible to wet soils. If they are to be planted in such a location, set them with the ball $1/3$ above the ground, and hill soil up to them.

Small fruit plants are usually sold bare root. To plant, follow these steps:

1. Soak the plants for several hours before planting them.

2. Trim the roots so that they fit in the planting holes.

3. Make mounds of soil in the bottoms of the holes so that the roots can be spread.

4. Backfill halfway with soil, fill the holes with water, and replace the remaining soil.

5. Soak the soil to settle it.

Growing small fruit can be an enjoyable part of your gardening experience. **Raspberries**, **currants**, or **blueberries** are certainly pleasant additions to the harvest as well.

The fruit grow on shrubby plants that take room. Plant in the garden or incorporate into the landscape. They require special care; the plants need to be acces-

sible so that you can prune, spray, and harvest the fruit.

CARE

Rake out the shrub beds as soon as there is a mild, sunny day. What a joy it is to be outside after the long winter. Collect the leaves and debris that have accumulated during the winter. Put the leaves into the compost pile or on the vegetable garden. Separate the trash. Take care not to disturb the emerging bulbs.

Notice any damage to the plants from the winter, such as broken branches or a rodent-feeding injury.

WATERING

Newly planted shrubs will need watering every few weeks if the weather becomes dry. Established shrubs usually require no watering until summer.

FERTILIZING

Apply a complete fertilizer such as 10-10-10, 1 pound per 100 square feet of shrub bed. A 1-pound coffee can holds 2 pounds of fertilizer.

 PESTS

Several overwintering pests of shrubs include aphids, mites, and scale insects. Control these insects with dormant oil. Aphids, mites, and scale insects are smothered by the thin coating of oil in the spray. Apply according to directions on the label. Do not use oil on **maples**.

As leaves begin to unfold, they will be infected by leaf spot diseases if the weather is wet.

Protect susceptible varieties such as **alpine currant**, **lilac**, and **honeysuckle** with thiophanate-methyl.

Weeds begin to be evident. Hoe out weeds as they appear. Apply preemergent herbicides to weed-free ground to prevent germination of weed seeds. DCPA or trifluralin are useful. Read the label. If your shrubs are not listed as safe, find a different herbicide.

As more forage is available to animals, they are less likely to damage your shrubs. Deer will feed on some shrubs until they are eaten to the ground, however. Keep the repellents or cages over the shrubs.

 PRUNING

Continue pruning deciduous shrubs. Prune **forsythia** when it finishes flowering. Pruning other spring-flowering shrubs now will remove flower buds. If the plants are badly overgrown, removal of $1/3$ of the oldest stems to the ground will improve them but will not severely reduce the bloom. Head these plants back when flowering has finished.

Rejuvenate **privet** hedges, **dwarf spireas**, and **red** and **yellow stem dogwoods** now. Cutting them to the ground will stimulate fresh new stems with leaves from top to bottom.

Finish spring pruning of **rasp-berries** and **blackberries** before the buds swell. Remove all the short and weak canes, leaving 6 to 8 canes per plant. Cut back remaining canes of **red raspber-ries** to 3 or 4 feet tall. On **black raspberries** and **blackberries**, cut back laterals on remaining stems to 10 or 15 inches long. After pruning brambles, tie them to their supports.

If you grow ever-bearing **rasp-berries** for the fall crop only, mow these plants to the ground now. The fresh new canes will produce berries in fall without further pruning.

Remove old, damaged, and dead canes from **currant**, **goose-berry**, and **blueberry** plants.

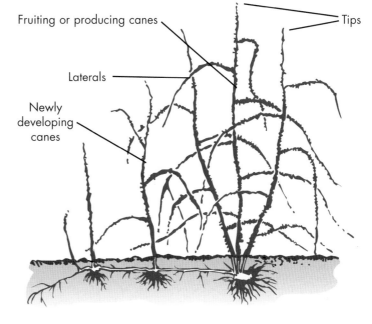

Typical raspberry or blackberry plant.

Tips

Fruiting or producing canes

Laterals

Newly developing canes

APRIL

SHRUBS

 PLANNING

Spring seems to start at the beginning of April when daylight-saving time begins. It stays light long enough for us to get out into the garden and do some things. The weather is milder, and warm winds blow from the south once in a while. Even though there are some winter encores, spring is definitely here. **Forsythias** are already in bloom.

It is planting time, but before you buy, make sure the plants will not become too big for their locations, and that they will grow and bloom as you expect them to.

Forsythia

 PLANTING

Spring is the best time to plant most shrubs. The soil is dry enough, and shrubs of all descriptions are available in containers, balled and burlapped, and bare root. Getting them in the ground now will allow them to begin making roots before the hot weather arrives. They will be well established before next winter.

Soak bare-root plants before planting them. These plants have been out of the ground since last fall and may have dried out a bit.

Containerized plants are grown in artificial soils that are quite different from the soils in your garden. If these are planted directly in the garden, they may have difficulty making roots out of the artificial soil. To help them do well, follow these steps:

1. After knocking these plants out of the containers, slice any circling roots.

2. Shake as much of the artificial soil mix from the ball as you can without damaging the roots.

3. Mix it with the soil going back into the planting hole.

After setting a balled-and-burlapped plant in the planting hole, remove the twine and burlap. Shove the burlap down to the bottom of the planting hole, or cut it off and remove it. Try to find balled-and-burlapped plants grown in a soil as nearly like the soil in your yard. Setting a ball of a very different soil in your soil will cause an interface problem.

• Water, air, and roots will not move freely into or from the ball.

• It will be too wet or too dry.

• Roots will not grow out of it.

If you have no choice, shave some soil from the ball, and mix it with the soil going back into the planting hole. Mixing the soils will reduce the difference and should help the roots survive and grow.

 CARE

Get to know about possible problems with your plants and any special requirements. Look them up in a good plant guide such as the *Manual of Woody Landscape Plants* by Mike Dirr or your *Gardener's Guide*. These books are available at libraries, botanic gardens, and arboreta for study.

WATERING

Newly planted shrubs will need water every 2 or 3 weeks if there is insufficient rain. Set a slowly running hose beneath the shrubs, and run it until the ground is saturated and the water begins to run off. A soaker hose or leaky pipe works, too.

Be careful not to overwater **yews**. They are more often killed by too much water than by not enough.

FERTILIZING

Shrubs can be fertilized once in spring. If you fertilized earlier, there is no need to fertilize again. If you have not yet applied fertilizer, apply 1 pound of 10-10-10 or a similar fertilizer per 100 square feet of shrub bed. Or apply a handful or two spread evenly beneath each shrub. Newly planted shrubs rarely need fertilizer the first year or two.

PESTS

Watch closely for aphids. They are the first insects to show up in spring, usually about the time the plants start making leaves.

Using insecticidal soap or acephate from a hose-end sprayer will eliminate them.

Fletcher scale may be a problem for **yews**. Eggs of these insects hatch about the time **Juneberry** and **saucer magnolias** are in bloom.

Spraying with insecticidal soap or summer horticultural oil will give the best chances of control at that time.

As leaves begin to unfold, they will be infected by leaf spot diseases if the weather is wet.

Protect susceptible varieties such as **alpine currant**, **lilac**, and **honeysuckle** with thiophanate-methyl fungicide.

Weeds may appear now. Hoe out weeds as they appear. Apply a preemergent herbicide. Two inches of shredded bark mulch will reduce the weed problem, but the ground must be weed-free before applying mulch or the weeds will grow right through it.

PRUNING

As soon as flowering shrubs have finished blooming, they can be pruned.

- Remove all dead or damaged branches.
- Renew by cutting out 1/4 of the oldest branches to the ground. This will generate new, vigorous shoots.
- Cut back the remaining branches to shorter shoots growing in the same direction as the longer stem.

There is still time to rejuvenate old woody shrubs and hedges with all the leaves at the tops. Cut these plants down to the ground. They will regrow with leaves from top to bottom.

HELPFUL HINTS

As spring-flowering shrubs bloom, visit a public park, botanic garden, or arboretum where these plants can be seen in bloom. The plants are usually well trained as well, so you can see how they should be pruned.

Classes are taught at many community colleges, park districts, garden centers, and other facilities that will instruct you in plant care. Take advantage of them. Many garden centers have trained staff people who can answer questions or demonstrate how to do certain gardening chores.

MAY

SHRUBS

PLANNING

Many of the most spectacular shrubs are in bloom—**rhododendrons**, **Koreanspice viburnums**, **lilacs**, and **vanhoutte spirea**. Some of the most fragrant are the **Koreanspice viburnums**, which are outstanding for a couple of weeks in May. When they are in bloom, the fragrance fills the air, especially in the evening. Open the windows and let it in! Isn't there some way to bottle it?

As the shrubs progress through the blooming season, make note of how they flower, whether they blend in with one another and other plants blooming at the same time. Also notice whether they are showing off at their best. White flowers against a white house may be lost, for instance.

Record all of your observations in a garden journal. A journal does not need to be fancy. A spiral notebook is good enough. Put the year at the top of a page. Then record the date you make an observation. Refer to your notes when you are making plans or contemplating a change.

Keep your garden plans in the journal, too, and list the names of things you plant, where they came from, and when you planted them. If you ever need to replace a **yew** in the middle of a hedge, you will know how important it is to know the variety and source are.

PLANTING

Containerized shrubs can be planted all summer. Nurseries and garden centers are aware of the popularity of plants in bloom and will usually have excellent displays of the various kinds while they are blooming.

If you see a **rhododendron** in bloom, for instance, and just must add one to your garden, now is the time to do it. **Rhododendrons** are extremely particular about their situation:

• Soil must be deep and well drained.

• The pH of the soil must be neutral or lower, though some kinds grow in soils with a higher pH.

• These shade plants need protection from midday sun in summer and winter.

Check the labels of the plants you buy. They provide planting instructions and often the peculiar requirements of the plants.

CARE

I like to carry my pocket knife as I tour the garden. I have a couple of pieces of old garden hose slit down one side so that they fit over my index finger and thumb, protecting them from being cut and from thorns or slivers. With one hand, I cut broken or diseased stems, old flowers, and insect-infested shoots as I see them. If I wear my gardening apron, I can deposit the offending pieces in the pouch for discarding in the compost or trash.

Rhododendron

WATERING

Sometimes late May turns dry. Be prepared to water new shrubs. A soaker hose or leaky pipe works well without getting the leaves wet. The water goes in the ground instead of over the walk, on the grass, or in the neighbor's yard.

FERTILIZING

Apply a balanced fertilizer such as 10-10-10 to your shrubs once in spring. One pound per 100 square feet under the plants is sufficient.

PESTS

As the temperatures rise, aphids and mites increase in numbers. Keep a close watch. Control these insects with insecticidal soap.

Oystershell scale insects can destroy shrub plantings.

Spray infested plants when the **vanhoutte spirea** is in bloom. Use insecticidal soap or summer horticultural oil, and repeat the treatment in 2 weeks.

Lilac borers attack **lilacs**. Spray **lilac** stems with lindane, permethrin, or acephate (from a hose-end sprayer) when the **vanhoutte spirea** is in bloom. Repeat in 4 weeks.

If your **mugo pine bush** jumps at you when you walk by it, it may be infested with pine sawflies. These caterpillars cluster on a shoot and all jump at the same time when disturbed. Put on a glove, and wipe the pine sawflies off the shoot. Or spray with carbaryl.

Continue spraying susceptible plants for foliar diseases as long as weather is wet.

Use thiophanate-methyl or triforine fungicides. (See the Pest Control Recommendations beginning on page 281.)

Weeds may appear at this time. Hoe out any weeds that show up. Pull those that you cannot reach with the hoe. Once shrubs develop a dense canopy of foliage, the weeds usually stop germinating. A 2- or 3-inch mulch of shredded bark will keep weeds out if the area was weed free before the mulch was applied.

PRUNING

As soon as **yews** and other evergreen shrubs have begun to grow, winter damage can be seen. Just because a stem has brown leaves does not mean it is dead, however. If these shoots are growing from the tips, do not remove them. Snip out any stems not growing now. The holes left where they were removed will fill in during the season.

Continue pruning spring-flowering shrubs as they finish blooming. **Lilacs** and **viburnums** need annual pruning to have fresh, new stems for prolific flowering each spring. Remove $1/4$ of the oldest stems all the way to the ground. Head back overly long stems to side shoots growing in the same direction.

HELPFUL HINTS

Throughout this book I mention applying an insect-control product when a certain plant is in bloom, when leaves are starting, flowers falling, or seeds ripening. Insects develop according to the weather. If the season is early, the bugs are early, too. Watching how plants are developing will tell you exactly when to treat for insects. This science is called *phenology*.

The correct timing for many insects was worked out by Donald Orton, and his book Coincide includes the details. See the bibliography at the end of this book for information on this and other references.

JUNE

SHRUBS

PLANNING

Some shrubs are still in bloom, but most of the spring-flowering kinds are finished.

Mock orange is the main flowering shrub in June. It has a magnificent fragrance that reminds me of the **orange** groves I lived near in Southern California when I was a youngster.

Mock orange

A large flowering shrub, **Japanese lilac**, flowers in June, too. It makes huge panicles of white flowers that are fragrant. If you like the fragrance as I do, they are great. If the fragrance bothers you, avoid them.

Leaves are fully out on most of the shrubs, and some have already set terminal buds. Take a good look at your plantings.

• Are they doing what you want them to do?

• Have they overgrown their current situations?

• Are they bare at the bottoms with all the leaves a fringe at the top?

• Did they flower as they should?

Sometimes corrective pruning will restore the plants and improve flowering. Sometimes replacement of the plants is the best option.

Make plans to do what is necessary to improve the plantings. You can do some of this work immediately. You may need to postpone other work until fall or next spring. List the things that need to be done. Plan carefully for replacement plants. Do not make the same mistakes again.

PLANTING

With the availability of container-grown plants, the planting season is limited only by extremely hot weather and by winter. In reality, plants are installed just about every month of the year by professional landscape contractors.

If you planned to do some planting in the spring but were unable to get to it, there is still time before the onset of hot, dry weather.

1. Prepare the planting site according to your plans. Container-grown plants tend to be small, and the inclination is to plant them too close together. If you follow your plan, they will be spaced properly. Although they may look a little funny, they will grow.

2. Dig the planting holes slightly less deep than and twice as wide as the containers.

3. After knocking the plants out of the containers, shake as much of the artificial soil off the balls, and mix it with the soil going back into the planting holes. Containerized plants are grown in artificial soil mixes. When these are planted in native soils, they stay too wet, and roots are not able to grow out of them into the surrounding soil.

4. Set the plants in the holes, backfill halfway, and fill the holes with water.

5. Replace the remaining soil, and water again to settle the soil.

WATERING

If June develops to be hot and dry, water all newly planted shrubs every week or more often if they wilt. Established shrubs may need water. Watch them for wilting, too. If the plants wilt, soak them thoroughly.

Berry plants setting fruit will need water to produce a full crop. Soak the **blueberries, raspberries, currants,** and **gooseberries** once every 10 to 15 days. Keep the leaves dry to prevent diseases.

FERTILIZING

Once the plants have made their seasonal growth, there is little need for fertilizer. Late fertilization may interfere with winter dormancy.

PESTS

Various insects may harm your shrubs. Treat aphids and mites with insecticidal soap as soon as you notice them. Control leaf-eating beetles and caterpillars with carbaryl.

Viburnum crown borers will destroy the plants if not treated.

Apply lindane or permethrin to the **viburnum** crowns when the **mock oranges** are blooming. Repeat every 3 weeks until August. Apply the second treatment for lilac borers.

Euonymous scale affects several other shrubs as well.

Spray **euonymous** with acephate from a hose-end sprayer, insecticidal soap, or summer horticultural oil when the **catalpa** and **Japanese tree lilacs** are in bloom.

Examine the plants for pests regularly. Several kinds of beetles, mealybugs, leaf hoppers, plant bugs, and others will sometimes become troublesome.

Treat plants if needed.

Once wet weather subsides, foliar diseases are less troublesome. Most leaf spot infestations take place in spring, and spraying now has no effect on them.

Weeds are sources of insect problems.

Hoe weeds out as you see them. Apply a shredded bark mulch to keep them out.

PRUNING

Hedges that have completed their first flushes of growth can be sheared now. Do not cut off all the new leaves. Shape the plants so that they are wider at the bottoms than at the tops. Bottom leaves that do not receive enough light will be shed, leaving the plants bare at the bottoms.

Remove old blooms from flowering shrubs. These plants can be pruned now as well. Hurry. They will soon set flower buds for next year. Late pruning will remove them.

HELPFUL HINTS

Once again, visit your favorite public garden to see what is in bloom now. Are there some things that would do well in your garden? If so, write the names down. Most of these gardens are excellent about tagging the plants. If you have questions, there are usually plant information people around who can answer them for you.

Become familiar with the botanic gardens, arboreta, and other public gardens in your area. They are some of the best places to learn about plants. Some local garden centers and nurseries are equally good. They construct display gardens and usually label the plants. Some have Master Gardeners on hand at certain hours, and the salespeople are happy to answer questions, too.

JULY

SHRUBS

PLANNING

Even though school has been out for weeks, summer does not seem to get here until the Fourth of July. Then the rush of spring is over, and it is vacation time.

It is time to enjoy the garden. The spring-flowering shrubs are finished for the season. Summer-flowering shrubs are less spectacular. They just seem to be there. Maybe it is because there are so many other things in bloom.

As I walk through the garden, I do not see the shrubs; they are providing the framework in which everything else exists. They are doing their jobs when they are not noticed. But if they were not there, they would certainly be missed.

Shrubs are the substance of landscape plantings. They create the transition from the lawn to the home. If the planting is well designed, shrubs point the way to the entrance of the home. They identify the boundaries of spaces—the public areas of your property and the private areas. They provide the background for the flowers and separate your yard from all the neighbors' yards. The flowers are a bonus.

PLANTING

July is not a good time to plant shrubs. They can suffer from the heat, and they have a tough time making roots when the foodstuffs are being used just to stay alive.

CARE

Blueberries and **raspberries** are ready for harvesting. Pick them as soon as they are ripe so that the birds do not get them first. You may need to put netting over the **blueberries** to keep the birds out.

WATERING

Make sure the shrubs get enough water during hot, dry weather. Soak them by laying the hose at the bases and letting water run slowly until the water runs off. Soakers and leaky pipe can be strung under the shrubs and all of them watered at one time.

Leaky pipe is a porous rubber hose that sweats water. It keeps the water where it will do the most good.

FERTILIZING

Shrubs do not need fertilizer during the summer. Most of them have finished their growth for the year. Forcing new growth may result in injury next winter.

PESTS

Japanese beetles make their appearance this month. They are slow-moving beetles, metallic green and bronze in color. They make lace of the foliage on certain shrubs and other plants.

Pick them off, and collect them in a plastic bag. Leave the bag in the sun for a few days to kill the beetles, and then dispose of it in the trash. Carbaryl controls them, but not until they have done a lot of damage.

Aphids and mites are always threats.

Spray for them whenever they appear. Use insecticidal soap.

Other leaf-eating beetles and caterpillars may be present in July.

Use carbaryl to control them.

Foliar diseases are not severe at this time of the season. Canker diseases begin to show up as dying twigs and branches as the weather becomes hot. These diseases invade the plants as a result of winter injury. They cannot be controlled now. Prune out dead twigs.

HELPFUL HINTS

Shrubs should not be burdensome plants in your landscape. They should mind their own business with a little pruning and some water if it is dry. If they are taking a lot of time, they may be poor choices for the spot where they are planted.

Properly selected shrubs will not outgrow their situations. They will not have serious disease or insect problems.

If your shrub plantings are causing you to have a headache, find out why, and make corrections.

Weeds harbor insects and diseases. Get rid of them as soon as they appear.

Birds may go after your berries.

Cover berry plantings with netting to prevent birds from getting the crop before you do.

PRUNING

Trim **yews** and **junipers**. Do not shear these plants unless they are in hedges. Clip out entire overgrown branches, leaving shorter ones in the same place. Use a knife or clippers. I prefer the knife and rubber-hose guards for my thumb and index finger.

Remove the old fruiting canes from brambles as soon as the berries are picked. They will not fruit again. Pinch back the tips of new canes on **black raspberries** and **blackberries**.

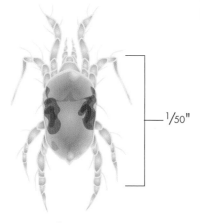

Spider Mite

1/50"

AUGUST

SHRUBS

PLANNING

By August, heat and drought may have taken their toll on the lawn and the flower garden, but the shrubs do not seem to mind, especially the evergreens and the **cotoneasters**. The plants with the tiny leaves are fine. A little water every couple of weeks is all they require at this time of the season.

Shrubs are great for attracting wildlife. Sitting on the porch, I watched several small birds, probably vireos or warblers, flitting around, catching something in the **tree lilacs**. They must have been small insects, but I never was able to see what they were. It was fun to see the birds so busy.

They suddenly flew off chirping nervously. The squirrel was arriving to see if he could figure a way to get to the bird feeder from there. It is placed far enough away that he cannot jump to it, but he still tries. He cannot get around the baffle on the post, either. For the time being, the seed is for the birds only.

Shrubs provide shelter for the animals. They provide seeds and evidently bugs, too. Later, some of the shrubs will have berries for the animals to eat. In return we get entertainment and company. Sometimes we need to just sit and enjoy what we have.

PLANTING

August is not a good time to plant shrubs. There are potted plants at the nurseries and garden centers, but the weather is too hot for them to get a good start. If you have no choice, plant now, but give the plants plenty of water, and syringe them a couple of times a day to cool them off.

CARE

Blueberries, **blackberries**, and **raspberries** are ripening now. At first there are just a few, enough for topping breakfast cereal in the morning or maybe ice cream in the evening. Pick them before the birds do. Try to avoid the temptation to pick a few and eat them every time you tour the garden. Take a pan, and pick some for the family, too.

WATERING

August can be very dry. If it is, water the shrubs every couple of weeks. Set a slowly running hose under the plants, and soak them until the water begins to run off. Soakers or leaky pipe put the water into the ground where it will do some good.

Pay particular attention to newly planted shrubs. They have small root systems struggling to get started. Water them when they need it, but do not drown them.

FERTILIZING

Do not fertilize shrubs now. Wait until after the first frost so that the plants are not delayed in becoming dormant for the winter. New growth forced now will not have time to harden off.

PESTS

Japanese beetles are still around, but in fewer numbers than a couple of weeks ago.

Pick them off, or spray with carbaryl if many are feeding on your plants.

Mites like hot weather. A few will become masses in just a few days.

Keep a close watch for them, and spray them if you see any. Use insecticidal soap or summer horticultural oil, or use dicofol or bifenthrin if they are out of hand and destroying your plants.

Mildew will appear on the leaves when the days are hot and evenings cool. These weather conditions bring on the heavy dew common in late summer. Mildew grows when leaves stay wet overnight. The disease is unsightly, but does little harm to the plants this late in the season. **Lilacs**, **viburnums**, **witch-hazels**, and some other varieties will be affected, especially if they are in the shade.

Use triforine or thiophanate-methyl fungicides to prevent the disease and to kill the fungus on the leaves. The leaves will still be marked up where they were injured by the disease. Usually, I ignore the problem.

Weeds are less troublesome now, but the ones that survive will produce seeds to start the problem again next year.

Keep hoeing!

PRUNING

Hedges can be sheared one more time this year. Do not remove all the new green growth. The plants need some leaves. If the plants are getting too big each year, consider cutting them back a little farther in the early spring so there is room for them to grow. If the plants are cut back to the same place every time, a knot develops at that point. Cut these knots off each spring, and cut a little farther out each time you shear during the season.

As soon as all the berries are gone from the brambles, pull out the old canes. Pinch the new tops of the **blackberries** and **black raspberries** at about 30 inches tall. Do not summer top **red raspberries**.

Remove diseased, damaged, or dead branches from all other shrubs. No severe pruning should be done to them now. It might force soft shoots that would be damaged by the winter.

Blackberry

HELPFUL HINTS

Sometimes, bugs are not worth spraying. If there are so few that they do no harm, let the natural predators handle them. Lady bugs and lacewings eat aphids, scales, and mealybugs. Assassin bugs and others feed on soft-bodied insects such as caterpillars. Many flies parasitize insect pests. Wasps and hornets catch insects to feed their young. Spraying insecticides harms the predators, too; use the least harmful material if you must spray.

Sometimes it is just as easy to snip off a single shoot if it is covered with aphids or to pick off the caterpillar or Japanese beetle as it is to mix and apply a pesticide. You should wear gloves to mix chemicals, and if you are squeamish, you can wear them to pick off the bugs too.

SEPTEMBER

SHRUBS

PLANNING

Labor Day is really the start of the fall season. School is back in session. Regular activities resume after the summer hiatus.

We have lost nearly three hours of daylight since the first day of summer. Meteorological fall started September 1, and official fall starts the third week of the month. (The date varies from year to year.)

Sumac is turning red. I see a few golden leaves on the **alpine currants**. And the pace of our activities quickens with the cooler weather. We sense along with other creatures that winter is not too distant and there are many things to do. Although there are still summerlike days ahead, the hint of fall is in the air, and the season is dwindling.

PLANTING

Fall is planting season. Almost all deciduous shrubs can be planted in the fall. The **rhododendrons** and the shrubby small fruit are best planted in spring, however.

Container-grown, balled-and-burlapped, and bare-root plants are once again plentiful in the nurseries and garden centers. The plants are not in bloom, but the labels should have good color pictures. Before you head to the nursery, know what you want. Otherwise, you may be swayed by the pretty pictures and glowing descriptions.

Bare-root plants have been out of the ground for a while and may have dried out a bit. Soak bare-root plants before planting them.

Container plants are grown in artificial soils that are quite different from the soils in your garden. After knocking these plants out of the containers, slice any circling roots, and shake as much of the artificial soil mix from the ball as you can without damaging the roots. Mix it with the soil going back into the planting hole.

To plant balled-and-burlapped plants, follow these steps:

1. After setting a balled-and-burlapped plant in the planting hole, remove the twine and burlap.

2. Shove the burlap down to the bottom of the planting hole, or cut it off and remove it.

3. Try to find balled-and-burlapped plants grown in a soil as nearly like the soil in your yard. Setting a ball of a very different soil in your soil will cause an interface problem.

4. If you have no choice, shave soil from the ball, and mix it with the soil going back into the planting hole. Mixing the soils will reduce the difference and should help the roots survive and grow.

CARE

Fall-bearing **raspberries** are ripening now. The berries seem to be sweeter when they ripen in cooler weather. Maybe they have more sugars because they develop more slowly. Pick them before the birds do. Be sure to eat a few fresh from the garden. Protect the bearing canes after these plants are picked off. They will bear again in spring.

Raspberries

If you are not interested in summer berries, mow these plants down to the ground in early spring. The new canes will bear in fall. This system eliminates a lot of work. Many pick-your-own farms are resorting to this method of growing **raspberries**. Large fall crops can be processed, frozen, or made into preserves.

WATERING

Fall usually brings more regular rainfall. If it turns out dry, water the shrubs every 3 weeks or so. Use a slowly running hose under the plants, or use soakers or leaky pipe. Make sure the ground is soaked to running off.

PESTS

Bug problems are less troublesome in fall. An exception is the whitefly, which is at a maximum late in the season.

Adults can be knocked down with pyrethrin or resmethrin sprays. The larvae under the leaves are susceptible to insecticidal soap. Freezing weather and leaf drop will solve the problem for the year. These insects do not overwinter here if the weather is severe. Usually, they are brought in on plants from elsewhere.

HELPFUL HINTS

Most shrubs are hardy and will stand winter weather without trouble. Newly planted shrubs and brambles may benefit from 4 to 6 inches of mulch over the roots. Applied now, the mulch will be attractive to voles, which will build nests in it. If they are close to a tasty shrub, they have it made for the winter, but the plants will not make it through the winter.

Wait until the ground has frozen before mulching these plants. The mulch should keep the ground frozen, preventing freezing and thawing. The best insulation is 6 inches of snow.

Mildew that shows up this late in the season does the plants no harm. It is unsightly, but not worth the effort to stop it. Affected leaves will still be unsightly even if the mildew is killed. Raking up old leaves in the fall might lessen the problem next year.

Weeds still appear. Hoeing is the solution.

The winter annuals and perennials germinating from new seed are starting now. They will survive the winter and be pests next spring if not removed. Grasses are the most trouble in the shrub border. They grow between the stems of the shrubs where they are impossible to hoe and hard to pull.

Spraying them with fluazifop-P-butyl grass killer while they are small kills grass but not broadleaf plants.

Begin thinking about how you will protect your shrubs from the ravages of wildlife this winter.

Look in your journal notes from last winter. Which treatments worked? Which ones were failures? You don't have notes from last year?

Start a journal. Throughout this book, I emphasize the importance of a gardening journal. Use a spiral notebook, and record anything you think might be useful to you in the future. Record successes, and record failures so that you do not repeat them.

Stock up on chicken wire or hardware cloth for cages and collars, and the repellents you will need to protect the plants from rabbits, mice, and deer.

PRUNING

Limit pruning to removing diseased, damaged, or broken stems. Late pruning may stimulate soft growth that will not harden off for winter.

OCTOBER

SHRUBS

PLANNING

Bright, sunny days and cool nights bring out the best of fall color. The **sumac** has been bright red for weeks. Now it is joined by **arrowwood viburnums, burning bushes, choke cherries, spicebushes, smoke bushes, hedge maples, fothergillas, witchhazels, amelanchiers**, and others too numerous to mention.

Visit your favorite botanic garden or arboretum to see plants in full color. Take your notebook and camera with you. Note the plants that might be appropriate in your garden. Keep in mind: something that looks the right size when it is out in the open might look a lot bigger when it is in your yard. Take a tape measure with you. You may want to measure the space in your yard before you leave, so you know how much room you have.

Once you have selected suitable plants, check with local suppliers for the availability of plants. Some plants that look really good are not grown for sale. Some are too hard to grow or to transplant. Others are seldom requested by home gardeners. Once in a while the nurseries have a similar selection that is much better than the species.

PLANTING

October is an excellent time to plant shrubs. The plants are dormant, so bare-root and balled-and-burlapped plants are being dug fresh every day instead of standing in a holding area where they have been since spring. Container plants are always in good condition. They can be planted anytime except when the ground is frozen.

Witchhazel

To plant bare-root or container-grown shrubs, follow these steps:

1. Dig planting holes as deep as and twice as wide as the roots on the plants.

2. Soak bare-root plants before planting them.

3. Knock container-grown plants out of the containers, slice any circling roots, and shake as much of the artificial soil mix from the ball as you can without damaging the roots. Mix it with the soil going back into the planting hole.

4. Backfill the planting holes halfway with soil.

5. Fill with water and then the rest of the soil.

6. Soak with water to settle the soil, and the plants are ready to begin making roots.

To plant a balled-and-burlapped shrub, follow these steps:

1. After setting a balled-and-burlapped plant in the planting hole, remove the twine and burlap.

2. Shove the burlap down to the bottom of the planting hole, or cut it off and remove it.

3. Try to find a balled-and-burlapped plant grown in soil similar to that in your yard. Planting a ball of a very different soil into the soil in your yard will cause an interface problem.

4. If you have no choice, shave soil from the ball, and mix it with the soil going back into

the planting hole. Mixing the soils will reduce the difference and should help the roots survive and grow.

5. Backfill the planting hole halfway with soil.

6. Fill with water and then the rest of the soil.

7. Soak with water to settle the soil once more, and the plant is ready to begin making roots.

CARE

As leaves fall, rake them up, and spread them over the beds in the vegetable garden or put them in the compost pile. Left under the shrubs, they can harbor diseases. Leaves that fall from the trees do not add to the disease problem, but they look messy and if left over winter are soggy and hard to get out.

WATERING

Unless fall is unusually dry, only the newly planted shrubs will need watering. Soak each thoroughly after planting and once or twice a month.

FERTILIZING

Starter fertilizer may be used the first time new plants are watered. Use a high-phosphate fertilizer such as Take Hold 10-52-17 or something similar. Use according to package directions.

PESTS

Most insect problems cease with a hard freeze and dropping of the leaves.

Deal with scales, and eggs of aphids and mites in spring using dormant oil.

Raking old leaves will reduce the carryover of diseases. Making sure the plants go into the winter fully dormant and well watered will reduce the chances of winter injury and canker diseases next year.

Grassy weeds and winter annuals such as chickweed may still be problems. Hoe them out or pull them as they show up.

No special animal problems occur at this time.

Check your materials for winter protection: chicken wire or hardware cloth for cages and collars, and repellents to protect the plants from rabbits, mice, and deer. Make an effective repellent by adding Tabasco sauce to a gallon of water. Add some soap or spreader-sticker so that it stays on the plants. Or buy a proprietary brand from the garden center.

PRUNING

Limit pruning to removal of diseased, damaged, or broken branches. Overly long branches that might be broken by the snow can be headed back. Sometimes plants make extra long, vigorous shoots that are too big for the plants. They look out of place and usually are too vigorous to set flower buds anyway.

HELPFUL HINTS

• Prepare to bundle up the upright evergreens and other plants that tend to be spread apart by the snow load. Use binder twine or burlap. Do not cover the plants with plastic. They will be cooked on sunny days even if the temperatures are low.

• If your evergreens along the front are hammered by snow sliding off the roof, consider building snow sheds to protect them. Make them of plywood sheets attached to sloping 2-by-4 frames, and set them over the plantings in fall. The snow that slides from the roof lands on the snow sheds and slides to the ground. Make the slope steep enough that snow does not stick to the roof of the snow shed. Snow is heavy, so the sheds must be strong enough to withstand the weight and the impact.

SHRUBS

PLANNING

Now that the leaves have fallen, examine the shrubs in your garden. It is easier to see the structure and the problems—borer damage, places where the mice and rabbits were gnawing last spring, and where the kids landed during the hide-and-seek game last summer.

Also note where pruning is needed. Determine which branches need to be removed after the plants have finished blooming next spring. By then the leaves will have made it very difficult to see.

Some of these items can be handled this winter. Others will need treating at the appropriate time next season.

Make notes in your journal. I hope my nagging has convinced you to start one.

PLANTING

There is time to plant as long as the ground is not frozen. Time is getting short, however. If you have some shrubs to plant and they are stored aboveground, they can be severely damaged by low temperatures. At 10 degrees above zero Fahrenheit, roots will be killed. Plant these shrubs as soon as possible. If a

cold snap is predicted and you cannot plant them, set them as close together as you can, ball to ball, and cover them with straw and a tarp. I have seen many fine plants ruined while they sat above ground waiting to be planted.

CARE

Fall cleanup is important to keep the plantings looking tidy. Be persistent. Usually, the day after you have picked up everything, a windstorm blows all the neighbors' leaves into your yard. Expect it, and you will not be quite so frustrated.

I have considered putting netting over the low-growing **cranberry cotoneasters** in front. That might keep out the big **sycamore** leaves that fall late and usually collect there. After everything else has dropped its leaves, that tree is full and green. Then suddenly, usually about the end of November, all the leaves drop. I think I will try that this year.

WATERING

It is important that shrubs go into winter well watered. Evergreens under overhanging eaves are especially vulnerable to desiccation in winter. Soak them before the ground freezes.

Cranberry cotoneaster

FERTILIZING

Fertilizer can be applied after the plants are fully dormant.

It will be available to the plants when roots begin to develop in early spring. Use a balanced material such as 10-10-10 or the equivalent. Apply 1 pound per 100 square feet of shrub bed.

PESTS

As the weather cools off, but before it freezes up, get ready for rabbits and deer.

Apply the repellent for rabbits and deer. It needs to dry after application before it freezes or it will not stick. Some years cold weather starts early, so be prepared.

Install the wire collars and cages for deer control. For larger areas or where fence is not practical, wire cages are the only sure way to protect valuable plants such as **yews**.

Snow fences will keep deer out of small areas, particularly if they think there is no room for them to land on the other side. Usually, a space 25 by 50 feet is safe. If the area is full of bushes, the deer may think it is not a safe place to land there, either. The fence needs to be tight to the ground. Even if deer think it is not safe to jump the fence, they will try to get under it. In fact, they are more likely to go under fences than over them.

Voles can attack shrubs.

Pull any old mulch away from the bases of the shrubs so that the voles do not get the idea that they can spend the winter there. Do not spread any fresh mulch until the ground is frozen.

PRUNING

Limit any pruning to removal of diseased, damaged, or broken branches. Start major pruning around Valentine's Day.

HELPFUL HINTS

• Before they freeze and burst, drain and roll up the hoses and soakers. The leaky pipes drain themselves, so they will not pop from freezing, but they will be stiff and tough to pull out of the shrub beds and roll up.

• Attractive shrub plantings, whether they are evergreens or deciduous, lend themselves well to decorating for the winter holidays. To avoid doing this when the temperature is zero and the wind is blowing, I usually string the lights as soon as the fall cleanup is finished. The weather is mild, and I can take my time doing it. It gives me time to test them to make sure they all work and to replace the ones that do not. In past years, trying to get the lights up the last minute resulted in frustration instead of enjoyment. In our town, the official beginning of the season is the day after Thanksgiving. That is when I turn on the lights the first time.

When the ground freezes, mulch the shrubs planted this fall as well as the brambles and berries. Use shredded bark, compost, or other materials you may find at reasonable cost.

• Bundle up the upright plants that are spread open by snow.

Install the snow sheds before the ground freezes and you cannot drive stakes.

Set up burlap screens to protect **rhododendrons** from winter sun and wind, and to protect shrubs from salt spray.

Prepare the places where snow can be piled. It cannot be piled on the shrubs without danger of breaking them. Any salt in the snow will burn the plants and filter into the soil.

Collect the garden tools, clean and sharpen them, and store them where you can find them when you need them.

DECEMBER

SHRUBS

CARE

Bundle upright evergreens with burlap or binder twine. Do not cover them with clear plastic or they will be cooked on sunny days.

Foundation plantings can be protected with snow sheds if snow tends to slide off your roof. In some parts of the country where it snows more than it does here, structures are used routinely to protect plants. They are usually made of plywood sheets attached to sloping 2-by-4 frames, then they are set over the plantings in fall. The snow that slides from the roofs lands on the snow sheds and slides to the ground. The slope must be sufficient so that the snow does not stick to the roof of the snow shed.

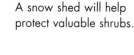

A snow shed will help protect valuable shrubs.

Snow is heavy; these structures must be strong enough to withstand the weight and the impact.

Because summer storage can be a problem, make the sheds so that you can knock them down and put them away.

WATERING

Make sure all the shrubs are well watered before the ground freezes. Take the hose out and water them, paying particular attention to the ones under overhangs. Evergreens, often expensive **yews**, are killed every year by desiccation. I see it all the time. Clients call in spring when the **yews** turn brown. Digging under the shrubs, I often find the ground powder dry. What a shame. Do not let your plants suffer in this way.

All newly planted shrubs are in jeopardy, too. Give them sufficient water, then drain and roll the hose back up. Keep it handy. If the winter is mild and

dry, you may need to water again in January.

FERTILIZING

Since the plants are fully dormant, fertilizer can be applied anytime the ground is not frozen or covered with snow. It will be available to the plants when roots begin to develop in early spring. Use a balanced material such as 10-10-10 or the equivalent. Apply 1 pound per 100 square feet of shrub bed.

PESTS

Get ready to protect your shrubs from animals.

Install all the cages, collars, and fences. If voles are evident, set out brodifacoum (D-con) in containers so that the other animals and birds cannot get the poison. See page 169 for ideas on making these containers.

PRUNING

Limit pruning to removing damaged branches. While the lights are on the bushes, pruning is difficult. There is the danger of cutting a wire. Removing branches may mean restringing the lights, too.

TREES

Trees create the framework and the backdrop for our landscapes. They provide shade and often have flowers. These large plants need to be carefully located in the planting plan. Their care as they develop will determine whether they become assets or liabilities.

Dwarf fruit trees can be fun in the garden, providing flowers in spring and fresh fruit, too. They require regular care to produce a luscious, wholesome crop.

Tree planting is a gift to future generations. Planting trees is hard work and can be a major investment. Planting must be done correctly at the proper time of year to increase the chances of the trees' survival.

Pruning to create the proper structure as trees grow is essential. Most home gardeners can prune small trees, but larger trees demand the expertise and the equipment of professional arborists.

Many pests can affect your trees. Keeping them under control requires intelligent use of available measures at the correct time. Nearly all pests have stages when they are susceptible to control measures. Treatments made at inappropriate times will not be effective.

CHAPTER EIGHT

DECIDING WHERE TO PLANT TREES

The mature sizes of the trees are important in selecting planting sites. Choose carefully because trees live a long time:

• Locate large shade trees away from the house so that they will have room to develop without severe pruning.

Deciduous shade trees provide shade during the summer and allow sunlight to get through in the winter. Place them on the south and west sides of the house. Evergreen trees and some deciduous trees that hold their leaves all winter should be set to the north. Avoid hiding the house with ornamental trees, but set them to frame the house.

• Use smaller trees under power lines.

A common error is situating large trees under power lines or in other restricted areas. As those under power lines grow, they encounter the lines and must be trimmed for clearance, and the shapes of the trees are ruined.

• Buy small trees that can grow to full size in small spots.

Many times big trees are planted in corners or on the patio next to the house. These trees begin to hit the structures, interfere with gutters, or hide windows, and must be severely pruned to fit. Japanese tree lilacs, ornamental pears, redbuds, hawthorns, and crabapples are 20 to 30 feet high at maturity. Narrow, upright (fastigiate) cultivars of many species can be planted in tight spaces next to buildings.

Plant fruit trees where there is room enough to care for them. For a full crop, they will need full sun, spraying, and pruning.

PLANTING TREES

Select trees that will grow without too many difficulties in your location:

• Do not plant trees that need acidic conditions if you have limy soil.

• Select plants that will grow in your climatic zone.

Some species are not hardy in all parts of the state. Even more important, subtypes of some common species may not be hardy in certain areas. Red maples grown from seed collected in Georgia are unlikely to survive in Rockford, Illinois, or Angola, Indiana. Redbuds from a southern mail-order nursery may be killed to the ground every winter in Battle Creek, Michigan, while native redbuds grow normally along the St. Joseph River in Berrien County.

Ask a local nurseryman about the source of the plants.

• Avoid soil incompatibility problems.

Buy trees grown in soil as nearly like that in your yard as you can find.

Most trees are grown in containers or are dug, then balled and burlapped. Follow these steps to plant a tree:

1. Dig the planting hole at the same depth as or slightly shallower than the depth of the ball of the plant. The hole should be at least twice the diameter of the ball.

2. In poor soil, set the plant higher, and hill up soil to cover the ball.

3. Remove the plant from the container.

4. Slice any circling roots. If the plants were growing in an artificial soil mix, carefully shake off as much of it as possible, and mix it with the soil from the planting holes.

5. Set the plant in the planting hole.

6. Remove the twine and burlap from a balled-and-burlapped tree, and shove it down in the hole.

7. Replace the soil.

8. Water thoroughly to settle the soil.

CHAPTER EIGHT

WATERING

Keep a newly planted tree watered the first year, but do not drown it.

During dry weather, give established trees at least 1 inch of water per week. Run a sprinkler to soak the entire area under the tree. Set a coffee can under the sprinkler to measure the amount of water. When the desired amount is in the coffee can, turn off the water. Large trees may be injured by drought even before the leaves look wilted.

PEST CONTROL

Diseases and insects will attack trees.

Some kinds of trees, such as crabapples and hawthorns, are very susceptible to diseases. Select cultivars that have disease resistance. Without resistance, trees will have diseases in wet spring weather. Many times the disease does not hurt the trees, but it is unsightly. Spraying as the leaves open in spring is helpful, but timing is important. Spraying large trees will need the services of a professional arborist.

Many sucking, chewing, or boring insects will invade trees. Some are annoying, but others are severely damaging and need to be controlled. Bronze birch borer, for instance, will kill white birches if not treated. Apply the correct material at the right time.

Fruit trees are very susceptible to insect and disease attack. Spray them at the right time to produce injury-free fruit.

Although trees are large plants, they are easily injured.

• Roots are often shallow, in the upper foot of soil.

Trampling roots will destroy them. Do not use black plastic under mulch because it suffocates them.

• Chemicals may injure trees, too.

Check that any lawn-care applications are safe for the trees before using them.

• Lawn mower or weed whacker damage to the trunks can allow canker diseases into the trees, girdling them several years later.

• Raised planters built around the bases of trees or mulch piled high on the trunks will keep them too wet, causing rotting of the bark and eventually loss of the trees.

Properly selected and well-maintained trees are assets. The wrong trees, poorly cared for, can become nuisances and may even be liabilities. Cost of repair or removal can be substantial. Give your trees the care they need.

PRUNING

As they grow, trees need pruning to develop into well-shaped, desirable plants. Small flowering trees need pruning to keep them attractive. Most gardeners can prune small trees, but professionals with the equipment and expertise to do the job safely should trim large ones.

Fruit trees require specialized trimming to develop the proper structure and productive wood. Some fruit on current season growth, others on wood produced the previous year. Various kinds need to be pruned at different times during the season.

JANUARY
TREES

 PLANNING

If you have big trees, examine them to make sure they are healthy and properly located. If some are in jeopardy, plan to replace them. Trees have finite lives. Big, old trees will live only so long and begin to deteriorate.

In treeless areas, you should try to plant trees as soon as possible. Follow these steps to help you make wise decisions in selecting and planting trees:

1. Draw a plan of your property on graph paper. Make it to scale if you can.

2. Locate trees on the plan so that they will provide shade, screening, and background, and will frame the house.

3. Go through the tree lists to pick out kinds that will fit your property.

 PLANTING

January is not the time to plant trees in the Midwest.

 CARE

After each storm, check the condition of your trees. Look for broken branches, splits where the limbs may be pulling the tree apart, or other injuries. Look closely around the bottoms of young trees for rodent damage.

 WATERING

If the winter is mild and dry, plants may dry out during the winter. On a mild day, water trees under overhangs or where the ground is exposed to sun and drying winds.

 FERTILIZING

Fertilizer can be applied during the winter when the ground is not frozen and the trees are dormant. Broadcast the fertilizer under the trees, or bore holes under the drip lines of the trees and fill them with the appropriate amount of fertilizer. The alternative is to hire a commercial arborist to fertilize the trees. Fertilizer applied now will be available to the trees as roots begin to grow in late winter.

 PESTS

Rabbits, voles, and deer are the most likely creatures to injure trees in winter. Rabbits and voles will feed on thin bark of young trees. They are able to girdle trees so that they die about the time they start leafing out in spring. Protect trees with collars around the bases. Make them tall enough so that rabbits cannot stand on the snow and feed over them.

Voles will take up residence in litter, mulch, or leaves around the bases of the trees, or under snow around them. Pull back anything around the trunks of the trees, and walk down the snow to pack it so that voles cannot run underneath it.

 PRUNING

Winter is a good time to prune large, established trees. Without leaves, the structure is easy to see. Experienced tree workers can tell the living from the dead wood even in winter. Hire certified arborists.

It is too early for pruning fruit trees or small flowering trees.

FEBRUARY

TREES

PLANNING

Notice the problems affecting your trees:

• Rabbits and voles will eat bark of young fruit trees, **pines**, and other thin-barked trees.

If rabbits can stand on the snow and reach over the protective collars, they can girdle the trees very quickly.

• Rabbits and deer will eat twigs that they can reach.

Dwarf fruit trees with low branches will be badly damaged if all the low branches are gone. The crop will be reduced, too. Small shade trees trying to get a start may be disfigured if they lose their branches and leader. This will set back their development for years.

• Ice and snow can damage trees. Following a storm, trees may need to be repaired.

List the things that need attention. Make plans to improve the protection next fall.

If you are planting fruit trees this spring, order them now. Fruit trees are often sold as dwarfs, but the kinds of roots are rarely described. The roots and interstock on which the trees are growing determine whether the plants will be small or whether they will be nearly as big as standard trees. Nurseries that specialize in fruit trees will specify the understock.

Dwarf ornamental plants often are sold the same way as fruit trees. **Crabapples** on dwarfing rootstock are not necessarily much smaller than standards of the same variety.

Grafted plants pose problems:

• Suckering from the rootstock may be severe, and the suckers must be removed.

• Sometimes the graft never heals because of incompatibility, and the top eventually breaks off.

• Many unusual tree cultivars are grafted because that is the only way they can be propagated. Cuttings do not root, or plants do not come "true" from seed. Where the plants can be obtained on their own roots, they are to be preferred.

WATERING

If the weather has been open and mild, the ground may have become quite dry. Trees planted last fall may benefit from watering. Frost will not go as deep in moist soil as in soil that is allowed to dry out. Even in winter, trees need water because they continue to make roots as long as the ground is not frozen.

FERTILIZING

Trees may be fertilized in winter if the ground is not frozen. Inject the fertilizer, or apply it in holes punched in the ground under the drip lines of the trees.

PESTS

Rabbits, deer, and voles can threaten your trees. Reapply animal repellents on a mild day. Be sure that the protective collars are still secure around tree trunks. Voles (meadow mice) prefer burrowing under the snow where they are protected from predators. Flatten the snow by walking it down, which will smash their tunnels. Usually, they do not dig them out again.

PRUNING

Valentine's Day is a good time to start pruning trees. The sap has not started to rise and is stored in the roots. All shade trees and all fruit trees except **peaches** can be pruned now.

Remove suckers, broken branches, branches crossing and rubbing others, and branches interfering with the house, power lines, or traffic. Preserve the leaders on shade trees so that they make a single, straight trunk.

MARCH

TREES

PLANNING

If you expect to plant trees this spring, it is not too early to decide what kinds to plant and where they will go. Placement of trees is too important to do on the spur of the moment. Consider how the trees will affect your property:

• Where do you need shade?

• Will the trees hold their leaves in winter and keep the snow from melting off the front sidewalk?

• Will they hide the picture window so that you cannot see out?

Answer these and other questions as you think about planting trees. Draw a scale diagram of your property, and locate the spots where trees will be helpful. Trees should frame your house, provide shade, and hide objectionable views.

Then decide on the kinds of trees you want in your yard, and draw the outlines of the trees at their mature sizes. Armed with this material, you are ready to start buying trees.

PLANTING

Spring is planting time! Any trees can be planted now, and some trees, such as **oaks**, **birches**, and others, are best planted in spring or can be planted only at this time of year. (See the planting chart for the kinds that must be spring planted.)

As soon as the soil dries enough that a handful can be squeezed into a ball and then crumbled, trees can be planted.

Trees are available bare root, balled and burlapped, or containerized.

To plant trees:

1. Dig the holes for planting as deep as and twice as wide as the roots of the plants.

2. Set the plants at the same depth they were growing or higher if the site is wet.

3. Fill the holes halfway with soil, fill the holes with water, and replace the remaining soil.

4. Water thoroughly again.

Small fruit plants are usually bare root. Here is the way to plant them:

1. Soak the plants for several hours before planting.

2. Dig the planting holes.

3. Trim the roots so that they fit in the planting holes.

4. Make mounds of soil in the bottoms of the holes so that the roots can be spread.

5. Backfill the holes halfway with soil, fill the holes with water, and fill with the remaining soil.

6. Water thoroughly again.

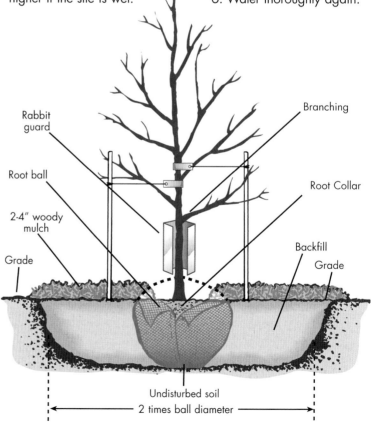

Rabbit guard

Branching

Root ball

Root Collar

2-4" woody mulch

Grade

Backfill

Grade

Undisturbed soil

2 times ball diameter

CARE

Newly planted trees in exposed locations may need to be staked to keep them from blowing over. Run the wire from the stakes through pieces of old garden hose to protect the bark of the trees. Remove the supports after 1 year. It left on too long, they may prevent the trunk from growing where they restrict it.

WATERING

Thoroughly water all newly planted trees immediately. If a landscape contractor plants your trees, determine whether the contractor will water the trees or whether it is up to you. These plants will need to be watered every 2 or 3 weeks in dry weather.

Established trees do not need water at this time of the season. Spring rains are generally sufficient to keep them watered.

FERTILIZING

Spring fertilization of trees promotes vigorous growth.

Fertilize large shade trees by applying a complete fertilizer such as 12-12-12 or something similar spread evenly under the trees at the rate of 15 to 20 pounds per 1,000 square feet of ground. Or apply the same amount of material in holes bored 12 inches deep every 3 feet in concentric circles under the trees. It may be easier to hire an arborist to inject the correct amount of fertilizer into the ground beneath the trees.

Fertilize established, bearing fruit trees at the rate of $1/4$ to $1/2$ pound of commercial fertilizer such as 12-12-12 per tree. Spread it evenly under the trees.

Do not fertilize newly planted fruit trees. Fertilizing them may cause rank growth and delay fruiting.

PESTS

Aphids, scales, and some mites may appear.

Apply dormant oil to control them. Read and follow carefully the directions on the package. Be sure that the temperature is above 32 degrees Fahrenheit when spraying oil, and that it will stay above freezing for 24 hours. Do not use oil on **maple** trees or any trees that have broken dormancy. Dormant oil is especially important for control of San José scale on **apple** trees. Before leaves emerge, spray insecticidal soap or dicofol to protect **honeylocust** from locust mites. Control maple bladder gall and eriophyid mites with malathion as the buds break and leaves begin to open.

Scab is a destructive disease of **apples**, **crabapples**, and other rosaceous plants.

Prevent scab by spraying with copper, chlorothalonil, mancozeb, or thiophanate-methyl fungicide. Start as buds break, and repeat every 10 to 14 days until dry weather. These same treatments will control cedar rust on these plants.

Anthracnose on **sycamore**, **maple**, **ash**, and **white oak** can be serious during a wet and cool spring.

The treatments noted here for the other diseases can be used to prevent this disease, too. Employ a commercial sprayer with the equipment to do the job. Usually, treatment is not recommended unless the trees are especially valuable because of the cost of the many treatments needed.

PRUNING

Pruning may continue on most trees. Exceptions are **oaks**, which are susceptible to wilt that is carried by beetles to open wounds, and **yellowwoods**, which bleed profusely if trimmed at this time.

TREES

PLANNING

April, the month in which Arbor Day falls, is officially a month for planting trees. That does not mean that you must wait until Arbor Day to plant trees, however. They can be planted as soon as the ground is workable. Nurseries are already hard at work digging and planting trees.

If you have decided what to plant and where to put them, start looking for your trees.

PLANTING

Trees are grown in containers, and are dug bare root or balled and burlapped. Soil compatibility problems may occur with containerized or balled-and-burlapped trees; there are no compatibility problems with bare-root trees.

Take these precautions:

• Containerized plants are grown in an artificial soil mix. If a tree in this soil mix is planted in common garden soil, the roots may have a tough time growing out of it into the surrounding soil. There are some technical reasons for this having to do with fluid dynamics.

Make the change gradual from the artificial soil to the surrounding soil. After removing the tree from the container, shake as much of the soil mix off the ball as you can, and mix it with the soil going back into the planting hole.

• Balled-and-burlapped trees may or may not have been grown in a soil like that in your yard.

Find a nursery that grows trees in your kind of soil. Otherwise, shave the balls of trees, and mix the soils as indicated for the artificial mix.

Follow these steps to proceed with planting:

1. Cut all circling roots from container plants.

2. Remove the twine and burlap from balled-and-burlapped plants.

3. Backfill the planting holes halfway with soil, fill them with water, and replace the remaining soil.

4. Soak again to settle the soil.

CARE

After planting, use any leftover soil to make a ring around the tree to hold water. Stake bare-root trees so that they do not blow over.

WATERING

Although April showers are usually sufficient for established plants, newly planted trees may need watering. After the initial

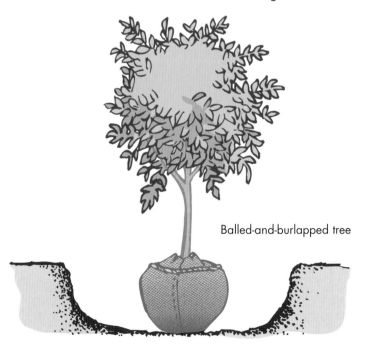

Balled-and-burlapped tree

soaking, water these plants every 2 to 3 weeks. Do not drown them, but do not let them dry up, either. If you are unsure whether to water them, dig down next to the ball, and see how wet the soil is. Unless it is too dry to make a ball and crumble it, water is not needed.

FERTILIZING

If your trees were not fertilized in March, follow the directions for fertilizing on page 197. Get the fertilizer into the ground either by dissolving it or by injecting it. The plants will not use it until it is in the vicinity of the roots and in solution. That means watering it in.

After applying fertilizer, irrigate to provide a measured 1 inch of water.

PESTS

Aphids are often the first insects to reach pest levels in the spring.

Before resorting to spraying them, wait to see whether natural controls will come into play. There are some that can help. Ladybugs and lacewings are efficient predators. Syrphid fly larvae can be found in aphid infestations consuming the pests. These predators find the infestation and quickly set

up housekeeping. If the weather is warm and moist, fungus diseases can crash an aphid population in days.

Do not use insecticides except for emergencies. Then select one that will do the least harm to the predators. Often, insecticidal soap is the preferred material.

Do not use insecticides on fruit trees when the blossoms are open. They will kill the bees needed for pollination.

Two serious borer pests are susceptible to control measures now.

Treat bronze birch borer with imidacloprid applied as a band around the trunks of **white birch** trees. Zimmerman pine moth is very destructive to **Austrian** and **Scotch pines**. Spray to cover trunks and branches with lindane or permethrin when the **Norway maples** and **amelanchiers** are in bloom. Read and follow instructions on the packages for these chemicals.

Continue to apply fungicides to control apple scab.

Use copper, chlorothalonil, mancozeb, or thiophanate-methyl fungicide, and repeat every 10 to 14 days until dry weather. These same treatments will control cedar rust on these plants. Spores of the rust diseases are being released from the alternate hosts, **junipers**, now. It is essential to protect the

apples, **hawthorns**, **crabapples**, and other susceptible trees.

Control peach leaf curl now. Apply captan fungicide to **peach** trees every 15 to 20 days starting before buds swell and until petal drop. It is the only way to prevent peach leaf curl. Any treatment later will be ineffective.

Squirrels will gnaw trees to sharpen their teeth. They may strip off long pieces of bark or may just chew branches.

There is little that you can do to discourage these pests.

PRUNING

Most shade trees may be pruned in April, but some (such as **maples** and **yellowwoods**) will bleed profusely. **Oak** trees should not be pruned now because of the possibility of the wounds being infected by the oak wilt fungus. Wait until late fall to prune **oaks**.

Prune **apricot** and **peach** trees just before they bloom. Severe pruning is needed every year to develop the new wood on which these trees flower.

MAY

TREES

PLANNING

You may note several things in your journal now:
- Which trees did you particularly enjoy this spring?
- Which ones could find a place in your garden?
- Where would a tree provide needed shade in your yard?

Record your thoughts before you forget them. Then dig out your garden plan to see where these trees will fit. If you are out of the mood to plant now, fall planting season is just a few months away.

PLANTING

Spring-dug plants are still available at the nurseries and garden centers. If these trees were dug before they leafed out, they can safely be planted now.

Plant containerized trees anytime during the season as long as temperatures are not excessive and there is sufficient water to keep them from desiccating.

To plant trees, follow these steps:

1. Dig the holes for planting as deep as and twice as wide as the roots of the plants.

2. Set the plants at the same depth they were growing or higher if the site is wet.

3. Fill the holes halfway with soil, fill the holes with water, and replace the remaining soil.

4. Water thoroughly to settle the soil.

CARE

Mulch around bases of newly planted shade and fruit trees.

Create tree rings for established trees. Tree rings are circles about 6 feet in diameter around the trunks, cleared of grass and weeds, and mulched with shredded bark or aged wood chips. Tree rings reduce competition for the roots and keep lawn mowers away from the trunks, so there is no scuffing or tearing of the bark. Lawn mower disease allows infection by cankers that can kill trees.

Thin fruit trees so that the load is not too great. Heavy fruit loads can break down the tree, and they can result in alternate bearing, fruit every other year. In late May or early June, thin **apples**, **peaches**, and **pears** to an average of 6 to 8 inches apart. Thin **apricots** and **plums** to 3 inches apart. (Thin **plums** in late June if possible.)

WATERING

If weather is dry, newly planted trees may need watering. Water these plants every 2 to 3 weeks. Do not drown them, but do not let them dry up, either. If you are unsure whether to water them, dig down next to the ball and see how wet the soil is. Unless it is too dry to make a ball and crumble it, water is not needed.

FERTILIZING

If your trees were not fertilized earlier, follow the directions for fertilizing on page 197. Get the fertilizer into the ground either by dissolving it or by injecting it. The plants will not use it until it is in the vicinity of the roots and in solution. That means watering it in.

PESTS

Aphids and mites will appear as soon as the weather warms up.

Let natural predators take care of the aphids. Control mites with insecticidal soap or dicoFol.

White birches need protection from bronze birch borers.

Spray with imidacloprid to thoroughly cover trunks and foliage when **vanhoutte spirea** finishes blooming. One application of imi-

A shady backyard offers a refreshing haven.

dacloprid is sufficient. Imidacloprid prevents birch leaf miner at the same time.

Susceptible trees need protection from flat-headed apple borers. Spray trunks and limbs of **crabapples**, **apples**, and other susceptible trees with lindane or permethrin about the time **irises** finish blooming.

As soon as petals fall from fruit trees, begin spraying them every 2 weeks with one of the all-purpose fruit tree sprays listed under captan in the Suggested Pest Control Materials on beginning page 281. These contain captan for diseases and an insecticide for insect control.

Add wettable sulfur if mildew becomes a problem.

Weeds will begin to appear now. Hoe or pull weeds from tree rings.

 PRUNING

Cut out all suckers sprouting from the bases on grafted shade and fruit trees. Ornamental **crabapples** grafted on dwarfing rootstock, for instance, will sucker and the suckers may overtake the top if not removed.

Proceed with major pruning of shade trees. Be aware that **maples** and **yellowwoods** will bleed profusely. Do not prune **oak** trees during the summer. The wounds could be infected with the oak wilt fungus.

Remove broken branches as you notice them. Hire professional arborists to remove large limbs damaged by storms and repair the wounds. Do not attempt heavy tree work without the equipment and expertise to do the job. Tree work is dangerous.

HELPFUL HINTS

Using sprays properly is important:
- Follow spray schedules carefully.
- Apply the right material at the right time.
- Follow directions on the package.

Paying attention to when indicator plants bloom will assure that applications are made at the right time even if the season is early or late.

Fruit on some plants is an annoyance. Sometimes fruit set can be prevented by spraying the trees at full bloom or shortly afterward. Spray **crabapples** with carbaryl 1 week to 21 days after petal fall. **Catalpas**, **mulberries**, **horsechestnuts**, **honeylocusts**, and **ginkgos** can be treated with other materials with varying degrees of success. Check with your Cooperative Extension Service offices for recommendations.

JUNE

TREES

PLANNING

At this time of year the differences in the various parts of the state can be the greatest. In Evanston, Illinois, on the Lake Michigan shore it is still cool with lake effect winds putting a chill in the air every afternoon. Downstate in Bloomington it can definitely be summer at the same time. In fact, the hotter it is inland, the stronger the lake effect will be as the rising hot air pulls the cold air inland.

Plants and pests are affected by these temperature differences so that recommendations based on the calendar are risky. Blooming dates of **mock orange** may be a week or more later in Beverly Shores than in Valparaiso, Indiana, and three weeks later than those in Evansville. In Michigan, **mock orange** blooming dates may be a week or more later in Stevensville than in Jackson, and three weeks earlier than those in Ludington. Recommendations in this book are based on average dates for the central part of the state. The far southern part will be about 2 weeks earlier, the far northwest, possibly 2 weeks later.

Keep a record of the dates certain plants flower each year, when leaves are fully out, when bugs appear, or when diseases show up. These records will be very helpful in planning tree-care activities.

PLANTING

Spring-dug and containerized trees can be planted as long as the weather is not unbearably hot and there is adequate water. Plant the trees as soon as possible after getting them home.

To plant them, follow these steps:

1. Dig the holes for planting as deep as and twice as wide as the roots of the plants.

2. Set the plants at the same depth they were growing or higher if the site is wet.

3. Fill the holes halfway with soil, fill the holes with water, and replace the remaining soil.

4. Water thoroughly to settle the soil.

CARE

The leaves are fully out, and the trees are beautiful in their summer finery. Or are they?

Most of us do not notice what is happening in the yard until the warm weather arrives and we begin to spend a lot of time outside. Then as we sit under a favorite shade tree, we suddenly notice all kinds of bad things.

The leaves have holes or brown spots, or the ground is becoming littered with perfectly good green leaves. What is happening? Our beautiful trees are being ruined.

First of all, no plant is perfect in every way. All trees are living creatures with other things that live on them. The most beautiful **oak** tree on close examination will be seen to have all kinds of things happening to it. As long as the tree is otherwise healthy, it can stand supporting all these guests.

Holes in the leaves are probably not from insects. Usually, they are tattered from frost damage as they were opening in spring. The more tender parts of the leaves are injured by late frost. Those parts die and fall out as the leaves continue to open.

The brown spots are anthracnose or another fungus disease. These diseases infect in cool, wet weather, and have done their damage by now.

The collection of leaves on the front lawn can be due to June drop, a normal adjustment in the density of the canopy by the tree. If too many leaves were developed in the cool spring weather, the tree may be unable to sustain them when hot, dry weather arrives.

Or have you noticed how the squirrels make their nests? They clip off leafy twigs, but drop most of them on the way to the nest. In either case, the actual reduction in the numbers of leaves in the tree is so small that it would be unnoticed if it were not for the leaves on the ground.

Another kind of June drop is the falling of tiny fruit from **apple** trees. This is a natural pruning as well. Usually, **apples** set too many fruit, and some are shed. Sometimes additional thinning is needed.

WATERING

As hot, dry weather arrives, be sure that trees get enough water. In the forest shade, deep soils and plenty of organic material reduce water loss. In the landscape, the trees are in lawns or beds, often with no protection over the roots and competition from the grass for water.

Apply 2 inches of water to the entire area beneath large shade trees every couple of weeks during droughtlike weather. Set a coffee can under the sprinkler to measure the water. Turn off the water when 2 inches are in the can.

Newly planted trees need water, too. Water the plants every week or so during dry

> ## HELPFUL HINTS
>
> Regular, timely care keeps trees in good condition. Neglected trees can be in jeopardy before anyone notices that they are in trouble. Weakened trees are susceptible to borers and diseases that can kill them.

weather. Do not drown them, but do not let them dry up, either. If you are unsure whether to water them, dig down next to the ball and see how wet the soil is. Unless it is too dry to make a ball and crumble it, water is not needed.

FERTILIZING

If your trees were not fertilized earlier, they may be fertilized now. Follow the directions for fertilizing on page 197. Get the fertilizer into the ground either by dissolving it or by injecting it. The plants will not use it until it is near the roots and in solution. That means watering it in.

If the trees were fertilized earlier, additional fertilizer is not needed at this time.

PESTS

Peach tree borers can severely damage **ornamental plums** as well as **peaches**.

When **mock orange** is blooming, spray **plums** and **peaches**

with permethrin to thoroughly cover the trunks and limbs, allowing spray to drench the ground around the trunks. Repeat in 4 weeks.

Continue spraying fruit trees every 2 weeks with captan or one of the all-purpose fruit tree sprays listed under captan in the Suggested Pest Control Materials beginning on page 281.

The foliar diseases such as anthracnoses, leaf spots, or scab cannot be prevented now. Treatment for them must be initiated as the leaves open.

Remember to treat them next year. Write down a reminder in your journal.

PRUNING

Cut out all suckers sprouting from the bases on grafted shade and fruit trees.

Proceed with major pruning of shade trees, but do not prune **oak** trees during the summer. Remove dead or broken branches as you notice them.

JULY

TREES

PLANNING

If you have doubted the value of shade trees for cooling your yard, take a drive through the open countryside on a hot day and then drive into a wooded area. The difference will be immediately noticeable. As trees give off moisture, they cool the air, and the shade prevents the soil and air beneath the trees from heating up.

Trees provide the same cooling effect around your home. If they shade the house, they reduce the heat load and the air-conditioning cost. In the yard, they create comfort zones where you can enjoy the outdoors without being cooked in the process.

To take full advantage of them, properly place the trees so that they provide shade at the right times of the day. Walk around the yard, and see where your trees are shading it. Decide where another tree or two would be helpful. Sit on your porch or patio at various times of the day to determine whether there is a time when trees would help.

Draw a plan of the yard, and locate the proposed trees where they will do the most good.

Then answer these questions:

• What kinds of trees would work?

• Will they fit your space?

• Will they interfere with utilities and power lines?

Make plans to visit a nursery or garden center next fall to pick out your trees and have them planted.

PLANTING

Containerized trees can be planted now. Although there are better times to plant trees, landscape contractors and nurseries can plant all summer with extra care, especially if the trees were dug or potted before they leafed out in the spring.

CARE

Fruit trees are a lot of work, but now as **peaches**, **apricots**, **cherries**, and summer **apples** are ripening, the troubles are forgotten and the results of all the efforts are realized. Pick the fruit at the peak of its quality as it ripens. Pick up fallen fruit as well. It attracts yellow jackets and other pests. Overwintering mummies (dried fruits still attached to the tree) can be sources of diseases the next year.

WATERING

It is important to properly water trees:

• Trees in the first year following planting need constant attention to be sure they have enough water.

Do not keep them soaked at all times, however. They need to dry out so that roots are not drowned.

• Roots will not grow in saturated soil.

Check the soil by digging next to the soil ball and seeing if the ground is wet. If a handful can be squeezed into a ball and crumbled, water is not needed.

Peach trees require a lot of work, but the rewards are sweet.

Wait a few days, and check again before watering.

• Established trees will need 1 inch of water a week.

If there is little rainfall, provide 2 inches of water every 2 to 3 weeks. Measure in a coffee can set under the sprinkler.

FERTILIZING

Do not fertilize trees at this time of the season. Fertilizer may interfere with the onset of dormancy. Semidormant trees can suffer severe winter damage if cold weather arrives early.

PESTS

Do not immediately assume that every insect you find is a bad one. Insects that feed on other insects are a diverse bunch. Twice-stabbed ladybug feeds on cottony maple scale; it is black with two red dots. Lacewing, syrphid flies, and several kinds of true bugs also feed on other insects.

Before you spray to get rid of these insects, identify them. Your local Cooperative Extension Service office can arrange to do so. Take or mail the insect in a pill bottle so that it is not

smashed on the way. I received many smudges that were once insects and was asked to identify them. Most of us have a hard time identifying smudges.

One of the worst pests of **apples** is the maggot. Adults begin to lay eggs on developing fruit now and will continue until the **apples** are harvested.

Spray every 2 weeks with one of the all-purpose fruit tree sprays, which contain both a fungicide and an insecticide. These are listed under captan on page 282. These sprays are effective, but must thoroughly cover the leaves and fruit. Sticky red balls hung in the trees offer little protection. The adults are attracted by scent, not color.

Japanese beetles may become a problem.

Spray carbaryl or cyfluthrin to combat a high number of Japanese beetles. If only a few are present, pick them off by hand. They do not bite.

Try not to let diseases get started.

Continue spraying fruit trees every 2 weeks with all-purpose fruit tree spray. Add sulfur if mildew is a problem.

Tree rings may have weeds.

Keep tree rings free of weeds that compete for water and harbor pests.

PRUNING

Remove water sprouts or suckers from all grafted trees. They can overtake the grafted top of the tree, reverting to the wild seedling. Grafted red-leaf **crabapples**, for instance, may lose all the red shoots, having been replaced by the green rootstock. The same can happen to flowering trees and fruit trees.

TREES

PLANNING

August 6 is midsummer, the halfway point between the summer solstice and the autumnal equinox. In Scandinavia, midsummer is celebrated on the longest day of the year, about June 21.

Some people insist that summer actually starts at the spring halfway point, which is May 5 or 6, and that winter begins on the fall halfway point, November 7. According to their calculations, the beginning of August is also about midsummer or about halfway through the growing season.

However you calculate it, summer is on the downside. There is still plenty of warm weather ahead, but we have lost an hour of daylight already. The evenings are cooling off, and dew is heavier at night.

Continue to care for your trees. **Peaches** and **pears** are being harvested this month. Soon the **apples** will be turning red, and leaves will be turning color.

Make plans for harvesting and storing the **apples**. Plan for disposing of leaves, too.

PLANTING

Do not plant trees now. In a few weeks, the fall planting season will be here, and there will be good selections of newly dug trees from which to select.

CARE

Trees generally are able to survive on their own in nature. When they are planted out of their natural habitat, they become more dependent on us to care for them.

Selecting trees that are well adapted to your part of the state and to your situation reduces the number of things you need to do to help them. For example, trees from bottomlands do better in heavy, wet soils; upland trees do better in dry situations.

- Evaluate how your trees stand the stresses of summer.

Are they equally adaptable?

- Keep track of how much care your trees demand.

If some take constant care and are just hanging on anyway, consider replacing them. For example, in some parts of the state that have alkaline soils, **pin oaks** and **red maples** barely survive because of these soils.

- Plant trees where the conditions are naturally favorable instead of trying to create the conditions artificially.

Pears can be harvested before they are fully ripe. Take them indoors, wrap them in newspaper, and store them in the basement or refrigerator. Take some out each day to ripen. The bugs and animals will not get them before you do, and none will overripen on the tree.

WATERING

In summer you may need to set priorities for the water you use. During droughts, most communities have water conservation plans that include limited watering or outright watering bans. Lawns usually can stand drought by going dormant and are easy to replace if they die out. One season, and they are back as good as new.

Trees take a lifetime to regrow. Where you have to make a choice, water the trees. Apply 2 inches of water to the entire area beneath the trees using a sprinkler. Measure the water in a coffee can. In a severe drought, you may need to water the trees every 2 to 3 weeks in a clay soil, every week in sand.

When the rains return, the grass may grow again. If it does not, you can reseed it. August is not a bad time to do that.

 FERTILIZING

Do not fertilize trees until they have lost their leaves in fall.

 PESTS

In some areas, Japanese beetles may be present in large numbers. Regularly apply carbaryl or cyfluthrin to control them. They may do a lot of damage in the meantime. If only a few are present, pick them off by hand. Beetle traps only attract more to your yard. If you use traps, set them as far away from your plantings as you can.

The larva of Zimmerman pine moth is a borer that invades the trunk at branch whorls. If not controlled, Zimmerman will girdle the trunk, killing the top. Apply permethrin in the middle of this month to susceptible **pines**.

First-generation fall webworm may be severe enough to spray in the southern part of the state.

Use *Bacillus thuringiensis kurstaki*, carbaryl, or acephate from a hose-end sprayer.

Control of apple maggot now is essential. Continue to spray **apple** trees with all-purpose fruit spray until the end of August. These are listed under captan on page 282. Check the label to see the waiting time between the last treatment and harvest.

By the end of the month, the leaves have done their jobs, and protecting them is not nearly as important.

Spray fruit trees for diseases the last time.

Weeds may appear in tree rings. Keep tree rings free of weeds and grass that compete with the trees for water.

 PRUNING

Summer pruning of **apple** and **peach** trees is especially helpful in keeping dwarf trees at the desirable size. Summer pruning does not stimulate vigorous growth the way winter pruning does.

Remove all water shoots and suckers from grafted trees. Suckers are continuing problems on these trees. Try diquat grass and weed killer on the suckers as they appear. It will kill the suckers, but not harm the trees if you keep the material off the trees themselves. Repeat the treatment every time the suckers start again.

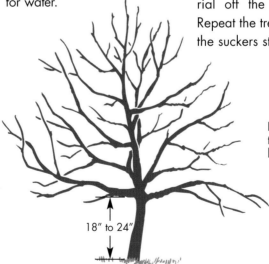

Prune apple trees to a central leader form.

18" to 24"

HELPFUL HINTS

Premature fall color in trees is often a sign of trouble. The trees may be overly dry or may have other problems. Often it is a sign of root damage or girdling. If one of your trees is already turning color, examine the collar to make sure it is sound. Girdling roots are often the cause of the trouble. Sometimes they are visible above ground, but they may be just below the soil surface. Remove girdling roots. If they are major roots, there may be some loss in the top of the tree. The alternative is loss of the entire tree from girdling.

September

TREES

PLANNING

Labor Day signals the start of a new season.

Our community has a list of tree walks. These walks wind through the town and list common and unusual trees along the route. Our city forester assembled the list, but any interested resident of the community could assemble one.

Every community has trees, some quite common and some unusual. Take a walk through your town, and notice the kinds of trees. It may surprise you if there are some you do not recognize. If not, you are the one to develop a tree walk. It is a fun way to spend some time this fall before the leaves drop. The neighborhood kids will appreciate it, and so will other residents who can learn about trees from your expertise.

If you have developed your planting plans, go to your favorite nursery to select and tag the trees. They will be dug at the appropriate time and delivered to your home. The nursery can plant the trees for you or set them where they are to go so that you can do the job yourself.

Keep in mind that some kinds, particularly **oaks** and **birches**, must be planted in the spring. Do not be disappointed if all the trees you need are not available.

PLANTING

As the summer weather moderates, conditions become more favorable for planting trees. Nurseries are beginning to dig a few of the earlier kinds. Once we have had a frost, the sales yards and garden centers will be full.

Containerized plants are available all season. They are usually smaller sizes than balled-and-burlapped trees, but can be planted anytime they are available.

Container plants are grown in artificial soils. To plant containerized plants, follow these steps:

1. Dig the planting holes.
2. Remove the plants from the containers.
3. Slice any circling roots.
4. Shake as much of the artificial soil off as you can without damaging the roots, and mix this with the soil going back into the planting holes.
5. Backfill the holes halfway, fill with water, and replace the remaining soil.
6. Water thoroughly to settle the soil.

To plant balled-and-burlapped trees, follow these steps:

1. Buy balled-and-burlapped trees from a nursery that has soil as nearly like the soil in your yard as you can find. This will make it easier for the roots to grow out of the balls.
2. Dig the planting holes.
3. Set the plants in the planting holes.
4. Cut the twine, stuff the burlap down in the hole, or cut it off and remove it.
5. If the soil in the balls is quite different from the soil in your yard, shave some off the balls and mix it with the soil going back into the hole.
6. Backfill the holes halfway, fill with water, and replace the remaining soil.
7. Water thoroughly to settle the soil.

CARE

Mulching trees with shredded bark or composted wood chips is beneficial:

- Mulch around newly planted trees prevents weeds and grass from competing with the tender new roots.
- Mulch preserves moisture.

• Mulch keeps lawn mowers away from the trees, preventing lawn mower disease.

Damage to the trunks of young trees often results in canker diseases that girdle and kill them many years later.

• Mulch can revive large, mature trees.

Mature trees decline because activities under them have damaged their roots. Mulches can save them, particularly **oaks** in urban areas. Mulch the entire area under the branch spread of the tree.

Avoid putting mulch next to the tree trunk.

 WATERING

Fall can be warm and dry. If it is, water new trees. If dry weather is extended, water large trees every 2 or 3 weeks. Apply 2 inches of water to the entire area beneath the trees. Measure the water with a coffee can set under the sprinkler.

 FERTILIZING

Do not fertilize trees at this time of the season. Wait until they have dropped their leaves. Using fertilizer now may delay the onset of dormancy and result in winter damage.

 PESTS

Cooley spruce gall adelgids cause swellings at the tips of branches of **Norway** and **blue spruces**, often killing them. Eastern spruce gall adelgids produce swellings at the bases of new shoots.

Control either insect with imidacloprid, cyfluthrin, or insecticidal soap. Soap will remove the blue from **blue spruces**.

Scale may threaten **magnolias**. Spray **magnolias** with acephate from a hose-end sprayer for scale at the end of the month.

Crown and root rot diseases can be initiated by piling soil or mulches high on the trunks of trees. The collars stay wet, and disease organisms are able to gain entrance. These diseases are slow to develop, but once the plant is infected, there is no cure. The tree eventually will die.

Do not allow mulch or soil to accumulate over the trunk of any tree.

Prepare now to protect your trees from deer and rodent damage. Rabbits and voles will feed on thin bark of young trees. They are able to girdle the plants so that they die about the time they start leafing out in spring.

Protect the plants with collars around the bases. Make them tall enough so that rabbits cannot stand on the snow and feed over them.

 PRUNING

Remove dead or damaged branches as they appear. Storm damage to large trees should be repaired by skilled commercial arborists.

OCTOBER

TREES

PLANNING

October is often the most beautiful month of the year, with clear, crisp days, cool nights, and a blazing display of color before freezing weather brings an end to the growing season. Nothing can compare with the fall colors of **maples**, **sweetgums**, **black tupelos**, and **oaks** as they put on one last display for the year.

Jack Frost is often given credit for this display, but frost actually can finish it before it begins. Freezing weather kills the leaves and stops the show. The bright, warm days that permit photosynthesis and lots of sugars in the leaves, combined with cool nights that prevent translocation from the leaves to other parts of the trees, result in the best fall color.

The reds and oranges are due to anthocyanin sugars in the leaves. The yellows of **birches** and **poplars** are carotenes that are always in the leaves but hidden by the green chlorophyll. Browns are tannins. Once the leaves are killed, the process stops, and the leaves fall.

If you have room in your garden for a **sugar maple**, it will give you a wonderful display every year. It is worth planning for.

PLANTING

Trees may be grown in containers, or they may be field grown and dug bare root or balled and burlapped.

Container plants are grown in an artificial soil mix. Roots of trees in this soil may have a tough time growing out of it into the surrounding soil. The change from the artificial soil to the surrounding soil needs to be gradual. To plant containerized trees, follow these steps:

1. Dig the planting holes.
2. Remove the trees from their containers.
3. Shake as much of the soil mix off the balls as you can, and mix it with the soil going back into the planting holes.
4. Cut all circling roots from container plants.
5. Backfill the planting holes halfway with soil, fill with water, and replace the remaining soil.
6. Soak again with water to settle the soil.

To plant balled-and-burlapped trees, follow these steps:

1. Buy trees grown in a soil like that in your yard from a reliable nursery.
2. Dig the planting holes.
3. Remove twine and burlap.

Red maples

4. If the soil is unlike that in your yard, shave the balls, and mix the soils as you did with the artificial mix.

5. Backfill the planting holes halfway with soil, fill with water, and replace the remaining soil.

6. Fill with water again to settle the soil.

CARE

Fluff up the mulch around your trees. Pull it away from the bases of the trees. Add mulch if needed. Use shredded bark or composted wood chips.

WATERING

Although October is generally a wet month, it can be very dry. Water new trees, and established ones if there is no rain for 2 weeks. Set a slowly running hose at the bases of new trees, and water until it begins to run off. Apply 2 inches of water to the entire area beneath established trees.

FERTILIZING

As soon as the leaves have dropped, fertilize trees.

For large shade trees, apply a complete fertilizer such as 12-12-12 or something similar spread evenly under the trees at the rate of 15 to 20 pounds per 1,000 square feet of ground. Or apply the same amount of material in holes bored 12 inches deep every 3 feet in concentric circles under the trees. It may be easier to hire an arborist to inject the correct amount of fertilizer into the ground beneath the trees.

Fertilize established trees only once every 1 or 2 years. Trees fertilized last spring should not be fertilized now.

Do not fertilize newly planted trees for the first 2 or 3 years unless planted in unusually infertile soil.

PESTS

Continue to control weeds around your trees.

Keep tree rings weed and grass free.

Voles will crawl through mulch and chew the bark of trees near the ground. They will attack any fruit trees, young shade trees, and **pines**.

Pull back mulch and other debris from the bases of young shade trees and fruit trees. If you see voles, set out bait stations with brodifacoum (D-con). Be sure that they are accessible to the voles but not to birds and other animals. Make small wooden boxes with a $3/4$-inch hole or two. Or use plastic butter or cottage cheese containers, cut a $3/4$-inch notch in the edges, add the brodifacoum (D-con), and replace the lids. Set the containers upside down where the voles have been active. Check regularly, and add brodifacoum (D-con) if needed.

PRUNING

Prune shade trees once they are dormant. Wait until midwinter to prune **apples** and **pears**, and just before bloom to prune **peaches**.

HELPFUL HINTS

Fallen leaves are valuable organic matter. They can be chopped with a mulching mower and left over the roots of the trees where they will recycle nutrients and add organic matter to the soil. If there are too many, collect them, and add them to the compost pile or spread them over the vegetable garden. The last resort is to send them to your community composting facility. Sometimes you can get the compost back for use in your garden.

NOVEMBER

TREES

PLANNING

When planning your garden, think about including trees that will provide winter interest. If you take some time looking at trees, you might eventually be able to identify them from the winter profile. Winter features are very important in our part of the country where the trees are bare for 5 months of the year.

With the leaves gone, trees take on a different character. On a sunny day take a good look at your trees. Notice their bark:

• Some trees such as **beech** or **white oak** have smooth bark even at old age.

• Other trees have smooth and peeling bark, such as **birch** and **paperbark maple**.

• Others have furrowed bark, sometimes deeply furrowed like **bur oak**. **Red oak** bark is smooth, becoming furrowed.

• Still other trees have bark that is shiny, such as **Japanese tree lilac**.

• The color of the bark can be white, brown, gray, black, green, or even mottled.

Branches can be ascending, descending, or radiating, or they can change with age.

Other features that provide interest are persistent fruit or leaves that stay on all winter. **Shingle oak** keeps its leaves.

Some **crabapples** keep their fruit. **Kentucky coffeetree** keeps its bean pods all winter.

The stark white of **paper birch** may be too cold, but the cinnamon-colored bark of **river birch** is soft and warm. Even in winter, trees provide a lot of enjoyment in the garden.

CARE

Mulching trees is beneficial for several reasons. We have discussed the value of mulches in keeping the soil moist, preventing weeds, and providing a buffer between the trees and the lawn mower.

Trees benefit in another way. Most trees have shallow root systems, especially in the heavy soils of the Midwest. But the roots do not exist on their own. They are accompanied by beneficial fungi in a symbiotic relationship:

• These fungi are called mycorrhizae (*myco* meaning "fungus" and *rrhizae* meaning "roots").

• The roots are invaded by the fungi, which grow out forming masses throughout the soil.

• The fungi become the effective roots for the plants, absorbing the water and fertilizers the plants need. The fungi receive sugars from the roots.

Shingle oak

• Organic mulch provides an ideal environment for the mycorrhizae. They thrive in it and quickly populate the mulch to derive nutrients.

• As the soil improves from the mulch, the mycorrhizae grow in it as well.

Providing a good organic mulch—and replenishing it regularly—is one of the nicest things you can do for your trees.

WATERING

Fall rains usually provide enough moisture for established trees. Newly planted trees may need watering before the ground freezes up. Set a hose under each new tree, and let it run slowly until the water begins to run off.

Do not let newly planted trees go into winter in dry soil.

FERTILIZING

Fertilize established trees when they are fully dormant. Fertilize large shade trees by applying a complete fertilizer such as 12-12-12 or something similar spread evenly under the trees at the rate of 15 to 20 pounds per 1,000 square feet of ground.

Fertilize established trees only once every 1 or 2 years. Trees fertilized last spring should not be fertilized now.

Do not fertilize newly planted trees for the first 2 or 3 years unless planted in an unusually infertile soil.

PESTS

Take precautions against rabbits. Install wire or plastic guards around trunks of young shade trees and fruit trees to protect them from rabbits. Make them high enough so that the rabbits standing on the snow cannot reach over them.

Protect trees from deer with fencing or repellents. Spray the trees with one of the proprietary materials containing thiram. Or spray with mixture of a bottle of Tabasco and a gallon of water. Add a little soap so that the mixture sticks to the plants.

Watch out for signs of voles.

Pull back the mulch 1 foot from trunks, and set traps for voles.

PRUNING

Prune shade trees anytime the plants are dormant. Prune fruit trees after midwinter.

HELPFUL HINTS

Trees provide shelter for birds during winter storms. Evergreen trees are especially helpful. You can help, too. Set up bird feeders, and keep them filled with the kinds of seeds that will attract the birds you want.

• Sunflower seeds: cardinals, blue jays, chickadees, nuthatches, purple finches, and possibly pine and evening grosbeaks.

• Thistles: finches, pine siskins, and doves.

• Cracked corn: crows, blue jays, cardinals, woodpeckers, doves, and pigeons.

• Suet or suet and peanut butter: woodpeckers, nuthatches, chickadees, blue jays, and starlings.

• Raisins and apple pieces (and **crabapple** trees with persistent fruit): robins, cardinals, blue jays, and cedar waxwings.

• Commercial seed mixes: juncos (on the ground), cardinals, blue jays, chickadees, nuthatches, doves, gold finches, and purple finches. (They can also attract sparrows, pigeons, and starlings. These imported weed birds often crowd out more desirable ones.)

If you can supply birds with fresh water in a heated container, they will stay around your yard all winter.

TREES

PLANNING

As the year ends, record the events that shaped it. Somewhere in your journal, note the weather events of the year:

- How did the year develop?
- Was the winter mild, terrible, or rather normal?
- Was spring early, late, wet, or dry?
- What were the conditions in the summer?
- What were the conditions in the fall?

All of these conditions affect the way your plants behave. They also affect the insects and diseases that can attack your plants. A severe winter can eliminate many overwintering bugs so that the season starts without them. It can eliminate the overwintering predators, too, so that the pest numbers could rise rapidly without any natural controls.

I have relied on the records of past seasons many times in trying to decide how to approach a season. Since my commercial clients in turn rely on me for guidance as they prepare for each season, having some definitive data on which to base my judgments is very helpful. In fact, I regularly write a column for a trade journal predicting what the next season may hold in store. Without having the masses of records, that would be difficult.

You never know where they will come in handy. Developing them a year at a time is easy.

Trying to reconstruct them is nearly impossible

PLANTING

As long as the ground is not frozen, trees can be planted. The roots should not be exposed to freezing temperatures while the plants are above ground. Roots are killed at temperatures that would have no effect on the tops of the trees.

CARE

Properly mulch your trees for the winter. Keep the mulch at least 1 foot from the trunks so that voles do not use it for a convenient place from which to feed on the bark.

WATERING

Water new trees well before the ground freezes up. Then drain the hoses, and store them where you can get to them in midwinter if you need them.

Persistent fruit can provide winter interest.

HELPFUL HINTS

To make Christmas truly memorable, why not decorate a living Christmas tree? Living Christmas trees are balled and burlapped or are grown in tubs so that they can be moved indoors, set up, and moved back out to be planted in the garden.

To get the best results from a living Christmas tree, follow these steps:

1. Before buying a tree, select the place in the garden where you will plant it.

2. Dig the hole before the ground freezes. Pile up the soil, and cover it so that it stays dry. Covering it with straw to keep it from freezing would help. Fill the hole with straw, and cover it as well.

3. Store the tree in a protected place after you get it until 1 or 2 days before Christmas. It should be in a place where it will not freeze, such as an unheated garage, porch, or cool basement.

4. Keep it indoors only about 5 days. Decide when it is most important to have the tree up. If it is before Christmas, for instance, plan to move the tree out the day after Christmas.

5. Acclimate the tree to cool weather on the porch or in the garage for a couple of days, then plant it.

6. Water it in thoroughly, and mulch it heavily.

Families have carried on this tradition while their children were growing up and now have trees that remind them of specific Christmases. You may not want to go through the trouble every year, but special Christmases may be worth it—the first Christmas of a newborn, a special anniversary, or a grandchild's visit.

When the holiday is over, throw a log on the fire, and relax. Garden catalogs are arriving, and spring is only 15 weeks away.

 FERTILIZING

Many commercial arboriculture firms prepare to fertilize trees in winter. These firms use equipment to inject the proper fertilizer analysis into the soil where it is in direct contact with roots. Roots will absorb the fertilizer all winter if the ground is not frozen. It will be ready for the trees to use in spring when growth begins.

 PESTS

Scales, mites, and aphid eggs may need to be controlled.

Spray with dormant oil to control these pests. Be sure the temperatures will be above freezing for 24 to 48 hours after application.

Rabbits may threaten your trees. Check the wire or plastic guards installed around trunks of young shade trees and fruit trees to protect them from rabbits. Make them high enough so that the rabbits standing on the snow cannot reach over them. Be sure they are securely attached at the bottoms, too. Rabbits will squeeze under them if they can.

If the weather has been wet, rain may have washed the repellents from trunks of the trees. Spray the trees again with one of the proprietary materials containing thiram. Or spray with a bottle of Tabasco mixed in a gallon of water; add soap so that the mixture sticks to the plants. Temperatures should be above freezing until the mixture dries or it may not stick.

VINE, GROUND COVERS, & ORNAMENTAL GRASSES

Vines and ground covers are utilitarian plants. They often serve as backgrounds for other, more conspicuous plants. Usually, they are neglected until something happens to them.

At Wrigley Field in Chicago, for instance, the vines on the outfield walls were taken for granted. They seemed to grow without difficulty, even though they had become part of the charm of the "Friendly Confines." When the Japanese beetles and leaf spot disease appeared one season, threatening the vines, the importance of these plants was immediately evident. Even the Chicago Cubs newsletter is named *Vineline*. Once the dam-age was done, it was too late to do anything that year to correct the situation. These troubles are now anticipated, however, and treatments applied before problems arise.

Some vines are so essential to the landscape that their loss changes the entire effect of the site. Not just the vines at Wrigley Field, but the ivy-covered walls of some institutions in our state create their personality.

Some vines are grown for their flowers, some for interesting fruit. Mostly, they are used to soften the harshness of architectural structures.

CHAPTER NINE

Vines do require care. Some are very aggressive, taking over if not restrained. Insect and disease incursions can become serious, even jeopardizing the plants. I have seen ancient vines on historic buildings killed to the ground by pests before the problem was recognized.

Ground cover plants simply cover the ground. There is nothing particularly outstanding about many ground covers. They are seldom used as specimen plantings. Ground covers are low-growing plants that are usually found in shady glens, on stream banks, on the forest floor, or in open, sunny meadows.

We plant ground covers in beds under trees where it is too dark for a lawn. We use them as facer plants in front of shrub plantings. We plant them on the tops of banks and over walls, and in places too small, too wet, or too hot for anything else. Sometimes, we use ground covers so that we have less grass to mow. Often, we plant them because they give us something more interesting to look at than turfgrass.

HELPFUL HINTS

Sometimes wisterias are reluctant to bloom. These vigorous plants would rather make leaves and stems when they are young. This vegetative growth uses up the stored carbohydrates faster than the plants can make them. Carbohydrates are the products of photosynthesis.

Some things that can stimulate the aggressive growth are fertilizing with nitrogen, mulching with fresh organic matter, and overly severe pruning. Cutting back the new growth to the spurs in the leaf axils now will help develop flower buds. Shade complicates the problem. Sometimes the plants can be shocked into blooming by deep cultivation that breaks shallow roots.

Weed control in some ground cover plantings must be done when the weeds are susceptible, but the damage to the ground cover is minimal. Most are so well suited to their circumstances that when used properly, they will keep weeds out. But then they may become invasive. At certain times of the season these plants may need pruning to keep them attractive.

Ornamental grasses have graced the natural landscape throughout history. They were here in the Midwest when the settlers arrived. Usually, they are well adapted to their situations, perfectly able to stand the weather, soils, and pests that they encounter.

Some ornamental grasses are exotics, while others are native plants. Both annual and perennial grasses have places in the landscape, but perennials are generally preferred.

These grasses require so little care that they can be planted and forgotten until they enliven the landscape with their presence. They take no staking, pruning, or pest control. Native kinds will stand any weather our state has to offer. They evolved with it.

Ornamental grasses do require care at certain times of the season, but with a little attention, they can provide four-season interest.

JANUARY
VINES, GROUND COVERS, & ORNAMENTAL GRASSES

PLANNING

January is a time for thinking about things to do in the garden.

The catalogs have arrived. Usually by now, you have scrutinized them and set them aside. Before you discard them, think about some places in the garden where you could use something different, and scan the catalogs for ideas.

The vines, ground covers, and ornamental grasses are used as background and, occasionally, as accents in the garden. They are utilitarian and serve many purposes.

Too many times our thinking gets into a single mode and familiar things are all we see.

• You may have areas of your yard and garden that lack something.

Is there a fence or a utility pole that is an eyesore, but you have never done anything about it? Maybe a vine would cover it.

• You may have areas in the lawn where grass refuses to grow.

Why fight it? Ground covers are adapted to such places. They take a lot less care and certainly look better than dried-up grass.

• You may be reluctant to plant ornamental grasses to solve a gardening problem.

Use vines to cover objects or to screen a view.

The ornamental grasses take almost no care. They are plant-'em-and-forget-'em plants. But they provide accents, screens, cut flowers, feed for birds, and winter effects. There are different sizes suitable for a variety of uses.

Make a drawing of your garden. Locate the troublesome areas where vines, ground covers, or grasses may solve problems. Then look at the catalogs again. You may need to do additional research on these plants before deciding which ones to try.

Before making a major investment in new kinds of plants, do a little experimenting:

1. Plan to buy a couple of each kind that interests you.

2. Set them out in a test garden to see how they behave.

3. Label them so that you know exactly what you planted.

4. Record your observations in your journal. If the idea of journaling bothers you, jot down a few things in a gardening notebook. List the name of each plant, where it came from, when you planted it, and how it does throughout the season.

CARE

Winter is here with a vengeance. There is little to do outside unless a January thaw occurs.

If there is a thaw, see how the plantings are surviving the winter. Herbaceous ground cover plants may be hidden under the snow or may have died down for the winter. The evergreen types stay green if protected from the sun and winter wind. Snow is the best protector.

If the winter has been mild and open, these plants may be dry by now. For instance, you may need to add a few inches of straw to keep **ginger** in an exposed spot out of the sun.

Vines can be pulled down by the snow. Make note of the ones that need better supports, and plan to build them in the spring.

The grasses that were knocked down by the snow might look messy, but it will not hurt them at all. Cut off those tops anytime, now or in spring.

WATERING

Mild, open weather can dry the soil even in winter, and evergreen ground cover plants may desiccate. Check the soil to see if it is dry. If so, water the plants on a warm day. Moist soil does not freeze as deeply as dried-out soil, either.

PESTS

Mice and rabbits will gnaw on the stems of vines and woody ground cover plants.

Apply a commercial repellent containing thiram. Or make a concoction of a bottle of Tabasco mixed in a gallon of water; add a little spreader-sticker or soap so that the stuff stays on the plants. Set out bait boxes of brodifacoum (D-con) to get rid of mice. Make sure other animals or birds cannot get into them.

PRUNING

Vines may be winter pruned; however, it is usually best to wait until the worst of the weather is over. Winter usually kills stems back from the tips. If the plants are pruned back too soon, more of each stem may be lost from cold injury.

FEBRUARY
VINES, GROUND COVERS, & ORNAMENTAL GRASSES

 PLANNING

By the beginning of February, things are generally looking up. The days are a little longer, and it is not quite dark as I drive home in the afternoon. We have gained an hour of daylight since the darkest days in December.

By the end of the month, a few warm, sunny days have melted some of the snow, and by afternoon the garden is a puddle. As soon as the frost is out of the ground, the puddles will drain away. Before long, the ground will be dry enough to do cleanup work.

 PLANTING

Sow seeds of some annual vines in peat pots under lights this month so that they will be large enough to set out in May. Follow these steps:

1. Sow **morning glories, cup-and-saucer vines**, or **black-eyed Susan vine** directly in the peat pots.

2. Moisten the soil.

3. Cover the pots with plastic wrap.

4. Set them under fluorescent lights lowered to the tops of the pots. This will keep them warm enough to germinate in about 15 days.

5. Remove the plastic as soon as the seedlings are up.

6. Clip off extra seedlings, and grow the plants under the lights until it is safe to set them out in the cold frame or garden.

Some ornamental grasses such as **fountain grass** and **northern sea oats** can be grown from seed started in the same way. If you are collecting seed from named cultivars, do not be surprised if the plants do not look like the parents. Do not thin these seedlings, but let all of them grow in the pots.

Thin seedlings by clipping out the extra ones.

CARE

Next month, dormant spraying, early planting, fertilizing, and pruning are on the calendar.

Do you have the equipment and materials you will need? Stores will begin stocking up on these items at the end of this month. Make a list of the things you will need, and get them before you need them.

WATERING

Evergreen ground cover plants and newly planted vines can dry out very quickly if exposed to mild temperatures and drying winds. Water these plants on a day while the temperatures are above freezing. A little water now may save these plants.

HELPFUL HINTS

Some ground covers are shallowly rooted and can be heaved out of the ground by freezing and thawing. When the soil is not frozen and fairly dry, gently firm any heaved ground cover plants back into the ground.

FERTILIZING

Do not fertilize spring-flowering vines now. It can delay or prevent blooming. Fertilize those that flower in summer and those that are not grown for their flowers as soon as the snow is gone if the ground is not frozen. Spread the fertilizer, and water or scratch it in so that it is not washed away by the next storm.

PESTS

Rabbits may still be pests.

Reapply the commercial rabbit repellent applied earlier this winter. The most effective are the ones containing thiram. Or make a concoction of a bottle of Tabasco mixed in a gallon of water, and add a little spreader-sticker or soap so that the stuff stays on the plants.

Mice may still be living among your plantings.

Refill the bait boxes of brodifacoum (D-con). Make sure other animals or birds cannot get into them. (Ideas for bait boxes can be found on page 239.)

PRUNING

By the middle of the month, a few warm, sunny days can make it feel as though spring is here. On one of those days, take your pruning shears out, and cut back some of the overgrown vines. Cut back **bittersweet** severely. It is a rambunctious plant and can quickly get out of hand. Prune other vines that bloom after the start of summer. Plants that bloom in spring already have set their flower buds, which would be removed if pruned now.

MARCH

VINES, GROUND COVERS, & ORNAMENTAL GRASSES

 PLANNING

March starts meteorological spring. The vernal equinox is not until the 20th or 21st, depending on the year, but in either case, spring is not far off.

Nighttime temperatures can still drop quite low, but the worst of the cold is over. Snow comes and goes instead of hanging around for weeks.

Think about getting the garden in shape for the season. Vines and ground covers do require some care throughout the season, but a lot of trouble can be prevented by starting them right. Ornamental grasses are almost self-sufficient during the season, but they need attention in spring.

 PLANTING

Dormant vines and grasses can be planted in the southern part of the state as soon as they are available in the garden centers. By the end of the month, plants should be available throughout the state.

Containerized plants are grown in artificial soils that are quite different from the soils in your garden. If these are planted directly in the garden, they may have difficulty making roots out of the artificial soil.

To minimize these problems, follow these steps:

1. After knocking the plant out of the container, gently loosen the roots from the ball, and spread them so that they do not circle the ball.

2. Knock as much of the artificial soil mix from the ball as you can without damaging the roots.

3. Mix it with the soil going back into the planting hole.

4. Set the plant in the planting hole at the same depth it was growing.

5. Backfill with half the soil, firm the soil, and fill the hole with water.

6. Replace the remaining soil, and soak it again.

If you started seedlings under lights last month, set them in the cold frame as soon as the danger of severe weather is over. These plants can be exposed to frost once they have been hardened off. If you think that the temperatures in the cold frame might drop below freezing, cover the frame with old blankets, or move the plants back indoors for the night.

Bring in the **Boston ivy** seeds that have been receiving the cold treatment, and set them under the lights to germinate.

Cut back ornamental grass, avoiding any new growth.

 CARE

Cut off the old tops from the ornamental grasses, and recycle them in the compost pile or on the vegetable garden. Be careful not to damage any early-starting green leaves.

Rake out the ground cover beds. Mow back winter-burned **purple wintercreeper**, **pachysandra**, **ginger**, **vinca**, or other herbaceous ground covers to remove damaged leaves.

WATERING

Spring is rarely dry, so established plants will probably need no watering. Soak new plants every few weeks unless rainfall keeps them wet.

FERTILIZING

Fertilize woody ground cover plants in sunny areas with a complete fertilizer such as 10-10-10 at the rate of $1/2$ pound per 100 square feet of bed. Wash any fertilizer off the foliage to avoid burning. Do not fertilize ground cover plants growing in the shade or tender herbaceous ground cover plants.

PESTS

Scale insects are especially damaging to some vines and ground covers.

Treat **euonymus** vines and ground cover plants with dormant oil. It may burn the foliage, but new growth will quickly hide the damage. Cover the undersides of the leaves. Make sure temperatures will stay above freezing at least 24 hours following application of the oil.

Sanitation is one way of reducing the disease problems in ground cover beds.

Rake out as many old, dead leaves as you can.

After cleanup, treat severe root and crown rot problems with fungicide drenches.

Use thiophanate-methyl to treat **English ivy** and **ajuga**. Treat **pachysandra** and **vinca** with either copper or mancozeb.

Creeping cotoneaster is susceptible to bacterial fire blight. Prune out any evidence of the disease from previous seasons, and treat with copper.

These disease-control materials are available at garden centers or hardware stores. Follow the directions on the packages carefully.

Ground cover beds must be kept free of weeds until they are dense enough to keep them out.

Before weed seeds germinate, apply preemergent herbicides. DCPA is the easiest to use. It can be applied to weed-free beds of all ground covers except **ajuga**.

Grasses in ground cover beds are hard to control.

Use fluaziflop-P-butyl grass killer around most ground cover varieties to kill the grass without hurting the other plants. Do not use fluazifop-P-butyl around ornamental grasses.

As soon as other things begin to green up, animals will move to them for better quality forage.

PRUNING

Prune **Jackman** and **Viticella clematis** plants now. Prune stems back to within a few inches long about the time the buds begin to swell. These shoots will bloom in July and August.

HELPFUL HINTS

Clematis plants bloom either on the canes produced the previous season or on new wood growing during the current year. Do not prune varieties blooming on old wood until the flowers have faded. These usually bloom in June. Within this group are the Lanuginosa, Patens, and Florida varieties.

In the spring, cut back hard the kinds flowering on new wood to develop vigorous new growth for prolific blooms. The **Jackman** and **Viticella clematis** varieties bloom on new wood.

APRIL

VINES, GROUND COVERS, & ORNAMENTAL GRASSES

 PLANNING

It is time to get ready for the gardening season:

- Have you made plans for renovating the ground cover plantings?

- Is there a spot that would look much nicer if it was covered with luscious green instead of struggling lawn all summer?

- How about vines to cover the old rail fence?

Complete your plans as soon as you can. It is time to get to work.

 PLANTING

Spring is the best time to plant ground covers, ornamental grasses, and most vines. These plants need time to make roots before the heat of summer and become well established before they are subjected to the stresses of a Midwest winter.

Almost all ornamental grasses, ground covers, and vines are grown in containers in artificial soils. This develops excellent root systems and allows planting almost all season. The artificial soils are quite different from the soils in your garden. If these are planted directly in the garden, the plants may have difficulty making roots out of the artificial soil.

To minimize problems, follow these steps in planting:

1. After knocking these plants out of the containers, slice any circling roots.

2. Shake as much of the artificial soil mix from the balls as you can without damaging the roots.

3. Mix it with the soil going back into the planting holes.

This procedure is especially important in planting small ground cover plants, which are often shallowly rooted anyway.

 CARE

Mulch new plants with shredded bark or composted wood chips. Refresh the mulch around established plants. Hoe out weeds so that they do not grow through the mulch.

Climbing hydrangea and **wisteria** are heavy plants that require substantial supports. Make sure that the structures on which they will grow are strong enough to hold them up. I have seen **wisteria** plants pull down porch railings, and **climbing hydrangeas** come crashing down because the support was inadequate. These vines will cling to masonry and siding of all kinds. They will pull off siding that is not securely attached or masonry in need of tuck pointing.

 WATERING

Water in any newly set plants. They will need watering every 1 or 2 weeks if the weather is dry.

Established ground cover plants are often shallowly rooted and will need watering, especially if under trees or shrubs that

Climbing hydrangea

compete for moisture. Apply a measured inch of water to ground cover beds early in the day so that the foliage dries before dark.

Established native grasses are able to survive the weather, whatever it is. Introduced grasses will need help, especially those such as **northern sea oats** and **fountain grass** that prefer moist soils.

FERTILIZING

Applying light fertilization every spring may benefit ground cover plants. Use 10-10-10 at $1/2$ pound per 100 square feet, and wash it off the foliage immediately.

Be cautious with fertilizers around vines and ornamental grasses. They are usually vigorous enough without additional help. If obviously deficient in nutrients, apply fertilizer lightly. Grasses will often become taller, weaker, and floppy if fertilized. Flowering vines may fail to bloom. Vigorous vines may become unmanageable and require excessive pruning to keep them from taking over.

PESTS

Aphids arrive about the time leaves show up. Control with insecticidal soap or acephate from a hose-end sprayer. Certain plants are sensitive to acephate, so read the label carefully.

Leaf spot diseases begin as the leaves start to open. You cannot see them yet, but unless they are controlled, you will see them later. If the weather is wet, spray the foliage of ground covers and vines with mancozeb or copper fungicides.

Crown rot or root rot of ground cover plants may be prevented. Use mancozeb or copper fungicides as soil drenches, or try thiophanate-methyl.

Before weeds appear, they can be prevented with a preemergent herbicide.

Apply DCPA to weed-free beds of all ground covers except **ajuga**.

Grasses can be removed with a selective grass herbicide.

Use fluazifop-P-butyl grass killer around most ground cover varieties to kill the grass without hurting the other plants. Do not use fluazifop-P-butyl around ornamental grasses.

PRUNING

Bittersweet and **trumpet vine** can be aggressive and difficult-to-handle plants. Prune them hard every spring and later in the season if they begin to take over. Other vines are much better behaved, but it is necessary to clean out the dead branches that result from the winter. **Boston ivy**, **English ivy**, **purple wintercreeper**, and **cranberry cotoneaster** all benefit from a spring trimming.

Low ground cover plants can be given a haircut with a power mower set at 3 to 4 inches high. Do this just before buds break. Remove the clippings. They will show up later as dead sticks in the planting. I have had calls in the past to come out and see what had killed the ground cover only to find the dead wood is from clippings that were not removed by the caretaker.

Do not be too hasty to remove the brown branches from **creeping juniper** ground cover plants. Even though the needles are dead, the branches may be very much alive and will grow as soon as the weather warms up. Wait until you are sure the branches will not grow from the tips before removing them.

225

 MAY

VINES, GROUND COVERS, & ORNAMENTAL GRASSES

 **PLANNING**

What a wonderful time of year! Everything is fresh and green. The air has a special fragrance to it. Mornings are warm and inviting. It is a joy to get up each morning and to go outside to see what is new.

Gardening is not just another enjoyable option for outdoor people, something to do when you happen to be outside. It is therapeutic. According to recent reports, doctors are prescribing gardening as therapy for their patients, and the doctors are heeding their own advice. In an American Medical Association survey of the members, more doctors garden for relaxation than play golf.

Consider these benefits of gardening:

- Gardening is fun.
- It is good exercise.
- It provides a creative outlet.
- It allows you to work off the pent-up frustrations of the day.
- It is not fattening.
- It is not immoral.
- It is not harmful to the environment.
- It is not divisive to the family.

Everyone can become a gardener. Caution! It is habit forming. Once you begin gardening, you will not be able to stop.

Boston ivy

 **PLANTING**

Ornamental grasses in containers, ground covers, and vines can be planted all summer if sufficient water is available. Grasses and vines are available in 1-, 2-, and 5-gallon sizes. The ground cover plants are usually sold in packs or in 4-inch pots.

These plants are grown in artificial soil. If plants are set into the holes and backfilled with the unmodified soil, they will be unable to make roots out of the balls. It will be as though they are sitting in pots of light artificial soil and cannot get out.

To minimize problems, modify the soil going back into the planting holes with some of the artificial mix.

1. After knocking the plants out of the containers, gently loosen the roots from the balls, and spread them so that they do not circle the balls.

2. Knock as much of the artificial soil mix from the balls as you can without damaging the roots.

3. Mix it with the soil going back into the planting holes.

4. Set the plants in the planting holes at the same depth they were growing.

5. Backfill with half the soil, firm the soil, and fill the holes with water.

6. Replace the remaining soil, and soak it again.

Plant seedling grasses and **Boston ivy** in the garden anytime the soil is dry enough.

Vines growing on walls or fences tend to thin out at the bottoms. Prune them to keep them full to the ground, but continuously renew the planting to keep it young and avoid the eventual loss as the plants all get old and die at the same time.

Interplant the newly started seedlings along the base of the wall or fence between the existing plants. As they take over, prune out the oldest canes.

CARE

Mulching ground covers and vines will reduce weeds and water loss from evaporation. It will mellow the soil, keeping it from compacting.

Use shredded bark or composted wood chips as mulch. Black plastic, weed-barrier fabric, and colored stones are not suitable mulching materials for ground covers or vines.

Annual vines need support. Before they become tangled messes, train them up strings, trellises, or other supports. Be sure that the supports are substantial to handle the weight of the vines.

WATERING

May can be a dry month. If it is, soak newly set plants every 1 or 2 weeks. Water established plants once a month or when they wilt.

FERTILIZING

If you did not use fertilizer in the spring, ground cover plants may benefit from light fertilization now. Use 10-10-10 at $1/2$ pound per 100 square feet, and wash it off the foliage immediately.

Do not fertilize ornamental grasses or vines. The grasses will become weak and will fall over. The vines may become excessively vegetative and refuse to flower.

PESTS

Aphids and mites arrive with warm weather. Control them with insecticidal soap or acephate from a hose-end sprayer. Acephate may damage certain plants, so read the label carefully before using.

If the weather is wet, leaf spot diseases may occur. Spray the foliage of ground covers and vines with mancozeb or copper fungicides to prevent leaf spot diseases.

Crown rot or root rot may affect ground cover plants. Use mancozeb, copper fungicides, or thiophanate-methyl as a soil drench to prevent crown rot or root rot.

Weeds may still appear. Hoe or pull weeds. Once the soil is weed free, prevent new weeds with a preemergent herbicide. DCPA is the easiest to use and can be applied to weed-free beds of all ground covers except **ajuga**.

You may need to eliminate grasses. Use fluazifop-P-butyl grass killer around most ground cover varieties to kill the grasses without hurting the other plants. Do not use fluazifop-P-butyl around ornamental grasses. It will kill them, too.

PRUNING

Limit pruning to plants that have already finished flowering. Pruning now will remove already developed flower buds or will delay flowering of those that bloom on new wood.

HELPFUL HINTS

If spring-flowering bulbs were planted in the ground cover beds, the leaves should be protected until they ripen. The beds will look messy for a while.

JUNE
VINES, GROUND COVERS, & ORNAMENTAL GRASSES

PLANNING

Meteorological summer begins June 1. The summer solstice, the official start of the summer season, is about June 21, depending on the year. I always feel that summer starts with Memorial Day. That is considered the latest date of last frost throughout most of this area.

In any case, it's summertime! New plants and established ones are in full leaf now, and the earliest ones are blooming.

Walk through the garden to see how things are doing, and make a few notes in your garden journal. Record how things have recovered from winter, the amount of dieback they sustained, the dates they began to bloom, and any other item that may be helpful in planning future plantings and care programs.

PLANTING

It is not too late to plant containerized grasses, vines, or ground covers. These plants are available at nurseries and garden centers throughout the summer. Get them into the ground as soon as possible so that they are well established before the onset of winter. Do not plant grasses any later than early

summer if possible so that they are well established before they begin to flower.

Planting now will give them plenty of time to make deep, strong root systems throughout the summer.

CARE

Keep the ground cover beds and the vines mulched with shredded bark or composted wood chips to conserve moisture.

Do not pile up mulch on the stems of the plants, or they will stay too wet and may begin to rot.

WATERING

Apply water as needed to keep the ground cover plants from wilting. If the small plants seem to wilt almost every day, follow these steps:

1. Pull up a few to see whether they are growing in the old artificial soil mixes they were planted in. If these plants are planted with the artificial soil-balls intact, the plants will not grow into the surrounding soil.

2. If they are, shake the mix off the roots, and replant them.

3. Soak them thoroughly to settle the soil.

FERTILIZING

Do not fertilize now if the plants were fertilized earlier in the season. Ground cover plants do benefit from spring fertilization. Grasses and vines should not be fertilized unless they show symptoms of nutrient deficiency. A soil test can be taken to determine the need.

Euonymus scale can destory euonymus and other plants.

PESTS

Euonymus plants, either vines or ground covers, can be destroyed by scale. It appears as little yellow dots on the upper surfaces of the leaves, and as little white things on the stems and undersides of the leaves. These insects can affect other plants, including **boxwood**, **bittersweet**, **honeysuckle**, and **ivy**.

Spray affected plants with acephate from a hose-end sprayer when the **catalpa** trees are in bloom. That is about the time eggs are hatching and the little crawler scales are exposed. Treat again about 2 weeks later.

Black vine weevil is a serious pest of **euonymus**. Spray with imidacloprid, allowing excess to saturate the ground beneath the plants when the **vanhoutte spirea** finishes blooming.

Leaf spot diseases will affect **Boston ivy** if weather is wet.

Be prepared to spray these plants with mancozeb or a copper fungicide as soon as any spots appear. Continue spraying to protect newly developing leaves as long as wet weather persists.

HELPFUL HINTS

• Enjoy your plantings. They are at their best as summer begins. Make note of any that are not performing as you expected. Either change the way they are handled, or replace them with something more suitable.

• Visit the nearest botanic garden, arboretum, or public garden to see things that might be appropriate for your garden. List them, noting especially how they grow and the size you can expect. Usually, there are people on the premises who can answer questions and help you find the plants that interest you.

Stem blight and root rot diseases may affect ground cover beds. Keep the soil moist but the leaves and stems dry.

Stem blight of **clematis** is a wet-weather disease. Spray affected plants with thiophanate-methyl fungicide during rainy periods.

Weeds continue to appear. Hoe or pull weeds. Once the soil is weed free, prevent more weeds with a pre-emergent herbicide. Use DCPA on all ground covers except **ajuga**.

Grasses may get into ground cover beds. Use fluazifop-P-butyl grass killer around most ground cover varieties to kill the grasses without hurting the other plants. Do not use fluazifop-P-butyl around ornamental grasses. It will kill them, too. Keep it off the lawn because it kills all grasses.

PRUNING

Prune your **spring-flowering clematis** as soon as they finish blooming. Give a haircut to herbaceous ground cover plants if they become overgrown and ragged. Head back woody ground cover plants anytime it is needed. Do severe pruning in winter or early spring.

JULY

VINES, GROUND COVERS, & ORNAMENTAL GRASSES

 **PLANNING**

July is vacation time. As you plan your vacation, plan for someone to take care of your plants while you are gone. Doing this is important for your plants, but it is equally important so that your property does not look as though no one is home.

If you plan to be gone for an extended time, several weeks or so, these tasks need attention:

• Watering the newly planted vines and ground cover plants

• Edging the ground cover beds

• Trimming the plants

• Removing spent blooms from the vines

Your choice of a care provider is professional or nonprofessional:

• Professional

A landscape contractor who has done work for you before will give your plants excellent care.

• Nonprofessional

Usually, a high schooler or a young person home from college for the summer is easy to hire. The person may not be trained in landscape maintenance, however, so you will need to show him or her what you expect. It is better to have the person well informed about how the plants should be treated before you leave. Start the person to work a week or so ahead of time so that adjustments can be made if necessary.

 **PLANTING**

Containerized vines and ground cover plants are available at garden centers and nurseries all summer. Plant them as long as adequate water is available.

 **CARE**

Use composted grass clippings, shredded bark, or composted wood chips to mulch around ground covers and vines.

Do not pile the mulch high on the stems of the plants. Stems that are kept wet will rot.

 **WATERING**

As the temperatures rise higher, the stresses on the plants increase, too. Plants need water for transpiration to cool themselves. Wilted plants cannot cool themselves, and internal temperatures can get high enough to kill leaves and twigs.

Apply water whenever the plants have begun to wilt. Thoroughly soak the ground. Use a sprinkler for ground cover beds. Set a slowly running hose at the bases of vines or ornamental grasses. Water until the water begins to run off.

 **FERTILIZING**

Fertilize summer-flowering vines as soon as they finish blooming.

Do not fertilize spring-flowering vines now while flower buds are being set. Fertilizing may stimulate vigorous growth and prevent bud set for next year.

 **PESTS**

Japanese beetle makes its appearance this month. As soon as you see any beetles, spray vines with imidacloprid or carbaryl. Repeat every 2 weeks if needed.

Aphids and mites will be troublesome in hot weather. Watch for signs of them, and treat immediately with insecticidal soap to cover the undersides of the leaves and the growing tips of the shoots. Repeat the treatment in 2 weeks.

Anytime the weather is wet, leaf spots may infect ground cover plants and vines. If the weather is wet, spray the foliage with mancozeb or copper fungicides.

Crown rot or root rot may affect ground covers. Use mancozeb, copper fungicides, or thiophanate-methyl as a soil drench to prevent crown rot or root rot.

Phomopsis tip blight may affect **creeping juniper**.

Control it with thiophanate-methyl.

Weeds will begin to grow in ground cover beds if they are not dense enough to shade out the seedlings. Thistles and grasses are especially difficult to keep out.

Pull or hoe the thistles as soon as they are noticed and before they are well established. Eliminate grasses with fluazifop-P-butyl grass herbicide. Keep it off the lawn and off ornamental grasses.

Creeping juniper

 PRUNING

Overgrown evergreen ground covers have made the most vigorous growth of the season; trim them now. These pruning scars will be covered by new growth, but the growth will not be so rampant that the plants will soon be out of bounds again. Try to head back overly long shoots by cutting to a shorter branch growing in the same direction. If the cut can be made beneath the shorter branch, the wound will be hidden.

When pruning these plants, use a hand clipper or sharp pruning knife. Do not shear these plants into unnatural forms.

HELPFUL HINTS

Some ground cover plants do poorly in full sun. Others are better in sun and do poorly in full shade. Sometimes as taller shrubs develop and provide more shade, the plants beneath them suffer. Most plantings can be expected to change over their lifetimes, and adjustments will need to be made.

If the plants that were in sun are now shaded, it is time to reevaluate and decide the changes that are needed.

AUGUST
VINES, GROUND COVERS, & ORNAMENTAL GRASSES

 PLANNING

Summer does take a toll on plants. Some survive better than others.

In your particular location, because of the soil, water, winds, light, or shade, the plants may be better or worse than you expected. Evaluate the plants, and plan for changes that may be indicated.

Some plants outgrow their situations, too. These plants may tolerate rejuvenation or may need replacing. Decide which is appropriate, and plan to take the action at the correct time.

 PLANTING

Plant containerized vines and ground cover plants anytime during the summer. Be sure there is sufficient water available. If the temperatures are predicted to be extremely high, postpone planting until they moderate.

Plant ornamental grasses no later than early summer to give them time to develop before they start to flower.

English ivy

 CARE

Refresh the mulch under vines and around ground cover plants. Fluff it up where it has become compacted. Add more where necessary.

Actively growing vines may need to be trained up their supports. **Boston ivy** and **English ivy** are just as happy growing along the ground as growing up a support.

To get these plants to climb, it may be necessary to tie them. To hold them to a wooden fence or trellis, staple twist ties to the support, and wire the vines. Do not tie them too tightly to avoid girdling them.

Some grasses may be too weak to stand without support. Surround them with tomato cages to keep them from falling over. Plan to treat them differently next year. It may be the water, too much or too little, the fertilizer, or the amount of light.

 WATERING

Apply water as needed to keep the plants from wilting excessively. If the plants wilt severely, they cannot cool themselves and will begin to die back. Do not keep the plants soaked, either. Allow the soil to dry until the plants just begin to wilt, and apply sufficient water to thoroughly wet the soil.

FERTILIZING

Do not fertilize vines, ground cover plants, or ornamental grasses at this time of the season.

PESTS

Mites are hot-weather pests. They cause the leaves to bronze and drop. Shoots and undersides of the leaves may be covered with webs. The mites may be seen crawling up and down on the webs. Check for mites by tapping a leaf over a piece of white paper. The mites will appear as tiny moving specks.

Treat severe infestations with dicofol. Use insecticidal soap on moderate infestations. Repeat the treatment in 5 days.

As long as weather is wet, fungicide treatments will be necessary to prevent leaf spot diseases. Severe leaf spot can completely defoliate vines in a few days. Spray the foliage with mancozeb, copper fungicides, or thiophanate-methyl.

Weeds still appear. Keep weeds under control by hoeing or pulling them. Once the ground cover plants are dense enough, weeds will cease being problems. Use DCPA pre-emergent herbicide to prevent more weeds after cleaning them out of the beds.

Mice will begin to look for places to nest when the weather starts to cool off. Do not provide them with convenient home sites next to your valuable vines or ground covers.

Pull the mulch back from stems, and set out brodifacoum (D-con) bait in bait boxes.

PRUNING

Limit pruning to removal of dead, damaged, or overly long branches.

Ground cover plants may be given a haircut if they are badly overgrown. Growth stimulated by late pruning may be winter injured, however.

HELPFUL HINTS

By the end of this month, the weather will be cooling off, and days will be noticeably shorter. Some of the plants will be changing color, and the approach of fall will be obvious.

One of the earliest vines to develop fall color is **Virginia creeper**. Poison ivy is early too, but few of us would grow it intentionally. It can be beautiful, intensely red, climbing to heights in wooded areas, up trees, or even up power poles. The linemen hate it.

Ornamental grasses should be in flower now. Notice the dates, forms, sizes, and colors of the various kinds, and record them in your journal. Some are excellent for cutting. Cut them before they fully mature and shatter.

Bittersweet and **euonymus** vines should be loaded with colorful fruit. Harvest them for use in arrangements. If they are not fully dry, hang them upside down in a cool, dry place for a couple of weeks. Once thoroughly dried, they will last a long time as decorations.

SEPTEMBER
VINES, GROUND COVERS, & ORNAMENTAL GRASSES

PLANNING

Labor Day signals the end of summer. Kids start back to school. Vacations are over. Fall activities begin.

September is a season of change. The weather starts out summerlike, and by the end of the month, fall is in the air.

This is the season for the ornamental grasses. Most of them are at their best now, fully in bloom and taking center stage in the garden. The greens of summer turn to the soft earth tones of fall, gorgeous in combination with golds, reds, and blues of the fall flowers.

What tasks do you need to do before the snow flies?

• Plant.

• Harvest.

• Prepare the garden for the coming winter.

Review your journal for notes made during the summer. Sometimes memories are short, and we forget things that were put off until fall. Make another list of the chores that must be done. This includes the things that need replacing, moving, eliminating, or renewing.

• Pick up the garden tools so that they are not lost over the winter.

PLANTING

Vines covering walls or fences need to be renewed continuously by interplanting small plants between the existing plants. Some vines such as **Boston ivy** drop seeds that produce many volunteer plants.

1. Dig these little plants, and set them among the older vines.

2. Selectively remove the oldest plants over time so that the planting never becomes really old.

3. Collect the little berrylike fruit containing the seeds from **Boston ivy** now.

4. Sow them in Styrofoam cups of artificial potting soil, and cover them with plastic wrap.

5. Put them in the refrigerator where they get temperatures of 40 degrees Fahrenheit or so for 3 months. This will break the dormancy and allow them to grow. They could be left outdoors for the winter with the same result.

Euonymus vines can be propagated by layering:

1. Select a long stem.

2. Make a shallow cut in it about midpoint, and bury the injury in the ground. The wound will heal, and roots will form from the callous tissue.

3. Remove the rooted part from the parent plant, and plant it elsewhere next spring.

Containerized ground covers and vines are available from nurseries and garden centers now. Water the plants well following planting.

Lily-of-the-valley

HELPFUL HINTS

Let the plants acquire dormancy on their own. They do not need any help. Dormancy can be delayed by fertilizing with nitrogen or by excessive pruning, however. Watering can delay dormancy if the plants have been dry all season. The sudden availability of moisture may cause them to begin growing. Any late growth is susceptible to winter damage.

Planting ornamental grasses this late in the season is not recommended.

CARE

Foliage of some ground covers begins to die down now. Mow off and rake out ripening leaves of **daylilies**, **lily-of-the valley**, and **sweet woodruff**. Dispose of them in the compost pile or on the vegetable garden where they may be spaded in. This improves the appearance of the beds and reduces the amounts of overwintering disease organisms.

WATERING

Water all newly set plants to thoroughly settle the soil. Water these plants every few weeks if the weather is dry.

Water established plants once a month, or if they show any signs of wilting. Plants protected by overhangs can dry out in spite of sufficient rain. Check them to make sure they are not dry even though plants in the open are wet enough.

FERTILIZING

Most vines and ground covers are best fertilized in the spring. Unnecessary fertilization will result in overly vigorous plants that will take more pruning and may not bloom.

PESTS

Although there still may be some insect activity now, the cooler weather slows them down, and moisture increases the diseases they suffer.

If hot weather persists, spray again for mites with insecticidal soap or dicofol. Cover the undersides of the leaves.

Most of the foliar diseases overwinter on old leaves.

Collect fallen leaves, and put them in the compost pile or on the vegetable garden to be spaded in.

Some grassy weeds germinate in the fall. Kentucky bluegrass spreads in fall by means of rhizomes. Both can invade ground cover beds. Winter annuals such as chickweed germinate now as well.

Remove them now. If they are not removed, they will be well established by spring and more difficult to eliminate.

Voles are beginning to seek out winter quarters.

Eliminate mulch within a couple of feet of vines. These animals will feed on the bark of plants if they can get to them without being exposed to the elements. Cover protects them from predators, too.

PRUNING

Prune vines in late winter or spring. The flowering habits dictate the best times.

Fall is not a good time to do any major pruning, but remove broken, diseased, or overly long branches now.

OCTOBER

VINES, GROUND COVERS, & ORNAMENTAL GRASSES

PLANNING

Fall color reaches its peak in October:

- A few of the vines add to it.

If not for its toxicity, poison ivy would be an outstanding vine. It and **Virginia creeper** turn flaming red in fall. Most other vines have little or no fall color.

- A few evergreen ground covers turn from green to purple in fall, but nothing spectacular. Deciduous ground cover plants are not much better.

Cranberry cotoneaster has plum-colored foliage in fall and is covered with bright red fruit.

European ginger maintains its bright green color until covered with snow. The fruit on **bittersweet**, **euonymus**, and the **cotoneaster** can be outstanding. If you are looking for fall color though, you will probably need to look elsewhere.

Vines do have many other attributes. They have excellent summer foliage, and some flower profusely.

Some ornamental grasses hold up well into winter with their flower heads persisting. The seeds of some provide for small birds in early winter.

Since there is little color from most of these plants, plan to supplement them with potted **mums** in fall. They will add touches of color to the beds for fall and can be removed and planted in the cutting garden or nursery beds in spring.

PLANTING

October is about the latest you will want to plant ground covers and vines. These plants will have a tough time making it through a severe winter unless they have adequate snow cover.

Mums

HELPFUL HINTS

By this time of the season, there is little that needs to be done for vines and ground cover plants. They are able to adjust for the coming winter on their own. If properly located with the right exposure and situation, they usually do just fine.

Most ornamental grasses are well adapted to Midwest conditions. If you are trying to grow something like **dwarf pampas grass**, you are aware of the requirements for keeping it alive over the winter.

If you have some exotic plants or have planted things where they are not well adapted, they could have problems. The solution is to avoid things that are problematic.

CARE

Mulch newly planted vines and ground cover plants after the ground freezes. The voles will get into it now and may destroy your new plants. After the ground freezes, these pests will have found their winter quarters, and there will be much less chance that they will decide to live next to your new plants.

Annual vines are finished with the first freeze. Cut them from their supports, and put them in the compost pile or on the vegetable garden where they can be spaded in.

WATERING

Soak new plants thoroughly to settle the soil and provide sufficient water for winter.

Soak established plants a couple of times before the ground freezes. Do not allow established plants to go into winter too dry, either.

PESTS

Weeds continue to appear. The ones most prevalent now are those that will survive the winter—grasses and winter annuals. They will still be here next spring if you do not get rid of them now. Keep hoeing.

Rabbits develop tastes for different plants. Sometimes they will gnaw on one kind one year and a different one the next year. They like to den under dense woody ground covers such as **cranberry cotoneasters**, **creeping junipers**, or **dwarf sumac**.

If they begin chewing on certain plants, apply a repellent containing thiram. Or mix a bottle of Tabasco in a gallon of water, and add soap so that the stuff sticks to the plants; spray the ones being damaged. The rabbit will get a tummy-ache if it persists in chewing on your plants.

PRUNING

Limit pruning to removal of dead, damaged, or overly long branches.

NOVEMBER
VINES, GROUND COVERS, & ORNAMENTAL GRASSES

Pachysandra along a walkway.

CARE

Since many ground cover beds are next to sidewalks, decide where snow can be piled so that it will not damage the plants. Piling it on woody ground covers such as **cranberry cotoneaster** and **creeping juniper** will break them down and may leave salt in the beds. Salt can severely damage herbaceous ground cover plants such as **pachysandra** and **ajuga**.

If there is danger that salt spray will be blown into the ground cover beds, set up fabric screens to intercept the spray. Tack burlap or geotextile to 2-by-2 stakes driven into the ground on the windward sides of the beds.

Be stingy with the salt. Shovel or plow the snow off the walks first, then spread salt down the middle of the walk so that it is less likely to get into the ground covers.

PLANNING

Some years, November is mild and dry. Other years it starts cold and snowy and never relents.

Even if the month begins with a vengeance, there usually are some breaks when milder days allow outdoor work. But you need to be ready:

• Cover mulching materials so that they stay dry and do not freeze solid.

• Rake out leaves as they drop so that they are not frozen in place, either.

• Collect and inventory tools so that they are not hidden under the snow when you need them.

WATERING

Continue to monitor the soil moisture content. Thoroughly water newly planted ground covers and vines—and established plants as well—before the ground freezes. A primary cause of winter injury is desiccation. Even when temperatures are below freezing, plants can lose moisture if they are warmed by the sun. Unless they can replace lost water, the tissues dry up and die. Evergreens are especially vulnerable.

Grasses, too, can be damaged by desiccation during the winter. The leaves dry up during the winter, and new roots are produced each year. But crowns exposed to drying winds or dry soils can be killed by freeze-drying if there is no moisture in the soil.

FERTILIZING

Do not fertilize ground covers, ornamental grasses, or vines at this time.

PESTS

Rabbits and voles may threaten your plants.

Protect susceptible plants from rabbit damage with repellents containing thiram, or with a bottle of Tabasco mixed in a gallon of water and sprayed on the plants. Set out bait boxes of brodifacoum (D-con) to combat voles. Make sure other animals or birds cannot get into them.

PRUNING

Limit pruning to removal of dead, damaged, or overly long branches.

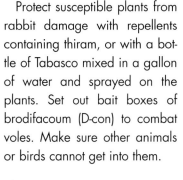

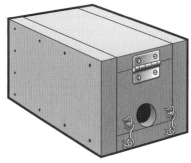

Bait Boxes

HELPFUL HINTS

Some trees drop leaves so late that they cannot be raked out of the ground cover beds before the snow flies. **Cranberry cotoneaster** and **dwarf sumac** plantings are notorious for collecting trash. Do not worry about it. These leaves do not carry any diseases that might cause problems for the ground covers. Rake them out in spring before the leaves pop open.

Make sure that the vines are securely fastened to their supports, and that the supports are strong enough. If they are not, they could be pulled down by the weight of snow and ice. Either secure them and reinforce the supports, or take them down and lay them on the ground for the winter. You may need to bundle them so that they are not blown all over the yard. In spring, refasten them to the refurbished supports.

Decorate ground cover beds of woody plants for the holidays. Lay strings of lights over the **cotoneasters**, **creeping junipers**, or **dwarf sumac** plants. They will complement the lights on the trees and shrubs.

DECEMBER
VINES, GROUND COVERS, & ORNAMENTAL GRASSES

 PLANNING

December finds just about all outdoor work finished and gardeners retired to a place next to the fire. Not that gardening is finished for the year. The catalogs are arriving, and there is time to peruse them with thoughts of what is new that can be tried next year.

Take a walk around the yard to be sure all is secure for the winter. Then warm up sitting by the window to watch the birds finishing the last of the seeds on the **northern sea oats** or enjoy the contrast of the snow and the bright orange berries on the last of the **bittersweet**. The cardinal on the feeder is a spot of crimson against the glistening white.

Think about the enjoyment plants and gardens provide, even when you are stuck indoors. As long as you can look out, you can appreciate what nature provides.

 CARE

As soon as the ground has frozen, spread the mulch to protect roots of newly planted vines and ground covers. Some evergreen ground covers such as **European ginger** and **pachysandra** will appreciate a cover-

ing of straw to protect them from winter sun and wind. Most garden centers will still have straw while they are selling Christmas trees. A couple of inches loosely laid over the plants will suffice. If there is sufficient snow cover, the straw will not be necessary.

 WATERING

Be sure that the plants have enough water before the ground freezes. Pay special attention to newly planted vines and ground covers.

 FERTILIZING

Do not fertilize vines, ground covers, or ornamental grasses in winter.

 PESTS

Protect susceptible plants from rabbit damage.

Use repellents containing thiram, or spray a mixture of a bottle of Tabasco in a gallon of water on the plants.

Protect plants from vole damage. Set out bait boxes of brodifacoum (D-con). Be sure other animals or birds cannot get into them. (See page 239 for ideas on making bait boxes.)

(See page 239 for ideas on making bait boxes.)

HELPFUL HINTS

Finish out the year by updating your journal. Summarize the good things and the things that did not work out as you had hoped. It is equally important to document failures so that you do not repeat them.

We gardeners are eternally optimistic. No matter how one season turned out, we are confident that the next one will be a winner.

As you contemplate the past and dream of next year, give thanks to the Creator who provides so many good things for each of us.

Walk down snow that accumulates next to susceptible plants so the voles cannot tunnel through it to the plants.

 PRUNING

Prune to remove damaged branches or those that are too long and being whipped around by the wind.

WATER &
BOG PLANTS

There is something about water that intrigues, soothes, and satisfies the soul. Whether you are sitting beside a quiet pool, hiking to a secluded waterfall, sailing on the big lake, or enjoying the fountain in the park, water comforts.

Within the last decade, water features have become the most popular new item in gardening. Water features can be as simple as a bird bath, a watering can that continuously fills, a tub with a few water plants, a backyard pond, or if you are so fortunate, the lake out your front door. The necessity of detention and retention ponds in new residential developments, the presence of barrow pits where soil for road construction was taken, and the accessibility of lakefront building sites have further stimulated the interest in water gardens.

The availability of equipment and supplies to build ponds and to care for them has made it simple to build ponds and to be successful in maintaining them.

Ponds cannot be set up and ignored, however. They take careful planning and a commitment to provide the necessities. Water gardens

constitute the most sophisticated kind of gardening. If done properly, these gardens will provide tremendous enjoyment. Plants, fish, even frogs, birds, and other animals will take up residence in and around a healthy pond.

The movement of the water and the other creatures will assure there is always something different to see in your water garden.

PLANNING

A water garden does not have to be elaborate. Keep it simple to start.

Although virtually everyone who has started a water garden has found it to be too small, starting too big has its drawbacks, too. A pond can always be enlarged, but if it is so big that it becomes burdensome from the start, you will be discouraged, missing out on the joy that the garden can provide.

A wash tub or barrel garden is sufficient to grow one water lily. A 3-foot-diameter pond will support a lily, submerged oxygenator plants, and fish. Larger ponds permit greater numbers of plants and fish.

Locating the pond will take thought. Keep these points in mind when deciding on the pond's location:

• It should be where the family relaxes and where people can see it from inside the house.

• It should be in the private area of the yard, protected from the view of the street and neighbors.

• If there are children in the neighborhood, it must be secure.

• It should not be placed below overhanging trees that would drop leaves into the pond.

Pond plants do best in a location where they receive sun at least 6 hours a day.

• It should be in a dry area. The pond will not sink in the mud, or if the water table rises, the liner will not be forced up by water pressure from below.

• It should be in the lowest part of the yard if that fits the other requirements. It is a more natural location.

If the spot collects runoff or tends to flood, some provision will need to be made to keep floodwater with its dirt and chemicals out of the pond.

Draw the water garden to scale on graph paper to be sure it will fit the location.

Ponds may be from 12 inches to several feet deep. A 3-foot-deep pond will not freeze completely, and it will allow fish and some plants to be overwintered. Shallow ponds will require removal of the plants and fish to winter quarters. Deeper ponds are less likely to

get too warm and oxygen-starved during hot spells.

Ponds may be constructed from many materials. The easiest to build are preformed plastic or fiberglass ones. Using flexible liners in holes dug directly in the ground allows creating freeform ponds of any shape or size. Many water garden firms offer catalogs listing all kinds, descriptions, and dimensions of pond liners.

Once you determine the location, size, and shape of the pond, you are ready to put the pond in place:

1. Lay out the pond outline. Use the preformed pond turned upside down, if it is symmetrical, or a garden hose to outline a freeform design.

2. Using a carpenter's level or transit, make sure the grade is level. The rim of the pond must be exactly level, or it will overflow before it is completely full.

3. Dig the hole to the proper depth and outline. The contour of a pond using a flexible liner must be exactly right. The liner will not correct errors.

4. Install the liner and edging, with the rim at least 1 inch or so above the ground level. This is to prevent surface water from running into the pond. Once a pond is operating and has reached equilibrium, any drainage water will upset it. The result can be algae bloom or

even contamination that could kill fish or plants.

PLANTING

For most small ponds, planting in containers eliminates some problems:

• It prevents the plants from getting out of hand.

• It allows lifting them for trimming, dividing, or storing for winter without having to contend with a mass of tangled roots.

• It makes setting them at the right depth easier.

• It simplifies cleaning the pond.

The containers can be boxes, tubs, or baskets. Most suppliers offer several types. The containers should have drainage so that water can flow in and out of them. Baskets should have a fine weave to prevent roots and rhizomes from escaping, and they will need to be lined with burlap to keep the soil from getting out.

Fill the containers with heavy clay soil. If they are too light to hold the plants upright, put bricks or heavy stones in the bottoms before filling them.

Submerged plants are essential to oxygenate the water. They remove carbon dioxide and minerals that would encourage algae while they provide shelter for smaller fish.

• Start with a bunch or two of one of the submerged oxygenator plants per square foot of surface water.

Many of them are very aggressive and will overtake the pond if allowed to do so. These plants should occupy no more than $1/3$ of the water volume.

• Plant a dozen or so in a small container, setting enough containers in the pond when you first establish the pond.

• If they become over-abundant, remove some of the containers.

Emerged plants are those that root in the hydrosol and reach to the surface. Water lilies, lotuses, and cattails are in this category. Leaves of water lilies and lotuses float on the surface, shading the water so that sunlight does not stimulate algae and providing fish protection from predators.

Plant emerged plants in large containers:

1. Fill the containers halfway with heavy garden soil that has a clay content of 20 to 25 percent.

2. Add fertilizer tablets, and push them into the soil.

3. Set the tubers or rhizomes so that the tips are level with the rim of the container.

4. Fill and firm the rest of the way with soil. The crowns or growing tips should be exposed.

5. Cover the soil surface with $1/2$ inch of pea gravel. This prevents soil from getting rooted out of the container by fish and fouling the water.

6. Saturate the soil.

7. Set the containers so that the plant crowns are at the minimum distance below the surface of the water. The warmth at the surface will hasten their development in the spring. As they begin to develop, they may be set lower in the water.

Free-floating plants such as water hyacinth, water lettuce, and duckweed do not root into the hydrosol, but drift around in the breezes and currents.

The leaves of emergent plants and free-floating plants should cover 50 to 60 percent of the pond surface. Free-floating plants can provide temporary cover until the larger plants mature. If they become too prolific, remove some of them.

Other creatures needed for pond health are scavengers, including fish, snails, and tadpoles. They clean up the leftover fish food, algae, and detritus. One scavenger per square foot of pond surface is about right.

HELPFUL HINTS

To perform regular maintenance operations, you may need to enter the water. Doing this disturbs the plants and the fish, upsetting the balance of the pond. Try to accomplish as much as you can each time. It will take time for the pond to settle down after you finish. The fewer times you enter the pond during the season, the less chance there is for permanent damage.

Having the proper attire makes working in the pond easier. Wear chest-high waders with soft soles. Lug soles may damage the pond liner. Inexpensive waders of this type are available with feet that fit into sneakers or mesh beach slippers such as Aqua Sox.

A properly balanced pond will clear the water in a few days after planting. If it does become cloudy, do not empty the pond. As soon as the organisms do their jobs, it will clear on its own.

Bog plants usually occupy saturated soils at the water's edge. Sometimes, they may actually stand in the pond. Plant them directly in the ground if it can be kept saturated.

Extending the pond liner beyond the edge of the pond several feet can provide an area for bog plants. Build a ridge around the pond so that the water from the bog area does not flow into the pond. You may want to plant them in individual containers to make it easier to keep them wet and to control them because some are very aggressive. These containers must be constructed in a way that the soil stays saturated.

CARE

Water and bog plants need the same kinds of care as any other garden plants, but the tasks may be modified for the specific environment.

Prune and trim so that dead or dying plant material is removed before it fouls the water. Do not neglect this regular chore. The plants must be kept in the proper balance with the needs of the pond. Too few or too many will result in imbalances and degradation of the water.

Remove some plants if they become too abundant. Duckweed can cover the water surface if not controlled.

Prepare plants for winter. Some plants are not hardy. Unless the pond is sufficiently deep, even hardy plants may need to be moved indoors for the winter. Fish can survive if the water does not freeze solid and if there is open water to allow air exchange.

FERTILIZING

Fertilize large plants such as water lilies with the proper amounts of fertilizer. Use special, slow-release fertilizers in pellet form, which do not increase the nutrient content of the water and result in algae problems. Use only fertilizers specially made for water plants.

WATERING

Maintain water levels throughout the season. If the levels are allowed to drop, they can result in fouling of the water and death of the plants and fish. During hot weather, aeration may be necessary to oxygenate the water.

PEST CONTROL

Most pests are controlled by scavengers and by careful maintenanceof the environment. Chemicals are difficult to use around ponds with fish populations.

JANUARY
WATER & BOG PLANTS

PLANNING

I have been looking at the new snow glistening in the morning sun. Steam is rising from the open water in the pond. In spite of the temperatures near 0 degrees Fahrenheit, the heater is doing its job. Without it, the pond would be frozen over, and I would be trying to melt a spot so the fish could get air.

When it warms up a little later, I will need to sweep some of the snow off the ice so that sunlight can get in. A pair of cardinals has been trying to get a little water without falling in, and some small birds have left tracks in the snow.

Many people feed birds in winter, but never think about giving birds something to drink. If the weather is severe, there may not be any water available for weeks. A few years ago we suf-

fered a severe bird kill because the only open water was runoff from the streets and roads. It was salty, but the birds used it anyway. Keeping the pond open helps them, too.

Stored away in the pond are the tender plants that would not make it through a good old Midwest winter. They are snoozing comfortably, unaware of the cold and snow. Others are at the bottom of the pond where they will not freeze. Before long, it will be time to think about any changes needing to be made in the pond and the plants for it.

As with any other kind of gardening, reviewing your records is a big help in knowing how the garden behaved last year and in planning for the new season.

Look through the latest water garden catalog to see what is new and interesting.

PLANTING

There is not much planting to do.

Later in spring, dividing and repotting will be necessary. Order the materials you will need: containers, fertilizer tabs, burlap, and soil if you have no extra in your own garden.

CARE

Check the overwintering plants stored indoors. They must be covered with water and not be allowed to dry out. If you are having trouble keeping them wet enough, cover the tops of the containers with plastic wrap. Leave the sides open so that they get air. If air is completely excluded, the soil will become rancid, and the plants will suffer.

HELPFUL HINTS

Keep the ice cleared of snow so that light reaches the plants. They will photosynthesize, removing carbon dioxide from the water and replacing it with oxygen. Be sure there is a good area of open water to allow toxic gases to escape.

If you do not have a heater and the ice freezes over, do not try to break a hole by chopping or pounding on the ice. That will send shock waves that may kill your fish. It may damage the pond liner, too.

Instead, pour boiling water on the ice to melt a hole. Sometimes a bucket of boiling water set on the ice will melt a spot. Refill with more hot water as it cools off.

When the weather is favorable, check the condition of the heater and the electrical connections. Sometimes animals have a taste for wiring and will gnaw on it.

FEBRUARY

WATER & BOG PLANTS

PLANNING

For most water gardeners just starting out, the main difficulty is maintaining the crystal-clear water like that in the glossy photos in catalogs and promotions. Therein lie the skills developed by those who have worked at learning how to manage these gardens.

Water gardens are probably the most demanding gardens in terms of the skills required to properly care for them. Caring for them is an art. Learning to handle your pond will take time, trial and error, and patience.

Fortunately, many places offer assistance to help you avoid some of the pitfalls. Most stores that specialize in water gardens employ people who can answer questions and have the supplies and materials to solve problems.

Clear water requires the right kinds and numbers of plants, scavengers, and time. Cloudy water is the result of algae that grow if the water is too rich in fertility and has too much light. These algae are not the same ones that grow in strands or like moss on the sides of the pond. Mosslike algae are controlled by scavengers that graze them. Scavengers will also eat leftover fish food so that it does not foul the water.

New ponds and ones just cleaned will turn cloudy. Plants will clear them in time. The submerged plants absorb the water's carbon dioxide and nutrients, starving the algae. Emerged and floating plants shade the water, reducing photosynthesis.

Do not drain your pond if it becomes cloudy. Allow it to age and reestablish the balance. In extreme cases, algicides and filters will speed up the process, but until the microorganisms and plant population are in balance, they are just temporary aids.

CARE

Pay attention to plants being kept indoors for the winter; do not allow them to dry out or become rancid. Add water as necessary to keep the plant containers flooded. If they are beginning to deteriorate, remove the cover, and let them air out. If the storage area is too warm, relocate the plants to a spot where temperatures are in the range of 40 to 50 degrees Fahrenheit.

Plants and fish wintering in the pond should be safe if they are below the freeze line and there is open water to release gases and reoxygenate the water. Keep at least the area over the plants free of snow so that the plants can photosynthesize on sunny days. That absorbs the carbon dioxide,

releasing oxygen into the water.

Check the heater often to be sure that nothing has happened to the wiring and that it is working properly. If the pond should freeze up, follow these steps:

1. Open a hole by melting the ice with hot water.

2. Or set a bucket of boiling water on the ice, which will eventually melt its way through. Add more water as it cools. Tie a line on the bucket to haul it out if it falls through the ice.

3. Do not chop or hammer a hole in the ice. The shock waves could harm the fish, and the pounding might damage the liner.

PESTS

Voles may hide in the mulch over the bog plants at the edge of the pond.

If there are signs of voles, set out bait boxes of brodifacoum (D-con). The voles may feed on the crowns of herbaceous plants when there is a shortage of forage for them.

Occasionally, wild animals will find the pond and go after the fish. Even in urban areas, predators that forage all year are becoming quite common.

Place wire over the open water to prevent this. Secure the wire around the edges so that the animals cannot pull it away.

MARCH

WATER & BOG PLANTS

PLANNING

Signs of spring are everywhere. The snow is melting; buds are swelling; the first robins have arrived. There is still winter weather to be sure, but the worst of the cold should be over.

As the sun intensifies, the water temperatures will rise, and certain things will happen in the pond. The plants begin to grow. The fish resume activity after the long winter stupor.

Water temperatures need to reach a certain level before reintroducing fish and plants overwintered indoors. A good practice is to record the dates and temperatures in your journal. Especially in spring, this information will give you an idea of when you can plan to do certain things each year.

You can guess at the water temperature, but for accuracy, it is better to use a thermometer.

Check the water temperature about once a week after the ice melts. After a few seasons, you will have enough data to determine averages.

• At 35 degrees Fahrenheit, remove the heater.

• At 45 degrees Fahrenheit, start the pumps.

• At 50 degrees Fahrenheit, release the last of the overwintered fish.

CARE

Check the condition of overwintering plants indoors. It will soon be time to prepare them for planting out. In the meantime, keep them cool and sufficiently covered with water.

In the garden, early bog plants are starting to grow. The **skunk cabbage** will flower shortly as will some of the other earliest plants. Pull back the mulch from these plants. Keep it handy in case winter stages a comeback.

Cut back the foliage left on plants around the pond before new growth emerges. Compost the material, or spread it over the vegetable garden where it can be spaded in later.

PESTS

Sanitation is the first defense against diseases. Remove old foliage and tops and debris floating on the surface of the pond. There will be time later to clean up and divide plants that overwintered in the pond.

Escaped pets, feral cats, and other wildlife may find the pond inviting, especially if the water level happens to be low. Use netting or a fence to protect fish from predation until the plants have grown enough to hide them.

TIME FOR REPAIRS

Ponds can sustain severe damage from ice or from freezing and thawing over winter. Repairs must be made before the season is very far along. Once things begin to grow, it will be difficult to keep everything under control while you carry out repairs. Repairs may require lowering the water level in the pond. Doing this while plants are still dormant and the fish are indoors or relatively inactive will be easier on them.

Here is a list of items that need attention at this time:
• Service pumps and filters.
• Clean the pumps and lubricate if required.
• Make sure all seals are intact.
• Clean or replace the elements in filters.

If water clarity is a continuing problem, you may want to invest in a biological filter or even in an ultraviolet sterilizer.
• Replace cracked hoses and tubing.
• Check the electrical service to your pond.

Winter weather or rodents may damage wiring. Mice are attracted to electrical wiring in winter and can gnaw through the insulation.
• Check seals around boxes and circuit breakers that were idle during the winter.

APRIL
WATER & BOG PLANTS

Water and bog plants will be set at different levels in the pond.

PLANNING

Spring is here with a vengeance. In the northern parts of the state, it will take a little longer for things to warm up, and there is still the possibility of a snowflake or two for another month or so. But the water in the pond is warmed by the ever-strengthening sun. Things are beginning to grow, and I heard frogs last night for the first time.

Review plans, schedules, or lists of jobs that need to be done this spring. You may have to work hard to finish everything before the start of the season.

PLANTING

The plants wintered in the bottom of the pond need attention:

1. Lift them, and trim off all dead and winter-damaged parts.

2. Before discarding any dead plants, check for new growth at the base.

3. If no new growth is forthcoming, replant the container with new plants using new soil and fertilizer tabs.

4. Cover the surface with pea gravel to prevent fish from rooting out the soil.

Divide crowded and overgrown plants. Pull the masses of oxygenator plants from the containers, clip off bunches of sprigs, and replant them in the same soil. Cover the surface with pea gravel.

Follow these steps to transplant and plant **hardy water lilies**:

1. Lift **hardy water lily** plants from the soil.

2. Wash them off.

3. Remove all open leaves.

4. Cut the rhizomes in $1/2$, discard the weaker parts, and trim long roots.

5. Replant with the crowns just below soil level.

6. Cover the soil with pea gravel.

7. Set the plants in the pond at the minimum depth until growth starts. Then set them at the maximum depth.

8. Plant new **hardy water lilies** now, too.

Spring is the time to divide all bog plants as well:

1. Carefully dig them up.

2. Rinse off the soil.

3. Pull apart clumps by hand, or cut them apart with a sharp knife or spade.

4. Cut apart tubers and rhizomes as described for **water lilies**.

5. Discard old, tired, or diseased parts.

6. Replant the best portions directly in the bog or in containers of fresh soil set in the bog.

When danger of a severe freeze is over, plant new hardy bog plants. After planting, mulch all bog plants to reduce water loss.

CARE

Trim back tops of bog and water-loving plants. Add them to the compost pile, or spread them on the vegetable garden for spading in later.

Set immersed water plants back on their ledges when there is no danger of a severe freeze. Or set plants on bricks, over-turned baskets, or boxes to the correct depth. Start them at the shallowest depth so that they are warmed by the sun to hasten development. As they grow,

---

HELPFUL HINTS

Check out all equipment before installing it in the pond for the summer. Test all pumps, filters, connections, pipes, hoses, tubing, and electrical wiring and boxes. It is easier to make repairs now before the equipment is installed than trying to get it apart and repaired when it is needed to keep the pond from having problems.

Once the pond is planted and stocked, disturbing it is unwise. Each time it is upset, it must go through the adjustment period again.

remove some of the supports until they are at their correct depths for the season.

WATERING

Bog plants must never dry out. They survive in saturated soil. The beds or containers must be watertight. Soak them whenever necessary to maintain their flooded condition.

FERTILIZING

Fertilize bog plants, being careful not to get any of the material in the pond. Excess nutrients will increase the algae bloom.

Fertilize **lilies** with tabs inserted into the soil. Do not use garden fertilizer to fertilize plants in the pond.

PESTS

Control of diseased plants is not complicated. Cut out any diseased portions of plants before setting them back in their summer locations.

As soon as the pond becomes active in spring, it will attract wildlife looking for an easy meal. Neighborhood cats, escaped pets, ferrets, minks, snakes, and turtles can decimate the fish population in a night or two. Blue herons arriving early in spring will find the fish in your pond easy pickings.

Install netting over the pond or fencing around it to keep out predators.

MAY

WATER & BOG PLANTS

PLANNING

Every few years draining and cleaning the pond may be necessary. Smaller ponds will need cleaning more often than larger ones, maybe every 2 or 3 years. This is a major job, requiring preparation and planning.

Spring is the best time to clean the pond. Overwintering plants and fish can be held out until the job is done. Overgrown plants wintered in the pond can be divided and thinned where needed. The health of the fish wintered in the pond can be determined and treatment made. The plants have plenty of time to become established before the onset of hot weather.

Assemble the materials you will need:

- Tubing to drain the pond
- Garden hose
- Plastic buckets
- A plastic dustpan
- A soft push broom
- A pump (not always needed)
- Water treatment chemicals for chlorine and ammonia (as the pond is being refilled)

- A soft net
- A bowl
- A children's wading pool or several large garbage cans
- Netting or towels to cover the containers
- Newspapers

Working in the pond can be made easier if you are properly attired. Wear chest-high waders with soft soles. Lug soles may damage the pond liner. Inexpensive waders of this type are available with feet that fit into sneakers or mesh beach slippers. To clean the pond, follow these steps:

1. Drain it, filling the holding containers with pond water first, and removing enough water (about 2/3 is usually enough) so that you can catch the fish.

2. Remove the containerized plants from the shelf.

3. Wrap the containers in wet newspaper, and set them in a shaded place.

4. Protect scavengers that may be trapped in them.

5. Catch as many fish as you can with the net and bowl, and put them in the holding pool.

6. Remove all the floating plants, and save bunches of each kind in the buckets of water.

7. Lift out the containerized immersed plants and **lilies**, wrapping the containers in wet newspaper. Store them in the shade.

8. Dip out the rest of the water.

9. Catch any remaining fish with the net, and transfer them to the holding pool.

10. Check for tadpoles and frogs in the mud. Transfer them to the holding pool. Cover the pool so that they cannot jump out.

11. Pour the water in the garden. Do not pour it down a drain.

12. With the water removed, carefully shovel out the rest of the mud with the plastic dustpan. Keep a bucket of mud to repopulate the pond. Watch for any small animals that may have escaped earlier. The mud can be added to the compost pile or spread on the vegetable garden for spading in later.

13. After most of the mud has been scooped out, scrub the bottom and sides of the pond with the soft brush. Add a little fresh water if needed. Rinse, and bail the dirty water.

14. Repair the pond. Examine the liner closely. Patches can be applied easily now. Masonry can be repaired or a butyl lining may be installed if repairs are not possible.

PLANTING

Now you are ready to recreate the pond:

1. Begin to refill the pond with the garden hose.

2. Unwrap the **lilies** and containerized immersed plants. Divide them if necessary, and replant them in the containers. Set the containers in the deepest part of the pond. Set them on bricks, overturned containers, or boxes to the right elevation so that the leaves are at the surface when the pond is full.

3. Once the larger plants have been set in the pond, add the bucket of bottom mud and water to the pond. This will reestablish the fish and other organisms more quickly.

4. Plant sprigs of the oxygenators in small containers, a dozen or so bunches per container, and set on the bottom of the pond.

5. Add plants such as **tropical lilies** wintered indoors. Divide and replant if necessary.

6. Then set the marginal plants on the shelf or on bricks to the right depth. Leave room to get into the pond.

7. Transfer the fish from the holding pool. Examine them for diseases or pests, and treat them if necessary. Transfer all the other beneficial organisms and scavengers.

8. Finish filling the pond.

9. Add the water treatments for chlorine and ammonia, and install the pump.

10. Finish replacing the marginal plants.

CARE

The pond will cloud up after cleaning until the plants are large enough to clear it.

Algicides may be helpful as temporary aids to clear the water.

WATERING

Make sure the bog plants are well watered. Mulch them to prevent water loss.

FERTILIZING

As the plants are set in the pond, fertilize them with the prescribed numbers of tabs. Fertilizer tabs especially for pond use are available at pond supply stores or by mail order. Do not use garden fertilizer in ponds because algae will grow.

PESTS

Remove leaves that turn yellow or show signs of diseases.

Filamentous algae can become excessive until the pond reaches equilibrium. Remove it with a stick to the compost pile.

Neighborhood cats, ferrets, escaped pets, minks, snakes, and turtles can decimate the fish population in a night or two. Blue herons arriving early in spring will find the fish in your pond easy pickings. Install netting over the pond or fencing around it to keep out predators.

PRUNING

Prune overgrown plants. Use care, and disturb the pond as little as possible if you must enter it to do the pruning. Remove excess oxygenators also.

JUNE

WATER & BOG PLANTS

PLANNING

By now the pond should have cleared itself from the annual cleaning in May, and the plants should be reestablished for the summer.

With all the spring work out of the way, evaluate the way things went. Make entries in your journal while the memories are still fresh.

Did you say you do not have a journal yet? Start one! It does not have to be fancy; a spiral notebook will do. Use it to record essential information:

• At the top of a page, enter the year.

• Along the margin, write the date each time you make an entry.

• Record how the plants withstood the winter.

Note the challenges involved in getting them back in the pond, the cleaning process and how it went, and any other pertinent comments.

• Record the difficulties so that you do not repeat them.

• Record the joys.

These are moments that need to be recorded. Life is full of frustrations. When something truly pleasant is going on, it needs to be noted. In the future you may look at the notes you wrote and remember a time that was exceptional.

After the work is over, isn't it a thrill sitting at the side of your pond, enjoying the fragrance of the **lotus**, and watching the fish lazily swimming in the crystal-clear water?

PLANTING

If the **lilies** and other deep-water plants do not provide enough shade yet, set floating plants in the pond to help out. Remove them later if the cover is too heavy.

Floating plants should occupy no more than one-third of a pond's surface.

Plant new **lilies** into the pond anytime in early summer as long as there is room. There is sufficient time for them to get started before it begins to get too hot.

CARE

Deadhead flowers after they are finished blooming to keep them from falling into the water. Remove leaves that turn yellow or are damaged by insects or diseases. Continuous care in removing organic matter will keep the pond clear.

WATERING

Hot, dry weather will increase evaporation and lower the pond level. Add water to maintain the level. It is better to add some every day than to make it up all at once. A major change in the water will affect the temperature and the population of bacteria as well as add chlorine.

The bog plants need to stay wet enough in hot weather, too.

FERTILIZING

Fertilize the large **water lilies** with tablets according to the sizes of the containers.

PESTS

Mites can cause problems on **lilies**. These tiny pests infest the undersides of the leaves.

Remove them with a strong spray of water.

Diseases are fairly easy to control.

Regularly remove discolored leaves. Doing this removes the disease and usually is sufficient to prevent any spread.

Filamentous algae and floating plants can become so abundant as to be weeds.

Remove the excess. Skim off the floating plants. Roll the algae on a stick, and remove it from the pond. Dispose of them in the compost pile.

By now the cover afforded by the floating-leafed plants should give fish enough protection from predators. Herons may still visit the pond if they found it easy pickings earlier in the year.

Use netting or wire to discourage them.

PRUNING

If floating-leafed plants are too large and covering more than 60 percent of the pond, remove some of the foliage. Oxygenators should occupy no more than a third of the water volume. Remove the excess as needed.

JULY

WATER & BOG PLANTS

PLANNING

A successful pond is one that minds its own business, providing maximum pleasure from a minimum amount of work. For this to happen takes planning, which in turn means understanding the dynamics of pond life.

All the elements of a pond—the water, plants, animals, and microorganisms—have functions.

The water provides support and essential components for the plants. These include carbon dioxide and the fertilizer elements.

• If these elements are lacking, the plants will not grow.

• If they are in excess, there will be a proliferation of vegetation, and the pond will become plugged up.

Usually, the plants in excess will be algae. Filamentous algae fill the pond with stands of green muck. Planktonic algae turn the water pea soup green.

• If the balance is correct, the beneficial plants have just the right amount of nutrients to do their jobs. The plants use up the nutrients and release oxygen into the water. The submerged oxygenator plants occupy about 30 percent of the water volume, and the floating-leafed plants shade 60 per cent of the water surface. There are no nutrients left for the algae.

The fish use the oxygen produced by the plants and release carbon dioxide for the plants to reuse. Scavengers remove any excess filamentous algae and leftover fish food. The bacteria in the bottom mud digest organic matter and convert chemicals into usable forms. The water stays clear.

If things begin to go out of kilter, the pond will deteriorate, and something will need to be done. This is where skill is important. As soon as changes appear, try to figure out what has happened:

Have the plants gotten overgrown? Are there too many fish? Are there too few oxygenators?

Sometimes immediate corrections are necessary. Often there is time to make plans for adjusting the various factors.

If you have made notes in the past, they can be helpful in evaluating the changes that have occurred and adjusting the pond to its optimum condition.

PLANTING

If the pond has insufficient cover or if the oxygenators are not filling 30 percent of the water volume, it is not too late to plant more of them. If some **lilies** have become overgrown and the leaves are beginning to stand

Seed pods of a lotus make great dried flowers.

up, remove some leaves by cutting them out with a sharp knife.

Lift containers of badly crowded plants, and divide the plants. Or make plans to divide them in the fall or spring. Note in your journal the ones needing attention.

Plant bog plants and marginals now, too.

CARE

Remove all yellowing leaves before they drop, as well as all faded blooms. Removing spent flowers can stimulate more flowers. The addition of dead organic matter to the water may turn it black.

If seeds are to be collected, leave those flowers on the plants until they ripen.

WATERING

Keep bog plants in saturated soil. If the weather is hot and dry, water these plants.

Check every few days to make sure the water level in the pond has not dropped. Add water to maintain the level. It is better to add some every day than to make it up all at once. A major change in the water will affect the temperature and the population of bacteria as well as add chlorine.

FERTILIZING

Fertilize deep-water plants every 3 to 4 weeks in summer with slow-release tablets available from water garden suppliers. The tabs are stuck into the soil in the containers where it is available for plant roots, but does not get into the water. Do not use garden fertilizer for ponds because it will dissolve in the water and stimulate the growth of algae.

PESTS

Aphids and whiteflies occasionally become pests in the water garden. If there are fish in the pond, chemical treatments are not advisable. Lady bugs will find the aphids, and certain wasps are predators of the whitefly larvae.

Obtain these insect predators through insectaria. Catalogs are available from garden centers and water garden specialists. Fish consume insect pests as well. Inspect your plants regularly, and remove severely infested leaves as soon as you notice the damage.

Several diseases can affect the foliage, especially during hot weather. Remove diseased leaves as they appear.

Weeds will appear in the marginal plantings. Pull them out as they appear to avoid their taking over. The weeds that appear in the pond are generally filamentous algae.

Roll up the strands on a stick, and pull them out of the pond. Let the mess drain on the edge of the pond so that any trapped scavengers can escape. Add the algae to the compost pile.

Herons and neighborhood cats can go after your fish.

If these predators appear, string fencing around the pond or netting over it. If the pond is elongated, herons can be discouraged from fishing in it by stringing a series of wires across the pond so the birds cannot wade along it.

PRUNING

Remove all ripening, damaged, or dead vegetation so that it does not accumulate in the pond.

HELPFUL HINTS

Summer storms can strip leaves from trees. Some trees seem to drop leaves all summer. Skim leaves off the pond before they sink to the bottom.

Be careful when mowing the grass around the pond. Collect the clippings, or run the mower so that the clippings are discharged away from the pond. If you employ a lawn service, make sure the operators are aware of the necessity of keeping the clippings out of the pond.

Any excess loading with organic matter will result in deterioration of the pond.

AUGUST

WATER & BOG PLANTS

PLANNING

Fish can provide an additional dimension to the enjoyment of your pond. They also are important parts of the pond ecology:

- They are colorful.
- They can be trained to come on demand for feeding and observing.
- They consume oxygen and release carbon dioxide for the plants.
- Some eat algae, keeping it at an acceptable level.
- They eat insects.

Mosquito fish in sufficient numbers will consume just about all the mosquito larvae in a pond. They will eat insect pests that could damage plants, too.

Planning is necessary before stocking the pond. Various kinds of fish require certain environments. Some fish are very tolerant; others are sensitive to conditions and will take more care. Some species are carnivorous and will eat your other fish. Some are happy in a shallow pond; others (like koi) need water at least 3 feet deep.

A deep pond will allow wintering the more hardy species outdoors. A shallow pond or less hardy species will demand a winter holding area indoors.

Many books are available describing the various options for stocking your pond, so I will mention only a few:

- Common goldfish

They are tough, will live up to 10 years, and can stay outside if the pond is deep enough and there is enough oxygen. A heater to keep the pond from freezing over is sufficient.

- Exotic goldfish

They should be brought in during the winter.

- Various kinds of carp, including koi

Koi are highly bred exotics that need special care. Water must be deep and crystal clear to enjoy them to the fullest. They can spend the winter outdoors if the pond is quite deep. The more valuable ones are usually moved indoors, though. Koi are rambunctious fish and will stir the bottom, clouding the water. They are heavy feeders, and good filters are needed to remove the mud and waste they create.

- Minnows and other small fish

They feed on the insects and are sometimes eaten by the larger fish. It is helpful to provide cover for the smaller fish. Cover also protects the larger fish from predators such as herons and escaped pets.

- Native fish, such as bluegills, minnows, crappie, and bass

They may stock natural ponds.

- Hybrid grass carp

These specialized fish are used to reduce weed problems in ponds that are completely out of control or are being managed poorly. These are large fish, and numbers must be carefully controlled to prevent the total elimination of vegetation in the pond. Permits are required before stocking ponds with grass carp.

PLANTING

Divide deep-water plants all summer if necessary. Once the pond has become stabilized for the summer, avoid upsetting it unless things are terribly wrong. In that case, make the corrections.

Leave sufficient time for bog and marginal plants growing in the ground to become reestablished before the season's end. Containerized plants moved indoors for the winter are not subjected to the same stresses.

Repopulate the pond with enough oxygenator plants to fill $^1/_3$ of the water volume and enough floating-leafed plants to cover $^2/_3$ of the surface. Use free-floating plants to fill in if needed.

CARE

Continue to trim off spent blooms and ripening foliage to prevent them from sinking into the pond. These materials will quickly degrade a pond, especially in hot weather when oxygen deficiencies can occur.

WATERING

Hot, dry weather can result in rapid evaporation from the pond surface and lowering of the water level. This can increase the mineral concentration in the pond, raise the water temperatures and reduce the oxygenation, expose the liner to sunlight, and cause other imbalances to occur. Ultraviolet light can ruin a liner very quickly.

Keep the liner covered with water or other materials where it is exposed at the pond edge.

Avoid adding large amounts of fresh water at one time. Adding water every day if needed is much less disruptive. If large amounts are added at one time, algae bloom or even fish kill may result.

FERTILIZING

Fertilize large, deep-water plants every 3 to 4 weeks in summer with slow-release tablets available from water garden suppliers. The tabs are stuck into the soil in the containers where it is available for plant roots, but does not get into the water. Do not use garden fertilizer for ponds because it will dissolve in the water and stimulate the growth of algae.

PESTS

Plants may suffer insect damage.

Remove the pests by cutting off the infested plant parts. Fish will eat insects washed off the plants into the water. Obtain predators of specific insect pests from suppliers or catalogs.

HELPFUL HINTS

Skim the pond to remove all leaves and other organic matter that blow onto the surface. As the season moves toward fall, there will be more and more leaves, old plant tops, seeds, and other debris. Keeping it from sinking in the pond will reduce the organic matter content, which will affect the pond oxygen level.

Leaves may show signs of disease infections. Clip them off.

Weeds may appear in bog plantings. Pull weeds as they appear. If it is necessary to walk in the bog, set planks or plywood sheets so that you do not sink and damage the plants.

Raccoons will occasionally fish in ornamental ponds. These animals are very difficult to dissuade once they develop habits. The only sure way of eliminating the problem is by trapping and relocating them. Contact your local animal control authorities.

September

WATER & BOG PLANTS

 PLANNING

Labor Day signals the start of a new season. Activities put on hold for the summer resume. School begins. Vacations are over, and there is less time to spend in the garden.

The weather can cool off quickly this month. There are $2\frac{1}{2}$ to 3 fewer hours of sunlight than there were in June. There may still be warm weekends when you can sit on the deck and enjoy your pond, but the relentless advance of the seasons cannot be ignored too long.

There is much to do to prepare the pond for the winter:

- Inventory your plants.
- List the ones that will need to be brought indoors.

Decide which plants are not worth saving. Sometimes saving plants is not worth the trouble. Many gardeners treat pond and bog plants like annuals, disposing of them in fall and replacing them with new ones in spring.

- Make arrangements to hold the plants that will be saved.

Tubs, buckets, or room for the containers must be acquired. Unless all the plant material and fish will be brought in for the winter, you will need a heater for the pond. If fish are to be wintered indoors, you will need a tank of the appropriate size.

Yellow flag iris may need supplemental watering if the weather is dry.

- List the materials and supplies you will need to take care of all the things that need attention.

If any propagation or replanting is to be done over winter, the soil needs to be stockpiled where it will not be frozen when you need it.

- Keep the list handy when you go shopping.

It may be wise to set up a calendar of the things you plan to do so there will be enough time to get them all finished this fall. A last-minute rush often leaves things undone because of lack of time or because they were forgotten.

 CARE

Continue to trim off spent blooms and ripening foliage to prevent them from sinking into the pond. These materials will quickly degrade a pond. There may be an abundance of old plant material as the plants get ready for winter. Keep it out of the pond to avoid problems later.

WATERING

The evaporation from the pond will slow down as the weather moderates, but the proper level must be maintained at all times. Water the bog plants if weather turns dry. Fall can be very dry throughout the Midwest.

FERTILIZING

Water temperatures affect the fertilizer needs of the plants. As the water cools down, stop fertilizing the plants. They will be going dormant and will need no fertilizer.

PESTS

Some insects overwinter on old plant parts.

Add all clippings, old leaves, plant tops, and other debris to the compost pile, or spread them on the vacated areas of the vegetable garden to be spaded in later.

Some foliage may become diseased.

Cut it off the plants, and add it to the compost pile or spread it over the vegetable garden.

SEPTEMBER TASKS

• Remove pumps and filters when the need for them is over.

This is usually when the water temperature gets down to 45 to 50 degrees Fahrenheit.

• Store them where they will not freeze.

They will need servicing during the winter to get them in shape for next season.

• Check the electrical supply to the pond.

Animals, lawn mowers, and the weather may have deteriorated the connections, insulation, or cables.

• Make needed repairs.

• Install and connect the heater.

It will not be needed for some time yet, but see that it works now, before you need it. Repair or replace it if it does not function properly.

Add grass clippings and old leaves to your compost pile.

OCTOBER

WATER & BOG PLANTS

 PLANNING

Before the memories of the season grow dim, record the events, thoughts, ideas, problems, and joys of the year. Journaling is something most of us try to avoid, but it is a good way to store information that would be lost if left to our imperfect memories.

How many times I have repeated the same dumb mistake because I did not recall having done it before. Our lives are so hectic that unless we write things down, they seem to fade into the foggy past. And unless jarred into the present, these ideas or thoughts are lost.

I recall . . . I forget what I was trying to recall! See, it happens all the time.

 PLANTING

As containerized plants are lifted for moving indoors, they can be divided, or the job can be left until spring.

Dividing now will result in less stuff to store over the winter, but you may be busier now than you will be in spring, and you may be just trying to finish out the season.

 CARE

As the days shorten and the weather turns cool, many plants will respond with a display of fall color or will simply dry up. Cut back the tops of these plants. Cut back stems of deep-water and emergent plants just below the water line. Cut back bog plants, leaving enough of the old leaves and stems to protect the crowns.

Lift tender bog plants that have grown in containers, and move them indoors before they freeze. Some tender plants are very difficult to winter over indoors.

Water gardens can be small or elaborate.

These can be discarded just like annuals and replaced next year.

Remove **tropical water lilies**, **lotuses**, and other tender deep-water plants before they freeze. Cut off dying foliage. Store them in their containers, or lift the tubers and rhizomes out of the containers and store them in containers filled with damp sand.

Move marginal plants and **hardy water lilies** from their shelves or supports, and set them into the deepest part of the pond. If the pond is too shallow for the plants to be below the ice line, store even hardy kinds indoors in tubs of water.

Plants with hollow stems such as **horsetail** and some **reeds** will rot if the stems fill up with water. They can usually be wintered in shallow water along with **cattails** and some other hardy plants. Native plants are perfectly able to stand the winter weather if their roots are in shallow water.

WATERING

Do not allow the level of the pond to drop at this time of the season. The plants and fish will need all the depth they can get to survive the winter.

Make sure the bog plants are well watered going into winter.

Plants in winter storage must never be allowed to dry out either.

• Check them often, especially after the heating season starts.

Heated air is very dry and can dry out the plants in a few days.

• Cover the containers with plastic wrap to keep them wet.

• Allow some air in the sides of the containers so that the soil does not become rancid.

PESTS

Wild animals looking for a quick and easy meal may find your pond. If they see the fish, they will try to catch them. Without the cover of the floating-leafed plants, the fish are exposed with no place to hide.

Provide the fish with pieces of 6-inch clay tile on the bottom of the pond in which to hide.

PRUNING

Remove all foliage from the deep-water and emergent plants. Trim back the submerged plants significantly. These plants usually die back during the winter with the excess plant material falling to the bottom of the pond where it decays the next season. If these plants are in containers, they can be lifted to make trimming easier.

Add all trimmings from deep-water, marginal, and submerged plants to the compost pile, or spread them on the vegetable garden to be spaded in.

HELPFUL HINTS

Before the leaves fall from the trees and shrubs, cover the pond with netting to catch them. Netting has at least two advantages:

1. Netting will save a lot of work next spring when leaves will have sunk to the bottom of the pond and removing them would be a messy job.

2. Netting will discourage some of the predators that might find the fish tempting.

As the leaves collect, remove the netting and empty the leaves into the compost pile or on the garden to be spaded in later. Replace the netting, and securely fasten it so that if animals decide to walk on it, they will not tear it loose.

NOVEMBER

WATER & BOG PLANTS

 PLANNING

The first snow has fallen. It did not stay around very long, but it was pretty while it lasted with its big, soft flakes that stuck to your eyelashes.

The pond is quiet now. Frost has killed back the last of the perennials, and only a few of the grasses have any green left. Tops of all the plants around the pond have been cut back, leaving tufts of old stems and leaves.

The netting is still stretched over the pond because the sycamore down the way still has most of its leaves. Those things stay until the last moment, then all fall at once. The wind picks them up and blows them around like so many kites. The leaves are almost as big as kites, too, and when they fill a pond, it is a mess. I hope they fall before the pond freezes over because I do not want to leave the netting on over winter if I can help it.

I have emptied the net on the garden a couple of times already. The net is a big help. I think I will stretch a net over the **cotoneaster** ground cover plants in front of the house next year. It is a chore to get the leaves out of them each spring, too.

Chickadees and juncos are back. Sometimes the chickadees stay around all summer, but the juncos are a sure sign that winter is on the way. The squirrels are extra furry this fall, and they have been especially busy. Does that mean a harder winter? We'll see!

 CARE

As soon as the ground gets a little frost, mulch the marginal plants with clean straw. This will keep them from freezing and thawing. That cycle is harder on them than the cold. As long as they stay frozen, they will be fine.

Watch the plants indoors, especially if it is quite warm where they are stored. If it is too warm, they may sprout or rot. Temperatures around 50 degrees Fahrenheit are probably about right. Cooler is better than hotter.

 WATERING

Make sure plants being wintered indoors are well watered. Marginals can be in containers of damp sand. Immersed or emerged plants must be in water.

Do not allow the bog plants outdoors to dry out if the weather is mild. Some winters are mild and open, and the plants can desiccate if the water evaporates. You may need to take out a hose and water them if they are dry.

 PESTS

Voles may decide to spend the winter in the mulch around some of your plants. They will nest next to tender shoots or stems and feed without going out into the weather.

If you see signs of voles, set out bait boxes of brodifacoum (D-con). Make sure the other animals and birds cannot get into them. Make small wooden boxes with a 3/4-inch hole or two. Or use a plastic butter or cottage cheese container, cut a 3/4-inch notch in the edge, add the brodifacoum (D-con), and replace the lid. Set the container upside down where the voles have been active. Check regularly, and add brodifacoum (D-con) if needed. See the diagram on page 239.

Protect shrubby plants with repellents sprayed on the stems and allowed to run down to soak the crowns. Try Tabasco, a bottle mixed in a gallon of water, and add some soap or spreader-sticker so that it stays on the plants. Keep this or any other sprays away from the pond.

DECEMBER
WATER & BOG PLANTS

 PLANNING

Some days it is too nice to hide indoors. Taking a walk around the garden and looking at the pond provide an excuse to be out.

While you are out, make notes in your journal. There I am again with that journaling stuff. I would not keep talking about it if it were not so important. But spring is only 12 weeks away, and there will be things to do before then. At least list the things that need to be corrected or changes you want to make.

 CARE

After touring the garden, check the status of the plants and fish overwintering indoors. Everything should be routine by now. As long as the conditions do not change, everything should be fine all winter. Do not leave it to chance, though. It is still important to check regularly.

 WATERING

The overwintering plants stored indoors must be covered with water and cannot be allowed to dry out. If you are having trouble keeping them wet enough, cover the tops of the containers with plastic wrap. Leave the sides open so that they have air. If air is completely excluded, the soil will become rancid, and the plants will suffer.

 PESTS

While you are outside, check for animal damage.

If you detect any, take proper control measures. Voles are the most damaging pests. Set traps, or make small wooden bait boxes with a 3/4-inch hole or two. Or use a plastic butter or cottage cheese container, cut a 3/4-inch notch in the edge, add the brodifacoum (D-con), and replace the lid. Set the container upside down where the voles have been active. It must stay dry. Check regularly, and add brodifacoum (D-con) if needed.

HELPFUL HINTS

Those of us who are able to garden and have the luxury of ponds, waterfronts, streams, or lakes need to be thankful for our blessings. These things give us pleasure, and they present us with responsibilities. We need to be good stewards of the land and water for which we have become responsible.

To be successful growing water gardens, we need to understand—more than with any other kind of gardening—the inter-relationships of the various elements of the garden, to nurture

them, and to provide what they need so that they can function.

Water gardening is an adventure. It is a learning experience. Once you embark on this journey, you will never be the same.

Each year will be different and will present new challenges. Study, ask questions, enjoy the fellowship of other pond gardeners, experiment, and keep records. You never know what the result may be. Someday you may want to write a book about your experiences with your water garden.

PLANTING CHARTS

Annuals

Variety	Sow Seed Indoors	Plant in Garden
Ageratum	Feb. 15 (light)	May 15
Alyssum	Mar. 15	May 15
Begonia	Jan. 15 (light)	May 30
Browallia	Feb. 10 (light)	May 30
Calendula	Apr. 1	May 15
Celosia	Apr. 10 (light)	May 15
Cleome	Apr. 15 directly in garden (light)	Apr. 15
Coleus	Mar. 1 (light)	May 30
Cosmos	Apr. 1 (or seed directly in garden)	May 30
Dusty Miller	Mar. 1	May 30
Flowering Cabbage	July 1	Sept. 1
Flowering Tobacco	Mar. 1 (light)	May 30
Four-O'Clock	Apr. 10 (or seed directly in garden)	May 10
Gaillardia	Apr. 1 (light)	May 30
Garden Pinks	Mar. 1	May 1
Geranium	Jan. 1	May 10
Gerbera	Feb. 1 (light)	May 30
Globe Amaranth	Apr. 1 (or directly in garden)	May 15
Gloriosa Daisy	Apr. 1 (or directly in garden)	May 1
Heliotrope	Feb. 1 (light)	May 30
Impatiens	Feb. 1 (light)	May 10
Lobelia	Feb. 10 (light)	May 10
Love-in-a-Mist	Feb. 15 (directly in garden or in peat pots; difficult to transplant)	May 1
Marigold	Apr. 1	May 10
Melampodium	Mar. 1	May 10
Morning Glory	Apr. 15 (directly in garden)	Apr. 15
Moss Rose	Mar. 15 (or directly in garden)	May 1
Nierembergia	Mar. 15 (light)	May 15

(Continued on following page)

PLANTING CHARTS

Annuals

Variety	Sow Seed Indoors	Plant in Garden
Pansy	Dec. 15	Mar. 15
Petunia	Feb. 1 (light)	Apr. 30
Salvia	Mar. 15 (light)	May 15
Snapdragon	Mar. 1 (or directly in garden)	Apr. 30
Sunflower	Apr. 15 (or directly in garden)	May 15
Verbena	Mar. 1 (light)	May 1
Zinnia	Apr. 1	May 30

Dates in this chart are based on the frost-free date for Zone 5b. For the southern part of the state, dates may be as much as 2 weeks earlier; for the far northwestern part of the state, the dates may be up to 2 weeks later.

Bulbs, Corms, Rhizomes, & Tubers

Variety	Plant in Garden	Depth (To top of bulb)	Spacing	Blooms	Overwinter?
Allium	Sept.-Oct.	2 to 3 inches	4 to 8 inches	May-June	Hardy
Autumn Crocus	June to Sept.	4 inches	6 to 8 inches	Sept.	Hardy
Caladium	May (Frost-free date)	Tuber at surface	12 inches	Foliage	Tender
Camass	Sept.	3 to 4 inches	5 inches	June	Hardy
Canna	May	6 inches	12 inches	Summer	Tender
Chionodoxa	Sept.	3 inches	4 inches	April	Hardy
Crocus	Aug.-Sept.	2 inches	3 inches	Mar.-Apr.	Hardy
Crown Imperial	Sept.	6 inches	8 to 12 inches	May-June	Hardy
Daffodil	Sept.-Oct.	6 inches	6 inches	May	Hardy
Dahlia	May	4 inches	12 to 24 inches	July-Oct.	Tender
Galanthus	Sept.-Oct.	3 inches	4 inches	Mar.-Apr.	Hardy
Gladiolus	Apr.-June	4 inches	9 inches	Summer	Tender
Iris (Bulbous)	Sept.-Oct.	3 to 4 inches	6 inches	Mar.-Apr.	Hardy
Lily	Sept.-Oct.	3 to 8 inches	12 inches	Summer	Hardy
Montbretia 'Lucifer'	May	3 inches	6 inches	Aug.	Semihardy
Muscari	Sept.-Oct.	3 inches	3 inches	Apr.-May	Hardy
Resurrection Lily	July	6 inches	6 inches	Aug.	Semihardy
Squill	Sept.-Oct.	2 inches	3 inches	May	Hardy
Summer Snowflake	Sept.-Oct.	3 inches	6 inches	May-June	Hardy

(Continued on following page)

PLANTING CHARTS

Bulbs, Corms, Rhizomes, & Tubers

Variety	Plant in Garden	Depth (To top of bulb)	Spacing	Blooms	Overwinter?
Tuberous Begonia	May	1 inch	12 inches	Summer	Tender
Tuberose	May	3 inches	6 inches	Aug.-Sept.	Tender
Tulip	Sept.-Nov.	4 inches	8 to 10 inches	Mar.-May	Hardy
Windflower	Sept.-Oct.	2 inches	3 inches	Apr.-May	Hardy
Winter Aconite	Sept.-Oct.	3 inches	3 inches	Mar.-Apr.	Hardy

Dates in this chart are based on the frost-free date Zone 5b. For the southern part of the state, dates may be as much as 2 weeks earlier; for the far northwestern part of the state, the dates may be up to 2 weeks later.

Vegetables

Variety	Sow Seed Indoors	Plant in Garden	Spacing In row	Between rows
Asparagus	Buy started plants	March 25	10	36
Bean, Snap	Seed directly in garden	May 10	18	24
Beet	Seed directly in garden	April 25	2-3	12
Broccoli	March 1	April 25	18	36
Cabbage	March 1	April 25	12	18
Carrot	Seed directly in garden	April 25	2	12
Cauliflower	March 1	April 25	18	36
Chard, Swiss	March 15 (or directly in garden)	April 25	4-6	18
Chinese Cabbage	March 10	April 25	12	24
Corn, Sweet	Seed directly in garden	May 10	9	24-36
Cucumber	April 30 (peat pots or directly in garden)	May 25	Hills 36 by 36	
Eggplant	April 15	May 25	18	30
Endive	March 15	April 25	9	18
Garlic, Clove	Plant directly in garden	September	3	12
Lettuce, Head	March 1	March 30	12	12
Lettuce, Leaf	March 15 (or directly in garden)	April 10	4	12
Muskmelon	April 30 (peat pots or directly in garden)	May 25	Hills 36 by 36	
Mustard	Seed directly in garden (or broadcast in beds)	April 10	2	12
Okra	May 1	May 30	12	36
Onion Set	Plant directly in garden	April 10	2-5	12

(Continued on following page)

PLANTING CHARTS

Vegetables

Variety	Sow Seed Indoors	Plant in Garden	Spacing In row	Between rows
Parsley	March 1	April 25	6	12
Parsnip	Seed directly in garden	April 25	2	12
Pea	Seed directly in garden	April 10	10	18
Pepper	April 25	May 25	18	24
Potato, Irish	Seed pieces directly in garden	April 10	12	24
Potato, Sweet	Slips directly in garden	May 25	12	36
Pumpkin	April 30 (peat pots or directly in garden)	May 25	Hills 72 by 72	
Radish	Seed directly in garden	April 10	1	12
Rhubarb	Buy started plants	March 25	36	48
Rutabaga	Seed directly in garden	April 10	6	18
Spinach	March 1	March 25	4	12
Squash, Bush	April 30 (peat pots or directly in garden)	May 25	Hills 36 by 36	
Squash, Vine	April 30 (peat pots or directly in garden)	May 25	Hills 72 by 72	
Tomato	April 1	May 10	36	36
Turnip	Seed directly in garden	April 10	4	12
Watermelon, Bush	April 30 (peat pots or directly in garden)	May 25	Hills 36 by 36	
Watermelon, Vine	April 30 (peat pots or directly in garden)	May 25	Hills 72 by 120	

Herbs

Variety	Sow Seed Indoors	Plant in Garden	Spacing In row	Between rows
Basil	April 30	May 30	12	18
Chives	March 1	March 25	12-by-12 clump	
Cilantro-Coriander	March 1 (or directly in garden)	March 25	1-6	20
Dill	March 1 (or directly in garden)	March 25	12	24
Fennel	March 1 (or directly in garden)	March 25	12	24
Horseradish	Buy divisions or roots	March	24-by-24 clump	
Mint	Buy started plants	March 25	12-by-12 clump	

(Continued on following page)

PLANTING CHARTS

Herbs

Variety	Sow Seed Indoors	Plant in Garden	Spacing In row	Between rows
Oregano	Buy started plants	March 25 clump	12-by-12	
Rosemary	Buy started plants	April 30	18	18
Sage	March 1	April 15	18	18
Salad Burnet	February 15 (or directly in garden)	October or March	12	12
Savory, Summer	April 15 (or directly in garden)	May 15	6	12
Savory, Winter	March 1	May 1	24	24
Sorrel, French	March 1 (or directly in garden)	April 15	12	12
Sweet Cicely	October 15 directly in garden, or buy started plants	March 25	12	18
Sweet Marjoram	April 15	May 10	6	12
Sweet Woodruff	October 15 directly in garden, or buy started plants	March 25	6	6
Tarragon	Buy started plants, or divide rhizomes in fall	March 25	12	18
Thyme	March 1, or buy started plants of named varieties	March 25	12-by-12 clump	

Dates in this chart are based on the frost-free date for Zone 5b. For the southern part of the state, dates may be as much as 2 weeks earlier; for the far northwestern part of the state, the dates may be up to 2 weeks later.

Lawns

Species	How to Start	When to Start	Uses
Colonial Bentgrass	Seed	Spring, summer, fall	Exotic lawns, fairways
Creeping Bentgrass	Seed or vegetative+	Spring, summer, fall	Exotic lawns, fairways
Creeping Red Fescue	Seed	Fall	Lawns, shade, poor soils
Kentucky Bluegrass	Seed, sod	Seed, spring or fall; Sod, spring, summer, fall	Lawns, fairways, sports fields
Perennial Ryegrass	Seed	Fall, spring	Lawns, sports fields
Tall Fescue	Seed	Fall, spring	Utility lawns, sports fields
Meyer Zoysia	Vegetative+	Spring	Lawns

+Sod, sprigs or plugs

Perennials

Variety	When to Plant	Spacing	Comments
Achillea	Seed, February 1 under lights. Plants, spring or fall	18 to 24 in.	Can be seeded in garden, transplanted in spring, fall.
Aster	Spring	24 to 36 in.	Started plants are available all season.
Astilbe	Spring or fall	24 in.	Can be seeded in garden, transplanted in midsummer.
Baptisia	Seed, August under lights. Plants, spring, fall	36 in.	Plants available all season.
Bee Balm	Spring, fall	36 to 48 in.	Started plants are available all season.
Bell Flower	Spring or fall	12 in.	May be seeded in midsummer. Named cultivars available as plants.
Bleeding Heart	Spring or fall	36 in.	Started plants, or seed in place.
Blue Star	Seed midsummer, plants, spring	30 to 36 in.	Container plants available all season.
Butterfly Weed	Spring	18 in.	Root cuttings or seed in spring, potted plants all season.
Columbine	Seed in fall, plants spring, fall	12 to 18 in.	Plants seeded indoors in Dec. can be planted out in spring.
Coneflower	Spring	24 to 36 in.	Divisions or plants. Potted plants available all season, or seed indoors.
Coreopsis	Spring	18 in.	Potted plants available all season.
Daylily	Spring, late summer	24 in.	Potted plants available all season.
Delphinium	Seed in August, plants, spring or fall	12 in.	Seed in garden, transplant in spring.
Ferns	Spring	6 to 24 in.	Started plants available all season, but best in spring so establish before winter.
Gaillardia	Seed under lights in January; plants, spring or fall	12 to 18 in.	Potted plants available all season.
Gay Feather	Spring	18 to 24 in.	Potted plants available all season.
Hardy Mums	Spring, fall	12 to 24 in.	Cuttings or plants in spring, blooming potted plants in fall.
Heuchera	Seed in August, plants spring or fall	8 to 12 in.	Potted plants available all season.
Hosta	Divisions, spring or fall.	12 to 18 in.	Potted plants available all season.
Iris	August	12 to 36 in.	Potted plants available all season.
Peony	Fall	36 in.	Divisions in fall, potted plants all season.
Phlox	Spring, fall	18 to 24 in.	Rooted cuttings or started plants, potted plants are available all season. Do not start from volunteer seed.

(Continued on following page)

PLANTING CHARTS

Perennials

Variety	When to Plant	Spacing	Comments
Purple Coneflower	Spring, fall	36 in.	Potted plants available all season.
Russian Sage	Spring, fall	18 in.	Potted plants available all season.
Salvia x *superba*	Spring, fall	12 to 18 in.	Potted plants available all season. May be seeded.
Shasta Daisy	Spring, fall	12 to 18 in.	Potted plants available all season.
Sedum 'Autumn Joy'	Spring, fall	18 to 24 in.	Potted plants available all season.
Speedwell	Spring, fall	18 to 36 in.	Potted plants available all season.

Roses

Variety	Uses	Spacing	Comments
Groundcover Roses	Low shrub landscape plantings	24 to 48 in.	True groundcover form, low and spreading. Plant spring or summer.
Harrison Yellow	Specimen	48 in.	Outstanding yellow in late May, June. Plant spring or summer.
Hybrid Tea Types	Rose garden, border garden, cutting, specimen (floribundas, grandifloras)	24 to 36 in.	Plant in spring bare root, or all summer from containers. Griffith Buck hybrid tea types are hardy to Zone 4.
Landscape Roses	Shrub borders, masses	24 to 30 in.	Winter-hardy, arching or upright shrubs. Plant spring or summer.
Miniature Roses	Edging, specimens, containers	12 in.	Tiny duplicates of the larger bush plants. Plant spring or summer.
Rugosa Types	Landscape borders, masses, hedges	24 to 36 in.	Tolerant plants, carefree and adaptable. Plant spring or summer.
Old-Fashioned Roses	Specimens, masses	4 to 10 feet	Large, often spreading. Spring-flowering. Newer hybrids—David Austin or English—are worth trying. Plant spring or summer.

PLANTING CHARTS

Ornamental Shrubs

Variety	Height	Spread	Blooms	Comments
Alpine Currant (*Ribes alpinum*)	3 to 6 feet	3 to 6 feet	Spring	Excellent hedges and low borders. Good in shade.
Arbor Vitae (*Thuja occidentalis*)	3 to 20 feet	3 to 6 feet	Conifer	Excellent tall hedges or screens. Globe types 3 to 4 feet high and wide.
Barberry (*Berberis* sp.)	1$\frac{1}{2}$ to 6 feet	3 to 6 feet	Spring	Blooms not showy. Good hedge and barrier. Many colors and forms.
Bluebeard (*Caryopteris* x *clandonensis*)	2 to 3 feet	2 to 3 feet	Late	Plant in early spring. Dainty blue flowers attract summer hummingbirds.
Boxwood (*Buxus* sp.)	2 to 4 feet	2 to 4 feet	March	Flowers not showy. Excellent broadleaf evergreen.
Cotoneaster (*Cotoneaster* sp.)	2 to 12 feet	6 feet or more	Spring	Tiny pink flowers and red berries in fall. Many forms for hedge and masses.
Dogwood (*Cornus* sp.)	6 to 20 feet	6 to 20 feet	Spring	Yellow, white, or pink blooms. Many forms. Colored bark on some.
Forsythia (*Forsythia* sp.)	3 to 9 feet	3 to 10 feet	Spring	Masses of yellow blooms. Large plants, need room.
Fragrant Sumac (*Rhus aromatica*)	To 6 feet	6 to 10 feet	Spring	Tall forms good for screen. Dwarf form excellent for masses. Tolerates full shade.
Holly (*Ilex* sp.)	10 to 15 feet	5 to 10 feet	Late spring	Inconspicuous white flowers. Red berries in fall. Some evergreen forms. Plant in spring.
Honeysuckle (*Lonicera* sp.)	3 to 10 feet	3 to 15 feet	Spring	Many forms and sizes. The workhorse of the landscape industry.
Hydrangea (*Hydrangea* sp.)	6 to 15 feet	6 to 18 feet	Summer	Plant spring or fall. Large showy flower clusters persistent. Good for cutting.
Juneberry (*Amelanchier arborea*)	15 to 20 feet	5 to 10 feet	Spring	Excellent native shrub.
Juniper (*Juniperus* sp.)	5 to 20 feet	5 to 20 feet	Conifer	Many forms and colors. Plant all season from containers.
Lilac (*Syringa* sp.)	4 to 10 feet	5 to 10 feet	Spring	Traditional spring-flowering shrubs. Many forms, sizes, and colors.
Mock Orange (*Philadelphus coronarius*)	3 to 10 feet	3 to 10 feet	June	Fragrant, white, orange blossoms. Dwarf forms easier to use.
Mugo Pine (*Pinus mugo*)	4 to 10 feet	8 to 20 feet	Conifer	Many sizes. Be sure you know which one you are getting.
Potentilla (*Potentilla fruticosa*)	1 to 4 feet	1 to 4 feet	Spring, summer	Yellow, white, or pink blooms all summer.
Privet (*Ligustrum* sp.)	5 to 15 feet	5 to 15 feet	Spring	Serviceable shrubs, tolerant of conditions and treatment. Sheared hedge or screen.

(Continued on following page)

PLANTING CHARTS

Ornamental Shrubs

Variety	Height	Spread	Blooms	Comments
Rhododendron (*Rhododendron* sp.)	3 to 6 feet	3 to 6 feet	Spring	Evergreen or deciduous plants. Gorgeous in flower. Plant in spring.
Rose-of-Sharon (*Hibiscus syriacus*)	10 feet	10 feet	Summer	Hollyhocklike flowers all summer on ungainly plants.
St. John's Wort (*Hypericum prolificum*)	1 to 4 feet	2 to 4 feet	July	Conspicuous yellow flowers on low plants.
Snowberry (*Symphoricarpos albus*)	3 to 6 feet	3 to 6 feet	June	Inconspicuous pink flowers followed by persistent white berries.
Spicebush (*Lindera benzoin*)	6 to 10 feet	6 to 10 feet	April	Fragrant yellow flowers. Tolerates deep shade.
Spirea (*Spiraea* sp.)	2 to 10 feet	2 to 10 feet	Spring, summer	Favorite, old-fashioned shrubs. Many, sizes, forms.
Summersweet (*Clethera alnifolia*)	3 to 10 feet	5 to 15 feet	Summer	Fragrant white clusters of flowers after almost everything else has bloomed out.
Viburnum (*Viburnum* sp.)	3 to 10 feet	3 to 10 feet	Spring, summer	White masses of blooms, some wonder, fully fragrant. Extremely serviceable plants, various sizes, forms.
Witchhazel (*Hamamelis* sp.)	15 feet	12 feet	Fall, spring	Plant in spring. Interesting flowers in late fall or early spring.
Yew (*Taxus* sp.)	4 to 20 feet	4 to 25 feet	Conifer	The Cadillac of shrubs, with rich green foliage and tidy form. Masses, hedges, specimens. Tolerant of severe shearing.

Small Fruit

Variety	Spacing	Fruit	Comments
Blackberries	4 by 6 feet	Summer or fall	Spacing depends on support system.
Blueberries	6 by 10 ft.	June, July	Blueberries require acidic soils. Protect from birds. Plant in spring.
Currants and Gooseberries	4 by 6 ft.	Summer	These plants are alternate hosts for white pine blister rust. Do not plant if white pines are growing in your area. Plant in spring.
Raspberries	4 by 6 feet	Summer or fall	Various kinds require different pruning methods. Ever-bearing types may be harvested spring and fall. Plant in spring.

PLANTING CHARTS

Trees

Alder (*Alnus glutinosa*)
Medium- to fast-growing, medium-sized tree, spreading, ascending. Alder is valued for its form, interesting bark, and suitability for wet areas. Height to 40 feet; spread to 20 to 30 feet.

Ash, American (*Fraxinus americana*)
Large, vigorous tree, fast growing and drought tolerant. 'Autumn Purple' cultivar is more adaptable to either wet or dry soils and has good purple fall color. Height to 100 feet; spread to about 50 feet·

Ash, Green (*Fraxinus pennsylvanica*)
Fast-growing, open tree, tolerant of adverse conditions. 'Marshall's Seedless', which has no seeds; 'Summit', which is upright and oval shaped; and 'Patmore', which is upright, compact, and more refined, are preferred to the species. Height to 60 feet; spread to 40 to 50 feet.

Bald Cypress (*Taxodium distichum*)
A deciduous conifer, broadly columnar when young, broadly rounded at maturity. Its feathery foliage appears late. Bald cypress is adapted to wet locations, but may suffer in alkaline sites. Height to 70 feet; spread to 40 feet.

Beech, American (*Fagus grandifolia*)
Splendid, slow-growing native tree that is outstanding in leaf, and in winter with beautiful light-gray bark. tlts surface roots may interfere with the lawn. Use it as a specimen in a tree bed. Height to 90 feet; equal spread.

Beech, European (*Fagus sylvatica*)
Dense, slow growing, with many cultivars from which to select. There is no finer specimen tree, and according to Dirr, it is "so beautiful that it overwhelms one at first glance." Use it as a specimen in a lawn or tree bed. Height to 75 feet; spread to 50 feet.

Birch, River (*Betula nigra*)
A borer-resistant birch with exfoliating cinnamon to pink bark. River birch is best as multistemmed, arching and graceful. Plant it only in spring. It is sensitive to pH of 7.4 and above. Height to 70 feet; spread to 40 feet.

Birch, White (*Betula platyphylla*)
Lovely white bark and relaxed pyramidal habit. The cultivar 'Whitespire' is borer resistant. Be sure that it is vegetatively propagated from the original tree. Plant it in spring only. Specimen height to 40 feet; spread to 25 feet.

Black Tupelo (*Nyssa sylvatica*)
One of our most beautiful native trees, with beautiful form and fall color. It suffers in alkaline soils above pH 6.5. Plant it only in spring. Use it as a specimen along the street or in the lawn. Height to 50 feet; spread to 40 feet.

Catalpa (*Catalpa speciosa*)
Fast-growing tree, picturesque with open, irregular crown, coarse texture. It has large leaves, white flowers in June, and beanlike pods in fall. It is very tolerant of conditions. Height to 60 to 80 feet; spread to 40 feet.

Chokecherry, Amur (*Prunus maackii*)
A rounded tree with exfoliating cinnamon-colored bark. It has clusters of white flowers in May and small fruit in August. One of the better cherries, it is rather carefree. Height probably to 35 feet in urban sites; spread to 30 feet.

Coffeetree, Kentucky (*Gymnocladus dioicus*)
Bold, open tree, somewhat coarse in winter. A large tree, it is suitable for open areas such as parks, golf courses, and multiple housing developments. Pods may be messy. The tree is adaptable to alkaline and droughtlike conditions. It is a good choice where it has room. Height to 90 feet; spread to 40 to 50 feet.

(Continued on following page)

PLANTING CHARTS

Trees

Cork Tree, Amur (*Phellodendron amurense*)
Medium tree with interesting bark in old age. It tolerates alkaline soils. Use the cultivar 'Macho' rather than the species. Height to 50 feet.

Crabapple, Flowering (*Malus* cv.)
Outstanding group of small flowering trees valued for flower, foliage, fruit, and form. Nothing can duplicate the beauty of a crab apple in flower. Use only varieties with resistance to foliar diseases. Use small-fruited varieties where fruit may be a nuisance. Because it is available in various forms and sizes, use it as a specimen, an accent, or in masses.

Dogwood, Flowering (*Cornus florida*)
Small tree with horizontal lines and layered effect. It is excellent in flower, foliage, fall color, fruit, and winter interest. It does best in a cool, shaded spot, protected from the heat of the day. Many cultivars are available. Height to 20, sometimes 30 feet; spread equal or greater.

Ginkgo (*Ginkgo biloba*)
Outstanding slow-growing, pest-free, site-tolerant tree with unique foliage and good fall color. It is actually a broadleaf conifer. Use only male trees because fruit has an objectionable odor. Height to 70 feet; spread to 40 feet or more.

Hackberry (*Celtis occidentalis*)
Good tree for city conditions with a form similar to that of an elm, but not as clean. Because it tolerates alkaline soils, grime, and air pollution, it can be used in rough locations. Witches' broom is a problem on the species. Broom-free cultivars are available. Height to 40 to 60 feet; equal spread.

Hawthorn (*Crataegus* sp.)
Dense, twiggy, small- to medium-sized trees. All are armed with thorns. Some thornless varieties are now available. It has attractive flowers and fruit but is subject to pests. Height to 25 feet; equal spread.

Hemlock, Eastern (*Tsuga canadensis*)
Graceful native evergreen tree, particularly suited to shaded sites, one of our best evergreens. It needs protection from winter wind. It can be sheared to any size. Height to 70 feet; spread to 25 feet.

Honeylocust, Thornless (*Gleditsia tricanthos inermis*)
Vase-shaped large tree with exceptionally fine foliage. It is tolerant of city conditions, but subject to pests. Although much overused, it is useful where better varieties will not grow. Many cultivars are available. Height to 70 feet or sometimes to 100 feet; spread about half that size.

Hop-Hornbeam (*Ostrya virginiana*)
Handsome small tree for urban plantings, graceful and rounded in form. Interesting fruit are similar to hops, thus the name. Height to 25 or 30 feet; spread about the same.

Hornbeam (*Carpinus caroliniana*)
Small tree best used in naturalized areas. It will stand flooding and alkaline soils. Use it as an understory tree or in a planter. It transplants best in spring. Height to 35 feet; equal spread.

Horsechestnut (*Aesculus hippocastanum*)
Handsome, dense tree, showy in flower. It is subject to foliar diseases. Height to 40 feet; equal spread.

Katsura Tree (*Cercidiphyllum japonicum*)
Pest-free, excellent tree for residential properties and parks, pyramidal to wide-spreading with apricot fall color. Transplanting is difficult but worth the effort. Plant it only in spring. It must be watered to become established in difficult sites. Height to 60 feet; spread to 30 to 60 feet.

(Continued on following page)

PLANTING CHARTS

Trees

Larch (*Larix decidua*)
Fast-growing deciduous conifer with a pyramidal habit, pendulous branchlets, and loose, open texture giving light shade. It has a striking appearance when leafing out in spring and good fall color. Height to 70, maybe 100 feet; spread to 50 feet.

Lilac, Japanese Tree (*Syringa reticulata*)
Good specimen or street tree for tight places. It has interesting bark, with fragrant clusters of white flowers in June. Height to 20 feet; equal spread.

Linden, American (*Tilia americana*)
Excellent, large native shade tree needing little attention. It has fragrant, conspicuous flowers. Suggested cultivars are 'Redmond', which is densely pyramidal, and 'Rosehill', which is fast growing with an open crown. Height to 80 feet; spread to 60 feet.

Linden, Littleleaf (*Tilia cordata*)
Relatively pest-free, excellent shade tree for almost any place a quality tree is needed. It tolerates alkalinity, pollution, and pruning. Many good cultivars are available. Buy it on own roots to avoid suckering problems. Height to 60 feet; spread to 40 to 50 feet.

Linden, Littleleaf Greenspire (*T. cordata* 'Greenspire')
Fast-growing tree with a dense, tightly pyramidal shape and compact foliage. Its flowers are very fragrant in early summer. Height to 50 feet; spread to 30 feet.

Magnolia, Saucer (*Magnolia soulangiana*)
Low-branched tree with 10-inch diameter flowers in early spring. Late frosts often spoil blooms just as they are at their peak, but it is still worth the effort to plant it. Plant it in spring in a protected area if possible. Height to 25 feet; spread equal or more at old age.

Maple, Norway (*Acer platanoides*)
Dense, rounded, symmetrical crown, shallow rooting. Growing grass under this tree is difficult. It tolerates city conditions but is subject to frost cracking, Verticillium, and scorch. Cultivars 'Emerald Queen' and 'Summer Shade' are preferable to species. 'Schwedler' with red leaves in spring and 'Crimson King' with red leaves all season are less tolerant. Height to 40 to 50 feet; equal spread or greater.

Maple, Silver (*Acer saccharinum*)
Fast-growing, rather soft tree subject to damage from wind, ice, and insects. Widely planted, it is useful if its limitations are taken into account. Although considered a short-lived tree, many 75- to 100-year-old individuals are still acceptable trees in the northern suburbs. Height to 80 feet; spread to 50 to 60 feet.

Maple, Sugar (*Acer saccharum*)
One of our finest native trees, slow growing, beautiful in fall. Pests seldom affect it. Cultivar 'Green Mountain' is more tolerant than species. Its size requires room. Height to 60 to 90 feet; spread to 40 to 60 feet.

Oak, Bur (*Quercus macrocarpa*)
Large, coarse, native tree, very adaptable to various soils. It needs room. Plant it in the spring. Height to 80 feet; spread to 80 feet.

Oak, English (*Quercus robur*)
Massive tree similar to native white oak. It may have insect and mildew problems. It must be planted in spring. Height to 75 feet; spread to 60 feet. Cultivar 'Fastigiata' is narrowly upright in habit, very useful in tight situations with height of 50 to 60 feet, but spread only to 15 to 20 feet.

Oak, Northern Red (*Quercus rubra*)
Moderately fast-growing tree, round topped and symmetrical with scarlet fall color. Plant it only in spring. It may be chlorotic in poorly drained or alkaline sites. Height to 75 feet; spread to 45 feet.

(Continued on following page)

PLANTING CHARTS

Trees

Oak, White (*Quercus alba*)
Slow growing and majestic. It is demanding and difficult to transplant. It needs an undisturbed site. It will tolerate alkalinity if soil is not disturbed and understory plants and litter are left in place to stimulate growth of mycorrhizae. Plant it in spring when leaves are mouse-ear sized. Height to 90 feet; spread to 60 feet.

Pagodatree, Japanese (*Sophora japonica*)
Fast-growing oval tree with masses of showy, white flowers in late summer. It may be considered messy when flowers fall, but it is worth a look. It tolerates difficult city conditions. Height to 50 feet.

Pear, Callery (*Pyrus calleryana*)
Small tree, tolerant of city conditions. It is covered with white flowers in spring; it has small fruit that is not messy. Height to 30 feet; spread to 20 feet. Cultivars are superior to species. 'Bradford', dense upright to rounded, reaches a height of 40 feet and a spread of 30 feet; it may split badly at mature size. 'Chanticleer', narrow upright, reaches a height of 35 feet and a spread of 15 feet. 'Trinity', tightly rounded, reaches a height of 30 feet.

Pine, Austrian, Scotch, White (*Pinus nigra, P. sylvestris, P. strobus*)
Magnificent evergreens widely planted as specimens and for screens. Scotch and Austrian pines are beset with pest problems. White pine remains relatively pest free, but suffers from alkaline and wet soils. Pines are absolutely beautiful where well cared for. Height to 40 to 60 feet; spread about half to equal at maturity.

Redbud (*Cercis canadensis*)
Small tree with showy pink flowers before the heart-shaped leaves appear in spring. It is shade tolerant and best planted in spring. Height to 25 feet.

Spruce, Norway, Blue (*Picea abies, P. concolor*)
Strongly upright, conical evergreens, even at maturity. Norways are drooping, used as screens or temporary specimens. Blues are stiffer and variable in color, green to blue; they are overused as specimens. Height to 60 feet; spread to 50 feet.

Sweetgum (*Liquidambar styraciflua*)
Strongly pyramidal when young, rounded at maturity. The star-shaped leaves turn yellow in fall. Plant it in spring or early summer. It is marginally hardy in Zone 4. Height to 75 feet; spread to 50 feet.

Tulip Tree (*Liriodendron tulipifera*)
A large native tree, handsome where allowed enough room. It has distinctive tulip-shaped leaves and flowers; it becomes golden yellow in fall. It can be brittle and suffer storm damage. Planting in spring is recommended. Although it is not a yard or street tree, it is often used that way. It is probably best used in large groupings, office parks, and multiple housing developments. Height to 150 feet in the wild; to 80 feet in urban locations; spread to 35 or 50 feet.

Yellowwood (*Cladrastis kentukea* [*lutea*])
Excellent small-spreading tree in flower and in leaf. It has drooping clusters of white blooms in June, and it is attractive to bees. It is a good choice for small properties. Height to 35 feet; spread somewhat greater.

PLANTING CHARTS

Vines

Variety	Size	Blooms	Comments
American Bittersweet (*Celastris scandens*)	Twining to 20 feet	June	Hardy native plant with showy fruit in fall. Male and female flowers on separate plants.
Boston Ivy (*Parthenocissus tricuspidata*)	Vining to 50 feet or more	Spring	Excellent vine with shiny leaves, common on the ivy-covered walls.
Clematis (*Clematis x jackmanii*)	5 to 15 feet	Summer	Outstanding flowers. Needs pruning for best blooming.
Climbing Hydrangea (*Hydrangea anomola* subsp. *petiolaris*)	Clinging to 50 or 80 feet	Late June	Probably the best of the flowering vines. Not timid, needs good support.
English Ivy (*Hedera helix*)	Clinging to 90 feet	Inconspicuous	Also used as ground cover. Best in shade. Incorporate new plants into planting to renew yearly.
Hyacinth Bean (*Lablab purpureus*)	15 to 30 feet	Summer	Vigorous annual vine with showy purple blooms. Start from seed.
Morning Glory (*Ipomoea purpurea*)	To 20 feet	Summer	Vigorous annual with large purple, red, or white blooms. Start from seed.
Wintercreeper (*Euonymous fortunei*)	40 to 50 feet	Inconspicuous	Also used as ground cover. Needs annual pruning. Subject to scale. Attractive, commonly used plants. Many forms.
Wisteria, Japanese (*Wisteria floribunda*)	20 to 30 feet	Spring	Hanging clusters of purple, pink, or white blooms. Sturdy vine that takes sturdy support.

Ground Covers

Variety	Size	Blooms	Comments
Ajuga (*Ajuga reptans*)	6 to 10 inches, spreading	Spring	Many colors, forms. Semievergreen. Best in shade.
Creeping Cotoneaster (*Cotoneaster adpressus*)	1½ feet tall, spreading 4 to 6 feet	Spring	Woody plant with glossy leaves, red fruit in fall.
European Ginger (*Asarum europaeum*)	6 to 10 inches, clumps	Inconspicuous	Neat mounds of shiny, bright green leaves One of the best in shade.
Gro-Low Sumac (*Rhus aromatica* 'Grow Low')	1 to 2 feet tall spreading to 10 feet	Spring	Excellent in tough places. Tolerates salt, sun, or shade. Good fall color and showy fruit.
Juniper (*Juniperus* sp.)	6 to 18 inches tall, spreading to 6 feet	Conifer	One of the toughest of all ground covers. Many colors, sizes.
Lily-of-the-Valley (*Convallaria majalis*)	6 to 12 inches	Spring	Fragrant flowers on aggressive plants. A favorite, but it dies down in late summer.

(Continued on following page)

PLANTING CHARTS

Ground Covers

Variety	Size	Blooms	Comments
Pachysandra (*Pachysandra terminalis*)	6 to 12 inches, spreading to 12 inches	Spring	Evergreen herbaceous plants, best in part or full shade.
Periwinkle (*Vinca minor*)	3 to 6 inches, creeping	Spring	Periwinkle-colored blooms, sun or partial shade. Very commonly used.
Purple Wintercreeper (*Euonymous fortunei* 'Coloratus')	6 to 12 inches	Insignificant	One of the most commonly used groundcovers. Semievergreen. Purple in winter.
Sweet Woodruff (*Galium odoratum*)	6 to 8 inches	Spring	Fragrant blooms, shade tolerant. Old-fashioned favorite.
Thyme (*Thymus vulgaris*)	2 to 6 inches	Late spring	Another old-fashioned favorite. Low spreading herb.

Ornamental Grasses

Variety	Size	Blooms	Comments
Blue Stem (*Andropogon gerardii Schizachyrium scoparium*)	2 to 10 feet tall, spread to 4 feet	August-September	Big and little blue stem are native grasses. Well adapted and trouble free.
Feather Reed Grass (*Calamagrostis acutiflora*)	4 to 5 feet tall	Midsummer	Upright, orderly plant. Blooms earlier than most grasses, holds flowers well.
Fountain Grass (*Pennisetum alopecuroides*)	2 feet tall and wide	Midsummer	Perennials and annuals. Red fountain grass is spectacular. Perennial kinds prefer hot weather and start late. Prefer moist soils.
Northern Sea Oats (*Chasmanthium latifolium*)	2 to 5 feet	Late summer	Warm-season plants will start late. Best in moist, fertile soils. Flowers last all winter and are excellent for picking.
Plume Grass (*Erianthus ravennae*)	To 12 feet	Late summer	Best in moist soils. Needs plenty of room. May escape cultivation. Good for dry arrangements.
Silver Grass *Miscanthus* sp.)	6 to 12 feet	Late summer, fall	Many cultivars with various forms, sizes. Maiden grass is one of the oldest and still one of the best.

PLANTING CHARTS

Submerged Oxygenating Plants

Variety	Size	Blooms	Comments
Canadian Pondweed (*Elodea canadensis*)	Up to 13-foot-long stems	Crimson, cream, just above surface.	Summer.One of the best oxygenators, native to the Midwest. Hardy. Can become invasive. Water depth 3 feet.
Curlyleaf Pondweed (*Potamogeton crispus*)	Up to 15-foot-long stems	Crimson, cream, just above surface.	Summer.Native to cooler parts of the Midwest. Long 15-foot stems of translucent 3-inch leaves. Needs trimming to keep under control. Water depth 3 feet.
Hornwort (Coontail) (*Ceratophyllum demersum*)	1 to 2 feet	Insignificant.	Rootless plant with 1- to 2-foot stems and stiff, forked, dark-green leaves. Water depth 2 feet.
Water Milfoil and Parrot's Feather (*Myriophyllum* sp.)	1 to 3 feet	Insignificant, yellow, held above water.	Two of several related species with delicate, feathery leaves. Excellent oxygenators. Hardy. Water depth 18 inches.

Floating Plants

Variety	Size	Blooms	Comments
Duckweed (*Lemna* sp.)	$1/2$ inches	Tiny, spring.	Tiny green plants with 2 leaves and single rootlet. Can take over in a short time. Provide shade early. Screen off from surface with net. Try the ivy-leafed variety, which is less invasive.
Frogbit (*Hydrocharis morsus-ranse*)	2 to 4 inches	Summer.	Tiny waterlilylike plants with white flowers. Overwinters on pond bottom as turions.
Water Hyacinth (*Erichhornia crassipes*)	6 to 12 inches	Summer.	This tropical can choke rivers in the South. Useful in the North. Lilac flowers with yellow eye. Overwinter indoors.
Water Lettuce (*Pistia stratiotes*)	6 to 12 inches	Insignificant.	Velvety, light-green leaves, clustered like leaf lettuce. Can get out of hand quickly. Winter indoors.

PLANTING CHARTS

Immersed Plants

Variety	Size	Blooms	Comments
Water Lilies, Hardy (*Nymphaea* sp.)	Spread 12 inches	Summer, many colors, forms	Hardy lilies available in dwarf, small, medium and large types. Larger ones take too much room in small ponds. Small kinds need 6 to 12 inches of water over crowns, larger kinds up to 3 feet. The flowers are borne at the surface of the water.
Water Lilies, Tropical (*Nymphaea* sp.)	24 to 36 inches	Summer, many colors	Tropicals are delicate plants, needing water 12 to 18 inches deep over the crowns. Tender plants must be wintered indoors. Tropicals almost always bear their flowers well above the surface of the water.
Lotus, American (*Nelumbo* 'Lutea')	2 to 3 feet above water	Summer, 6- to 8-inch	This is the only lotus native to North America. It is ideal for pond culture.
Lotus, Sacred (*Nelumbo nucifera*)	1 to 7 feet above water	Summer, many colors, fragrant.	Incredible flowers and heady aroma Familiar seed pods in fall. Must be grown in containers or will take over. Winter below ice line or indoors.

Marginal Plants

Variety	Size	Blooms	Comments
Arrow Arum (*Peltandra sagittifolia*)	15 to 20 inches	Yellow in summer.	Bright green, arrow-shaped leaves. Winter below ice line or indoors. Water depth 2 inches.
Arrowhead (*Sagittaria sagittifolia*)	To 36 inches tall, half as wide	White in midsummer.	Large plants. Need containers to keep from spreading. Winter below ice line or indoors. Water depth 10 inches.
Cattail (*Typha angustifolia*)	18 to 36 inches	Spikelike in summer. Brown.	Familiar plants of wet areas. Try dwarf kinds. Grow in containers. Water depth 10 inches.
Iris (*Iris* sp.)	To 36 inches	Yellow, purple, white in spring.	Common native plants of wet sites. Need to be dried off for winter. Sink pots in garden, mulch, and move back in spring. Water depth 2 to 3 inches.
Pickerel Weed (*Pontederia cordata*)	18 inches	Spikes of blueflowers in summer.	Native plant with heart-shaped leaves. Robust. Winter below ice line or indoors. Water depth 5 inches.

SUGGESTED PEST CONTROL MATERIALS

These pest control materials are suggested ones only. It is the option of the gardener as to whether to use any of these materials. In general, chemicals are the last resort for pest control. When all other means are exhausted, chemicals will provide control to reestablish the balance. Maintaining a tidy garden and healthy, vigorous plants will make the presence of pests much less likely. Most years, we use no pesticides in our garden. Only rarely are they necessary. But when troubles do appear, it is a comfort to have the materials available to get things back in order.

This table lists pest control materials by the common name followed by the capitalized commercial trade names. The materials and the brand names are suggestions for your convenience only. If the material suggested is not available at your garden store, check the common name. Any product with the same common name is satisfactory, if it is labeled for the use and the plants on which it is to be applied. This list is not complete and is not intended to endorse, nor to discriminate against similar materials not listed.

It is unlawful to use any pest control materials in a manner not specifically indicated on the label. **Read the label** prior to buying any pest control material to make sure it is labeled for the use to which you intend to put it, and follow all directions carefully.

Insecticides

Common Chemical Name	Brand Name(s)
acephate	Orthene; Ortho Bug-B-Gon
Bacillus thuringiensis israelensis	Gnatrol
Bacillus thuringiensis kurstaki	Dipel; Thuricide; B. t.
Bacillus thuringiensis san diego	Potato Shield; Colorado Potato Beetle Beater
bifenthrin	Ortho Rose and Flower Insect Killer
carbaryl	Sevin; Ortho Bug-B-Gon Garden and Landscape Insect Killer
cyfluthrin	Bayer Advanced Garden PowerForce Multi-Insect Killer; Bayer Advanced Lawn PowerForce Ant Killer
deltamethrin	Bonide Delta Eight Insect Control; Enforcer Home Pest Control; Hi-Yield Kill-A-Bug II
dicofol	Kelthane; Hi-Yield Kelthane Spray
disulfoton	Bayer Advanced Garden 2-in-1 Systemic; Ferti-lome Systemic Insect Granules; Hi-Yield Di-Syston Systemic Granules
esfenvalerate	Ortho Bug-B-Gone Garden and Landscape Insect Killer

SUGGESTED PEST CONTROL MATEERIALS

Insecticides

Common Chemical Name	Brand Name(s)
halofenozide	Grub-X; Hi-Yield Kill-A-Grub
horticultural oil	Bonide All Seasons Spray Oil; Dormant and Summer Oil Spray; Ortho Volk Oil Spray; SunSpray Ultrafine Oil
imidacloprid	Merit, Bayer Advanced Garden Tree & Shrub Insect Control; Bayer Advanced Season Long Grub Control
insecticidal soap	Safer's Insecticidal Soap; Schultz Garden Safe Insecticidal Soap Multi-Purpose Insect Killer
lindane	Ortho Borer and Leafminer Spray
malathion	Ortho Malathion Plus; Ferti-lome Mal-A-Cide Lawn and Garden Insect Control
metaldehyde	Bonide Slug, Snail, & Sowbug Bait (+carbaryl); Ferti-lome Eliminate; Ortho Bug-Getta Snail and Slug Killer; Spectracide Snail and Slug Killer
permethrin	Bonide Borer-Miner Killer; Do-It-Best Multi-Purpose Garden Insect Killer; Eight Vegetable, Fruit, and Flower Spray; Gordon's Bug No More; Hi-Yield Kill-A-Bug II; Ortho Bug-B-Gone Garden and Landscape Insect Killer; Spectracide Bug-Stop Multi-Purpose Insect Control
pyrethrin	Ferti-lome Quick-Kill, Home Garden and Pet RTU; Gordon's Garden Guard; Hi-Yield Rose and Flower Spray; Hi-Yield Tomato and Vegetable Spray; I-Bomb; Ortho Indoor Insect Fogger; Schultz Garden Safe Houseplant and Garden Spray (+canola oil); Spectracide Houseplant and Garden Insect Spray; Spectracide Rose and Flower Insect Spray; Spectracide Tomato and Vegetable Insect Spray.
resmethrin	Ferti-lome Whitefly & Mealybug Killer; Spectracide Bug Stop Insect Control Granules
Steinernema carpocapsae	Biosafe (insect-attacking nematode)
trichlorfon	Dylox; Bayer Advanced Lawn 24-Hour Grub Control

Fungicides

Common Chemical Name	Brand Name(s)
captan	Bonide Captan; Dragon Captan; Bonide Complete Fruit Tree Spray (+malathion +carbaryl); Ferti-lome Fruit Tree Spray (+malathion); Ortho Home Orchard Spray (+malathion, +methoxychlor)

SUGGESTED PEST CONTROL MATEERIALS

Fungicides

Common Chemical Name	Brand Name(s)
chlorothalonil	Bonide Fung-onil; Bravo; Dragon Daconil 2787; Ferti-lome Liquid Fungicide; Ortho Daconil 2787
copper	Bonide Copper; Dragon Copper; Ferti-lome Blackspot; Hi-Yield Bordeaux; Phyton 27
mancozeb	Bonide Mancozeb; Dragon Mancozeb
maneb	Hi-Yield Maneb Garden Fungicide
PCNB	Ferti-lome Insecticide and Fungicide (+malathion); Terrachlor
potassium bicarbonate	Bonide Remedy
sulfur	Bonide Liquid Sulfur; Bonide Sulfur; Ferti-lome Sulfur
thiophanate-methyl	Bonide Benomyl; Dragon 3336; Ferti-lome Halt
triforine	Funginex; Orthenex (+acephate, +resmethrin)

Herbicides

Common Chemical Name	Brand Name(s)
dacthal	DCPA
diquat	Ace Grass and Weed Killer; Spectracide Systemic Grass and Weed Killer (with fluazifop-P-butyl)
fluazifop-P-butyl	Fusilade
glyphosate	Roundup; Roundup Original; Aquamaster
oxyfluorfen+pendimethalin	Ornamental Herbicide II; Progrow
trifluralin	Treflan; Preen

Animal Repellants and Controls

Common Chemical Name	Brand Name(s)
brodifacoum	D-con
thiram	Arasan

BOTANICAL GARDENS
IN THE MIDWEST

ILLINOIS

Cantigny Foundation
1 South Winfield Road
Wheaton, 60187
(630) 260-8158

Chicago Botanic Garden
1000 Lake Cook Road
Glencoe, 60022
(847) 835-5440

Fell Arboretum at Illinois State University
Normal, 61790-9000
(309) 438-2085

Garfield and Lincoln Park Conservatories
300 North Central
Chicago, 60624
(312) 746-5995

Illinois Central College
East Peoria, 61635
(309) 694-8446

Kishwaukee College
21193 Malta Road
Malta, 60150-9699
(815) 825-2086

Klehm Arboretum & Botanic Garden
2701 Clifton
Rockford, 61102-3537
(815) 965-8146

Luthy Memorial Botanic Garden
2218 N. Prospect Road
Peoria, 61603
(309) 686-3362

National Shrine of Our Lady of Snows
442 S. Mazenod Drive
Belleville, 62223
(618) 397-6700

Quad City Botanic Center
2525 Fourth Avenue
Rock Island, 61201-9008
(309) 794-0991

Robert Allerton Park
515 Old Timber Road
Monticello, 61856
(217) 244-1035

Southern Illinois University at Edwardsville
Edwardsville, 62026-1099
(618) 692-3311

Sun-Star Botanical Garden
201 N. 34th
Decatur, 62521
(217) 422-7156

The Morton Arboretum
4100 Route 53
Lisle, 60532-1293
(630) 719-2401

University of Illinois Arboretum
Urbana, 61801
(217) 333-2126

Washington Park Botanical Garden
2500 South 11th Street
Springfield, 62703
(217) 753-6228

INDIANA

Foellinger-Freimann Botanical Conservatory
1100 South Calhoun Street
Fort Wayne, 46802
(219) 427-6440

Garfield Park Conservatory
2450 South Shelby Street
Indianapolis, 46203
(317) 327-7184

Hayes Regional Arboretum
801 Elks Road
Richmond, 47374
(317) 962-3745

Indiana University Northwest
3400 Broadway
Gary, 46408
(219) 980-6500

Oakhurst Gardens
1200 North Minnetrista Parkway
Muncie, 47303-2925
(765) 282-4848

BOTANICAL GARDENS IN THE MIDWEST

IOWA

**Better Homes and Gardens
Test Gardens**
1716 Locust Street
Des Moines, 50309-3023
(515) 284-3994

**Dubuque Arboretum and
Botanic Gardens,**
3800 Arboretum Drive
Dubuque, 52001
(563) 556-2100

Reiman Gardens
Iowa State University
1407 Elmwood Drive
Ames, 50011
(515) 294-2710

MICHIGAN

**Applewood—
The C. S. Mott Estate**
1400 East Kearsley Street
Flint, 48503
(810) 233-3031

Beal Botanical Garden
Michigan State University
East Lansing, 48824
(517) 355-9582

Dow Gardens
1018 Main Street
Midland, 48640
(517) 631-677

**Fernwood Botanical Garden
and Nature Preserve**
13988 Range Line Road
Niles, 49120
(616) 695-6491

Frederik Meijer Gardens
3411 Bradford NE
Grand Rapids, 49546
(616) 957-1580

Hidden Lake Gardens
6280 West Munger Road
Tipton 49287
(517) 431-2060

Leila Arboretum Society
928 West Michigan Avenue
Battle Creek, 49017
(616) 969-0270

Nichols Arboretum
University of Michigan
Ann Arbor, 48109-1115
(313) 763-4033

**Slayton Arboretum of
Hillsdale College**
Hillsdale, 49242
(517) 437-7341

**University of Michigan Matthei
Botanical Gardens and
Arboretum**
1800 N. Dixboro Road
Ann Arbor, 48105
(734) 998-7061

MISSOURI

Missouri Botanical Garden
St. Louis, 63166-0299
(314) 577-5111

**University of Missouri
Botanic Garden**
Columbia, 65211
(573) 882-4240

OHIO

**Cincinnati Zoo and
Botanical Garden**
3400 Vine Street
Cincinnati, 45220
(513) 475-6106

**Cleveland
Botanical Garden**
11030 East Boulevard
Cleveland, 44106
(216) 721-1600

Dawes Arboretum
7770 Jacksontown Road SE
Newark, 43056-9380
(740) 323-2355

**Ohio State University
Chadwick Arboretum**
Columbus, 43210-1096
(614) 688-3479

Toledo Botanical Garden
5403 Elmer Drive
Toledo, 43615
(419) 936-2986

WISCONSIN

**Boerner Botanical Gardens,
Milwaukee County Parks**
9400 Boerner Drive
Hales Corners, 53130-2299
(414) 525-5601

Green Bay Botanical Garden
2600 Larsen Road
Green Bay, 54307-2644
(920) 490-9457

Olbrich Botanical Gardens
3330 Atwood Avenue
Madison, 53704
(608) 246-4550

**University of Wisconsin
Arboretum**
1207 Seminole Highway
Madison, 53711
(608) 262-2746

SUPPLIERS

This is not a complete list of suppliers and it is provided only for your convenience. It does not imply endorsement of the firms listed, nor does it discriminate against firms not listed.

CATALOG MAIL-ORDER SEED SUPPLIERS

Alberta Nursery and Seeds
P. O. Box 20
Bowden, AB T0M 0K0
Canada
Phone: (403) 224-3544
Fax: (403) 224-2455

W. Atlee Burpee Co.
300 Park Avenue
Warminster, PA 18974
Phone: (800) 888-1447
Fax: (800) 487-5530

E & R Seed Co.
1356 East 200 South
Monroe, IN 46772
Write for catalog.

Gurney Seed & Nursery
Gurney Building
Yankton, SD 57078
Phone: (513) 354-1491

Harris Seeds
355 Paul Road
Rochester, NY 14624
Phone: (800) 514-4441
Fax: (877) 892-9187

Holmes Seed Co.
P. O. Box 9087
Canton, OH 44709
Phone: (800) 435-6077
Fax: (330) 492-0167

Ed Hume Seeds, Inc.
P. O. Box 73160
Puyallup, WA 98373
Phone: (253) 435-4414
Fax: (253) 435-5144

Johnny's Selected Seeds
955 Benton Avenue
Winslow, ME 04901-2601
Phone: (207) 861-8377

J. W. Jung Seed Company
335 S. High Street
Randolph, WI 53957-0001
Phone: (800) 247-5864
Fax: (800) 692-5864

Lindenberg Seeds, Ltd.
803 Princess Ave.
Brandon, MB R7A 0P5
Canada
Phone: (204) 727-0575
Fax: (204) 727-2832

Nichols Garden Nursery
1190 Old Salem Road NE
Albany, OR 97321
Phone: (800) 422-3985
Fax: (800) 231-5306

Park Seed Company
1 Parkton Avenue
Greenwood, SC 29647
Phone: (800) 213-0076
Fax: (800) 275-9941

Pinetree Garden Seeds
P. O. Box 300
New Gloucester, ME 04260
Phone: (207) 926-3400
Fax: (888) 527-3337

R. H. Shumway
334 W. Stroud Street
Randolph, WI 53956-1274
Phone: (800) 342-9461
Fax: (888) 437-2733

Seed Savers Exchange
3076 North Winn Road
Decora, IA 52101
Phone: (563) 382-5990
Fax: (563) 382-5872

Seeds of Change
P. O. Box 15700
Santa Fe, NM 87506
Phone: (888)762-7333

Thompson and Morgan
P. O. Box 1308
Jackson, NJ 08527
Phone: (800) 274-7333

Tomato Growers Supply
P. O. Box 60015
Ft. Meyers, FL 33906
Phone: (888) 478-7333
Fax: (888) 768-3476

SUPPLIERS

CATALOG MAIL-ORDER SEED SUPPLIERS

Totally Tomatoes
334 West Stroud Street
Randolph, WI 53956-1274
Phone: (800) 345-5977
Fax: (888) 477-7333

Vermont Bean Seed Co.
334 West Stroud Street
Randolph, WI 53956-1274
Phone: (800) 349-1071
Fax: (888) 500-7333

West Coast Seeds Ltd.
Unit 206 - Ontario Street
Vancouver, BC V5X 3E8
Canada
Phone: (604) 952-8820
Fax: (604) 482-8822

FRUIT PLANT SUPPLIERS

Applesource
1716 Apples Road
Chapin, IL 62628
Phone: (800) 588-3854
Fax: (217) 245-7844

Hilltop Nursery
P. O. Box 578
Hartford, MI 49057
Phone: (800) 253-2911
Fax: (616) 621-2062

Raintree Nursery
391 Butts Road
Morton, WA 98356
Phone: (360) 496-6400
Fax: (888) 770-8358

Hartmann's Plantation
310 60th Street
Grand Junction, MI 49063
Phone: (269) 253-4281
Fax: (269) 253-4457

Miller Nurseries
5060 West Lake Road
Canadaigua, NY
14424-8904
Phone: (800) 836-9630

Stark Bros. Nurseries
P. O. Box 1800
Louisiana, MO 63353
Phone: (800) 325-4180

SUPPLIERS OF BENEFICIAL INSECTS

ARBICO
P. O. Box 8910
Tucson, AZ 85738-0910
Phone: (800) 827-2847
Fax: (520) 825-2038

Rincon Vitova
P. O. Box 1555
Ventura, CA 93022-1555
Phone: (800) 248-2847
Fax: (805) 643.6267

Global Horticultural, Inc.
135 Lake Avenue
Riverhead, New York 11901
Phone: (877) 369-6411
Fax: (905) 563-3191

The Bug Store
113 West Argonne
St. Louis, MO 63122-1104
(800) 455.2847

BIRD NETTING, FLOATING ROW COVERS, AND RABBIT FENCE

Bird-X, Inc.
300 North Elizabeth Street
Chicago, IL 60607
www.bird-x.com

Gempler's
P. O. Box 44993
Madison, WI 53744-4993
www.gemplers.com

**Indiana Berry and
Plant Company**
5218 West 500 South
Huntingburg, IN 47542
www.inberry.com

Forestry Suppliers, Inc.
P. O. Box 8397
Jackson, MS 39284-8397
www.forestry-suppliers.com

Hummert International
4500 Earth City Expressway
Earth City, MO 63045-1329
www.hummert.com

Snapdragon Industries
600 Old Bristol Road
New Hampton, NH 03256
www./ezrabbitfencing.com

GLOSSARY

AAS: All-America Selections. Awarded to plant varieties that have given outstanding performance in trial gardens throughout the country.

Alkaline soil: soil with a pH greater than 7.0. The converse of acid soil; alkaline soil often has high limestone content.

All-purpose fertilizer: Powdered, liquid, or granular fertilizer containing nitrogen (N), phosphorus (P), and potassium (K). It is suitable for application to most plants.

Annual: A plant that starts from seed, grows, flowers, and produces fruit and seeds in 1 season. Zinnias, marigolds, lettuce, corn, and beans are examples.

Anthracnose: A fungal disease characterized by discolored, often dead, angular spots on leaves, stems, or fruit.

Artificial potting soil: A commercial blend of peat moss, composted bark, perlite, or other materials used instead of soil as a growing medium for containerized plants.

Average date of last frost: Frost-free date (as compared to latest date of last frost). On average, frost will not occur after this date 50% of the time.

Balled and burlapped: Describes a tree or shrub grown in the field on which the soilball was wrapped with protective burlap and twine when the plant was dug for relocation.

Banding: An application of fertilizer or pesticide to the soil in a narrow strip alongside the plants as opposed to broadcasting over the entire planted area. Similar to side-dressing. (See side-dress.)

Bare root: Describes plants lifted for transplanting with no soil attached to the roots. (Often mail-order shrubs and trees arrive with their roots covered by moist peat, sphagnum moss, sawdust, or similar material, and wrapped in plastic, etc.)

Barrier plant: A plant that has intimidating thorns or spines and is sited purposely to block foot traffic or other access to the home or yard.

Beneficial insects: Insects that prey on pests. They may be flying insects, such as ladybugs, parasitic wasps, praying mantids, and soldier bugs, or soil dwellers such as predatory nematodes, spiders, and ants.

Berm: A raised, elongated, hill-like soil mass used as a barrier or to screen out undesirable sights and sounds. Often planted with trees, shrubs, and grass.

Biennial: A plant that requires 2 seasons to produce seed. It grows a rosette of foliage from seed the first year, produces a flower, fruit, and seed the second year, and dies. Examples include hollyhocks, parsley, angelica, and carrots.

Blackleg: A fungal disease characterized by black discoloration of the plant stem at and above the soil line.

Black rot: A fungal disease characterized by black discoloration and rotting of the fruit of grapes, or apples, etc.

Blossom-end rot: A leathery-brown spot which develops on the bottoms of tomatoes or peppers due to unfavorable growing conditions. Usually, limited to the first few fruits early in the season, and is self correcting.

Bolt: To produce flowers or seed prematurely.

Bract: A modified leaf structure usually subtending the flower, resembling a petal, and often more colorful and visible than the actual flower, as in dogwood or poinsettia.

GLOSSARY

Bulb: A specialized underground bud consisting of a thick flat stem, rudimentary leaves, and flower buds and roots, as in a lily bulb or an onion.

Cane: A woody, often hollow stem, usually unbranched arising from the ground. Stems of brambles are referred to as canes.

Canopy: The crown of a tree, usually referring to its volume and including branches and foliage but not the trunk.

Catfacing: Malformed fruit caused by poor pollination.

Chlorosis: Yellowing of young leaves due to failure to develop chlorophyll. Often due to high soil pH or nutrient deficiencies.

Clubroot: A disease characterized by swollen, club-like roots on plants such as cabbage or broccoli.

Cold hardiness: The ability of a plant to survive anticipated low temperatures in a particular geographic area.

Companion planting: Growing 2 crops in the same space or growing plants of several different varieties next to each other to conserve space; i.e., radishes are often sown in the same rows as carrots, or squash with corn.

Composite: A plant characterized by flower heads consisting of petalless disk flowers surrounded by ray flowers each with a colorful petal. Sunflowers, daisies, and dandelions are composites.

Compost: Organic matter that has undergone progressive decomposition by microbial and macrobial activity until it is reduced to a spongy, fluffy texture. Added to soil of any type, it improves the soil's ability to hold air and water, and to drain well.

Compound leaves: Leaves consisting of several-to-many leaflets attached to a single central stalk.

Corm: A subterranean, bulblike stem with buds at the top and rudimentary rots at the base, as in gladiolus.

Cross-pollination: Fertilization of a flower of one plant by the pollen of another closely related plant, as opposed to self-pollination.

Crown: The center part of a plant; the point at which the leaves and stems of a plant join the roots.

Cultivar: A **culti**vated **var**iety. The correct nomenclature for a variety that is purposely developed and persists under cultivation.

Deadhead: To remove faded flowers from plants to improve their appearance, abort seed production, and stimulate further flowering.

Deciduous plants: Trees and shrubs which lose their leaves in the fall.

Desiccation: Drying out of plant tissues, due to the inability of roots or stems to provide adequate water. Can be due to drought or wind.

Determinate: Growth characteristic of tomato varieties that set terminal flowers thus stopping further growth. Determinate plants form low bushes with all of the fruit formed about the same time, and thus are convenient for processing.

Dibble: A small, hand-held, pointed stick used to make holes in soil for planting seedlings or bulbs. Also, to poke a hole in the soil with a dibble for planting.

Dioecious: Plants bearing both male and female flowers. Typical of vine crops.

Division: A portion of a perennial plant split apart to create several smaller segments. Useful for controlling the plant's size and for acquiring more plants; it is also essential to the health and continued flowering of certain plants. Each divided segment is a division.

Dormancy: The period, usually the winter, when perennial plants temporarily cease active growth.

Dormant: referring to plants which have ceased active growth.

Drainage: Capacity of soil to drain away water.

Established: The time at which a newly planted tree, shrub, or flower has recovered from transplanting.

Evergreen: A plant which retains its foliage throughout the year; foliage persisting and functioning for two or more seasons.

GLOSSARY

Fallow: To keep soil free of all plants for a season or more, thus reducing subsequent weed, disease or insect problems.

Fertilizer: Any substance used to add plant nutrients to the soil.

Foliage: Leaves

Foliar: referring to the leaves of the plant.

Floret: A tiny flower, usually one of many forming an inflorescence such as a spike, a panicle or a head.

Frass: A mass of shredded plant parts and often insect parts due to feeding by insect pests.

Frost-free date: Average date of last frost (as compared to latest date of last frost).

Full sun: Receiving all available sunlight from sunrise to sunset.

Fungicide: A pesticide used to control fungus diseases.

Germinate: To begin growth as a plant from a seed.

Graft (union): The point at which the bud or shoot (scion) is inserted into a groove or slit in the parent plant (stock) where it continues to grow. Fruit trees, roses, and many ornamental trees are grafted.

Green manure: Temporary planting of fast-growing vegetation to be plowed into the soil adding organic matter and improving soil condition.

Growing season: The average number of days between the last freeze of spring and the first freeze of autumn.

Harden off: To gradually expose plants grown indoors or in a greenhouse to lower temperatures, making it possible for them to withstand colder conditions. Also applies to plants exposed to adverse conditions such as low fertility, low temperatures, or drying causing stunting, and sometimes premature flowering.

Hardscape: The permanent, structural, non-plant part of a landscape, such as walls, sheds, pools, patios, arbors, and walkways.

Healing in: A method of storing plants in the ground until conditions are favorable for planting. Plants are laid on their sides in a shallow trench and covered with soil so only the tips of the plants are exposed.

Herbaceous: Plants having fleshy or soft stems that die back with frost; the opposite of woody.

Herbicide: A pesticide used to modify or kill plants.

Hilling-up: Mounding soil around the base of a plant for various purposes: i.e. to blanch celery or Belgian endive, to protect perennials from adverse weather, or potatoes from sun, etc.

Hill planting: Several plants set in close proximity creating a "hill," the hills widely spaced in rows. (As opposed to row planting in which plants are evenly spaced along the row)

Hybrid: a plant that is the result of intentional or natural cross-pollination between two or more plants of the same species or genus.

Indeterminate: Growth characteristic of tomato plants that set flower clusters along a vining stem, never setting terminal flowers. They grow indefinitely producing fruit throughout the season until killed off by frost. These varieties are excellent for growing on trellises or stakes.

Insecticide: A pesticide to control insects and related pests.

Latest date of last frost: The date after which frost does not occur in a locality.

Leader: The central, vertical shoot of a plant.

Leaf axil: The angle between the upper side of a leaf or stem and the supporting stem.

Lifting: Digging up or pulling plants as in harvesting or removal for transplanting.

Mulch: A covering of straw, compost, plastic sheeting, etc. spread on the ground around plants to reduce water loss, prevent weeds, and enrich the soil (if the mulch is a natural substance).

GLOSSARY

Naturalize: (*a*) To plant seeds, bulbs, or plants in a random, informal pattern as they would appear in their natural habitat; (*b*) to adapt to and spread throughout adopted habitats (a tendency of some nonnative plants).

Nectar: The sweet fluid produced by glands on flowers that attract pollinators such as hummingbirds and honeybees for which it is a source of energy.

Open pollination: Plants pollinated naturally by whatever pollen happens to blow onto them. These varieties come true from seed; that is, collected seed will produce a plant identical to the one the seed was collected from. Hybrid varieties do not come true from collected seed.

Organic material, organic matter: Any material or debris that is derived from plants. It is carbon-based material capable of undergoing decomposition and decay.

Overwinter: To survive winter; to tolerate the winter conditions without injury.

Partial shade: Filtered sun all day or shade part of the day.

Peat moss: organic matter from peat sedges (United States) or sphagnum mosses (Canada, Europe), a major portion of artificial soil mixes, often used to improve soil texture.

Peat pot: Small pot formed out of peat moss. Often used for starting seeds.

Perennial: a plant that grows from a seed, developing the plant for the first year, and flowering and producing fruit and seeds thereafter. Examples include peonies, daylilies, or hostas, and woody plants.

Pesticide: A substance used to control insects (insecticide), fungi (fungicide), and weeds (herbicide) etc.

pH: A measurement of the relative acidity (low pH) or alkalinity (high pH) of soil or water. Most garden plants prefer a pH of 6.0 to 7.0 on a scale of 1 to 14.

Pinch: To remove tender shoot tips to encourage branching, compactness, and flowering in plants, or to remove insect pests clustered at growing tips.

Plug: A plant grown in plug of soil, in a small pot, or in a plug tray for later transplanting.

Pollen: the yellow, powdery grains in the center of a flower. A plant's male sex cells, they are transferred to the female plant parts by means of wind or animal pollinators to fertilize them and create seeds.

Pollination: Fertilization of female part of a flower by pollen from the male part of a flower.

Potbound: The condition of a plant that has been confined in a container too long, its roots having filled the soil mass. Also called rootbound.

Raceme: An arrangement of single stalked flowers along an elongated, unbranched axis.

Rhizome: A root-like subterranean stem lying horizontally in the soil, with roots emerging from its lower surface and growth shoots from a growing point at or near its tip, as in bearded iris.

Rogue: To uproot or destroy things that do not conform to a certain standard.

Root cutting: A small, thin, root used for propagation.

Root division: Section of a root system used for propagation.

Root flare: The transition at the base of a tree trunk where the bark tissue begins to differentiate and roots begin to spread just before entering the soil. This area should not be covered with soil when planting a tree.

Rosette: A circular cluster of leaves.

Rototill: To till the soil using a rototiller.

Row cover: Sheets, blankets, or plastic covers placed over susceptible plants to prevent frost damage, or insect damage, i.e. miners attacking Swiss chard or cucumber beetles feeding on vine crops. Floating row covers are mats of spun-bound polypropylene that are very light, need no supports, and do not crush plants under them.

GLOSSARY

Scaffold: Horizontal branch on a tree.

Scald: Condition in which plant leaves dry out and become papery at the edges.

Seedbed: Finely tilled soil suitable for sowing seed. Also a bed so prepared.

Self-seeding: Refers to plants that spontaneously drop seeds, thus perpetuating themselves. Often an undesirable characteristic.

Semi-evergreen: Tending to be evergreen in a mild climate but deciduous in a rigorous one.

Shearing: The pruning technique whereby plant stems and branches are cut uniformly with long-bladed pruning shears (hedge shears) or powered hedge trimmers. It is used when creating and maintaining hedges and topiary.

Side-dress: To apply fertilizer next to the rows of plants at about half the normal rate, thus avoiding damage from fertilizer touching the growing plants. Sidedressing is usually applied about mid-season after the preplant fertilizers have begun to run out.

Slow-acting fertilizer: Fertilizer that is water-insoluble and therefore releases its nutrients gradually as a function of soil temperature, moisture, and related microbial activity. Typically granular, it may be organic or synthetic.

Soil types: Sand, silt, clay or loam, etc., describing the coarseness or fineness of the soil.

Stamen: Male part of a seed-bearing flower.

Succulent growth: The sometimes undesirable production of fleshy, water-storing leaves or stems which results from overfertilization.

Suckers: Undesirable vertical shoots arising from roots or branches of plants. Also called water sprouts. Some plants produce suckers as a result of pruning or a wound.

Tender perennial: A perennial plant which is unable to tolerate the winter temperatures in a particular climate.

Till: To work the soil by spading, digging, cultivating, rolling, etc.

Tilth: The physical condition of the soil.

Tuber: A short, thickened underground stem, often with small scale-like buds from which arise new plants. Dahlias and potatoes develop from tubers.

Variegated: Having various colors or color patterns. The term usually refers to plant foliage that is streaked, edged, blotched, or mottled with a contrasting color, often green with yellow, cream, or white.

Variety: A cultivar.

Vegetative propagation: Propagation by means of cuttings, divisions, or grafting.

Water sprouts: Vigorous, undesirable, vertical sprouts growing from the base, trunk, or scaffold branches of a tree.

Whip: Small, single-stemmed, whiplike tree. Used to start a planting.

White grubs: Fat, white, larvae of May beetles, June bugs, or Japanese beetles, residing in the soil and feeding on plant (especially grass) roots.

Wilt: A fungal or bacterial disease that causes plants to wilt and die.

Wings: (a) The corky tissue that forms edges along the twigs of some woody plants such as winged euonymus; (b) The flat, dried extension of tissue on some seeds, such as maple, that catch the wind and help them disseminate.

Woody plant: Any plant developing stems that persist from year to year.

Zone: A region that differs significantly in climate and temperature from adjacent areas.

PHOTOGRAPHY & ILLUSTRATION CREDITS

ILLUSTRATIONS
Bill Kersey, Kersey Design

PHOTOGRAPHY

Thomas Eltzroth: pages 22 (celosia, bottom of page); 26; 27; 32; 45 (tulip, top of page; wax begonia, bottom of page); 50; 53; 63; 68; 69 (tomato collection, top of page); 78; 82; 84; 86; 88; 91; 92; 95 (close-up of zoysia, top of page; lawn landscape, bottom of page); 96; 108; 112; 133; 144; 166 (lacecap hydrangea, top of page); 169; 178; 183; 184; 188; 204; 226; 231; 232; 236; 238; 241 (water lily, top of page; Japanese iris landscape, bottom of page); 260

Neil Soderstrom: pages 28; 30; 31; 37; 38; 52; 56; 67; 74; 93; 99; 123; 124; 127; 128; 134; 139; 147; 148; 153; 159; 160; 163; 164; 220; 222; 259

Jerry Pavia: pages 7 (top of page, pansy); 22 (zinnia, top of page); 54; 64; 118 (purple coneflower, top of page; perennial landscape, bottom of page); 131; 142 (Bourbon rose, top of page; rose landscape, bottom of page); 157; 166 (barberry landscape, bottom of page); 176; 186; 218; 258

Liz Ball and Rick Ray: pages 59; 69 (harvest bench, bottom of page); 141; 170; 191 (ginkgo, top of page; weeping spruce, bottom of page); 201; 210; 212; 214; 224; 234; 254

Andre Viette: page 216 (clematis, top of page; miscanthus and hosta landscape; bottom of page)

Cathy Barash: page 252

Ralph Snodsmith: page 174

Netherlands Bulb Association: page 58

BIBLIOGRAPHY

American Horticulture Society Encyclopedia of Garden Plants, The, Christoper Brickell, Editor, Macmillan Publishing Company, NY, 1993.

America's Garden Book, Bush-Brown and Bush-Brown, Scribners, NY, 1953.

Ball Red Book, Geo J. Ball, Inc., West Chicago, IL, 1974.

Big Book of Gardening Skills, The, Garden Way Publishing, VT, 1993.

Book of Outdoor Gardening, Smith & Hawken, Workman Publishing Co., NY, 1996.

Coincide, Donald Orton, American Nurseryman, Chicago, IL, 1989.

Complete Guide to Water Gardening, Peter Robinson, American Horticulture Society, DK Publishing Co., NY, 1997.

Creative Water Gardener, The, Andrew Wilson, Sterling Publishing Co., NY, 1995.

Garden Ponds, David Papworth, Salamander Books, Ltd., London, UK, 1984.

Holland Bulb Forcer's Guide, August DeHertogh, Michigan State University, 1977.

Illinois Gardener's Guide, James A. Fizzell, Cool Springs Press, Nashville, TN, 1997, (Revised, 2002).

Indiana Gardener's Guide, Tom Tyler and Jo Ellen Myers Sharp, Cool Springs Press, Nashville, TN, 1998.

Manual of Herbaceous Ornamental Plants, 4th Edition, Steven M. Still, Stipes Publishing Co., Champaign, IL, 1994.

Manual of Woody Landscape Plants, 4th Edition, Michael A. Dirr, Stipes Publishing Co., Champaign, IL, 1990.

Michigan Gardener's Guide, Timothy Boland, Laura Coit, and Marty Hair, Cool Springs Press, Nashville, TN, 1997.

Midwest Fruit & Vegetable Book, James A. Fizzell, Cool Springs Press, Nashville, TN, 2001.

Month-by-Month Gardening in the South, Don Hastings and Chris Hastings, Longstreet Press, Inc., Atlanta, GA, 1997.

New Illustrated Encyclopedia of Gardening, T. H. Everett, Editor, Greystone Press, New York, 1966.

Ornamental Grasses, Peter Loewer, Better Homes and Gardens Books, Des Moines, IA, 1995.

Rating and Raising Indoor Plants, Virginia Beatty, Publications International, Ltd., Skokie, IL, 1975.

Successful Rose Gardening, Better Homes and Gardens Books, Des Moines, IA, 1993.

Vegetable Gardening in the Midwest, C. S. Voit and J. S. Vandemark, University of Illinois College of Agriculture Circular 1331, 1995.

Water Garden, The, Peter Robinson, Sterling Publishing Co., NY, 1995.

PLANT INDEX

INDEX

INDEX

INDEX

INDEX

INDEX

INDEX

INDEX

MEET JAMES A. FIZZELL

James A. Fizzell is best known as the "Staff Horticulturalist" on Chicago's WGN radio where he answered gardening questions for more than 40 years. As the president of James A. Fizzell & Associates, the author provides consulting services to the commercial horticulture industry. Fizzell's projects include such important landmarks as Wrigley Field, home of the Chicago Cubs, Chicago's O'Hare and Midway airports, and the Chicago Park District.

For nearly 30 years, the author served as the horticulturist with the University of Illinois Extension Service. In that capacity, Fizzell wrote gardening columns for 200 newspapers in the Midwest and hundreds of articles for horticultural trade publications.

Fizzell holds two degrees in horticulture from the University of Illinois. The esteemed horticulturalist has received many honors including the prestigious Linnaeaus award by the Chicago Horticulture Society for lifetime service to horticulture. The author's contributions include his instrumental role in developing the Master Gardener Program in Illinois and in forming the Illinois Landscape Contractors Association and the Illinois Arborist Association.

The author and his wife, Jane, enjoy gardening in their northern Illinois home on Garden Street.

ENJOY THESE OTHER HELPFUL BOOKS FROM COOL SPRINGS PRESS

Cool Springs Press is devoted to state and regional gardening and offers a selection of books to help you enjoy gardening and bird watching where you live. Choose Cool Springs Press books with confidence.

Illinois Gardener's Guide
ISBN# 1-88860-899-4 • $24.99

The Gardening Book for Ohio
ISBN# 1-59186-047-4 • $24.99

Michigan Gardener's Guide
ISBN# 1-93060-420-3 • $24.99

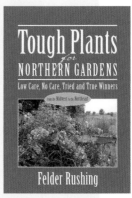

Tough Plants for Northern Gardens
ISBN# 1-59186-063-6 • $24.99

Illinois Bird Watching
ISBN# 1-59186-170-5 • $16.99

Ohio Bird Watching
ISBN# 1-59186-168-3 • $16.99

Michigan Bird Watching
ISBN# 1-59186-167-5 • $16.99

Can't Miss Water Gardening
for the Midwest
ISBN# 1-59186-154-3 • $18.99

COOL SPRINGS PRESS
A Division of Thomas Nelson Publishers
Since 1798

www.coolspringspress.net

See your garden center, bookseller, or home improvement center for these Cool Springs Press titles. Also, be sure to visit www.coolspringspress.net for more great titles from Cool Springs Press.